Perspectives on Western Sahara

Barcelona
Portugal
Madrid
Spain
Lisbon
Seville
Algiers
Casablanca
Morocco
Algeria
Western
Sahara
Mauritania
Mali
Dakar
Senegal
The Gambia
Bamako
Burkina
Faso

Perspectives on Western Sahara

Myths, Nationalisms, and Geopolitics

Edited by
Anouar Boukhars
and Jacques Roussellier

ROWMAN & LITTLEFIELD
Lanham • Boulder • New York • Toronto • Plymouth, UK

Published by Rowman & Littlefield
4501 Forbes Boulevard, Suite 200, Lanham, Maryland 20706
www.rowman.com

10 Thornbury Road, Plymouth PL6 7PP, United Kingdom

Copyright © 2014 by Rowman & Littlefield

All rights reserved. No part of this book may be reproduced in any form or by any electronic or mechanical means, including information storage and retrieval systems, without written permission from the publisher, except by a reviewer who may quote passages in a review.

British Library Cataloguing in Publication Information Available

Library of Congress Cataloging-in-Publication Data Available

Anouar Boukhars.
Perspectives on Western Sahara : Myths, nationalisms, and geopolitics / edited by Anouar Boukhars and Jacques Roussellier.
p. cm.
Includes bibliographical references and index.
ISBN 978-1-4422-2685-2 (cloth : alk. paper) -- ISBN 978-1-4422-2686-9 (electronic)

∞™ The paper used in this publication meets the minimum requirements of American National Standard for Information Sciences Permanence of Paper for Printed Library Materials, ANSI/NISO Z39.48-1992.

Printed in the United States of America

Contents

Acronyms   vii
Foreword   xi
Introduction   xv

Part I: Setting the Context

1. A History of the Conflict in Western Sahara   3
   Osama Abi-Mershed and Adam Farrar
2. The Identity Question: Who Are the Sahrawis and What Is Their "Home?"   29
   Joshua Castellino and Elvira Domínguez-Redondo

Part II: The Background for the Current Impasse

3. Morocco's Saharan Policy   55
   I. William Zartman
4. The Emergence and Politics of the Polisario Front   71
   Stephen J. King
5. The Algerian Foreign Policy on Western Sahara   91
   Laurence Aïda Ammour
6. The Evolving Role of the United Nations: The Impossible Dual Track?   119
   Jacques Roussellier
7. Diplomatic Struggle in Africa and Europe over the Western Sahara Conflict   141
   Antonin Tisseron
8. The Evolution of US and Moroccan Policy on Western Sahara : From Conflict to Cooperation   163
   Ambassador Edward M. Gabriel and Robert M. Holley

Part III: Dynamics of Optimal Solutions

9. Dynamics of Intergroup Conflicts in the Western Sahara   187
   Anouar Boukhars
10. Self-Determination for Western Sahara : The Evolution of a Concept   209
    Samuel J. Spector

11	The Use and Development of Natural Resources in Non-Self-Governing Territories *Glynn Torres-Spelliscy*	235
12	Refugees, Humanitarian Aid, and the Displacement Impasse in Sahrawi Camps *Aomar Boum*	261
13	Western Sahara: A Conflict on the Fringes of New Regional Dynamics *Khadija Mohsen-Finan*	277

Conclusion: A Realistic Solution to the Western Sahara Conflict 297
J. Peter Pham

Index 307

About the Contributors 323

Acronyms

ACSRT African Center for Studies and Research on Terrorism
AFP Agence French Presse
AIS Islamic Salvation Army
ALM Moroccan Army of Liberation
ALN National Liberation Army (Algeria)
AMU Arab Maghreb Union
ANC African National Congress
ANP National People's Army
APN National People's Assembly (Algerian)
AQIM Al-Qaeda in the Islamic Maghreb
AU African Union
CEMOC General Staff Joint Operations Committee
CEN-SAD Community of Sahel-Saharan States
CMPI Main Military Investigation Center (Algiers)
CNDH National Human Rights Council (Morocco)
CNRT National Council of Timorese Resistance
CORCAS Royal Advisory Council for Saharan Affairs (Morocco)
CRI Regional Investment Center
DEPT Department of Economic Studies and Financial Forecast (Morocco)
DRS Department of Intelligence and Security (*Département du Renseignement et de la Sécurité*) (Algeria)
DSI *Direction de la Sécurité Intérieure,* or DSI (Algeria)
ECOWAS Economic Community of Wester African Stakes
EU European Union
EXIM Export-Import Bank (US)
FAR Royal Armed Forces—Kingdom of Morocco
FLN National Liberation Front
FLU Fusion and Liaison Unit (Algeria)
FPA Fisheries Partnership Agreement
GAM Free Aceh Movement
GCF *Groupement des gardes-frontières*
GCTF Global Counterterrorism Forum
GIA Armed Islamic Group
GPRA Provisional Government of the Algerian Republic
GSPC Salafist Group for Preaching and Combat
GWOT Gobal war on terrorism

HCE High State Council (*Haut Comité d'État*) (Algeria)
IC Identification Commission (MINURSO)
ICG International Crisis Group
ICJ International Court of Justice
IER Equity and Reconciliation Commission—Kingdom of Morocco
IMF International Monetary Fund
LOGA Law on the Governing of Aceh
MINURSO United Nations Mission for the Referendum in the Western Sahara (*Mission des Nations Unies pour l'Organisation d'un Referendum au Sahara Occidental*)
MNLA National Movement for the Liberation of Azawad
MoU Memorandum of Understanding
MTNM Northern Mali Tuareg Movement
MUJAO Movement for Unity and Jihad in West Africa
NCT National Transition Council (Libya)
NEPAD New Partnership for Africa's Development
NGO nongovernmental organization
NSGT non-self-governing territory
OAU Organization of African Unity
OCP Office Chérifien des Phosphates (Morocco)
OCRS Common Organization of the Saharan Regions
OHMYM Office National des Hydrocarbures et des Mines
OPEC Organization of Petroleum Exporting Countries
OPIC Overseas Private Investment Corporation (US)
PAM Party of Authenticity and Modernity
PESG Personal Envoy of the Secretary-General
PJD Justice and Development Party
Polisario, or Polisario Front Popular Front for the Liberation of Saguia al-Hamra and Rio de Oro (*Frente Popular de Liberación de Saguía el Hamray Río de Oro*)
PSOE *Partido Socialista Obrero Espanol*
PUNS Partido De La Union Nacional Saharaui
PVLs Provisional Voters Lists
SADR Sahrawi Arab Democratic Republic
SRSG Special Envoy of the Secretary-General
SM Sécurité Militaire
SPLA Sahrawi Peoples Liberation Army
SRCS Sahrawi Red Crescent Society
SRSG Special Representative of the Secretary-General
TSCTI Trans-Sahara Counterterrorism Initiative
UAS Union of African States
UEMOA West African Economic and Monetary Union
UMA Arab Maghreb Union (same as AMU)
UN United Nations
UNGA United Nations General Assembly

UNHCR United Nations High Commissioner for Refugees
UNSC United Nations Security Council
UNSG United Nations Secretary General
UNTAET United Nations Transitional Administration in East Timor

Foreword

This volume of essays speaks to a continuing political debate that is increasingly important in a global community riven by emerging ethnic and cultural tensions. Rather than greater integration within societies, we are witnessing in Africa, the Arab countries, and South Asia a growing emphasis on differences among peoples. The resolution of the Western Sahara conflict, within that context, may help us better appreciate how constructive engagement among participants might, abetted by genuine advocacy for peace, possibly provide lessons for other leaders and analysts as to how to reverse troubling situations before they worsen.

One conflict that has gone on for far too long is the situation in the Western Sahara. In any discussion of this issue, there are scores of proponents on both sides who can marshal facts and opinions as to what must and should be done to resolve the conflict, rarely focusing on what can be done after more than 38 years of an inconclusive state of affairs.

On the one hand, for nearly fifty years, the kings of Morocco, supported by a wide national consensus, have constantly affirmed that their country, as far as the contested status of the Western Sahara territory is concerned, would never accept any outcome that might stop short of endorsing Moroccan sovereignty, let alone result in the independence of the territory.

In the middle is the international community, which early on, through the United Nations General Assembly (UNGA), in its first resolution of December 16, 1965, proposed that Spain, the then UN administering power in the territory, "takes all necessary measures" to decolonize the territory, while entering into negotiations on "problems relative to governing." The UNGA subsequently adopted seven more resolutions between 1966 and 1973 reiterating the need to hold a referendum on self-determination, in line with the Declaration on the Granting of Independence to Colonial Countries and Peoples.

And then, on the other hand, is the Polsario Front, which with the full support of Algeria, argues that the initial resolution supporting a referendum on self-determination is cast in stone, a rather immovable goal despite the fact that decades later it remains out of grasp.

As soon as Spain announced its plan to organize a referendum on self-determination in early 1975, King Hassan II immediately referred the case to the International Court of Justice (ICJ) and called for the "Green

March" the day after the publication of the Court opinion in order to prevent any step toward the independence of the "southern territories."

As is detailed in relevant chapters, after several years during which the Organization of African Unity (OAU) tried unsuccessfully to solve the conflict in accordance with the Moroccan initiative, UN Secretary General Pérez de Cuéllar convinced King Hassan II on July 20, 1985, to accept self-determination referendum based on the wishes of the inhabitants of Western Sahara under UN auspices. Subsequent negotiation led to the adoption of the UN Settlement Plan that went into effect in April 1991.

During this entire period, either before or after any agreement or negotiation, the Moroccan authorities have never left any doubt that they had a very restrictive interpretation of the referendum as a mere "confirmation" of continued Moroccan sovereignty.

Conscious of that essential and unavoidable factor, Mr. Pérez de Cuéllar seems to have been convinced early in the process that autonomy could be a preferable and more practical option for Western Sahara.

Nevertheless, the process engaged under the UN Settlement Plan, and, in particular, voter identification for the proposed self-determination referendum went ahead for almost a decade but without any credible outcome as the result of parties' procrastination, the intricacies of their political goals, or other constraints.

Soon after his appointment, UN secretary-general Kofi Annan nominated James Baker III as his personal envoy in order to try to unlock the impasse. From March 1997 to April 2004, his mediation did not not achieve any concrete result as long as the notion of a referendum on independence was included in any of the options proposed.

As the post-World War II era was followed by the Cold War and then its passing, political realities evolved, as noted in the chapter on the multiple definitions for satisfying self-determination, the UN Security Council, in its Resolution 154 adopted on April 20, 2004, recalled that "a mutually acceptable political solution" is the only way out, thereby, in fact, allocating the option of a referendum focused on the independence option to the diplomatic netherworld.

It has always been evident that key members of the Security Council, for fear of triggering a regional conflict or undermining the Moroccan regime's stability, would refrain from imposing the mandatory organization of a referendum by the UN whose result, being unacceptable to one party, might eventually lead to a new international crisis. None of these countries would like to be faced with such a situation in which the Security Council would have to condemn one party as well as to consider the option of a mandatory (under chapter VII of the UN Charter) military intervention in Western Sahara. Furthermore, with the emerging crisis in the Sahel region, it is even more obvious that major international as well as regional powers will not change their mind.

As argued in several chapters, this is why autonomy still appears to be the only possible option if one wants to get the acquiescence of Morocco, it being understood that an accommodation with Algeria would be key to securing the agreement of the Polisario Front.

It is evident, that if a satisfactory formula for self-determination is to be reached among the parties, some sort of referendum will remain on the table, with the understanding that such a ballot could not clearly include the option of independence, which remains unacceptable to Morocco. It might be possible, however, to deal with the nature and degree of powers devolved to the Western Sahara territory, as called for in Morocco's autonomy initiative of 2007.

It is in this context of devising a solution acceptable to the region and to the global community that this book contains many valuable insights and contributions. While one cannot ignore the challenge that any solution short of independence being accepted by Algeria and the Polisario Front poses, more constructive engagement on this issue can only be helpful. As the authors point out, the international community and the Security Council's continued monitoring of the evolution of the situation on the ground, increasing their visible support for positive efforts to achieve a serious and credible solution, can, in the growing instability in the region, lead to reasonable progress and a mindful solution.

Bernard Miyet
Former UN Under-Secretary General for Peacekeeping Operations

Introduction

Of war men ask the outcome, not the cause. —Seneca

The Western Sahara conflict has been one of the most complex and stubborn disputes in the modern era. After more than thirty-eight years of war and diplomacy, the parties to the conflict are no closer to reaching a mutually satisfactory settlement. The standoff between Morocco and the Popular Front for the Liberation of Saguia al-Hamra and Rio de Oro (Polisario)—a Sahrawi independence movement founded in 1973 and based in Algeria—has triggered disastrous human, economic, and political consequences across North Africa and beyond. From the onset of the war in 1975 until the 1991 ceasefire, the fighting between Morocco and the Algerian-backed Polisario, has caused the displacement of thousands of people, the killing of thousands of fighters, and the division of the territory into a heavily fortified Moroccan zone constituting 85 percent of the territory, protected by defensive walls (called the "Berm") built in the mid-1980s and manned by 150,000 soldiers. The Polisario controls the remainder of the area.

Besides the terrible human and economic costs, the conflict has also negatively impacted trans-Saharan security. The United Nations Secretary General (UNSG) recently warned about the vulnerability of the Sahrawis in the Polisario-controlled refugee camps in northwest Algeria to radicalization and terrorist infiltration.[1] It is the first time that the UN head acknowledged what many experts have been describing for years as a "ticking time bomb."

Understanding the various dimensions of the conflict and the political challenges that hinder its resolution is therefore one of the most important tasks confronting scholars, analysts, and practitioners of peace and security studies. Thus far and with very few exceptions, studies of the conflict have been politicized and dominated by activist scholars. Activist-oriented research can be useful when scholars don't allow their biases to affect the rigor of their research. Unfortunately, the Western Sahara conflict confirms the exception rather the rule. This disturbing trend where partisanship and preconceived dogmas are often substituted for scholarship has not been limited to academia.

There is a growing cottage industry of policy analysts and bloggers whose sole task is to propagate their constructed narrative of the conflict and demolish the other side's understanding of events. In the midst of this zero-sum contest, lines are sharply drawn and sensible ideas are suppressed. What the conflict is and how it should be resolved is shaped by what side of the conflict you support. Challenges to this zero-sum view are not fashionable and carry risks of ironically being branded as partisan. Worse, scholars or policy analysts, whose analysis of the conflict dynamics and conclusions do not fit with the "consensus" developed by one camp or the other, can be subjected to smear campaigns aimed at undermining their academic or professional credentials.

This Western Sahara collection aims to transcend the current stale debates and strident partisan wrangling over who is to blame for the impasse on resolving the conflict. In so doing, it brings the best informed scholars and policy analysts of conflict resolution, natural resources, and security studies to contribute to a collaborative work that fills a critical knowledge gap. For the first time, leading scholars and practitioners of the Western Sahara come together to present a range of approaches and methodologies that recognize multiple views and perspectives. A unique collaboration of Algerian, Moroccan, French, Spanish, British, and American authors, this edited volume serves as a comprehensive primer for students, teachers, researchers, and practitioners of conflict studies as well as international law and security.

IS HISTORY A GOOD START?

For Osama Abi-Mershed and Adam Farrar, the history of the Western Sahara showcases complex interactions between local (Sahrawi), regional (Moroccan), and neighborly (Spanish) dynamics and concerns. The territory has attracted different actors for various reasons that are linked to both expansionist and nationalist interests and narratives.

In the midst of the turmoil brought about by the pressure of the Ottoman Empire in the East during the last half of the nineteenth century, economic downturn due to natural causes and the increased presence of European predatory colonial interests in the west and south, and its reaction of self-imposed diplomatic isolation, Morocco's Alawite sultanate seemed to have conceded sovereignty over its southern territories. In this political vacuum and economic uncertainty, a combination of Spanish concern for commercial competition from other European powers in the Western Sahara region and political competition and interference by Europeans in Moroccan affairs led to the creation of a Spanish protectorate in the Western Sahara. In 1956, Morocco's freshly independent and postcolonial state with its nationalist narrative over the southern territories shaped its claim over Western Sahara, while, at the same time, native Sahrawi national aspirations emerged even stronger. Morocco's internally driven agenda on the Western Sahara created new regional and diplomatic implications for its claim, focused in part by Morocco's irredentist claims to the Spanish Sahara and Spain's other possessions within what was considered the natural boundaries of Morocco. As Spain's regional weight receded after World War II, a new dynamic replaced the traditional triumvirate, leaving international organizations and proxies of the global superpowers a freer hand in the *de facto* internationalization and prolongation of the conflict, in particular after the inconclusive outcome of the desert war between Morocco and pro-Sahrawi independence Polisario forces. The search for a political settlement based on a self-determination referendum remained complex and elusive as the post–Cold War context (and perhaps the Arab Spring's new demands) reinforced Morocco's national claim of the Sahara's relevance to regime survival, thereby weakening the Sahrawi independence option, further entrenching the stalemate in the absence of effective international pressures to settle the dispute. While not underestimating the use of historical analysis in conflict resolution, concludes Abi-Mershed, history is no substitute to the critical answer to the core of the Western Sahara dispute: Who are the Western Sahara people and who can decide the future of the contested territory?

SETTING THE HISTORICAL AND SOCIOLOGICAL CONTEXT OF THE CONFLICT

Joshua Castellino and Elvira Redondo reframe the structural foundation of the dispute as a clash between, on the one hand, the prescription of self-determination embodied in the 1975 International Court of Justice advisory opinion on Western Sahara and legacy of the Westphalian system, and, on the other hand, the reality of the definitions of governance, territory, and people. Hence, the historical and sociological context suggests the "the role and existence of structures of governance facilitating legal and political support for the legitimacy of colonial expansion and titles" as opposed to the primacy of ethnicity and specific precolonial administrative systems. Indeed, Castellino and Redondo see Saharan communities building organization and identity on structures other than territorial foundations that are so critical to the application of Westphalian sovereign statehood claims.

Indeed, the distinction in the Sherifian Empire between a domain of sovereignty (*Bled el-Makhzen*) and a domain of suzerainty or dissidence (*Bled es-Siba*) underpins Morocco's irredentist claims over the Western Sahara in stressing the Sultan's role and power as spiritual rather than temporal. Similarly, the *Bilad Shinguitti* system—a loose governance structure based on customary law in a region that included Mauritania and the Western Sahara—could not qualify as a conventional and functioning state. None of these indigenous interpretations of tribal structures could fit in the European legal and political notion of statehood.

> Questions concerning the demographics in the region, and the nature of the Sahrawi identity remain key to resolution. —Castellino and Redondo

Yet, Castellino and Redondo note that there is some evidence that the transient and nomadic population of Western Sahara, with a much wider pattern of migratory movements than the Western Sahara and their practice of political autonomy, paid religious allegiance to the Moroccan sultan. Thus the decolonization paradigm (see Roussellier) of independent statehood, free association, or integration misjudges the complexities of historic ties and Sahrawi identity, which remain key to resolution of the conflict. Though territoriality is one of the elements that define people's identity, it cannot prevail over other factors pertaining to postmodern tribalism, which begs the question of international law protection for such independent quasi-states.

Samuel Spector articulates cogently a similar assessment of the inherent limitations of the decolonization process and the prevalence of the self-determination paradigm. Linking self-determination and self-government in international law and practice, Spector proposes to reexamine Morocco's Autonomy Initiative of April 2007 as a conflict resolution tool and entry point to negotiations. While the plan exhibits "acceptable outcomes under the law of self-determination," in its current iteration, it fails however to define organizational details about securing popular consent to such a political arrangement, which is critical for a lawful and legitimate resolution to the conflict. Innovative solutions to the conflict may have to overcome the narrow lens of the decolonization and self-determination framework with an integrating comprehensive and negotiated political settlement as the foundation for lasting settlement of conflict.

Illustrative of several options for self-determination are the cases of the former New Zealand colonies of Cook Islands and Niue, Aceh (an autonomous territory within Indonesia), New Caledonia (a colony of France), and Bougainville (an autonomous territory within Papua New Guinea). These and others provide trends for a fresh look at international legality and the resolution of postcolonial conflicts involving self-determination such as Western Sahara. In some instances (Cook Islands and Niue) full autonomy has been achieved through some form of popular consent but without direct referendum, which still met the United Nations General Assembly's (UNGA) approval. In others (such as Aceh) a lesser degree of autonomy as well of popular consent still led to negotiated compromise; or incremental devolution of power is agreed with no fixed date for a statutory referendum (New Caledonia and Bougainville). Roussellier adds that none of the eleven UN (formerly League of Nations) Trust Territories achieved self-determination on the basis of a referendum on the three options of independence, free association, or integration/status quo; though for six of them a plebiscite or referendum took place, which could be construed as a direct or indirect vote on independence.

The legality and practice of acceptance for free association status never depended on guarantees for local government's exclusive control over certain specified powers but rather on freely expressed choice of the population of the territory. In comparison, the Moroccan Autonomy Plan for the Western Sahara provides for an autonomy statute that would result from negotiations between parties to be submitted to "the populations concerned" without a specific time frame. The plan further assumes that such popular consultation would allow for the free exercise of self-determination by the people of Western Sahara in accordance with international legality as defined by the UN Charter and body of UN Resolutions. Spector warns that the plan's failure to specify voting procedures and voter eligibility for securing popular consultation—on which depends the realization of self-determination for the Western Sahara territory—is likely to remain a fundamental weakness for effective conflict resolution and should be addressed either in negotiations or in future iterations of the Autonomy Plan.

> [T]he need for a prompt and effective resolution of issues concerning the use and development of the natural resources of the territory has never been more urgent. —Glynn Torres-Gillepscy

Control over the territory and power sharing are at the center of the self-governance debate for the Western Sahara people. The territory's natural resources remain a hotly contested issue that has a specific legal and political setting. According to Glynn Torres-Gillepscy, the natural resources of the Western Sahara, though largely unexplored, represent significant opportunities for the territory's economic development. Within one of the least densely populated and most environmentally challenged areas in the world, Western Sahara is neither an economic wasteland nor an insurmountable challenge for its development. Despite obvious potentials (large phosphate deposits, potential oil reserves, and abundant coastline fishing), political conflict over juridical and factual control of the territory has deprived the Sahrawis from realizing the full economic potentials from the exploitation of these resources. While there is a broad agreement that Morocco cannot be the *de jure* administrator (or administering power) of the territory (Roussellier even noted that the UN has not quite decided whether Spain was no longer the territory's administering power in terms of the UN Charter), some have argued that it should be considered a de facto administrator (with corresponding de jure powers by analogy), but others suggested that, owing to Morocco's occupying power in the territory under international law, the laws of occupation should govern the use of natural resources.

Both approaches, however, indicate that in principle the unresolved issue of sovereignty should not prevent the economic development of Western Sahara's natural resources as long as the interest of the territory's population are taken into account and the peoples of the territory are consulted. Furthermore, Torres-Gillepscy notes, the prevailing *opinion juris* regarding the meaning of "permanent sovereignty over natural resources" in non-self-governing territories does not specify that a prohibition of economic development based on the exploitation of natural resources in these territories is detrimental to the well-being of the peoples of these territories. Rather, natural resources development in non-self-governing territories is predicated upon the achievement of two tests: the proposed activities are carried out in the best interests of, and are done in consultation with, the people of the territory.

EXPANDING CONFLICT DYNAMICS: NATION-BUILDING AND GEOPOLITICS

Khadija Mohsen-Finan, expanding on Mershed and Farrar's historical relativism and Castelliano and Redondo's idiosyncratic characterization of the conflict, identifies not only colonial legacy and border disputes as the root causes of the conflict but also subsequent regional competition for a defined sphere of influence. Indeed neither this hegemonic factor nor the need to consolidate young states like Morocco and Algeria through nationalist claims can explain alone the emergence of the Western Sahara conflict without the recognition of a new player: Polisario, a "liberation" movement that was born out of a transnational ideology and later embraced a narrative of statehood and independence for Western Sahara.

Morocco articulated a discourse around the need to correct history and recover lost territories, enabling Hassan II to turn the Sahara issue into a matter of national interest, which could be used as a political platform to reengage left-wing opposition, divert challenges to the monarchy, and secure broader participation in government institutions. For I. William Zartman, Morocco's claim over the Western Sahara is existential, part of a national and historical identity and not essentially the result of territorial expansionism. It is as much the expression of strategic and self-definition anxiety as it is an interest-based foreign policy priority for the kingdom. Though strategies and tactics have evolved or even shifted, Morocco's policy on Western Sahara has "evolved in consonance with both the changing international status of the territory and with the evolving domestic political situation."

The Western Sahara's existential resonance is also intimately connected to domestic policy and regime survival tactics as part of a mutually reinforcing dynamic in which the political and governance status of

Western Sahara had to be synchronized and harmonized with Morocco's domestic and political reforms agenda. In this context, notes Zartman, Morocco's policy on the Western Sahara has remained a prerogative of the royal executive and the security establishment. This policy-making process is also rooted in Morocco's own politically uncontested experience of postcolonial transition from territorial fragmentation to a retrocession process within historic borders.

For Algeria, as Laurence Aïda Ammour observes, its war of independence has left deep nationalistic and militaristic marks on the Algerian political culture, including domestic and foreign policy. The country's unwavering stand on the Western Sahara conflict over four decades of changes in international relations and structure demonstrates not only the extent to which the management of this conflict is rooted in "the emergence of a political culture of belligerence structured around the army," but also from intense diplomatic and strategic competition for regional hegemony with Rabat.

As Algerian foreign policy predated the birth of the Algerian state in the anticolonial struggle, the Algerian military continues its historic monopoly on formulating and executing foreign policy. Despite generational change, institutional memory and ideology ensure that the Algerian military, security apparatus, and the executive will continue to see Morocco as the main adversary, implying a regional balance of power has to be maintained in the Western Sahara. The military's belief that it is the only true heir to the country's identity as well as the only guarantor of the state as a nation has left deep-seated and long-held hostility toward Morocco. Algeria's pro-Sahrawi activism is evidently a financial, diplomatic, and political burden, undermining Algiers' aspirations as regional and ideological unifier, but it is also instrumental in containing Morocco's territorial claims in the Sahara. However, warns Ammour, the deteriorating security situation in the Sahel, the Libyan crisis, and European pressure to strengthen intra-Maghreb cooperation following the Arab Spring weakened Algeria's policy to exclude Morocco from regional security arrangements.

SELF-DETERMINATION REFERENDUM OR POLITICAL REFEREE ON AUTONOMY?

According to Mohsen-Finan, Morocco's initial support for a self-determination referendum to end the Spanish presence in the Sahara was quickly reversed out of concern that the referendum could reinforce nascent Saharan nationalism in the territory and start a genuine independence process. This led the Moroccan monarchy to subsequently seek a regional framework for the resolution of the dispute by seeking a united front with Algeria and Mauritania against Spain. However, beyond the facade of unanimity to bury colonization, ulterior motives prevented a speedy settlement of the conflict. Morocco's territorial concessions to both Algeria and Mauritania, which effectively scaled down Rabat's grand vision of Greater Morocco, were expected to be matched by recognition of its claim to the Spanish Sahara in the name of territorial integrity.

> [V]arious UN peace plans essentially did nothing to change the situation.... They merely shifted the conflict to the diplomatic arena. The situation became so inextricable that the UNSC routinely refused to make any decisions on the thorny issue of Western Sahara. —Mohsen-Finan

In 1981, Mohsen-Finan recalls, Hassan II launched a new diplomatic, military, and political strategy. The monarchy was heavily dependent on the financial support of the Gulf monarchies as well as the United States and France in the armed conflict with the Algerian-backed Polisario, while opposing any direct negotiations. In this context, accepting self-determination in principle, the king effectively transformed a guerilla war (Morocco was losing) into a war of attrition through the building of several defensive walls. Morocco shifted the Western Sahara conflict to a new international law ground and placed it within a regionalization policy based on the integration of the Saharan people into Morocco. Algiers could not accept, however, to discuss a self-determination process as framed by Rabat without appearing to surrender. Thus, the UN–proposed settlement plan in the late 1980s allowed Algiers a policy shift from supporting negotiations between Morocco and Polisario to an honorable exit, ensuring continued support for the Polisario without ceding to Morocco's terms of negotiations. Furthermore, the multilateralization of the conflict suited also Spain.

As Antonin Tisseron observes, the Spanish stand on the Western Sahara issue remained noncommittal as far as the main conflict stakeholders' positions are concerned. Madrid reiterated that a final status for the territory should be the result of a negotiated outcome among the different parties and be consistent with the right to self-determination as guaranteed by a UN-supervised referendum. Spain would rather stand behind the UN, the European Union (EU), or the United States as it seeks to avoid antagonizing Algeria or Spanish public opinion.

Zartman argues that Morocco's strategy—from a border dispute with Algeria and military conflicts with pro-Western Sahara independence forces in 1970s and 1980s to the hope of a UN-blessed referendum of confirmation for Western Sahara integration with the kingdom in the 1990s—has embraced an offensive bargaining strategy in the 2000s. Furthermore, Roussellier points out, the emergence of *realpolitik* at the UN (out of concern for the internal stabilization of Morocco) created a dual track approach: the self-determination paradigm and the political settlement option.

At the same time, progress in domestic politics was expected to match compromise (autonomy proposal) in political negotiations over Western Sahara. Since its annexation of the territory, Morocco implemented a complex, three-pronged strategy focusing on military, sociopolitical, and diplomatic tactics, of which only the latter proved to be less convincing. In this regard, Tisseron notes that Black Africa has been the most vocal in criticizing Morocco's Saharan policy and its annexation of Western Sahara, which contradict two critical principles of the African Union (AU): self-determination and acceptance of colonial borders. To be sure, combined diplomatic and economic efforts by Morocco to strengthen relations with Africa and post–Cold War geopolitical factors have effectively weakened Africa's support for Polisario and the Sahrawi Arab Democratic Republic (SADR) in the mid-1990s. But despite significant support for Morocco's autonomy plan among African states, Tisseron argues, Algeria enjoys considerable influence within the AU thanks to its financial commitment and proactive diplomacy at the regional and multilateral level.

On balance, Zartman observes, Morocco has shown varying degrees of diplomatic skills in defending its referendum strategy. Its ability to raise the Saharan issue as a domestic concern tied to the monarchy, which has identified its goal as integration into the political system, and, on the diplomatic scene, to link persuasively Western Sahara retrocession (be it under autonomy status or otherwise) with the country's stability, guarantees Morocco a policy success while its failure will have the worst outcomes.

> A remnant of the Cold War, the conflict in the Western Sahara historically has not been a priority for US diplomacy. Despite the shift in US policy under President Clinton, the United States has failed thus far to take clearly identifiable actions that make a negotiated solution more attainable. —Edward M. Gabriel and Robert M. Holley

For Holley and Gabriel, Morocco's offer of a negotiated political settlement based on a large degree of autonomy for the Western Sahara meant a major policy adjustment in Rabat as well as a substantial shift in position in Washington. The initial Framework Agreement developed by James Baker was possible as a result of US policy shift and subsequent Moroccan commitment to embrace a new approach to conflict settlement.

Lack of progress on voter registration for the UN-led referendum process, lingering frustration in the US Congress at Morocco's increasingly contentious position, and growing questions about US participation in UN peacekeeping missions in general led to strained US-Morocco relations on the Western Sahara. At this critical juncture a new approach was felt necessary in Washington and a formal US interagency policy review was initialed in early 1999. The review by the State Department effectively took stock of the referendum impasse, even with a resolution of the voter registration disagreement, and concluded that a winner-take-all outcome would be counterproductive to US interests and threaten stability in the region. Instead, the review—notwithstanding lingering doubts among senior State Department officials about Morocco's claim and commitment to moving away from the current "do-no-harm" status quo—promoted a political compromise that would guarantee Morocco's sovereignty together with substantial degree of self-governance as a legitimate instrument of the realization of self-determination. The results of the policy review, however, were treated with some ambivalence at the State Department: for some, it was a strategic shift in the region; for others, a tactical improvement in US-Morocco relations. Eventually a formal endorsement in the Bush and the later Clinton and Obama administrations led to the current UN diplomatic initiative.

Morocco's reaction to the first Baker plan was to support a political compromise even it if meant abandoning the long-held position of integrating the territory and carrying the risk of further demands for self-rule by other regions, hoping that a resolution of the conflict would help build a more stable and economically vibrant Maghreb region. The second Baker Plan—which would have allowed the autonomous government to enact laws without reference to the Moroccan constitution and without clear indication of a final vote—prompted a Moroccan refusal. The proposal failed to secure the support of the Bush administration, which insisted on a political compromise (autonomy) within Moroccan sovereignty and on avoiding any imposed solution, a position that the United Nations Security Council (UNSC) later echoed. The United States (Bush, Clinton, and Obama administrations) officially endorsed the Moroccan autonomy initiative but the Algerian-backed Polisario consistently rejected the plan, even threatening a return to hostilities. With no concrete steps by the United States and continued impasse at the UNSC, tens of thousands of Sahrawi refugees remained condemned to a bleak life in the refugee camps, which remain vulnerable to destabilization and terrorist and criminal infiltration. Yet, writes Steven King, the Polisario "remains caught up in a revolutionary vision that may no longer be viable given international concerns with stability and security in the region and beyond." How the movement readjusts and reinvents itself "will largely determine its survival and the sustainability of Sahrawi nationalism," adds King.

While Holley and Gabriel underlined the link between Sahrawi refugee camps and regional stability, Aomar Boum argues that the issue of Sahrawi refugees is not peripheral or mainly humanitarian for the Western Sahara conflict. It is both a moral and political tool for different narratives as well as diplomatic games. For Rabat, the refugees are "captive prisoners" in desolate camps run by the Polisario under the watchful eye of the Algerian military. For the Polisario, they are the national liberation vanguards of the future Sahrawi state, which they will create upon their return to the Western Sahara territory. More than clashing memories of political refugees versus detainees' narratives, the refugees are powerful vehicles for Polisario's search of international empathy for its humanitarian survival and political cause.

Refugees are as much a political statement of the collective expression of national identity and statehood as a bargaining chip in granting the Western Sahara conflict international visibility against Morocco's assumed goal of national solution through a prolonged status quo. In the Polisario narrative, displaced Sahrawi women, children, prisoners as well as disabled and elderly men are no longer symbolic disenfranchised victims; they are effectively turned into active participants of anticolonial struggle (against Morocco) and "organized agents in state formation." This public relations strategy is the basis for Polisario's humanitarian support network. Despite significant Sahrawi transnational displacement and migration, Sahrawi camps support Polisario's memory of loss and exile. Environmental challenges, mismanagement, isolation, economic struggles, illicit activities, organized crimes, and possible links with regional terrorist organizations, warns Boum, may offer a direct challenge to the "human face" of the Western Sahara conflict. Worse, according to King, these same challenges, compounded by rising discontent in the camps and diplomatic deadlock, threaten the very "nature of Sahrawi nationalism."

WHAT DOES THE FUTURE HOLD FOR MOROCCO'S AUTONOMY PLAN AND WESTERN SAHARA'S INTERNAL SITUATION?

For Mohsen-Finan, the Moroccan autonomy plan, lacking specificity and clarity about transfer of powers to the territory, implies regional autonomy and an "asymmetrical system of territorial organization." Granting autonomy would also mean implicit acknowledgment of the Sahrawi identity, which the Polisario has claimed to embody as a liberation movement and a state. This could also be construed as a victory for Polisario and could prompt similar self-rule demands by other regions in Morocco.

The emergence of a new generation of Sahrawis in the territory—who refuse both elites co-opted by Morocco (in the context of autonomy) and support for Polisario—ushers in a new context of reference and political demands. At the same time, leveraging self-determination and therefore independence, the new Sahrawi generation re-asserts social and economic aspirations in the broader context of a right-based approach, which the international community has to take into account. Similarly, Anouar Boukhars observes that "the fading of the old guard is rapidly giving way to a new and unpredictable generation of protesters." Boukhars sees the emergence of a new generation of Sahrawis who are more individualistic and prone to violence than the previous generation, and politically agnostic (neither integration with Morocco nor independence on Polisario's terms).

> The inability of tribal leaders and political elites to address catalysts of conflict and mediate crises when they emerge demonstrated the dangerous absence of traditional and political structures for conflict resolution. —Boukhars

For Boukhars, ethnic cleavages, tribal tensions, and socioeconomic grievances—which are the results of far-reaching demographic, social, political, and economic changes since Morocco's annexation of the territory in 1975 and through successive waves of migration—reinforce opposing groups' demands and further entrench separate identity and interests-driven aspirations, a foreboding about a worsening security situation as well as uncertain societal and economic development in the territory. Yet, the Western Sahara was spared large scale ethnic strife, politically motivated insurrections, and socioeconomic demonstrations that have spread throughout North Africa during the "Arab Spring."

NOTE

1. Afua Hirsch, "Mali Conflict Could Spill over into Western Sahara, Warns Ban Ki-moon," *Guardian*, April 9, 2013.

Part I

Setting the Context

ONE
A History of the Conflict in Western Sahara

Osama Abi-Mershed and Adam Farrar[1]

The present and ongoing conflict in Western Sahara is regularly described as one of the more intractable legacies of European colonization in North Africa. At the heart of the territorial dispute between Morocco and the Frente Polisario lie uncompromising geopolitical interests and incompatible historical claims that have been aggravated by the use of military force and by decades of largely unproductive diplomatic maneuvering on the part of international bodies and regional or foreign powers. This chapter will review the origins of the conflict by examining the historical weight of colonial rule, incomplete decolonization, and irredentist ambitions on the current regional divisions and disagreements over the former Spanish Sahara. Moreover, it will supplement its analysis of modern political developments with a broad overview of the economic and sociocultural exchanges that historically have interconnected and incorporated the communities and agglomerations extending from present-day Morocco to Mauritania.

To this end, the first section of the chapter aims to contextualize Morocco's historical links and claims to Western Sahara, beginning with the conquest and unification of the region by the Almoravids in the eleventh century. It will highlight specific and fundamental episodes in the annals of Moroccan-Saharan relations, such as the "Saharan" origins of the Saadian and Alawite dynasties of Morocco, and the intermittent expansion of their respective political jurisdictions into the "Lands of the Sudan" from the fifteenth to the eighteenth centuries. By the same token, the chapter seeks also to provide the historical backdrop for the emergence of a "national" Sahrawi identity and its existing claims for sovereignty and self-determination. While the crucible of anticolonial struggles was a critical factor in the maturation of the modern Sahrawi identity, the emergence of local political and cultural-linguistic particularities predates the colonial chapter and may be traced to the distinct progress of Hassaniya society since the fourteenth century.

In the late fifteenth century, Moroccan-Saharan relations were tested by the arrival of Portuguese and Castilian ships and men of war, seeking to commandeer the lucrative trans-regional trade and commerce. In the course of the sixteenth century, the contest between expanding Iberian imperialism and nativist resistance would bring about new forms and structures of political authority in Morocco. In addition, the early Iberian footholds on African soil would serve as the nuclei for the implantation of larger European settlements, and eventually grow into the overarching colonial administrations of the nineteenth and twentieth centuries. Thus, the second section will relate the history of European colonial implantations in North and Atlantic Africa since the mid-fifteenth century. It will situate the creation of the Spanish Sahara within the larger context of European imperial rivalries in the nineteenth century, which culminated with Spain's takeover of Río de Oro in 1884 and the establishment of French and Spanish protectorates over Morocco in 1912.

The third section will summarize anticolonial and nationalist responses to European colonialism, and examine the place of Spanish Sahara in the emergent nationalist discourse of Morocco following the kingdom's independence in 1956. The brief and "forgotten" Ifni War of 1957 will serve as the backdrop against which to analyze Morocco's claims to the territories of Saguia el-Hamra and Río de Oro and Spain's motives for retaining them through the 1960s. Spain's restitution of Sidi Ifni to Morocco in 1969 will further complicate the unresolved status of the Spanish Sahara and mobilize the rise of Sahrawi nationalist movements, such as the Harakat Tahrir in 1970 and the Frente Polisario in 1973. It will conclude with the key events of 1975, namely, the Green March and the ensuing Madrid Accords, by which Spain withdrew from the Sahara and negotiated a tripartite agreement with Morocco and Mauritania.

The fourth section will concentrate on the escalation of the conflict in Western Sahara after 1975, which was marked by the proclamation of the Sahrawi Arab Democratic Republic, by Morocco's "indirect" war with neighboring Algeria, main backer of the Frente Polisario, and by the growing internationalization of the conflict with political and diplomatic interventions by the Organization of African Unity (OAU) and eventually the UN. Finally, it will consider the status of the former Spanish Sahara since the UN-brokered cease-fire of 1991, and will briefly assess the record of its Mission for the Referendum in Western Sahara (MINURSO) in finding a peaceful resolution to the conflict.

THE LONG ARC OF HISTORY

The African Crusade

The emergence into the light of history of the region that came to be known as Western Sahara is often considered to have occurred in the late nineteenth century, with Spain's imperial "acquisition" of the coastal region of Río de Oro in 1884.[2] In reality, the chapter on the making of the modern Western Sahara opens significantly earlier, and was impelled by profound historical interactions between Moroccan, Iberian, and local Sahrawi elements and forces. The decisive merging of the three regional factors began in the mid-eleventh century CE, when the Sanhaja Almoravids (Al-Murabitun) burst forth from their strongholds (*ribat*) in the Mauritanian Adrar to capture Morocco (Maghrib) and incorporate Muslim Iberia (Andalus) into their imperial possessions.[3] For the next two centuries, the Almoravids (r.1040–1147), and their successors the Almohads (r.1121–1269), governed a Western Mediterranean empire founded on the unprecedented political integration of the Atlantic Sahara, Morocco, and Andalus: a tripartite administrative union whose architectural equivalent was exemplified in the commissioning of the "official" Almohad mosques in Marrakesh (Al-Kutubiyya), Rabat (Hassan), and Seville (now, La Giralda).[4]

The ambition to rule a unified Western Mediterranean realm, encompassing Iberia, North Africa, and the Sahara, would survive the collapse of the Almohads. Their Maghribi successors, the Marinids (r.1244–1465), made several attempts to recreate it, but the dynasty lacked the resources and the overarching religious legitimacy to succeed, and in the course of the thirteenth century, Morocco's new rulers would relinquish effective control over the former Saharan possessions of the Almohads to the south of the Oued Sous.[5] Likewise, Ferdinand III of Castile asserted himself as the effective inheritor of the Almohad dominions by virtue of his conquest of the heartland of Andalus.[6] Ferdinand was a prime champion of the "African Crusade," or the prolongation of the ongoing *Reconquista* into Africa to reclaim the once-Christian provinces of Rome. He died in 1252, while preparing to cross the Straits and invade Morocco.[7]

The political and ideological mobilizations for the African Crusade, as an extension of the policies of the *Reconquista* proper, were integral to the consolidation of the autonomous Catholic dynasties in Iberia, and led to the eventual division by agreement of North and Atlantic Africa into respective Spanish and Portuguese spheres of interest. Aside from religious dogma, foremost in the calculations of the Catholic monarchs was access to the trans-Saharan networks of trade and to the desert's legendary abundance in gold.[8]

The gold mines of the Sahara had compelled European imaginations since the establishment of Arab rule in Iberia and Sicily. Beginning in the late thirteenth century, European mariners attempted to circumnavigate Cape Bojador (Ras Boujdour)—then, the southern limit of the mapped world—in a bid to tap into the "golden trade of the Moors."[9] Abraham Cresques captured the fascination of Europeans with Africa's mythical "rivers of gold." His *Catalan Atlas* of 1375 depicts the ill-fated voyage of Captain Jaime Ferrer, who sailed around Cape Bojador in search of *al Riu de l'Or*, believed to lie somewhere to the south of Morocco.[10] With European naval technology and power in clear ascendance by the late fourteenth century, the search for the fabled *Río de Oro* developed into state-sanctioned policies, especially by the ruling houses of Portugal and Castile, where royal subventions enticed a growing number of explorers to venture along African coasts in search of fortune and fame.[11]

Portuguese explorations resulted in the establishment of several military outposts, or *fronteiras*, along the African coast to the mouth of the Senegal River, notably in 1445 on the Island of Arguim, off the shore of present-day Mauritania.[12] African gold, captives, and slaves began to be sold in Portuguese marketplaces, and intensifying naval and commercial rivalry between Portugal and Castile over these commodities prompted Pope Calixtus III's *Inter Caetera* of 1456 to demarcate their respective zones of operation north and south of Cape Bojador.[13] The precedent was set for the formal recognition of exclusive rights of exploitation and control over the Muslim lands of North Africa and newfound overseas territories. The Treaty of Alcáçovas-Toledo, signed by Portugal and Castile-Aragon on September 4, 1479, ended the War of the Castilian Succession and divided the Western Mediterranean Basin and the Atlantic Ocean into discrete zones of influence.[14] To this extent, the treaty inaugurated the colonial principle of exclusive territorial reserves, with discretionary license to intervene in the affairs of indigenous populations therein.

Alcáçovas also marked the entry in force of European imperial encroachments upon the sovereignty of Morocco and the Atlantic Sahara. It recognized Castile's dominion over the Canary Islands, and awarded Portugal monopoly of navigation, conquest, and trade in all the ocean south of Cape Bojador, in "coasts or lands discovered and to be discovered, found and to be found."[15] It confirmed, moreover, Portugal's rights over the Atlantic coast of Morocco, as well as its freedom to undertake the conquest of "the Kingdom of Fez." By then, Portugal and Castile—having already established fortified trading posts at Alcácer-Ceguer (El-Ksar as-Sghir, 1458), Tangier (1464), Arzila (1471), and Santa Cruz de Mar Pequeña (Foum Agoutir, 1476)—were well on their way to carving lucrative inroads into trans-Saharan networks, and suffocating the local commercial and naval outlets of Morocco.[16] After 1479, the Iberian powers intensified their drive to dominate the Atlantic and West Mediterranean coasts with military garrisons and naval bases. Portugal now established *fronteiras* in southern Morocco at Safi (Asfi, 1488), Azamor (Azemmour, 1513), and Santa Cruz do Cabo de Aguer (Agadir, 1505). The Spaniards, meanwhile, established a fortified settlement (*presidio*) at the mouth of the Oued Draa (1499) and at Villa Cisneros (Dakhla, 1502). Later, the lower course of the Draa would mark the boundary between French Protectorate Morocco and the Southern Spanish Zone (Cape Juby).[17]

The Consolidation of Sharifian Authority

Local Sufi and maraboutic (*murabit*) orders decried publicly the manner in which the ruling Wattasids (Banu Wattas, r.1472–1554) of Fez were prosecuting the war effort against the Iberians.[18] According to *Dawhat an-Nashir*, the biographical narrative of Muhammad ibn 'Ali ibn 'Askar, in 1511, the *murabit* Shaykh al-Matghari of Oued Draa, in conjunction with the followers of the venerated Sufi *imam* Muhammad al-Jazuli (d.1465) of Afoughal, channeled popular grievances against the Wattasids, proclaiming that the inept dynasty had lost its legitimacy to rule over Muslims. They called on the communities of southern Morocco to transfer their allegiance (*bay'a*) to the Saadian Sharif (pl. *shurafa'* = holy men of Prophetic descent) Muhammad al-Mahdi al-Qa'im bi-Amri'llah (d.1517) and his sons Ahmad al-A'raj (d.1557) and Muhammad ash-Shaykh (d.1557). Their divine charisma (*baraka*) and extraordinary, even miraculous, abilities alone would save Muslims from annihilation.[19]

Between 1518 and 1525, Al-Qa'im's sons organized effective propaganda and military campaigns against the Wattasids, their local allies, and tribes that had submitted to the Christian powers. Saadian forces razed the Spanish *presidio* at Santa Cruz de Mar Pequeña in 1524, and in the following year, seized Marrakesh.[20] In 1536, Sharif Ahmad al-A'raj inflicted an irrevocable defeat upon the Wattasids at Bir 'Uqba (or Bu 'Uqba). Now turning their full attention to the Portuguese, Saadian forces captured their stronghold at Agadir in 1541, and forced the evacuation of Azamor and Safi. By 1545, they controlled most of the former Wattasid realm, and in 1549, Muhammad ash-Shaykh marched into Fez, the capital of the fallen dynasty. By 1554, only the *fronteiras* closest to Portugal and Spain (Al-Ksar as-Sghir, Tangiers, Asila, Ceuta, and Mellila) remained under Christian control. Portugal's last-ditch effort to subdue Morocco ended with its disastrous 1578 defeat at Oued al-Makhazin (Al-Ksar al-Kbir = Alcácer-Quibir).

Moroccans ascribed the decisive success of the Saadians (r.1554–1659) to their Prophetic descent and their spiritual sanctity.[21] Henceforth, the notions of *bay'a* and *baraka* became mainstays for the exercise of political authority in Morocco, as did the prominence of the divinely sanctioned ruler in protecting the integrity of his Muslim subjects and preserving the unity of his lands. The Saadians based their political legitimacy on the integration of temporal power with religious authority and divine sanction. In time, the central state apparatus would become known as the *makhzan*, to connote the effective political synthesis between the spiritual and fiscal dues owed to the person of the Sharif.[22] Indeed, Sharifian houses have ruled Morocco to this day: the Saadians until 1659, followed by the incumbent Alawite line.

The Saadian victory at Oued al-Makhazin propelled the remarkable career of Moulay Ahmad al-Mansur ad-Dhahbi (r.1578–1603), so named (ad-Dhahbi = Golden) for the ransoms of gold he commanded in exchange for the many Portuguese nobles his soldiers had seized during the battle. With the Catholic powers at bay, Al-Mansur revitalized the political imperialism of a foregone era to reclaim the patrimony of the Almoravids and Almohads in the south, and restore Morocco's control over the western axes of the trans-Saharan commerce. The expansion of Al-Mansur's political and religious authority over Saharan Africa after 1590 has since provided much historical substance for Morocco's more contemporary claims to Western Sahara, though it must be noted as well that historical relations and exchanges between Morocco and Saharan Africa were not limited to geopolitical interests and calculations. The following paragraphs will show that, through their growing integration into trans-Saharan networks of trade over the span of centuries, socioeconomic, intellectual, and communal exchanges between North and Atlantic Africa tended to transcend political or administrative considerations.[23]

Trans-Saharan Exchanges

With the establishment of Arab rule in North Africa and the Western Mediterranean in the course of the seventh and eighth centuries, the internal African commercial networks were integrated to the long-distance trade routes of the Muslim world, and regular transaction across the Sahara expanded considerably. Sub-Saharan Africa supplied the Muslim economy with spices, amber, gum arabic, kola nuts, animal skins, cowries, precious stones, and ivory. It imported in return jewels, textiles, copper, silver, pearls, wheat, and finished products. The focal commodities of the trans-Saharan traffic, however, were gold, salt, and slaves.[24] As early as the eighth century, the gold mines of Bambuk (Senegal), Bouré (Guinea), Lobé (Ghana) and Akan (later known as Africa's Gold Coast) had grown vital to the markets and monetary regimes of Idrisid Morocco, Umayyad Andalus, and Aghlabid Ifriqya. In the Land of the Blacks (As-Sudan), Arab merchants claimed, gold grew in the earth as carrots did.[25]

Trans-Saharan trade routes were also gateways for sociocultural and intellectual exchanges between the Muslim Mediterranean and the communities of the African Sahel (As-Sahil).[26] In the wake of the establishment of Arab rule in North Africa, the language and faith of the conquerors were carried into the Sahel along with the commodities of the trans-Saharan exchange. By the early tenth century, the main Saharan crossroads had developed into prosperous and renowned centers of Muslim urbanity: Sijilmasa, Tahert, Taghaza, Awdaghust, and Timbuktu. The local Zenata and Sanhaja tribes, who controlled the key oasis settlements along the western trade routes, were gradually Islamized and Arabized. But the main thrust of Islamization in the Sahara occurred in the eleventh century, when, as we have seen, the Almoravids began to preach their doctrine among the Lemtuna and Jadala clans, before expanding north and taking the Zenata towns of Sijilmasa and Awdaghust in 1054.[27] By 1058, the Almoravids had reached southern Morocco, settling first in Aghmat before establishing nearby their future capital of Marrakesh, sometime between 1061–1062 and 1070.[28] At the height of their power, the Almoravids ruled a unified empire that stretched from Valencia in Andalus to Kumbi Saleh, the former capital of the Empire of Ghana. In parallel fashion, the arrival of the Arab Banu Hassan tribes of the Ma'qil clans and their settlement in the Tafilalt domains of the Sanhaja in the fourteenth century, widened the use of Arabic among the local populations, altered the ethnolinguistic profile of southern Morocco, the western Sahara, and Mauritania, and deepened cultural and intellectual ties between these provinces.[29]

Following the political fragmentation of the Almohad Empire after 1269, Marinid and Wattasid command over the Saharan trade routes became tenuous and was increasingly disrupted by Portuguese and Spanish incursions.[30] But as mentioned earlier, the Saadian victory at Oued al-Makhazin in 1578 provided the dynasty with the occasion to restore its authority over the western part of the Sahara. Moulay Ahmad al-Mansur prepared his invasion of the Sudan by securing the oases of Tuwat, Timimun, and Ghurara between 1583 and 1588, before setting out for the salt mines of Taghaza and the gold reserves of Sudan. In 1590, Saadian infantry and cavalry, under the command of the converted Spanish eunuch Jawdar Pasha (d.1606), began the long and arduous trek across the desert, in the direction of Timbuktu. It reached the Niger River in 1591 and followed its course to Gao, where it met the powerful Songhai army at Tondibi. Jawdar's convincing victory destroyed the Songhai as a regional power, and brought the cities of Gao, Timbuktu, and Jenne within Morocco's orbit.[31]

The Saadian triumph did not last long, however, and soon after the death of Al-Mansur in 1603, Morocco lost control of the central valley of Niger and was itself rent by a civil war of succession. Europeans exploited the reigning political anarchy to reestablish military enclaves in the north of the country. By 1659, the year of the demise of the Saadian dynasty, Timbuktu, Jenne, and Gao had slipped from Morocco's sway, and local tribal groups, once again, vied for dominance over the trans-Saharan routes.[32] The Banu Hassan capitalized on the waning power of the Saadians to wrest control of the trade in gold, salt, and slaves from the Sanhaja. The thirty-year War of Shar Buba (1644–1674) resulted in the submission of the Sanhaja, and opened the way for the Arabization of the western Sahara and Mauritania, where the Arabic Hassaniyya dialect remains the mother tongue of the local Arabo-Tamazight communities now recognized as the Sahrawis.[33]

Over the next two centuries, the succeeding Alawite Sharifs would struggle to repair the unity of the *makhzan*, and reassert its control over dissident provinces (*blad as-siba*) and remote Saharan trading posts and depots. Moulay Ismail (r.1672–1727) relied on his formidable black troops, *'abid al-Bukhari*, to impose his authority over *blad as-siba*, and extend his influence to Tuwat and Taghaza, and as far south as the Emirate of Trarza, in modern-day Mauritania, where Ali Chandora (r.1703–1727), the incumbent emir, swore fealty to Ismail in return for the sultan's investiture of authority.[34] Ismail's successors, however, lacked his capabilities and resolve, and the Alawite Sultanate entered a period of rampant political turmoil, economic dislocation, and demographic decline due to widespread famine and epidemics. Confronted with deepening territorial fragmentation and increased European political and economic intrusions, the Alawite *makhzan* turned inward, opting to restrict its dealings with external powers. It was in this context of diplomatic insularity and weakened centralized authority that Alawite sultans signed protocols by which they appeared to concede their sovereignty over the southern territories. Notably, in the peace treaty of May 1767 with Spain, Sultan Mohammed ibn Abdallah (r.1757–1790) acknowledged that lands and seas south of Oued Nun did not recognize his authority. Similarly, in March 1799, Moulay Sliman (r.1792–1822) signed an accord with King Charles IV, in which he conceded that Saguia el-Hamra and Cape Juby were beyond his dominion. Not surprising, such documents have figured prominently in contemporary debates concerning the validity of Morocco's claims to Western Sahara.

COLONIAL RULE

Morocco's version of isolationism ended abruptly in July 1830 with the French conquest of Algiers, especially as the colonial regime exerted greater pressure on the Sharifian Sultanate to divert its commerce to French-held Algerian ports. The defeat of Moulay Abd ar-Rahman (r.1822–1859) at Oued Isly in August 1844, exposed the military weakness of the *makhzan* and drove the sultan to seek British support to ward off the growing French threat.[35] Britain demanded trade concessions in return, specifically the dismantling of the sultan's monopolistic controls over local trade. European assaults on the sultan's monopolies accelerated during the Crimean War, as France joined Britain in compelling the *makhzan* to liberalize its economy and commerce. On December 9, 1856, Abd ar-Rahman acquiesced to the Treaty and Convention on Commerce and Navigation, which abolished most state monopolies, reduced import duties on British goods, imposed maximum duties on Moroccan finished goods, and stipulated that the clauses of the agreement could extend to other nations.[36]

The Treaty of 1856 devastated the economy and commerce of Morocco. Moroccans saw prices on basic foodstuffs double and triple within months of the Treaty, and regarded the latter as proof of the growing corruption and ineptitude of their government.[37] In 1858, impoverished rural Moroccans rose up and attacked local European concessions. The government of Spain seized on a border incident in Melilla in late 1859 to land an army at Martil and occupy Tetuan in February 1860, before marching on to Tangier.[38] The British government intervened and placated the Spaniards by forcing Sultan Mohammad IV (r.1859–1873) to accept the Terms of Wad-Ras on April 26, 1860. The Spaniards withdrew from Tetuan in return for territorial annexations around Ceuta and Mellila, and for the restoration of their former southern enclave of Santa Cruz de Mar Pequeña.[39] Unable or unwilling to determine the exact location of the ruined *presidio*, Spain opted finally to rebuild it at the mouth of Oued Nun, more than one hundred nautical miles north of the original location.

The *makhzan* was now effectively bankrupt, its economy greatly leveraged by European interests, and its political authority increasingly contested by provincial chiefs (*qaids*) who withdrew their allegiance to the Sharifian ruler. The more independent-minded of them entered into personal agreements with European officials or traders. Such was the case with the *qaid* of Sus, who granted the Scottish merchant Donald Mackenzie the right to establish a trading post (Port Victoria) for his North-West Africa Company in the Cape Juby Strip (Tarfaya).[40] Attempts by Sultan Moulay Hassan (r.1873–1894) to deter Mackenzie and preserve his commercial monopolies bore little fruit. The latter, instead, expanded his operations and made known his project to establish a second trading post in Río de Oro. This prompted the government of Spain, alarmed by the growing weight of Britain and France in Moroccan affairs, to land forces there and obstruct Mackenzie's venture with concessions of its own: the Canaries-African Fisheries Company (*Sociedad Pesquerías Canario-Africanas*), established at Villa Cisneros (Dakhla) in 1881, and the Spanish Society of Africanists and Colonists (*Sociedad Española de Africanistas y Colonistas*), founded in Río de Oro in 1884. This was the prelude for Spain to proclaim on December 26, 1884, its protectorate over Río de Oro, from Cape Bojador to Bahia del Oeste (Ras Nouadhibou) in Mauritania, with Villa Cisneros as its administrative center. The Royal Order was later validated by European concert at the Conference of Berlin, and in 1887, Spain expanded its Protectorate to Saguia el-Hamra.[41]

The establishment of the Protectorate of Río de Oro incited the *makhzan* to reaffirm the authority of the sultan over the dissonant southern provinces, and to reinstate allegiances and tributary payments from local leaders.[42] A vigorous Alawite military expedition into the Tafilalt in 1893 prompted the Sahrawi *qaid* of Tindouf Ma' al-Aynayn (d.1910) to seek weapons and funds from Moulay Hassan to wage war against the colonizers. Ma' al-Aynayn swore to uphold the laws of the sultan in the Western Sahara and Mauritania, and in 1895, his warriors seized Port Victoria. Seeking to avoid embroilment in the growing conflict, the British government agreed to sell the North-West Africa Company to the sultan. The ensuing Anglo-Moroccan Treaty of March 13, 1895, stipulated that "the territories stretching from Oued Draa to Cape Bojador, and known as Tarfaya, [belonged] to Morocco."[43] Eighty years later, the government of Morocco would submit the text of this Anglo-Moroccan agreement to the International Court of Justice (ICJ) in its bid to garner support for its claims of sovereignty over Western Sahara. The ICJ, however, ruled that other contemporaneous British and French diplomatic documents contradicted the letter of the agreement and disputed the sovereignty of Morocco over Río de Oro.[44] For example, when the governments of France and Spain signed the Convention of Paris in 1904 to demarcate the border between Río de Oro and French Mauritania, they recognized Spain's freedom of action in the territories of Saguia el-Hamra and Cape Juby, "which are outside the borders of Morocco." Similarly, the same borders, as well as the perimeter of the enclave of Ifni, were confirmed and ratified by the French protectorate authorities in 1912.

In 1910, France gained the definitive military upper hand against Ma' al-Aynayn in southern Morocco, and in the following year, Sultan Abd al-Hafid (r.1908–1912) ended his opposition to French protection, thus paving the way for colonial troops to occupy his capital, Fez.[45] On March 30, 1912, the Treaty of Fez proclaimed officially the establishment of the French Protectorate of Morocco, and on November 27, Spain followed suit with the Treaty of Madrid, which formalized its protectorates in the Rif and in the south.[46] Resistance to Spanish and French forces in southern Morocco and the Sahara was now taken up by the "Blue Sultan" Ahmad al-Hiba (d.1919), son of Ma' al-Aynayn.[47] Allied with the powerful *qaids* of the Glawa, Al-Hiba entered Marrakesh in August 1912, where he was proclaimed Sultan of Morocco. But on September 6, 1912, Al-Hiba's forces were routed by a French column at Sidi Bou Othman. Soon after, Franco-Spanish accords would formally approve the boundaries between French Mauritania and Spain's Moroccan and Saharan possessions.[48]

NATIONALISM, RESISTANCE, AND DECOLONIZATION

Colonial policies in Morocco and the Sahara were intended to arrest, if not stifle, the political and social development of local institutions and populations. Still, Moroccan and Saharawi societies underwent fundamental political and ideological transformations in the interwar period (1919–1939); changes that would feature prominently in shaping the postcolonial conflict over Western Sahara and complicating the prospects for its diplomatic resolution. To begin, the field of colonial politics was greatly polarized in the interwar decades, and exacerbated by the rise of radical authoritarian and socialist parties in Europe. The Bolshevik Revolution in Russia, combined with the peace settlements of Versailles, encouraged the development of irredentist activism inspired by ultra-nationalism or by proletarian populism. Fascist and Marxist-Leninist agitation found fertile grounds in Europe's colonies, where questions of territorial sovereignty and ethnic or cultural identity were always highly charged. In the 1920s, local anticolonial agitation was increasingly integrated to a worldwide network of like-minded associations and international solidarities. European Communist or Socialist parties and intercolonial unions would articulate "indigenous" concerns in terms of an ideological struggle for the liberation of exploited masses from unjust capitalistic exploitation, especially in the context of the global economic crisis of 1929, which made living conditions in the colonies even more tenuous for the colonized populations.[49]

At the same time, political and cultural nativism was strengthened by the popularization of public education, literacy, and print media in the colonies. Anticolonial activists were heartened by the establishment in 1919 of the League of Nations to provide mutual guarantees of political self-determination and territorial integrity to great and small states alike. The mandatory system offered hope that the colonial empires in Africa were not intended to be permanent, and that international opinion had recognized that the purpose of colonial rule was to create new African nations able to stand on their own in the modern world.[50]

Finally, anticolonialism was also motivated by developments within Arabo-Muslim society itself, namely, the rise of religious reformist movements, like the Salafiya, and the development of the secular ideology of pan-Arabism. The Salafis enounced a religious nationalism based on the cultural authenticity and political autonomy of the Muslim personality. Pan-Arabism, on the other hand, aimed for the creation of a secular independent Arab state. Its exponent in Arabophone Africa in the interwar years was the Syro-Lebanese intellectual, Shakib Arslan, publisher of *La Nation Arabe*.[51] Arslan pioneered the ideology of pan-Maghribism, and argued that it was imperative for the peoples of North Africa to consolidate their shared language, heritage, and history, and unite in the face of European oppression.

These various ideological and structural trends would translate into novel frameworks for anticolonial expressions in the North African possessions of France and Spain, and would facilitate the emergence of new forms of political affiliation, grounded in nationalist identification rather than time-honored allegiances of faith and kinship. Indeed, in Morocco, the survival of the political sovereignty of the sultan during the anticolonial struggle would depend on his ability to link his traditional Sharifian authority to his country's rising nationalist agenda. The revolt of Abdelkrim al-Khattabi (1920–1926) and the establishment of the Federated Republic of the Rif in 1922 had demonstrated amply to the *makhzan* the capacity for provincial movements to crystallize, under the impact of anticolonial mobilization, into protonationalist groupings.[52] Likewise, in the late 1950s, Moroccan authorities were perhaps the first to be surprised by the manifestation of an autonomous and separatist "national" Sahrawi identity.

As the wave of decolonization swelled in the decade following the Second World War, the question of the boundaries of independent Morocco began to loom large in the rhetoric and vision of the nationalist campaign. The emergent Moroccan national identity—based on shared language, heritage, and history—superseded the territorial limits imposed by the French and Spanish Protectorates. Yet, while the majority of Moroccans rejected clearly the fragmentation of their country into French and Spanish zones, there was far less consensus among them on the final scope and composition of "historical Morocco." Allal al-Fasi (d.1974), head of the widely popular nationalist party Al-Istiqlal (Independence), is credited with advancing the idea of the independent "Greater Morocco," encompassing the totality of the French and Spanish Protectorates, the Rif and *plazas de soberanía* (Ceuta, Melilla, Chafarinas, Alhucemas, Vélez de la Gomera) in the north, as well as neighboring territories that had come under the jurisdiction of the sultan in precolonial centuries: from Sidi Ifni and the Oued Draa, south to the Senegal—including the Canary Islands, the Sahara, Mauritania and Mali (Timbuktu)—and east to comprise the provinces of Colomb-Béchar and Tindouf in French Algeria.[53]

The independence of the Kingdom of Morocco in March–April 1956 only heightened such irredentist expectations, to be satisfied by diplomatic or forceful action. Negotiations resolved the status of the International Zone of Tangier in October 1956, but in the following year, elements of the Moroccan Army of Liberation targeted Spanish installations in the southern enclave of Ifni. The Agreements of Angra de Cintra to end the "forgotten" War of Ifni (*Guerra olvidada*) in April 1958 awarded Morocco the Tarfaya Strip, but Spain retained control of Sidi Ifni and integrated the administrations of Río de Oro and Saguia el-Hamra into that of the Spanish Sahara.[54] Far from being a meaningless military operation, the Ifni War demonstrated the lengths to which the newly independent Moroccan state, still in the throes of crafting and imposing a national narrative over its territory, would go to support its claim over the Río de Oro and the Saguia al-Hamra. It also was a tangible demonstration of native Sahrawis' emergent anticolonial and nationalist sentiments.

The actions of the Army of Liberation—and its reorganization in 1958 as the Saharan Liberation Army—inspired the formation of similar paramilitary units and revolutionary movements aiming to obtain independence or Moroccan sovereignty for the disputed Spanish possessions: in 1966, the Front for the Liberation of the Sahara from Spanish Domination (*Frente de Liberacíon del Sahara bajo Dominacíon Española*); in 1967, the Movement for the Liberation of Seguia el-Hamra and Río de Oro (*Harakat Tahrir Saqia al-Hamra wa Wadi al-Dhahab*), founded by Muhammad Embarak Bassiri;[55] in 1969, the pro-Moroccan Revolutionary Movement of the Blue Men (*Mouvement Révolutionnaire des Hommes Bleus* = Morehob), created by Edouard Moha (Mohammed R'guibi); finally, in 1973, the Popular Front for the Liberation of Saguia el-Hamra and Río de Oro (Polisario) (*Frente Popular de Liberación de Saguía el Hamra y Río de Oro* = Frente Polisario), cofounded by Brahim Ghali and El-Ouali Mustapha Sayed.[56]

In the early 1960s, the territorial imperatives of Greater Morocco, and the government's rejection of colonial borders, would embroil the kingdom in regional conflicts, and confound its relations with the UN, the Arab League, and the OAU (African Union [AU] after 2002). In November 1960, Morocco refused to recognize the independence of Mauritania and objected to its admission to the UN and the Arab League. In 1963, the newly established OAU adopted the principle of *uti possidetis* (as you possess) to settle the status of colonial boundaries by preexisting treaty rather than by force.[57] In the same year and in contravention of *uti possidetis*, the War of the Sands (*Guerre des sables*) pitted Morocco against newly independent Algeria in battles over the provinces of Tindouf and Béchar.[58] The failure to achieve a clear victory, combined with the increasing implausibility of fulfilling the project of Greater Morocco, convinced a growing number of Moroccan officials of the futility of military maneuvers without diplomatic sanction and the need to moderate their government's irredentist claims. Gradually, the kingdom sacrificed its larger territorial ambitions in order to focus more intently on the Spanish Sahara.[59] After 1965, Morocco would also seek to mend its relations with the internatil community—which had largely sided with Algeria during the War of the Sands—and to explore political solutions to the growing conflict over the Sahara. Thus, as Spain's regional leverage receded irrevocably, it was effectively supplanted by interventions on the part of international organizations, primarily, the UN, Arab League, and OAU, but also by the global superpowers and their local Cold War proxies.

The earliest foray by the UN into the Saharan conflict produced General Assembly Resolution 1514 (XV) of December 14, 1960, which declared the Spanish Western Sahara a "non-self-governing territory to be decolonized."[60] It was followed with Resolution 2072 (XX) of December 17, 1965, which invited Spain to take immediately the necessary measures for the liberation from colonial domination of the territories of Sidi Ifni and the Spanish Sahara, and to negotiate the sovereignty of these two territories. Spain and Portugal voted against Resolution 2072, while South Africa, France, the United Kingdom, and the United States abstained. Further, General Assembly Resolution 2229 (XXI) of December 20, 1966, requested Spain to organize, under UN supervision, a referendum on self-determination in the Spanish Sahara.[61] The resolution was subsequently registered on the agenda of the Fourth Commission of Decolonization, and occasioned seven additional resolutions by the General Assembly between 1966 and 1973. Since 1966, the official position of the UN has favored the referendum on self-determination for the Sahrawi population, not to be revised until 1999 in favor of a negotiated political settlement.

In 1969, international pressure convinced Spain to restore Sidi Ifni to Morocco, but it was the military successes of the Frente Polisario, beginning with its raid on the Spanish military post at El-Khanga in May 1973, which gradually forced the Spanish government to acknowledge formally UN General Assembly (UNGA) Resolution 2229.[62] It accepted the proposal for a referendum to determine the future status of the Spanish Sahara, and requested that the plebiscite be conducted under the supervision of the UN. In December 1974, Spain initiated the prerequisite census survey in the Sahara to determine the list of eligible participants in the vote for self-determination. The census registered 73,497 inhabitants, but failed to take into account the Sahara's nomadic communities or the number of Sahrawi refugees in neighboring countries.[63] Morocco thus protested Spain's methods and activities, and referred the matter to arbitration by the ICJ at The Hague. On October 16, 1975, the ICJ issued its Advisory Opinion, which recognized unanimously that the territory of Río de Oro and Saguia el-Hamra was not *terra nullius* (belonging to no one) before its colonization by Spain. The Advisory Opinion further acknowledged,

> The existence, at the time of Spanish colonization, of legal ties of allegiance between the sultan of Morocco and some of the tribes living in the territory of Western Sahara. They equally show the existence of rights, including some rights relating to the land, which constituted legal ties between the Mauritanian entity, as understood by the Court, and the territory of Western Sahara. On the other hand, the Court's conclusion is that the materials and information presented to it do not establish any tie of territorial sovereignty between the territory of Western Sahara and the Kingdom of Morocco or the Mauritanian entity. Thus the Court has not found legal ties of such a nature as might affect the application of General Assembly resolution 1514 (XV) in the decolonization of Western Sahara and, in particular, of the principle of self-determination through the free and genuine expression of the will of the peoples of the Territory.[64]

While the court's ruling favored the right to self-determination for the people of the territory of Western Sahara, the mere acknowledgment of "the existence . . . of legal ties of allegiance between the sultan of Morocco and some of the tribes living in the territory," was sufficient for King Hassan II (r.1961–1999) to consider his claims vindicated. Within hours of the verdict by the ICJ, the Moroccan government issued the statement that,

> the opinion of the Court can only mean one thing: the so-called Western Sahara was part of Moroccan territory over which the sovereignty was exercised by the Kings of Morocco and that the populations of this territory considered themselves and were considered to be Moroccans. . . . Today Moroccan demands have been recognized by the legal advisory organ of the United Nations.[65]

Claiming the court had ruled in Morocco's favor, Hassan II unveiled his plan to conduct a "Green March" (*al-masira al-khadra'*) into the Spanish Sahara to induce Spain to relinquish the territory to Morocco. The Green March mobilized hundreds of thousands of Moroccan civilians to gather in Tarfaya, from where they began to cross into the Sahara on November 6. It is estimated that approximately 350,000 civilians, supported by about 20,000 soldiers crossed the border, forcing the Spaniards to withdraw south by several kilometers. The United Nations Security Council (UNSC) was quick to condemn Morocco's unilateral actions in the Sahara. However, on November 14, 1975, the Spanish government relented and signed the Agreements of Madrid, thereby ceding administrative control of the territory to Morocco (northern two-thirds) and Mauritania (southern third), after a transitional period of tripartite administration. Spain retained its economic concessions over local fisheries and the important phosphate mines of Bou Craa. In December 1975, Moroccan troops entered El Aaiún (renamed Laâyoune), while Mauritanian troops occupied Tichla and Lagouira.[66] In February 1976, Spain withdrew officially from the Sahara, as Moroccan troops arrived in Dakhla (Villa Cisneros). Already, Moroccan and Mauritanian military operations had resulted in the exodus of thousands of Sahrawis to refugee camps in the region of Tindouf in Algeria.

THE INTERNATIONALIZATION OF THE CONFLICT

The Campaigns of the Frente Polisario

The Polisario Front opposed the Agreements of Madrid, and announced the formation of the Sahrawi Arab Democratic Republic (SADR)—which existed as a government in exile in the refugee camps of Tindouf—with El-Ouali Mustapha Sayed, General Secretary of the Polisario, as its appointed president.[67] The government of Algeria, equally opposed to the agreements, approved of the SADR, as did a majority of OAU member states. Algeria began to fund, arm, and support the Frente

Polisario, thus provoking the rupture of diplomatic relations with Morocco.[68] Adding to Morocco's diplomatic malaise during this time was the publication of reports by human rights groups, such as Amnesty International and International Federation of Human Rights, documenting abuses committed by Moroccan troops against Sahrawi civilians, including arbitrary arrests, summary judgments, targeted assassinations, and the resort to torture during interrogations. On January 27–29, 1976, an Algerian force advanced into Western Sahara as far as the oasis of Amgala, where it clashed with Moroccan infantry for the first time since the War of the Sands. The Algerians suffered heavy losses and withdrew across the border. The two North African countries remained on high military alert until 1982, but succeeded in avoiding further direct confrontations.[69]

The battle plan of the Polisario Front was to concentrate its military effort against the relatively weaker forces of Mauritania, while simultaneously striking at the economic lifeline of Western Sahara and crippling its production and transport of phosphates. The Polisario was generally successful in its operations against Mauritanian positions, and in June 1976, it seized international headlines following its spectacular, albeit costly, raid within the capital, Nouakchott.[70] By 1978, Mauritania's position was severely deteriorated and its economy verging on bankruptcy. A *coup d'état* on July 10, brought the Military Committee for National Salvation to power in Nouakchott, and the Polisario offered a conditional ceasefire. On August 15, 1979, the Military Committee for National Salvation accepted the conditions of the Polisario Front, and committed to withdrawing its troops from Western Sahara and renouncing its claims to any part of the territory. Moroccan forces, however, moved quickly into Mauritania's former zone and annexed the southern portion of the Sahara. The Polisario now directed all its efforts against Morocco, and in the course of 1977–1980, it scored a series of politically significant military successes, targeting not only positions within Western Sahara (Dakhla in August 1979, Samara and Mahbès in October 1979), but also conducting raids on Moroccan soil, as in the attacks on the southern towns of Tan-Tan in January 1979 and Labouirat in September 1979.[71]

In March 1980, the stinging Moroccan defeat at Jebel Ouarkziz convinced the royal military command of the urgency of a new strategic plan. Beginning in August, the government initiated the construction of a fortified defensive wall, encompassing at first the main economic hub of Laâyoune-Samara-Bou Craa.[72] The Moroccan Wall—approximately 1,700 miles in length and consisting of a series of berms of sand and stone, up to seven feet in height and guarded with barbwired trenches several feet deep—was designed to seal off the mineral-rich regions of Western Sahara from infiltration by Polisario combatants. It is manned by some 90,000 troops, and its approach is prohibited by a barrier mine-belt several hundred feet wide. Surveillance and intervention units, equipped with sensory and night vision equipment, monitor all movements along its perimeter. The Moroccan Wall proved very effective in protecting the "Southern Provinces" from guerilla incursions and containing the Polisario forces, especially after Morocco and Libya signed the Treaty of Oujda in August 1984, by which the latter agreed to suspend its military and diplomatic support for the Polisario.[73]

The Creation of Mission of United Nations for the Organization of a Referendum in Western Sahara

In September 1984, Hassan II followed up on his successful diplomatic negotiations with Libya by stating before the General Assembly his government's acceptance in principle of oversight by the UN of the referendum on self-determination.[74] Two months later, however, he resigned in protest from the OAU when the Polisario Front was awarded a seat as the representative of the SADR.[75] With its field of military maneuvers now notably constrained, the Polisario accepted OAU Resolution AHG104 of 1983, which named the Kingdom of Morocco and the Polisario Front "parties to the conflict" and urged them "to undertake direct negotiations with a view to bringing about a cease-fire to create the necessary conditions for a peaceful and fair referendum for self-determination of the people of Western Sahara, a referendum without any administrative or military constraints, under the auspices of the Organization of African Unity and the United Nations."[76]

Between July 1985 and August 1988, joint UN-OAU initiatives finally produced the "Settlement Proposals" for a peaceful resolution of the conflict.[77] The proposals were reiterated in the UN General's Report S/22464 of April 19, 1991, and adopted by UNSC Resolution 690, which established the Mission of United Nations for the Organization of a Referendum in Western Sahara (MINURSO).[78] The proposals, now known as the "Settlement Plan," mandated MINURSO to "monitor the cease-fire, identify eligible voters for participation in the referendum, and create the conditions and modalities for the supervision and conduct of the referendum." The required preliminary cease-fire took hold on September 6, and following agreement with the United Nations Secretary General (UNSG), both sides suspended military operations. The application of the resolution was soon obstructed again by the difficulty of identifying the voters who were eligible to participate in the referendum. In seeking to secure a pro-independence vote, the Polisario Front aimed to limit registration to the residents identified by the census of 1974 and their descendants, while Morocco countered that Sahrawis settled in Morocco and Moroccans residing in Western Sahara were equally eligible.[79] According to Erik Jensen, former head of MINURSO, Morocco and Polisario considered their respective positions to be "closed to compromise":

For Morocco the right to vote had to be comprehensively based on the principle of *jus sanguinis*, extending to all Saharan tribes linked to the former Spanish Sahara; for the Polisario, it should be narrowly defined, mainly according to *jus soli*, but in effect largely limited to those counted in the Spanish census of 1974. . . . The consequences of one interpretation or the other's prevailing are recognized by both as determinant in a winner-take-all referendum, with the unnuanced choice between integration with Morocco and independence under Polisario.[80]

By then, the global strategic balance had shifted dramatically, following the collapse of the Soviet Union and Eastern Bloc, and the US-led war against Iraq. In the new unipolar world order, the conflict in Western Sahara assumed novel dimensions for Morocco and the Polisario.[81] For the latter, the disappearance of the USSR and Eastern Bloc was tantamount to the loss of some of its main political and military backers, and indeed, in the course of the 1990s, international recognition of the SADR diminished considerably.[82] On the Moroccan front, overwhelming popular discontent with the monarchy's decision to participate in the Gulf War revived the specter of popular insurgency and military dissent at home.[83] Consolidating its control over the Southern Provinces became imperative for a throne under popular pressure to embark upon constitutional reforms, guarantee a state of law, and advance toward parliamentary monarchical governance. Moreover, from the perspective of Hassan II, the war against the Polisario had paid great political dividends in effectively keeping army commanders distracted from domestic ambitions since the attempted military coups of the 1970s.[84] Such considerations would lead to a noticeable hardening in Hassan II's position on Western Sahara during the remaining years of his reign.

In March 1997, the UNSG appointed former US Secretary of State James Baker III as his personal envoy for Western Sahara (S/1997/236).[85] Baker visited the region on April 23–28, 1997, and succeeded in convening Sahrawi and Moroccan negotiators in Houston on September 14–16. The meetings produced the Agreements of Houston, which scheduled a referendum in 1998.[86] Again, the drawing of the Provisional Voters List faltered over the identification of eligible candidates. To break the stalemate, Baker proposed wide local autonomy for the Sahara within the framework of the Moroccan state, the prerogatives of which would be limited to matters of defense and international relations. When the Polisario Front and the government of Algeria rejected the plan, the UNSG proposed a new initiative in 2003 (Baker II), which provided for the self-determination of Western Sahara after a three-year period of provisional administration by a governing body elected by the people listed in the Provisional Voters Lists.[87] A referendum would then allow an electorate, formed by the members of the Provisional Voters Lists and the residents in the territory since 1999, to opt for independence, integration, or autonomy within Morocco. The plan was approved unanimously by the Security Council (S/2003/565) on the condition of acceptance by all parties. On April 23, 2004, however, Morocco's new ruler, King Mohammed VI (r.1999–), rejected the transition arrangements and the option of independence in Baker II, and the former Secretary of State resigned his position.[88]

The failure of the Baker initiatives epitomized the inability of the UN to propose a solution acceptable to the belligerent parties, and exposed the weakness of its mandate to instigate meaningful negotiations and provide effective incentives for compromise. In the meantime, the government of Morocco continued to move away from the option of a referendum on self-determination in Western Sahara. In November 2005, on the occasion of the thirtieth anniversary of the Green March, Mohammed VI announced his plan to grant autonomy to Western Sahara within Moroccan sovereignty.[89] In March 2006, he revitalized the Royal Advisory Council of Saharan Affairs (CORCAS) by including among its 140 members tribal notables, women, and representatives of civil societies. The task of the CORCAS was to offer proposals concerning the autonomy of Western Sahara, while Morocco would preserve the portfolios of national defense, foreign affairs, and currency. The following month, the UNSC S/1675 (2006) reaffirmed its commitment to assist the concerned parties achieve a just, lasting, and mutually acceptable political solution that would provide for the self-determination of Western Sahara in the context of arrangements consistent with the principles and purpose of the Charter of the United Nations. To this end, it extended the mandate of MINURSO until October 30, 2006.[90]

Early in 2007, Morocco presented its proposed Autonomy Initiative, which was countered by the Polisario Front's restatement of the referendum process. These proposals then formed the basis for UN-sponsored negotiations under the auspices of the Personal Envoy of the Secretary General (PESG). On June 18, 2007, the first round of negotiations for a definitive solution to the question of Western Sahara took place in Manhasset, New York, between representatives of Morocco (including the president of the CORCAS) and the Frente Polisario, on the invitation of the UNSG and according to UNSC Resolution 1754. However, on April 21, 2008, Personal Envoy Peter van Walsum expressed his opinion that the independence of Western Sahara was no longer "a reachable goal."[91] He added that the option of a referendum on self-determination seemed unrealistic in the absence of "pressure on Morocco so that it abandons its demand for sovereignty." On April 30, the UNSC adopted Resolution 1813, which renewed the mandate of MINURSO to April 30, 2009, repeating the fundamental principles expressed during the previous resolutions, but especially making "its own for the parties to display proof of realism and a spirit of compromise to maintain the impetus of the process of negotiation."[92] Meanwhile, on the occasion of the thirty-fourth anniversary of the Green March, Mohammed VI warned that on the issue of Western Sahara, "one is either a patriot or a traitor. There is no middle ground between patriotism and treason."[93]

CONCLUSION

This chapter has presented the history of the conflict in Western Sahara as a contextually grounded trilateral interaction between Moroccans, Sahrawis, and Iberians—who would later be replaced by the international community. This is in contrast to conventional narratives that cast both the history of the territory and the conflict in a unidirectional colonial/anticolonial binary. Furthermore, by examining the trilateral interactions that have occurred, and continue to occur within the Sahara since the eleventh century, this chapter aimed to give greater depth and complexity to the historical narrative by linking actions to context and interest, and portraying them as reactions to other actors vying for the territory. In short, this chapter has attempted to add to, rather than detract from, the conflict's present and historical complexity. Yet, the length and depth of the history presented here should not be interpreted as supporting arguments that the territory known as "Western Sahara" is to be forever steeped in conflict, or that there is a clear, linear historical trajectory from the eleventh century to the present day. Instead, through a combination of interest-based territorial expansionism, colonial imagination, and eventually nationalism and national self-determination, this chapter has attempted to show how different actors have conceived of the territory as desirable for different reasons. Furthermore, it has argued that different actors' interests should be viewed as dynamic and responsive to their respective domestic politics and circumstances as well as foreign relations. Through this lens, the history of the conflict is not of a "clash of civilizations" between Europeans, Moroccans/Arabs, and Sahrawis, but consists rather of a series of multilayered political conflicts stemming from competing interests and projects focused on the territory.

The long arc of the history of the conflict in Western Sahara engenders a certain frustrating ambiguity as to how it should be resolved. The present stalemate is largely a result of the intractability of the present triumvirate's positions. The internationalization of the conflict from solely Iberian elements to international and regional organizations and the United States, France, Spain, and Algeria, has both served to add resources to resolving the conflict as well as to insert additional interests that seem only to have prolonged the conflict. For its part, and since the Ifni War of 1957–1958, Morocco has demonstrated its willingness to shed blood and expend treasure for a territory it deems an integral part of its national cohesion. Additionally, the kingdom has sought allies within the international community to bolster its claims to the desired parts of Western Sahara, as demonstrated by the construction of its Sand Wall. On the other side, the Polisario Front, speaking for Sahrawi rights to self-determination, has insisted that any referendum regarding the future of Western Sahara must contain the option for independence. Morocco's rejection of an independent Western Sahara and the international community's indecisiveness and unwillingness to exert pressure on Morocco and the SADR otherwise perpetuates the present *status quo*.

Framing the conflict as a stalemate, however, tends to cast the situation as static. But this chapter also endeavored to show that despite recurrent conflict within a triumvirate of actors and a lengthy stalemate of twenty-two years, the conflict is dynamic. Although the balance of power may not have shifted significantly since the 1991 cease-fire and creation of MINURSO, there is a dynamism to the conflict as actors' international and local interests, and international and local contexts change. The reciprocal and ripple effects of local and international developments require that historical analyses take note of the fundamental transformations on the ground over time, starting with the shifts in the demographic profile of Western Sahara. The changing demographics of Western Sahara are eroding what has constituted since 1974 the core issue for any negotiated settlement: the identification of eligible voters in the referendum. The prospects for its ultimate feasibility have started to resemble, in the words of Erik Jensen, an elusive desert mirage: "who is a Sahrawi, who is a Western Saharan, and who should be entitled to vote? Who should be the determining self in the act of self-determination?"[94]

Despite the conflict's dynamism, there is a certain tendency within the literature on Western Sahara to draw upon history as a means by which to offer prognostications and solutions to resolve the conflict.[95] Within the literature, three broad trajectories tend to prevail: maintenance of the status quo stalemate, resolution, or renewed war between Moroccan and Sahrawi armed forces. As an example of another type of outcome, Stephen Zunes and Jacob Mundy contend in their book, *Western Sahara: War, Nationalism and Conflict Irresolution*, that "conflicts involving settler colonialism have tended to conclude in one of three ways: total independence for the natives, total subjugation of the natives by the colonizer, or independence based on an alliance between natives and renegade settlers."[96] Zunes and Mundy favor the third option which would see a growing solidarity among Moroccan settlers and Sahrawis transform into a united Moroccan-Sahrawi demand for an independent state for Western Saharans, that is, all such individuals, Moroccan and Sahrawi, living within the territory of Western Sahara.

The purpose of citing the proposal of Zunes and Mundy is not to evaluate it for its validity, but to distinguish this chapter from other historical analyses of the conflict in Western Sahara. As a descriptive chapter focusing on the depth and complexity of the interactive history, no predictions or solutions will be offered based on historical analysis.

This is not to separate the utility of history from conflict resolution or absolve the interested parties to the conflict from knowing the history of the conflict. History cannot answer the "core question" of the conflict; but where history can be useful, and where this historical outline situates itself, is in raising questions about the conflict's roots and the narratives employed by different actors involved. Knowing first which questions to address seems the prudent way forward.

NOTES

1. The authors wish to thank Dorothée Kellou for her invaluable and meticulous help in editing and researching this chapter.
2. See, for example, Thomas K. Park and Aomar Boum, *Western Sahara: The Roots of a Desert War* (Westport, CT: L. Hill Park, 1983); Tony Hodges, *Historical Dictionary of Morocco* (Lanham, MD: Scarecrow Press, 2006).
3. More precisely, the Almoravid dynasty originated among the Lamtuna and Jadala (Juddala) clans of the Sanhaja confederation. See Jamil M. Abun-Nasr, *A History of the Maghrib in the Islamic Period* (Cambridge: Cambridge University Press, 1987).
4. Andrew Petersen, *Dictionary of Islamic Architecture* (London: Routledge, 1996), 193.
5. Scott Alan Kugle, *Rebel between Spirit and Law: Ahmad Zarruq, Sainthood, and Authority in Islam* (Bloomington: Indiana University Press, 2006), 86.
6. Between 1225 and 1248, Ferdinand's forces captured the Guadalquivir valley (*al-Wadi al-kabir*) and much of the Levante (*sharq al-andalus*), the political, economic, and demographic core of Muslim Spain.
7. Joseph F. O'Callaghan, *The Gibraltar Crusade: Castile and the Battle for the Strait* (Philadelphia: University of Pennsylvania Press, 2011), 11.
8. See John France, *The Crusades and the Expansion of Catholic Christendom, 1000–1714* (London: Routledge, 2005).
9. See E. W. Bovill and Robin Hallett, *The Golden Trade of the Moors: West African Kingdoms in the Fourteenth Century* (Princeton, NJ: M. Weiner Publishers, 1995).
10. John Wright, *The Trans-Saharan Slave Trade* (London: Routledge, 2007), 42.
11. Virginia Thompson and Richard Adloff, *The Western Saharans: Background to Conflict* (London: Croom Helm, 1980), 5.
12. M. D. D. Newitt, *A History of Portuguese Overseas Expansion, 1400–1668* (London: New York, 2005), 24.
13. Newitt, *A History of Portuguese Overseas Expansion*, 52.
14. *Treaty of Alcáçovas-Toledo (1479)*, http://avalon.law.yale.edu/15th_century/sppo01.asp.
15. Bailey W. Diffie and George D. Winius, *Foundations of the Portuguese Empire, 1415–1580* (Minneapolis: University of Minnesota Press, 1977), 152.
16. Hugh Thomas, *The Slave Trade: The Story of the Atlantic Slave Trade, 1440–1870* (New York: Simon & Schuster, 1997), 76.
17. Newitt, *A History of Portuguese Overseas Expansion*, 112.
18. Clifford Edmund Bosworth, *The New Islamic Dynasties: A Chronological and Genealogical Manual* (Edinburgh: Edinburgh University Press, 1996), 48.
19. See Muhammad ibn 'Ali Ibn 'Askar, *Dawhat al-nasir* (Dar al-Magrib, Morocco: li-l-Ta'lif wa-l-Tarjama wa-l-Nashr, 1977).
20. Thompson and Adloff, *The Western Saharans*, 5.
21. Abun-Nasr, *A History of the Maghrib in the Islamic Period*, 214.
22. Abun-Nasr, *A History of the Maghrib in the Islamic Period*, 164.
23. Ralph A. Austen, *Trans-Saharan Africa in World History* (New York: Oxford University Press, 2010), 44.

24. A. Adu Boahen, J. F. Ade Ajayi, and Michael Tidy, *Topics in West African History* (Burnt Mill, Harlow, Essex, England: Longman Group, 1986), 7.
25. J. F. Ade Ajayi and Michael Crowder, *History of West Africa* (Burnt Mill, Harlow, Essex, England: Longman Group, 1985), 156.
26. The Sahel refers to the southern rim of the Sahara, the ecological and climatic zone of transition between desert and savannah.
27. Abun-Nasr, *A History of the Maghrib in the Islamic Period*, 80.
28. The earlier date is recorded by 'Ali ibn Abi Zar' al-Fasi in *Rawd al-Qirtas* and 'Abd ar-Rahman ibn Khaldun in *Kitabu l-'ibar*. In *Al-Bayan al-Mughrib*, Ahmad ibn 'Idhari al-Marrakushi relates the foundation of the city to the year 1070.
29. C. H. M. Versteegh and Mushira Eid, *Encyclopedia of Arabic Language and Linguistics* (Leiden: Brill, 2005), 170.
30. Abun-Nasr, *A History of the Maghrib in the Islamic Period*, 115.
31. Ajayi, et al., *History of West Africa*, 297.
32. Elias N. Saad, *Social History of Timbuktu: The Role of Muslim Scholars and Notables, 1400–1900* (Cambridge: Cambridge University Press, 1983), 54.
33. Alexander Mikaberidze, *Conflict and Conquest in the Islamic World: A Historical Encyclopedia* (Santa Barbara, CA: ABC-CLIO, 2011), 242.
34. Frank Trout, *Morocco's Saharan Frontiers* (Geneva: Droz, 1969), 140–42, and Mikaberidze, *Conflict and Conquest in the Islamic World*, 429.
35. Abun-Nasr, *A History of the Maghrib in the Islamic Period*, 299.
36. For the text of the Convention on Commerce and Navigation, see Great Britain, Parliament, *List of Treaties of Commerce and Navigation between Great Britain and Foreign Powers: Containing Most-Favored-Nation Clauses, Stating the Period When Terminable, and Showing Whether They Apply to the British Colonies* (Ottawa: Maclean, Roger & Co., 1880), 38–40.
37. Kenneth L. Brown, *People of Salé: Tradition and Change in a Moroccan City, 1830–1930* (Cambridge, MA: Harvard University Press, 1976), 120.
38. Phillip Chiviges Naylor, *North Africa: A History from Antiquity to the Present* (Austin: University of Texas Press, 2009), 161.
39. Naylor, *North Africa*, 161.
40. See F. V. Parsons, "The North-West African Company and the British Government, 1875–95," *Historical Journal* 1, no. 2 (1958): 136–53; Michael Brett, "Great Britain and Southern Morocco in the Nineteenth Century," *Journal of North African Studies* 2, no. 2 (1997), 1–10. The remains of Mackenzie's trading post (Casa del Mar) remain visible to this day.
41. Thompson and Adloff, *The Western Saharans*, 5.
42. Harry Hamilton Johnston and J. G. Bartholomew, *A History of the Colonization of Africa by Alien Races* (Charleston, SC: Bibliolife, 2009), 191.
43. Michael Brett, "Great Britain and Southern Morocco in the Nineteenth Century," *Journal of North African Studies* 2, no. 2 (1997): 1–10.
44. According to the ICJ Advisory Opinion of October 16, 1975, the Anglo-Moroccan Treaty constituted merely an agreement by Great Britain to refrain from disputing future territorial claims in southern Morocco by the sultan. It did not amount, therefore, to formal British recognition of Morocco's existing sovereignty over these territories. See International Court of Justice, *Western Sahara: Advisory Opinion of 16 October 1975*, October 16, 1975, www.icj-cij.org/docket/files/61/6197.pdf.
45. Abun-Nasr, *A History of the Maghrib in the Islamic Period*, 370.
46. Trout, *Morocco's Saharan Frontiers*, 203.
47. Thomas K. Park and Aomar Boum, *Historical Dictionary of Morocco* (Lanham, MD: Scarecrow Press, 2006), 153.
48. C. R. Pennell, *Morocco since 1830: A History* (New York: New York University Press, 2000), 158.
49. See Robert Stuart, *Marxism and National Identity: Socialism, Nationalism, and National Socialism During the French fin de siècle* (Albany: State University of New York Press, 2006).

50. Neta Crawford, *Argument and Change in World Politics: Ethics, Decolonization, and Humanitarian Intervention* (Cambridge: Cambridge University Press, 2002), 293.

51. See Shakib Arslan, *La Nation Arabe* (Farnham Common, Buckinghamshire, England: Archive Editions), 1988.

52. Hsain Ilahiane, *Historical Dictionary of the Berbers (Imazighen)* (Lanham, MD: Scarecrow Press, 2006), 107.

53. Naylor, *North Africa*, 230.

54. On April 19, 1961, El Aaiún became the capital of Spanish Sahara.

55. On June 17, 1970, Spanish Foreign Legionnaires opened fire on pro-independence Sahrawis and *Harakat Tahrir* activists in the Zemla district of El Aaiún (Zemla Uprising). In the ensuing round-up of suspected *Harakat Tahrir* militants, hundreds of individuals were arrested, among them Muhammad Bassiri, who was never seen again and is believed to have been tortured and killed by his Spanish captors.

56. See Anthony G. Pazzanita, *Historical Dictionary of Western Sahara* (Lanham, MD: Scarecrow Press, 2006).

57. Gino J. Naldi, *The Organization of African Unity: An Analysis of Its Role* (London: Mansell, 1989). The international law principle of *uti possidetis* stipulates that territory and other property remain with its possessor at the end of a conflict, unless otherwise provided for by treaty. Thus, the principle of *uti possidetis* prevails in the absence of a treaty regarding the possession of property and territory taken during conflict.

58. Nicole Grimaud, *La politique extérieure de l'Algérie (1962–1978)* (Paris: Karthala, 1984), 198.

59. Ali Abdullatif Ahmida, *Beyond Colonialism and Nationalism in the Maghrib: History, Culture, and Politics* (Houndmills, Basingstoke, Hampshire, UK: Palgrave, 2000), 203.

60. See Dietrich Rauschning, Katja Wiesbrock, and Martin Lailach, eds., *Key Resolutions of the United Nations General Assembly, 1946–1996* (Cambridge: Cambridge University Press, 1997).

61. Rauschning, Wiesbrock, and Lailach, *Key Resolutions of the United Nations General Assembly*.

62. Erik Jensen, *Western Sahara: Anatomy of a Stalemate* (Boulder, CO: Lynne Rienner Publishers, 2005), 79.

63. Jensen, *Western Sahara*, 154.

64. International Court of Justice, *Western Sahara: Advisory Opinion of 16 October 1975*.

65. Press release of the Permanent Mission of Morocco to the United Nations on October 16, 1975, quoted in Thomas M. Franck, "The Stealing of the Sahara," *American Journal of International Law* 70, no. 4 (October 1976): 711. See also, Jacob Mundy, "Neutrality or Complicity? The United States and the 1975 Moroccan Takeover of the Spanish Sahara," *Journal of North African Studies* 11, no. 3 (2006): 285.

66. Alan J. Day, and Judith Bell, *Border and Territorial Disputes* (Detroit: Gale Research, 1982), 166.

67. Thompson and Adloff, *The Western Saharans*, 20.

68. Jensen, *Western Sahara: Anatomy of a Stalemate*, 30.

69. Stephen O. Hughes, *Morocco under King Hassan* (New York: Ithaca Press, 2006), 252.

70. Pennell, *Morocco since 1830*, 342.

71. Pennell, *Morocco since 1830*, 342.

72. Jensen, *Western Sahara*, 34.

73. Thomas M. Leonard, *Encyclopedia of the Developing World* (New York: Routledge, 2006), 1169.

74. Andreu Solà-Martín, *United Nations Mission for the Referendum in Western Sahara* (Lewiston, NY: Edwin Mellen Press, 2007), 34.

75. Naldi, *The Organization of African Unity*, 39.

76. Organization of African Unity, 19th Summit, "OAU Peace Plan on Western Sahara (Addis Abbaba, June 6–12, 1983)," AHG/Res. 104 (XIX), www.arso.org/03-3.htm.
77. Jensen, *Western Sahara*, 124.
78. Jensen, *Western Sahara*, 43.
79. Jensen, *Western Sahara*, 41.
80. Jensen, *Western Sahara*, 13.
81. Robbin F. Laird and Erik P. Hoffmann, *Soviet Foreign Policy in a Changing World* (New York: Aldine, 1986), 291.
82. Toby Shelley, *Endgame in the Western Sahara: What Future for Africa's Last Colony?* (London: Zed, 2004), 199.
83. Phyllis Bennis and Michel Moushabeck, eds., *Beyond the Storm: A Gulf Crisis Reader* (Brooklyn, NY: Olive Branch Press, 1991), 20.
84. Anthony H. Cordesman, *A Tragedy of Arms: Military and Security Developments in the Maghreb* (Westport, CT: Praeger, 2001), 89.
85. Cordesman, *A Tragedy of Arms*, 142.
86. Solà-Martín, *United Nations Mission for the Referendum in Western Sahara*, 75.
87. Yahia H. Zoubir and Haizam Amirah Fernández, *North Africa: Politics, Region, and the Limits of Transformation* (London: Routledge, 2008), 200.
88. Zoubir and Fernández, *North Africa*, 192.
89. Zoubir and Fernández, *North Africa*, 285.
90. Zoubir and Fernández, *North Africa*, 194–95.
91. Zoubir and Fernández, *North Africa*, 194–95.
92. United Nations Security Council, "Resolution 1813 (2008) [on the Western Sahara]," (S/RES/1813), www.un.org/ga/search/view_doc.asp?symbol=S/RES/1813(2008).
93. "Discours de Sa Majesté le Roi à la Nation à l'Occasion du 34ème Anniversaire de la Marche Verte, Ouarzazate, 6 Novembre 2009," in Anna Khakee, "The Western Saharan Autonomy Proposal and Political Reform in Morocco," *NOREF Report* 10, no. 46 (June 2011).
94. Jensen, *Western Sahara*, 13.
95. Stephen Zunes and Jacob Mundy, *Western Sahara: War, Nationalism, and Conflict Irresolution* (Syracuse, NY: Syracuse University Press, 2010), 254–65.
96. Zunes and Mundy, *Western Sahara*, 264.

TWO

The Identity Question: Who Are the Sahrawis and What Is Their "Home?"

Joshua Castellino and Elvira Domínguez-Redondo

The situation in northwest Africa in general and the Western Sahara in particular is intriguing since it brings to light the complexities of identity and its interplay with the politics of possession. In examining the historic and ethnographic profile of the Sahrawi and their presence in the Western Sahara, this chapter seeks to provide insights into understanding the impasse for the realization of the right to self-determination of the only African territory still on the list of the UN decolonization process; it also sets the scene for the analysis of the International Court of Justice (ICJ) Advisory Opinion coming in the following chapters.

The Western Sahara conflict reflects the tenuous link between territory and identity in international law. The following pages seek to demonstrate the nuances that form that identity, and then to examine this complexity against the rather single dimensional backdrop of the right of self-determination as presented in public international law. It is argued that the concept of self-determination is well defined in the Western Sahara and derives from the 1975 ICJ's Advisory Opinion, and more generally, can be extrapolated from the three options outlined in the 1960 General Assembly Resolution 1514(XV). These "solutions" however, break down completely on the criteria used to determine the identity of those who may be provided the option of determining the fate of the territory. This is a central issue since, in the language of self-determination, the issue of the governance of a territory is to be determined via the consent of the governed.

In an attempt to trace the lineage that forms part of the identity of a typical person in the region, the opening section begins with a brief historical sketch of the experiences of the Sherifian Empire and the Bilad Shinguitti, through to the colonial influence.[1] This is followed by an examination of the effects of colonization on the region, and on the identity of the nomadic peoples of the desert. The final section will look at some of the issues of definition that were raised with respect to territory and identity in the *Western Sahara Case (Advisory Opinion)*[2] adjudicated before the ICJ in 1975. Particular attention is given to the principle of *uti possidetis*,[3] which in conjunction with the intertemporal rule of law, has often been used to foreclose the issue of reexamination of the boundaries of former colonies. Application of these principles hinders resolution of conflicts such as the one in Western Sahara, by using a legal framework that evolved around the model created by European states that won their freedom from the Roman Catholic Church after the Peace of Westphalia in 1648.[4]

THE GEOPOLITICAL BACKDROP OF WESTERN SAHARA'S TERRITORY AND PEOPLES: THE FORMATION OF MOROCCO AND MAURITANIA

Strands of history and shared visions inevitably contribute to the identity of peoples within any given territory.[5] In this section, some of the influences that have shaped the identity of the "people/s" of North Western Africa are traced. It is not the purpose of these pages to provide a thorough historical account of North Africa, but rather to question the importance of ethnicity and the existence of precolonial structures of governance in the context of the pending realization of the right to self-determination in Western Sahara.[6]

Self-interested colonial accounts of history have often focused on the analyses of ethnic groups existing in the Maghreb and elsewhere,[7] downplaying or ignoring the role and existence of structures of governance facilitating legal and political support for the legitimacy of colonial expansion and titles.[8] North Africa is a fascinating place for a study of "national" identity and its expression within the form of the territorial state. Prior to this political formation, communities in this region, as elsewhere, displayed a range of different forms of organization that challenge the basis of the territorial expression of identity that is so central to the discourse of sovereign statehood. At the heart of this challenge is the notion of two entities prominent in ancient northwest Africa—the Sherifian Empire (precursor to modern Morocco) and the Bilad Shinguitti[9] (precursor to the Islamic Republic of Mauritania), both of which came under the colonial influence of France and Spain. Using the terminology of the ICJ, this section will present a "photograph"[10] of the organization of political allegiance in the region, focusing on these two entities first, and culminating with an assessment of the effect of colonization on the region. This will provide an overview of how the notion of ethnicity developed and was "accommodated" through colonial rule into the two modern territorially based states.

Sherifian Society

Societies can often be classified according to the extent and manner in which the central government can impose its will on their members.[11] The system that prevailed under the Sherifian Empire presented a picture close to anarchy to European viewers,[12] but nonetheless had a complex system of allegiances and vassalages in constant movement, leading to a relatively stable equilibrium. The empire as such, came into being after a series of Berber and Arab kingdoms were formed and dissolved with great rapidity on the Tunis-Kairouan-Tlemcen-Fés axes. These struggles are documented elsewhere[13] but it suffices for our purposes to conclude that the empire was built on the ashes of the Almoravids and Almohads dynasties. It differed from European "states" in existence at the time, since it was built on a system of allegiance to the sultan, considered the spiritual head of the region. Under him, myriads of tribes functioned more or less autonomously, with Berber tribes in the hinterland and Arab tribes closer to the centers of power and the imperial cities of Fés, Casablanca, and Marrakech.[14] As pointed out by Dunn,

> migratory movement of pastoral populations has been a continuous theme in the history of Morocco and the Western Sahara for almost a thousand years ... the major thrust of these movements has been from the fringes of the Sahara northward into the Atlas and beyond to the fertile Atlantic coastal plains. The Saharan environment was a constant factor in setting in motion tribal migrations. Extended periods of drought, famine, and epidemic, alternated with population growth to seek new homes. The more abundant pastures on and beyond the slopes of the Atlas invariably attracted them towards the north.[15]

This migration of indigenous Berbers from south to north began to be tempered by countermovements from north to south in the face of Arab expansionism, with the constant movement of people making for a "lack of unity" in the system[16] counterbalanced by the spread of Islam. Islam arrived with the Arabs and gradually spread to Berber tribes. It has been suggested that the Berbers were only superficially Islamized;[17] in any case, with the exception of small pockets of Jews, in the region prior to colonization, and of Europeans, who came much later with the colonial drive, the entire region of the Maghreb was Muslim. The Islam practiced in the region was unique and encompassed a "complex and ramified network of religious brotherhood and saint cults, with regular pilgrimages and loose but extensive hierarchies" which were primarily tribal.[18]

The maintenance of order was left to local tribal people themselves, "generally (though not universally) self-defined in kin terms, in which virtually all adult males were warriors and which maintained order by a complex system of . . . balances, operating simultaneously at various levels of size."[19]

These balances and counterbalances worked externally among tribes, but also created internal balances that regulated life within the tribe. The system relied on mediators and arbitrators, usually governed by tenets of Islam, who were exempt from the feuding ethos of the tribes. According to Gellner, the lineages were the nearest the system had to an aristocracy.[20] Thus, the Sherifian Empire was "perched precariously on top of a mass of tribal communities which resembled each other, and which indulged, in such qualitative diversity as existed only with restraint and discretion, as indicated."[21]

The most intriguing aspect of the empire from the perspective of ties of territorial allegiances was the relationship between the center and the peripheral regions. It is difficult to define the territory that can be considered "peripheral" owing to the indeterminate nature of the allegiances. Alliance to the political and religious authority of the sultan was given more weight than control over territory, explaining the absence of precise territorial limits of what would subsequently become Morocco.[22] The basic structure generally described in the literature suggests that the empire was divided into two broad and fairly distinct parts, the *Bled el-Makhzen* and the *Bled es-Siba*. The payment of tax was essentially what differentiated these two sections of the society, a distinction described as a domain of sovereignty (*Bled el-Makhzen*) and a domain of suzerainty (*Bled es-Siba*).[23] The lands immediately surrounding the urban areas, and the predominantly Arab tribal lands around them were all part of the *Bled el-Makhzen* or "the land of governance"; they paid taxes to the sultan and provided the backbone of his army. The *Bled es-Siba*, on the other hand, or the "land of dissidence and disorder" in Arabic, was composed mainly of Berber tribes who refused to pay taxes to the sultan yet had no problem in accepting him as spiritual head of the region.[24] This distinction in the comprehension of the sultan's role as spiritual rather than temporal forms the basis of Moroccan irredentist arguments with regard to the Western Sahara.[25]

Hart draws a parallel made in the work of Lahlabi, who compares the whole issue of the relationship between center and periphery to a Rousseausque idea of "social contract" with its related concept of "opting out," since the issue hinged, in the words of Hart, solely on the "consent of the governed."[26] Thus, the *siba* partially opted out of this contract, in that while recognizing the sultan as spiritual head of the territory, they did not recognize him as temporal head. The sultan seems to have recognized this partial opting out: while military expeditions were undertaken into the *Bled es-Siba* for rent collection, these were irregular.[27] The structure held together on acceptance of the sultan as a direct descendant of Prophet Mohammed and, therefore as head of the Muslim community in the region. According to one author, the entire region "belonged" to the sultan according to *shariah* law.[28] Islam remains the strongest contemporary thread in the identity of the peoples of the region, who subscribe to the beliefs of the Orthodox Sunni Islamic school of faith and the Maliki rite (though clearly not accepting the "sovereignty" of the sultan).

A fundamental issue regarding the Western Sahara conflict, namely, the determination of external boundaries of the Sherifian Empire, is virtually impossible to establish due to the vast amount of contradictory data. The Spanish have fiercely defended the proposition that the empire extended only up to the River Draa and no further south; Morocco claims that the Western Sahara and even parts of Mauritania and Algeria were included in the larger *Bled es-Siba*. However, it is important to note that the seat of the sultan was not territorial: his court moved around the region, though primarily restricted to the *Bled el-Makhzen*.[29] Terrasse suggests that the *Bled el-Makhzen* was not a firm bloc or coherent force, but a coalition maintained by the force of profiting elements such as the *makhzen* itself, as well the *guich* (warring military tribes that largely formed the backbone of the sultan's army).[30] He contrasts this against the *Bled es-Siba*, portrayed as ridden by ancient clan rivalries, tribes, and moieties marked by feuding and infighting that prevented united opposition to *makhzen* forces. Thus, Moroccan politics before the arrival of the French were "ceaseless efforts of the *makhzen* to impose its authority upon the rebellious tribes of *siba* land, and their constant defense of their independence."[31] There is also a suggestion that the divide was ethnic in that the *siba* consisted mainly of Berber tribes while the *makhzen* was dominated by Arabs. One of the claims as to why Islam failed to provide a unifying effect was that the Berbers were only superficially Islamicized, and still practiced their old natural paganism.[32] *Shariah* law and the establishment of *makhzen* administration settled their internal disputes using customary laws regulated by tribal councils, and were governed through *jema'as*[33] marked by something akin to a democratic spirit. The Spanish gave representation to the Sahrawi by legitimizing their organization into *jema'as*, including them within the mechanisms of colonial governance. Before we examine the questions of the ties between this entity and the territory defined as the Western Sahara today, it is important to explore the nature of the other entity that originally laid claim to the territory of the Western Sahara, that is, the Bilad Shinguitti, presented by Mauritania as the precursor of the Mauritanian state.

Bilad Shinguitti

The Bilad Shinguitti presents an equally fascinating platform for questioning the primacy of the principle of territoriality in state-dominated discourse. It did not have a defined territory or fixed population at the time of the Sahara's colonization by Spain. Unlike the Sherifian Empire north of it, it could not be identified as having a single authority that tribes swore allegiance to or contested taxes against, therefore not fulfilling one of the criteria customarily accepted as fundamental for states to be considered as such, namely, the existence of an effective government.[34] The Shinguitti functioned differently; and while the Mauritanian argument was negated by the court and its territorial claim to the territory subsequently dropped,[35] it nevertheless directly challenged the perception of territorially based identities within international legal discourse.

At the time of the colonization of the Western Sahara, Mauritania defined itself in the following terms:

> (a) Geographically, . . . lying between, on the east, the meridian of Timbuktu and, on the west, the Atlantic, . . . bounded on the south by the Senegal river and on the north by the Wad Sakiet El Hamra. In the eyes of both its own inhabitants and of the Arabo-Islamic communities, that region constituted a distinct entity.
> (b) That entity was the Bilad Shinguitti, . . . which constituted a distinct human unit, characterized by a common language, way of life, and religion. It had a uniform social structure, composed of three "orders": warrior tribes exercising political power; marabout tribes engaged in religion, teaching, cultural, judicial, and economic activities; and client-vassal tribes under the protection of a warrior or marabout tribe. . . . The most significant feature of Bilad Shinguitti was the importance given to the marabout tribes, who created a strong written cultural tradition in religious studies, education, literature and poetry; indeed its fame in the Arab world derived from the reputation acquired by its scholars.[36]

Mauritania also enunciated that there were two types of political systems within *Bilad Shinguitti*: one consisting of emirates, and the other of tribes independent of the emirates. Neither group bore any tie of territorial allegiance to the Sultan of the *Sherifian Empire*, although he might have been acknowledged as spiritual head.[37] Mauritania argued that one of the emirates, the Emirate of Adrar, around the town of Shinguit, was a center of Shinguit culture and proved an attraction for the nomadic Sahrawi tribes.[38] The argument presented was that at the time of colonization of the Western Sahara by Spain, the Emir of Adrar was the most important political figure of the north and northwest *Shinguitt* (which by implication included the Western Sahara). It also mentions the testimony of Captain Cervera who concluded a treaty with the Emir at Ijil, by which Spain would have recognized the Emir as sovereign over the stated lands.[39] The parties to that treaty, according to Mauritania, included not just the Emir but also several tribal chiefs, not only from Adrar but also from the west of the Emirate. It is these tribal chiefs that allegedly represented the tribes within the Western Sahara, and hence the origin of the claim of a territorial link between the Emir and the nomadic tribes that traversed the desert immediately north of the Emirate.

It is relatively uncontested that the emirates and tribal groupings were autonomous; they signed treaties with explorers without "higher consent" of the sultan of the Sherifian Empire. Nonetheless, "the emirs, sheikhs, and other tribal chiefs were never vested by outside authorities and derived their powers from the special rules governing the devolution of power in the Shinguitti entity."[40] Each emirate or tribal group was "autonomously administered," and the rulers derived their power from the *Jama'a*—the locally elected participatory system that functioned as a governing council for each tribe. This is particularly relevant in view of the spirit of self-determination that draws on the American Declaration of Independence, often considered to be an early articulation of the principle concerning the legitimacy that emanates from the consent of the governed.[41] It appears from the evidence presented by the Mauritania before the ICJ as well as by the work undertaken by Gellner and others on the subject, that the Saharan tribes[42] had a degree of autonomy that would have fulfilled these conditions. Thus, the argument presented suggested that identity in the Western Sahara was in the guise of allegiance to the system of the Bilad Shinguitti. This system, short of a conventional state, pertained to a loose governance structure that formed part of the customary law for a region including Mauritania and the territory of the Western Sahara. This "system," Mauritania claimed, was interrupted by the arrival of the colonialists, and it is to this influence that we turn to in the next paragraphs.

The interpretation of international standards in relation to the largely uncontested evidence about the tribal governance structure within the *Bilad Shinguittii* presented in the 1975 ICJ case by Mauritania highlights the rigidity of international law principles and the difficulty to try to apply its principles and rules to entities preceding the postcolonial state.

Mauritania recognized that the Shinguitti could not be assimilated to the notion of modern state "nor to a federation, nor even to a confederation, unless one saw fit to give that name to the tenuous political ties linking the various tribes."[43] It also explained that the tribes and the four emirates "were a community having its own cohesion" and distinctive characteristics, "and a common Saharan law concerning the use of waterholes, grazing lands and agricultural lands, the regulation of inter-tribal hostilities and the settlement of disputes."[44] Nonetheless, demonstrating how much it was embedded in the international law discourse, Mauritania itself pleaded that these facts were not sufficient basis to assert sovereignty or the international personality of the Shinguitti.[45] The colonial interpretation of the tribal structures explained by Mauritania was not regarded as evidence of an existing system of governance but rather, as threatening of order, and therefore not fitting the European notion of statehood. This is evidence of the continued impact of Eurocentricism of international law, whose basis was accepted despite its derivation from a monolithic and unequal vision of law.[46] This characteristic, coupled with the problematic acceptance of externally imposed boundaries, hinders the extent to which international law could ever adequately resolve self-determination disputes in Africa.[47] The idea of state at the heart of international legal discourse of self-determination is located within a fixed European context, but it remains questionable whether this is the only entity capable of guaranteeing that the consent of the governed makes for legitimate government. As argued later, the conditions inherent to the Saharan region contributed to a form of life and governance that could not fit the European conceptual model of state.

Colonial Influence

As in other parts of the world, boundary regimes were a colonial phenomenon introduced in the Maghreb to limit the sphere of influence of competing colonial powers.[48] The main effect of this colonization on the Sherifian Empire was the transformation of its internal structure from its original form to that of the independent state of Morocco in 1956. Within close proximity to Europe, Morocco was strongly influenced by European events. The first of these was plausibly the *Reconquista* when Christian forces pursued Andalusians into the Maghreb from 1505 onward.[49] Rézette suggests that Christian and Arabic chronicles described the Atlantic in the thirteenth century as "a shadowy ocean, peopled by monstrous animals and subject to terrible tempests; from which no one ever returned."[50] With the discovery of Lanzarote between 1312 and 1335, the Canary Islands had become a source of constant pillage by Europeans including Portuguese, Catalans, Majorcans, and Norman "expeditions." But it was only after the fall of Granada in 1492 that Spain and Portugal first began to land on the coasts of northwest Africa.

This process was accompanied by the expulsion of 500,000 Muslims and Jews by Philippe III from Spain between 1609 and 1612. It was under the pretext of protection of these peoples that Portugal and Spain began to exert influence on the northwest tip of Africa. European vessels had been fishing south of the Iberian Peninsula for centuries prior to this but had refrained from launching themselves along the Atlantic coast, "despite the desire to appropriate at the source, the 'gold of the Sudan' monopolized by the Mohammedans."[51]

By 1912 though, France and Spain had established respective protectorates over the region carving it into three segments along different axes.[52] The 1912 *Treaty of Fés* set the boundaries of the three states that were to come into existence on withdrawal of the colonial powers. Thus, the main effect of colonization on the Sherifian Empire was that it united territories subsequently known as Morocco, into a single unit. The French protectorate also ensured that the Bled es-Siba was absorbed into the Bled el-Makhzen and within a period of less than thirty years, the fabric of the society was altered by the French, rendering "anomalous the traditional patterns of government. The *makhzen* no longer needed an army to collect taxes, and, in any case, it was not permitted."[53]

The Treaty of Fés also laid down the modern boundary of Mauritania. Inhabited by people referred to as Moors in popular literature,[54] they derived their identity from the French colonization of the territory of the Bilad Shinguitti. After the conquest by France of parts of the Sahara, the term "Moor" came to be formally used to describe people of the region. So in terms of the crystallization of identity, French influence was significant. The distinction of *bidani* versus *sudani*—central to internal precolonial "Mauritanian" identity[55] was replaced at "national" level by the creation of a supervening identity that papered over the differences and "united" them under the sobriquet of Moorism. The parallel between the Moroccan and Mauritanian experience is striking: the colonial power superimposed a territorial state and a corresponding identity to go along with it that was nonindigenous to the region. In the words of Stewart:

> Prior to the carving out of the territory which is known today as Mauritania, the Moors inhabited an area vaguely known as the Shinqit, and the lands to the south of the Shinqit, inhabited by Wolof, Toucuolots, Bambara, and Sarakolès, marked the beginning of the *Bled es-Sudan* which was beyond the pale of Moorish politics and only marginally involved in the historical traditions of the Shinqit.[56]

Modern political parties in Mauritania owe their existence to French efforts to create a viable political entity.[57] Other data confirms the colonial influence in the region and the irrelevance of boundaries in the formation of identity. At the independence of Morocco in 1956, Mauritania was the subject of irredentist claims from Morocco, voiced at the time by Allal el-Fassi, who suggested that Mauritania, Algeria, Mali, and all of the Rio de Oro constituted integral parts of Morocco. These claims were taken up within Mauritania by umra Ould Babana who was supported by some of the tribal groups in the north. Babana was expelled from the territory and, after visits to Paris and Cairo, finally settled in Rabat to champion the irredentist movements that sought to unite the entire region of northwest Africa under the aegis of the Maghreb.[58] In addition, there seems clear indication that precolonial identity was localized, especially in the case of Berber tribes who followed ideals that facilitating participation in public affairs, where contact between governed and governing was closer than in many larger entities. The arrival of colonial powers and their need to demarcate spheres of influence in the territory forced people to begin identifying on a "national" level. While in the past allegiance in Mauritania focused on the tribe, with little awareness of the central power (if any) involved, the emphasis was forcibly shifted to a central administrative power. Thus, colonial presence removed local aspects of identity in a bid to "unite" differences under the umbrella of the sovereign state. Thus,

> the colonial experiment in Mauritania reflects many of the same features of colonial administration and politics which are found in other countries in North and West Africa. These include indirect rule, a policy of divide and rule, the creation of new, broader political entities by the incorporation of minority groups under a single administrative unit, the introduction of the metropolitan language and culture, the consolidation of colonial administration and the undermining of traditional authority.[59]

Hence under French influence, the territories immediately to the north and south of the region recognized as the Western Sahara, took on the guise of modern states. Meanwhile the Western Sahara (Spanish Sahara) came under the influence of Spain, which was more concerned about having a safe coast to protect its interest in the Canary Islands.[60] As a result, it did not set up the kind of colonial state discussed earlier.

TERRITORY AND IDENTITY IN THE WESTERN SAHARA

One of the most visible complexities of "identity" within the western fringe of the Saharan desert is the nomadic nature of the population in search of survival, thereby preventing fixed "territorial" links from crystallizing. The influence of a sea-faring colonial power seeking to control the coast, and a modern decolonized state with a historically powerful past linked to religion complicate questions of identity. The Western Sahara situation poses questions about territoriality, identity, and statehood that must be addressed to understand the nuances attached to a solution of this conflict.

Before colonization, it was not possible to speak about the "national identity" of the Sahrawi people. The term "Sahrawi" derives from the Spanish Sahara and would have not existed before the mid-twentieth century.[61] Meaning "Saharan" in Arabic, the term Sahrawi has a broader literal meaning than the one normally conferred.[62] The distinction between "Sahrawi" and "indigenous Western Sahara" is also used or ignored for different problematic purposes by Western Saharan nationalists and Morocco.[63] This nomadic people(s) had their own mechanisms of social, political, and economic organization dependent on belonging to a tribe or *cabila* and the status within it. As acknowledge by the ICJ:

> In the Western Sahara case at the time of Spanish colonization, the nomadic tribes of the region were clearly organized politically and socially under chiefs competent to represent them.[64]

Different tribes inhabited the area of the Western Sahara over the years, settling to varying degrees: archaeological evidence demonstrates that the Bafour lived there from about 5000 to 2500 BCE. The desertification of the area would have driven the Bafour southward while, during the first millennium BC, the first Berber nomads, the Sanhaja, began migrating into the territory from the north.[65] During the eleventh century, the Almoravid followed their Berber leader Yusuf ibn Tashfin who consolidated the earlier introduction of Islam during the eighth and ninth century. The king of the Almoravid Empire reached the plains of northern Morocco, founded Marrakech in 1062, and completed the Almoravid conquest of Morocco in 1069 by taking Fez.[66] The Maqil, a Bedouin Arab people, penetrated Western Sahara in the eleventh century.[67] Over the years, different dynasties such as the Saadian and the Alaouite achieved different degrees of control over the tribes of the region. Descendants of the Maqil, the Beni Hassan, warrior people constituted by a group of tribes claiming Yemeni ancestry, established themselves in the area and absorbed the Berber Sanhaja population who were subject to a process of Arabization.[68] Some scholars still use the colonial anthropological accounts of Saharan tribes as divided into neat castes between which significant inequalities existed (mainly the Arab Hassans as warriors, the Zawaya as scholarly classes, and the shepherds).[69] Modern readings of this literature suggest this neat separation is problematic.[70]

Supreme authority among the Sahrawi was exercised through the *Eit-al-arbain* or Assembly of the Forty. This consisted of a government of forty members, elected among their own tribes who were in charge of common matters such as defense or the delimitation of pasture areas, as well as how to settle disputes between different tribes based on customary law, Sahrawi tradition, and *shariah* law.[71]

Internally the tribes were organized into fractions—groups of families of the same tribe who lived in the same settlement and moved together. Crafters, musicians, and slaves not belonging to the tribe were integrated into these nomadic settlements keeping significant social distances from its members. The internal administration of the tribe was exercised by the *jema'a*, an assembly formed by chiefs of each group, normally the most elderly who complemented and limited the powers of the *chej*, supreme authority of the tribe. This social, economic, and political reality suffered a radical transformation with the appearance of the Spanish, who distorted and manipulated traditional Sahrawi structures to consolidate power.[72]

The Western Sahara borders the Atlantic coastline and shares borders with Morocco (north) and Mauritania (south) with a small common border with Algeria.[73] As with most African countries, the borders of the state were agreed to and drawn by France and Spain, who divided the region between themselves. While Spanish rights over the Western Sahara were acknowledged in the 1884–1885 *Berlin West Africa Conference*, Spanish presence antagonized French interests in the Maghreb.[74] In addition, the loss of the Caribbean and Pacific territories in 1898 (Cuba, Puerto

Rico, Philippine Islands, and Guam) resulted in Spain's urgent and clear recognition of its vulnerability and the need for it to secure its border in Western Africa to protect its Canary interests.[75] This led to the agreements between Spain and France signed in 1900, 1904, and 1912,[76] which gave the Western Sahara its current geographic parameters.

International law recognizes 1884 as the year when the Spanish declared a "protectorate" over the Western Sahara,[77] recategorized as a province of Spain in 1958. It is claimed that this protectorate was declared after agreements were signed with independent tribes. The boundaries of the protectorate included Rio de Oro and Sakiet el-Hamra. The only dispute with respect to territorial implications in relation to the protectorate surrounds the exact demarcation of the Bled es-Siba prior to Spanish acquisition. This is significant since the Bled es-Siba is uncontested as a part of the Sherifian Empire. The crux of the Moroccan territorial argument is that the Bled es-Siba included Rio de Oro and Sakiet el Hamra, while the Spanish suggest it was restricted to the Draa River Valley that forms the modern boundary between the Western Sahara and Morocco. Thus a central part of the dispute concerns the location of the seam between the Bled es-Siba and the Shinguitti, and whether there existed between these two entities a space corresponding to the Western Sahara.

At this point, it is important to reiterate the nature of the territory in examining the kinds of ties that could have existed which might be relevant in determining the identity of the people. From this discussion, it remains uncertain as to whether the nomadic population of the Western Sahara had religious allegiance to the sultan, while it can be clearly ascertained that they enjoyed a fairly autonomous political structure. The sparsely populated, largely Berber tribes seemed to have traversed the region following definite migratory routes largely dictated by the presence of water wells. The relations between tribes were governed by certain accepted customs and traditions, which could be considered indications of legal customs and norms.[78] Included within this parameter were issues such as the use of migratory routes, access to wells, burial grounds, and agricultural land. It is also important to note that the tribes themselves did not restrict their existence to the territory currently known as the Western Sahara but traversed parts of southern Morocco, Mauritania, and even parts of Algeria.[79] This continued through the colonial period when boundaries ascribed to the region were more permeable than in postcolonial states. Nonetheless, with territoriality being the basis of the modern colonial states to the north, south, and east of the Western Sahara, there was an increasing trend toward sedentarism among the peoples within this territory too. Still, nomadism remained central to the identity of these peoples. In ascertaining the nature of identity in the Western Sahara with respect to the two claimants to the territory, the chief problem faced is that the Western Sahara was not a self-contained unit. Rather, it functioned largely as a frontier-less entity whose peoples had close relations with the two entities that neighbored it. Of course, the key question within this case is the nature of allegiance between the peoples of this area and the two entities in question.

Any number of possible scenarios arises. First, the region could have been part of the Bled es-Siba, which extended all the way north toward the imperial cities of the Sherifian Empire. There is a fair amount of evidence presented for this view in the case before the ICJ.[80] Were this the case, it would still leave open the larger question of whether being part of the Bled es-Siba necessarily means that modern Western Sahara should form a part of modern Morocco. Such a line of argument would reflect the rule of *uti possidetis juris*,[81] based on a historic fact of territorial possession which could not be said to be demonstrably "effective" in light of the constant rebellions of the *siba* against the *makhzen*.

The second plausible scenario is that the territory and the tribes within it were part of the culture of the Bilad Shinguitti which encompassed, besides modern day Mauritania, the territory north of it, that is, the Western Sahara, and extended southward toward the *Bled Sudan* where "Black Africa" could be said to commence.[82] Were this the case, and once again the evidence presented is reasonably comprehensive, it would need to be examined whether the tribes had any allegiance to pax Shinguitti. This is difficult to determine from this distance of time. Nonetheless were it to be accepted, it suggests a form of identity and allegiance based on lifestyle rather than territoriality. Of course, it needs to be pointed out that this option in the current climate does not now exist with Mauritania having withdrawn its claim to the region.

A possible third scenario is that the tribes of the region were politically independent of both the entities. They did not form a part of the Bled es-Siba and although perhaps acknowledging the sultan's spiritual leadership, they did not accept his temporal leadership over their lands. Nor did they have any links to the Bilad Shinguitti of whom they functioned independently. They could have subscribed to a system of allegiances and vassalages similar to the Shinguitti culture, partly dictated by an existence in the same desert, but did not pay political homage to any of the tribes or emirates in the *Shinqit*. This scenario is not difficult to imagine since the Bilad Shinguitti consisted of fairly autonomy tribes. Within this scenario though, the tribes would be required to be completely politically independent of both entities while perhaps subscribing to various facets of culture that emanate from a common heritage (namely, Berberic), common religion (namely, Islam), and a common lifestyle (dictated by the Saharan desert).[83]

As the 1975 case before the ICJ progressed, an idea developed which focused on bifurcation of the territory between the two claimants. Thus, the northern tribes would be accepted by Mauritania, as part of the Bled es-Siba while the southern tribes were conceded by Morocco as being part of Shinqit culture. With this compromise, it would have seemed that the homogeneity of the territory as a unit was now being questioned. Some authors have interrogated the wisdom of trying to ascertain the existence of ties and their nature in the region.[84] For them the territory of the Western Sahara, as a unit of colonial rule, ought to have the option in a referendum of opting for one of three options presented by the international law of self-determination, namely: (a) Emerging as a sovereign independent State; (b) freely associating with either Morocco or Mauritania; or (c) integrating with either Morocco or Mauritania.[85] For these authors, the legality or otherwise of historic ties would be subjugated to the process of the people of the territory deciding which of these three options they would prefer. However, such an oversimplification would misunderstand the complexities of identity, further legitimize the colonial boundaries, and force identities to conform to them. It is perhaps not wholly convincing that the tribes in the Western Sahara existed completely independent of the Sherifian Empire as well as the Bilad Shinguitti. The works of Gellner and others suggests that there are significant links in the culture of the Berbers, which spread across the width of the entire region that could be recognized as the Maghreb. These scholars emphasize that this unity in Berber culture spreads beyond twentieth century externally imposed state boundaries. At the same time, the discourse of statehood is openly challenged in this case since even though the Berbers may have had a relatively uniform culture, they nonetheless did not function as a single entity.[86] It is an uncontested fact that, during any given period in pre-Spanish Sahara, intertribal conflict was fairly frequent, suggesting few external allegiances of any kind between the different tribes. Nonetheless, as far as internal governance was concerned, each tribe had its own internal mechanisms overseeing life within the tribe. Thus, the idea of a supreme power that united the peoples of the region is arguably flawed. And the imposition of statehood on different tribes has not been a process that was accepted without great resistance.[87] Of course, it needs to be stressed that this particular phenomenon is not peculiar to the Western Sahara but fairly common in most postcolonial territories. While imposition of artificial boundaries has been a challenge faced in most decolonization struggles, it is accentuated in the Western Sahara due to the nature of the population. In the case of sedentary populations, boundaries have a greater effect on a solidification of identities within particular newer territorial regimes. However, in the case of nomadic populations, boundaries can prove to be even more artificial.

THE CRUX OF THE MATTER: TERRITORY VERSUS IDENTITY

Traditionally nomadic, the Sahrawi have wandered across northwest Africa including Morocco as well as Mauritania for centuries never constrained by borders. In 1956 Mauritania and Morocco, both of whom had by this stage gained their independence, called for the self-determination of Spanish Sahara.[88] Both countries were certain that exercise of this right would see the region amalgamated into their respective states. This claim was not surprising since the nomads had traversed across the region throughout history and shared a greater Maghreb identity that encompassed northwestern Africa. With statehood within predetermined boundaries increasingly becoming the only legitimate expression of national identity, both Mauritania and Morocco believed they had a good claim to the territory, which they regarded as unviable as a "state" by itself. While both countries squabbled, the UN renewed calls for self-determination,[89] a right upheld by the ICJ in 1975. The Western Sahara is the only African territory still under consideration by the UN Decolonization Committee.[90] From an international perspective, historically there was no discussion about the application of the right to self-determination to this territory and for many years the celebration of a referendum looked like a prospective solution on how Sahrawis would realize such a right.

The decolonization of "Spanish Sahara" was first demanded by the United Nations General Assembly (UNGA) in 1965.[91] Calls for the hosting of a referendum to allow the realization of the right to self-determination of the Sahrawi were repeated by the UNGA between 1966 and 1975, when the Moroccan government decided to seek an advisory opinion on the links between itself and the territory before the ICJ. For this purpose, a basic settlement plan agreed by Morocco and the Polisario came into existence in 1988.[92] However, the process of identifying who had a right to vote in the previously proposed referenda has been a key factor in explaining why the process to realize the Sahrawi right to self-determination has continuously stalled.[93] Opening a debate over "Who Is a Western Sahrawi" has provided the Moroccan government with the opportunity to question the category altogether.[94] Thus a major difficulty, one expressed as a self-determination question posed as early as in 1918 by Robert Lansing,[95] is that someone must decide who the people are who can subsequently be called upon to decide their future, as demonstrated in the UN bid to try to ascertain the identity of the people. However, exercise of this right is a complicated process and today, decades since the first international political interest in the region, the task of ascertaining *who* the Sahrawis are and *how* the area might determine its political future remains unresolved. Questions concerning the demographics in the region and the nature of the Sahrawi identity remain key to resolution. To add to the complexity, nearly half the populations that could be considered Sahrawi have lived as refugees in Algeria since 1976 while the others continue to live as a minority population under Moroccan rule.[96] The transnational education program promoted by the Polisario in Libya and Cuba has led to the existence of Sahrawi refugees in those countries.[97] Pablo San Martin argues that the strategic relationship of the Polisario with Latin America[98] and particularly Cuba has also contributed to the "Hispanization" of the refugee population.[99]

While one reading of public international law is that the question of self-determination is easily resolved, the norm itself has been of limited utility to the dispute due to a lack of any clear mechanism through which such a process can be undertaken. Closer legal analysis of the term highlights the problematic root of it. As analyzed elsewhere, one of the key interlinked concepts to the norm is the doctrine of *uti possidetis*.[100] This Roman law interdict, by implication, treats territory as a possession that may change title; and in the case of most territories in the international community, has changed hands throughout the course of history. Framing a legal rule that allows the possessor to keep possession suggests certain rigidity that cannot allow modification. Decolonization was such a modification, and in this process, this question, previously considered foreclosed, was forced open. With the international community treasuring "order" above all else, this change was strictly regulated. As a result, the entities that came out of the decolonization process were often unrecognizable from the precolonial reality. However, as far as *international* law at that stage was concerned, these entities were now considered full-fledged states, and took their national identities from the territory allocated to them. This is precisely what transpired in the Western Sahara.

Indigenous systems were overrun by colonization, which created the territory of the Western Sahara. Above and below it geographically, the two ancient entities maintained an overall identity, though much altered by French state-building processes. However, in this specific zone of the desert, nonconducive to sedentary life, this process was not as easy. In addition, the Spanish were not overtly concerned with initiating this process. As a result, when the Spanish were forced to abdicate under international pressure, the normal process of decolonization stalled. This cause has subsequently been taken up by the Polisario. Their case however remains problematic in the context of the current discourse, since it too, is based on the territorial assumption that takes as a given the land of the "Western Sahara." The question therefore remains as to whether it is possible in the context of modern international politics to maintain an identity that is not based on a territorial assumption, and still be entitled to "statehood." For the Western Sahara, its fate has long depended on the political maneuvering of the two parties—the Moroccan government and the Polisario—as they seek to negotiate their differences of *who* the people are that need to be consulted in determining the population eligible to vote in the plebiscite deciding the political destiny of the territory.

The advisory opinion of the ICJ in 1975 in this matter demonstrates the difficulties in seeking a legalistic interpretation of identity that is the result of shared experiences of peoples over centuries.[101] It is also significant that the nature of international law and the dispute resolving mechanism of the ICJ could not accommodate the view of the Polisario—barred from proceedings since it was not a state. In addition, the choice of a date as being "critical"—in this case the date the Spanish arrived in the Western Sahara—is contentious. The differences between peoples cannot be subsumed to a restrictive territorial definition of identity. In this vein, some authors speak about the Western Sahara conflict as an "imaginary" one:

> The conflict is imaginary at its most fundamental level—not imaginary in the sense that it is fiction, but in the sense that is largely based on ideas. In the material world, both sides agree that the dispute is over a piece of land. Yet abstractly, at the level of the "metaconflict," the dispute stems from mutually exclusive differences in the self-perceptions that ground Moroccan and Western Saharan nationalism.[102]

Moroccan nationalism sees Western Sahara as part of the original Moroccan territory, manipulated by the maneuvering of colonialism. Its Western Sahara aspirations represent another attempt to reshape Morocco through the validation of colonial boundaries.[103] Some others claim that Sahrawi nationalists represented by the Polisario see themselves as a distinct people with exclusive rights over the territory. They have, through millennia of continuous habitation, "constructed themselves as the natives, whereas Moroccans are the settlers."[104]

While it is impossible to deny that territoriality is *one* of the factors in determining a people's identity, it is dangerous to subordinate all other factors to it. The norm of *uti possidetis* that shaped the postcolonial world has played an important role in maintaining peace and security and preventing newly independent regions from fragmenting. The question that needs to be posed today in a scenario of postmodern tribalism is whether these independent quasi-states should still be afforded protection under this norm despite the inherent defeat that it constitutes to the principle of self-determination.

CONCLUSION

The full realization of the right to self-determination by the Sahrawis is no closer to resolution today than in 1988, when the Polisario Front and Morocco agreed to UN proposals to resolve the conflict using a referendum. The prolonged attempt to find a political solution to the conflict[105] through the mediation of the first Personal Envoy of the Secretary-General, James Baker III, ended with his resignation.[106] UN Security Council Resolution 1754 (2004) sought to provide new impetus to the process of moving away from a referendum, leading to current negotiations under the auspices of the Secretary General's Personal Envoy. While Morocco has offered an autonomy proposal, the Polisario retain their position of independence through referendum, with the stalemate continuing. Today, only solutions not involving the independence of Western Sahara are accepted for negotiations by Morocco, indicating that the referendum option supported by the Polisario is no longer tenable. Thus while the Western Sahara case, as described in another chapter in this book, has provided content and shaped the contours of the right to self-determination, this has not helped it become a beneficiary.

Self-determination has always been about a right that will enable people to control their own political destiny. As we have seen from this chapter, debates around "who are the people" and "what is self-determination" and how it should be expressed continue to obscure solutions. At the heart of the norm of self-determination is the idea that a government can be considered legitimate when it has been formed with the consent of the people. If an elected government bears closer proximity to the populations within a specific area that government is likely to be considered more legitimate to one that is further away, irrespective of the historical perspectives. This principle is heightened in the Western Sahara where historical perspectives are clouded and open to interpretation. From our perspective therefore, the Sahrawi have the clear right to self-determination in an external sense. They ought to be allowed to continue the stalled decolonization process, while guarantees should be sought that any and every government that rules the territory will guarantee the human rights of every individual and be particularly mindful of the significant population with Moroccan origins who have settled in the region who should be allowed and encouraged to participate fully in political and public life. This would require that the government that emerges would necessarily have to justify its legitimacy against *all* those within the jurisdiction, making issues of identity less relevant to the need to provide effective governance and the trappings of a modern state.

NOTES

1. Especially drawing on the work of Ernst Gellner and Charles Micaud, eds., *Arabs and Berbers: From Tribe to Nation in North Africa* (Lexington, MA: Heath, 1972).

2. See International Court of Justice, *Western Sahara: Advisory Opinion of 16 October 1975*, October 16, 1975, 12.

3. For a discussion on the principle of *uti possidetis juris*, see Joshua Castellino and Steve Allen, *Title to Territory in International Law: A Temporal Analysis* (Aldershot: Ashgate Publishing Limited, 2003); Joshua Castellino, "The Territorial Integrity and the 'Right' to Self-Determination: An Examination of the Conceptual Tools," *Brooklyn Journal of International Law* 33, no. 2 (2008): 503–68.

4. All cited websites were last accessed on November 4, 2012.

5. Thomas Franck, "Clan and Super Clan: Loyalty, Identity and Community in Law and Practice," *American Journal of International Law* 90, no. 3 (1996): 359–83.

6. For a full historic account, see J. M. Abun-Nasr, *A History of the Maghrib*, 2nd ed. (Cambridge: Cambridge University Press, 1975).

7. See generally Joshua Castellino and Kathleen Cavanaugh, *Minority Rights in the Middle East: A Comparative Legal Analysis* (Oxford: Oxford University Press, 2013).

8. See A. Laroui, "African Initiatives and Resistance in North Africa and the Sahara," in *General History of Africa: Africa under Colonial Domination*, vol. 7, ed. A. A. Boaher

Who Are the Sahrawis? 47

(Berkeley: University of California Press, 1989; Paris: UNESCO, 2000), 89. Citations are to the UNESCO edition.

9. Spelled by some authors as "Blad Shinqit," as in C. C. Stewart, "Political Authority and Social Stratification in Mauritania," in Gellner and Micaud, *Arabs and Berbers*, 375–93. In these pages the spelling used in the ICJ judgment, which refers to it as "Bilad Shinguitti" or "Shinguitti country," will be used.

10. International Court of Justice, *Report 554: Border Dispute Case: Burkina Faso v. Mali*, December 22, 1986, para. 30.

11. Gellner and Micaud, *Arabs and Berbers*, 16.

12. See Spanish argument in referring to the tribes of the Sahara, found in the International Court of Justice, *Western Sahara: Advisory Opinion*, 44–45, para. 96–97; see also Edmund Burke III, "The Image of the Moroccan State in French Ethnological Literature," in Gellner and Micaud, *Arabs and Berbers*, 177.

13. See R. Rézette, *The Western Sahara and the Frontiers of Morocco* (Paris: Nouvelles Editions Latines, 1975), and Abun-Nasr, *A History of the Maghrib*.

14. R. Dunn, "Berber Imperialism: The Ait Atta Expansion in Southeast Morocco," in Gellner and Micaud, *Arabs and Berbers*, 85–107.

15. Dunn, "Berber Imperialism," 85.

16. Gellner and Micaud, *Arabs and Berbers*, 17.

17. Roger le Tourneau, "North Africa to the Sixteenth Century," in *Cambridge History of Islam*, eds. P. M. Holt, K. S. Lambton, B. Lewis (Cambridge: Cambridge University Press, 1970), 2A: 216. See also H. Monès, "The Conquest of North Africa and Berber Resistance," in *General History of Africa: Africa from the Seventh to the Eleventh Century*, vol. 3, eds. M. Elfasi and M. Hrbek (Berkeley: University of California Press, 1989; Paris: UNESCO, 2000), 224–45. Citations are to the UNESCO edition; "Stages in the Development of Islam and Its Dissemination in Africa," Ibid., 56–91.

18. Gellner and Micaud, *Arabs and Berbers*, 17.

19. Gellner and Micaud, *Arabs and Berbers*, 18.

20. Gellner and Micaud, *Arabs and Berbers*, 18.

21. Gellner and Micaud, *Arabs and Berbers*, 18.

22. A. Bahaijoub, *Western Sahara Conflict: Historical, Regional and International Dimensions* (London: North South Publications, 2010), 262.

23. A. Laroui, "Morocco from the Beginning of the Nineteenth Century to 1880," in *General History of Africa: Africa in the Nineteenth Century until the 1880s*, vol. 6, ed. J. F. Ade Ajayi (Berkeley: University of California Press, 1989; Paris: UNESCO, 2000), 478. Citations are to the UNESCO edition.

24. On the distinction, see International Court of Justice, *Western Sahara: Advisory Opinion*, 44–45, para. 96.

25. See D. Hart, "The Tribe in Modern Morocco: Two Case Studies," in Gellner and Micaud, *Arabs and Berbers*, 25. See also Bahaijoub, *Western Sahara Conflict*, 134–35.

26. Lahlabi as quoted in Hart, "The Tribe in Modern Morocco," 28. See also Hart, "The Social Structure of the Rgibat Beduoins of the Western Sahara," *Middle East Journal* 15 (1962): 515–27.

27. A fact also acknowledged by all the parties in the International Court of Justice, *Western Sahara: Advisory Opinion*.

28. See Burke quoting Terrasse in Gellner and Micaud, *Arabs and Berbers*, 177.

29. Hart, "The Tribe in Modern Morocco," 26.

30. H. Terrasse, *Histoire du Maroc des Origins à l'Etablissement du Protectorat Français* (1950), as cited by Burke III, "The Image of the Moroccan State in French Ethnological Literature," 177.

31. Burke III, "The Image of the Moroccan State in French Ethnological Literature," 177.

32. Notably Burke III quoting Terrasse, Burke III, "The Image of the Moroccan State in French Ethnological Literature," 356–58. See previous note 16.

33. The word *jema'a* has been spelled differently by different authors but one imagines that the words *jema'a* and *jama'a* derive their meaning from the same root. For

the sake of accuracy we shall use the two separate terms in appropriate places with the caveat that they mean one and the same.

34. See Joshua Castellino, *International Law and Self-determination* (The Hague: Martinus Nijhoff Publishers, 2000), 75–80.

35. Political factors also saw the withdrawal of Mauritania's claim to the Western Sahara. See J. Chopra, "Breaking the Stalemate in the Western Sahara," *International Peacekeeping* 1, no. 3 (1994): 303–19; Yahya Zoubir and Daniel Volman, "The United States and Conflict in the Maghreb," *Journal of North African Studies* 2, no. 3 (1997): 10–24.

36. International Court of Justice, *Western Sahara: Advisory Opinion*, 57–58, para. 132.

37. International Court of Justice, *Western Sahara: Advisory Opinion*, 45, para. 99.

38. International Court of Justice, *Western Sahara: Advisory Opinion*, 58, para. 133.

39. International Court of Justice, *Western Sahara: Advisory Opinion*, 58, para. 133.

40. International Court of Justice, *Western Sahara: Advisory Opinion*, 58–59, para. 134.

41. See Thomas Franck, "The Emerging Right to Democratic Participation," *American Journal of International Law* 86, no. 1 (1992): 46–91.

42. This is used to mean the tribes that existed in this part of the Saharan Desert, rather than the *Sahrawi* tribes—which is used here to refer specifically to the tribes that Polisario claims to represent and that seek to realize their right to self-determination.

43. International Court of Justice, *Western Sahara: Advisory Opinion*, 59, para. 135.

44. International Court of Justice, *Western Sahara: Advisory Opinion*, 59, para. 136.

45. International Court of Justice, *Western Sahara: Advisory Opinion*, 59, para. 135.

46. Arguing that current international law is still shaped according to neocolonialist principles, see A. Anghie, "The Evolution of International Law: Colonial and Postcolonial Realities," *Third World Quarterly* 27, no. 5 (2006): 739–53.

47. Siba N. Grovogui, *Sovereigns, Quasi Sovereigns and Africans: Race and Self-Determination in International Law* (Minneapolis: University of Minnesota Press, 1996).

48. On the colonial drawing of borders see Castellino, *International Law and Self-Determination*, 109–44.

49. For a historical account, see Rézette, *The Western Sahara and the Frontiers of Morocco*, and Abun-Nasr, *A History of the Maghrib*.

50. As quoted in Rézette, *The Western Sahara*, 51.

51. As quoted in Rézette, *The Western Sahara*, 51.

52. See Gellner and Micaud, *Arabs and Berbers*, 13.

53. J. Seddon, "Local Politics and State Intervention: Northeast Morocco from 1870 to 1970," in Gellner and Micaud, *Arabs and Berbers*, 109–39.

54. The term "Moor" comes from Latin and has been applied at various times to Muslim peoples from Andalusia to the Senegal Basin. On the epistemology of the term see Stephen Zunes and Jacob Mundy, *Western Sahara: War, Nationalism, and Conflict Irresolution* (Syracuse, NY: Syracuse University Press, 2010), 93.

55. See Stewart in Gellner and Micaud, *Arabs and Berbers*, 375–98.

56. See Stewart in Gellner and Micaud, *Arabs and Berbers*, 377.

57. See Stewart in Gellner and Micaud, *Arabs and Berbers*, 379.

58. For a deeper reading on the issues of the Greater Maghreb and the politics within the formation of such a customs union see Rézette, *The Western Sahara and the Frontiers of Morocco*, 36–90, and Abun-Nasr, *A History of the Maghrib*.

59. See Stewart in Gellner and Micaud, *Arabs and Berbers*, 382.

60. Rézette, *The Western Sahara and the Frontiers of Morocco*, 5469; "Separate Opinion of Vice President Ammoun," International Court of Justice, *Western Sahara: Advisory Opinion*, para. 85.

61. Zunes and Mundy, *Western Sahara*, 93.

62. Zunes and Mundy, *Western Sahara*, 93. The most pragmatic definition of Sahrawis according to Zunes and Mundy would define them as "the Hassaniyyah-speaking people who claim membership among at least one of the social groupings found in and around the area now known as Western Sahara."

63. Zunes and Mundy, *Western Sahara*, 92–95.

64. International Court of Justice, *Western Sahara: Advisory Opinion*, 39, para. 81.
65. E. Jensen, *Western Sahara: Anatomy of a Stalemate*, 2nd ed. (London: Rienner, 2012), 9.
66. Jensen, *Western Sahara*, 10.
67. Jensen, *Western Sahara*, 10.
68. Jensen, *Western Sahara*, 10. See also Zunes and Mundy, *Western Sahara*, 95–98.
69. A. Mera Miyares, "El Sahara Occidental: Un Conflicto Olvidado?," *Institut de Drets Humans de Catalunya* (2007): 4.
70. Zunes and Mundy, *Western Sahara*, 94.
71. Miyares, "El Sahara Occidental: Un Conflicto Olvidado?," 4.
72. Miyares, "El Sahara Occidental: Un Conflicto Olvidado?," 4; Zunes and Mundy, *Western Sahara*, 95, 101.
73. For guidelines of the areas comprised as Western Sahara, see UN Cartographic Section, "Map of Western Sahara," no. 3175 rev. 2 (January 2004), www.refworld.org/docid/460b64d02.html; UN Cartographic Section "MINURSO," no. 3691 rev. 67 (April 2012), www.refworld.org/docid/4fbf7a8f2.html.
74. Miyares, "El Sahara Occidental: Un Conflicto Olvidado?," 4–6.
75. Ironically enough it was a Cuban born veteran, Francisco Bens, who led the real colonization of the Saharan territories. See Pablo San Martin, "¡*Estos locos cubarauis!*: The Hispanization of Sahrawi Society (. . . after Spain)," *Journal of Transatlantic Studies* 7, no. 3 (2000): 249–51; Ignacio Fuentes Cobo, "La Dimensión Militar y Diplomática del Conflicto del Sahara Occidental: Colonización y Descolonización," in *El Conflicto del Sahara Occidental*, eds. Ignacio Fuente Cobo and Fernando M. Mariño Menéndez (Madrid: Instituto de Estudios Interancionales y Europeos "Francisco de Vitoria," Escuela de Guerra del Ejército, Ministerio de Defensa, 2003), 12–13.
76. Rézette, *The Western Sahara and the Frontiers of Morocco*.
77. On pre-1884 sporadic attempts to establish settlements in the Saharan coast by Europeans since early fifteenth century, see Jensen, *Western Sahara: Anatomy of a Stalemate*, 11–12.
78. See generally, Ernst Gellner, *Saints of the Atlas* (London: Trinity Press, 1969), 41–68.
79. See Rézette, *The Western Sahara and the Frontiers of Morocco*, 111–26.
80. This is primarily the argument presented by the Government of Morocco in the Pleadings to the Western Sahara Case. See Castellino, *International Law and Self-determination*, 238–52; International Court of Justice, *Western Sahara: Advisory Opinion*, 42–45, para. 90–99.
81. See literature cited in note 3.
82. This is the argument presented by the government of the Islamic Republic of Mauritania in the International Court of Justice, *Western Sahara: Advisory Opinion*, 40–42, para. 84–89.
83. International Court of Justice, *Western Sahara: Advisory Opinion*, 40–42, para. 100–102. This argument, by default, was presented by the Government of Spain.
84. Notably Judge Dillard (Dissenting Opinion), International Court of Justice, *Western Sahara: Advisory Opinion*, 116–26; Thomas Franck, "The Stealing of the Sahara," *American Journal of International Law* 70, no. 4 (1976): 694–721; Malcolm Shaw, "The Western Sahara Case," *British Yearbook of International Law* 44 (1978): 134–44.
85. As given by UNGA, 947th Plenary Meeting, Official Records, "Resolution 1514 (XV): Declaration on the Granting of Independence to Colonial Countries and Peoples," December 15, 1960, http://daccess-dds-ny.un.org/doc/RESOLUTION/GEN/NR0/152/88/IMG/NR015288.pdf?OpenElement.
86. See Dunn, "Berber Imperialism," 85–108.
87. This remains true to this day for the Berbers of the region. Several recent news report highlight a "revival" of Berber identity vis-à-vis Arabs facilitated by the "Arab Spring." See, for example, "Springtime for Them Too? The Berbers Join the Arab Revolt," *The Economist*, August 13, 2011, www.economist.com/node/21525925 (accessed September 20, 2012); Casper Wuite, "The Politics of Identity: A Berber Spring in

Algeria?," *Fair Observer*, August 4, 2012, www.fairobserver.com/article/politics-identity-berber-spring-algeria (accessed September 20, 2012); C. J. Chivers, "Amid a Berber Reawakening in Libya, Fears of Revenge," *New York Times*, August 8, 2011, www.nytimes.com/2011/08/09/world/africa/09berbers.html?_r=2 (accessed September 20, 2012). See also literature cited in note 16.

88. Franck, "The Stealing of the Sahara," 694.

89. See especially UNGA, 30th Session, 2318th Plenary Meeting, Official Records, "Resolution 3292 (XXIX): Question of Spanish Sahara," December 13, 1974, http://daccess-dds-ny.un.org/doc/RESOLUTION/GEN/NR0/738/94/IMG/NR073894.pdf?OpenElement.

90. Known as the "Committee of the 24," the Special Committee on Decolonization, in charge of monitoring the implementation of the Declaration on the Granting of Independence to Colonial Countries and Peoples, was created by the UNGA Resolution 1654 (XVI) on November 27, 1961. Its members increased from 17 to 24 in 1962 and it has kept its popular name of the "Committee of the 24," although the number of its members has varied over time. The latest report of the Committee at the time of writing these pages was UN document A/67/23 (July 2012).

91. UNGA, 1398th Plenary Meeting, Official Records, "Resolution 2072 (XX): Question of Ifni and Spanish Sahara," December 16, 1965, para. 2, http://daccess-dds-ny.un.org/doc/RESOLUTION/GEN/NR0/218/35/IMG/NR021835.pdf?OpenElement. The UNGA requested the Spanish government "to take immediately all necessary measures for the liberation of the Territories of Ifni and Spanish Sahara from colonial domination." The UNGA reiterated its demands for a referendum between 1966 and 1975 in its Resolutions: 2229 (XXI) of 20 December 1966, 2354 (XXII) of 19 December 1967, 2428 (XXIII) of 18 December 1968, 2591 (XXIV) of 16 December 1969, 2711 (XXV) of 14 December 1970, 3162 (XXVIII) of 14 December 1973, 3292 (XXIX) of 13 December 1974 and 3458 (XXX) of 8 December 1975.

92. The initial settlement proposals accepted by Morocco and Frente Polisario on August 30, 1988, were the basis of the UNSC Resolution 609 of April 29, 1991, establishing the UN Mission for the Referendum in Western Sahara (MINURSO). For the text of the 1988 settlement plan, see UNSC, Official Records, "The Situation Concerning Western Sahara: Report of the Secretary General," prepared by Secretary-General Javier Pérez de Cuéllar, S/21360 (June 18, 1990), www.un.org/ga/search/view_doc.asp?symbol=S/21360.

93. On the process of identification of voters that followed the 1988 agreements, see Anna Theofilopoulou, "The United Nations and Western Sahara: A Never-ending Affair," *United States Institute of Peace*, Special Report 166 (July 2006): 4–8.

94. Zunes and Mundy, *Western Sahara*, 91.

95. See Joshua Castellino, "Territoriality and Identity in International Law: The Struggle for Self-Determination in the Western Sahara," *Millennium* 28, no. 3 (1999): 525.

96. Zunes and Mundy, *Western Sahara*, xxi.

97. On the categorization of students in Libya and Cuba as refugees, see Elena Fiddian-Quasmiyeh, "Invisible Refugees and/or Overlapping Refugeedom? Protecting Sahrawis and Palestinians Displaced by the 2011 Libyan Uprising," *International Journal of Refugee Law* 24, no. 2 (2012): 263.

98. As early as in 1978, Panama was the first Latin American country to open a SADR Embassy, followed by Mexico in 1979; Cuba and Costa Rica (1980); Venezuela, Bolivia, and Peru (1982); Ecuador (1983); and Colombia (1984). Central American countries joined in the second half of the 1980s (Nicaragua, Honduras, El Salvador) and by the end of the decade the whole Caribbean had established diplomatic relationships with the SADR. In 2000, Paraguay joined the list. See Ahmed Buhari, "Una Deuda Pendiente de América Latina: el Sahara Occidental," *Fundación Vivián Trivias*, Cuaderno no. 20 (2005).

99. Pablo San Martin, "¡*Estos locos cubarauis!* the Hispanization of Sahrawi society (. . . after Spain)," *Journal of Transatlantic Studies* 7, no. 3 (2000): 249–63. The Cuban

student program for Sahrawi refugees has funded the studies of about 10,000 Sahrawis and has been accused by Morocco of being a tool of indoctrination. For a documentary on the topic see, *El Maestro Sharaui*, directed by Nicolás Muñoz, 2010.

100. See the literature cited in note 3.

101. Steve Ratner, "Drawing a Better Line: *Uti Possidetis* and the Borders of New States," *American Journal of International Law* 90, no. 4 (1996): 590–624.

102. Zunes and Mundy, *Western Sahara*, xxiii.

103. Zunes and Mundy, *Western Sahara*, xxiii.

104. Zunes and Mundy, *Western Sahara*, xxiv.

105. Anna Theofilopoulou, "Western Sahara," *The Global Dispatches*, January 31, 2011, www.theglobaldispatches.com/articles/western-sahara (accessed September 20, 2012).

106. See United Nations Security Council, "Resolution 1429 (2002) [on the Western Sahara]," (S/RES/1429), www.un.org/ ga/search/view_doc.asp?symbol=S/RES/1429(2002), in which the Security Council expressed "its readiness to consider any approach which provides for self-determination that may be proposed by the Secretary-General and the Personal Envoy." As a result, Baker drafted a "Peace Plan for Self-Determination for the People of Western Sahara," available in Annex II of United Nations Security Council, Official Records, *Report of the Secretary-General on the Situation Concerning Western Sahara*, prepared by Secretary-General Kofi Annan, S/2003/565, 2003. On the different governmental positions over this plan, see Theofilopoulou, "The United Nations and Western Sahara: A Never-ending Affair," 9–13.

Part II

The Background for the Current Impasse

THREE
Morocco's Saharan Policy

I. William Zartman

Moroccan policy toward the Sahara is captured in that specifically Moroccan term that characterizes Morocco's independence process—"retrocession" or the return of territories piece by piece to Moroccan sovereignty. Although there could be many reasons—material and strategic—for Morocco to pursue its manifest destiny, these are all adjunct to the central conviction that the territory involved *is* Moroccan and simply should return home. In other words, below the good reason is the real reason, below the position is the interest, and the two levels are identical. This means that by extension the issue is existential, not as an expansion on the national self but as part of the national self, and is regarded so by the population and its leaders alike; it is the basis of membership in the Moroccan political system and the primary—even if not the sole—foreign policy interest.[1]

On this central pillar, however, strategy and tactics have evolved in consonance with both the changing international status of the territory and with the evolving domestic political situation. For the first two decades of its independence the Moroccan government adopted an *aggressive claiming* strategy, developing its own internal sense of its claims and seeking their international acceptance. This period ended with the occupation of the Spanish Sahara by Moroccan troops following an agreement with Spain in 1975 and opened into a *defensive confirming* strategy that had deep resonance with changes in domestic politics in which Morocco sought to confirm its de facto control of the former Spanish colony. Particular tactics changed with the circumstances, first as the military situation changed over the 1970s and into the early 1980s, then as bilateral relations with Algeria evolved over the 1980s, and third as the UN took over in 1991 with a cease-fire and a call for a referendum. Morocco launched an *offensive bargaining* strategy in the beginning of the 2000s as the new monarchy of Mohammed VI took hold, then once again preparing a significant step in the evolution of domestic politics, making a move of compromise between the two sides' official positions that it hoped would lead to conclusive political negotiations. Through these changes in strategy, the goal has remained constant but its particular form has vacillated between the direct expression of retrocession to the indirect one of anything-but-independence, the latter only crystallizing as "autonomy" under Mohammed VI. In all this the means to the goal has ostensibly oscillated between negotiation and referendum, where both are always present and both rest on the factual assumption of military occupation.

Throughout these phases, Morocco's Saharan policy has had an intimate connection to domestic affairs and has been used to orient and support a consensus around the monarchy. But it has also had its impact on directions of domestic policy, which needs to proceed in harmony with the Saharan issue. On the level of policy making, the dossier has always remained under direct royal control once the goal was adopted by Mohammed V soon after independence. The policy had its impact on the foreign ministry and was carried out by the interior ministry and the army but it never left the hands of the palace.

AGGRESSIVE CLAIMING

The whole political system in Morocco took two decades to define what is meant by its *Saharan irredenta*, a process that was in turn conditioned by the particular way in which the country attained its independence. Morocco recovered its independence from the French and Spanish (and international) colonizers in pieces. The palace and the Independence (Istiqlal) party negotiated the return of the larger French Protectorate and the smaller Spanish Protectorate in the north in March 1956, followed soon after by the International Zone of Tangier. The government then pressed for the return of the Southern Spanish Protectorate of Tarfaya in 1958, followed in 1969 by Spain's Atlantic enclave of Ifni (the Mediterranean enclaves of Ceuta [Sebta], Melilla, and associated islands have still not returned to Morocco and are the subject of a tacit truce, rattled a bit from time to time).[2] Over these territories, Morocco's claim and the retrocession process of reconstituting its historic limits were uncontested.

Beyond lay the Sahara, of contested status, with no clear indication of the limits for continuing retrocession. Claims over the lands to the south were long advanced by the leading nationalist party, the Istiqlal, maps in hand, but became Moroccan policy only in 1958 when enunciated by Mohammed V in a speech at Mhamid on February 25, to undercut the Istiqlal by making their positions his own. At that time, all the territory was still under French colonial control, except for the two Spanish territories of Saqiet el-Hamra (Red Creek) and Rio del Oro (River of Gold). The Istiqlal's map showed western Algeria (Tindouf and the Tuat), northern Mali, and all of Mauritania as the claimed territory, although there was never any boundary for the claims except for the Senegal River in the case of Mauritania.[3] Here, the basis of the claims was very different from the previous retroceded territories. It lay in the historic conquests of Sultan Ahmed al-Mansour in the late sixteenth century,[4] maintained by the assertions that in an area bereft of legitimate civil authority, the prayers said in the name of the sultan of Morocco constituted a sign of sovereignty. Morocco's sovereignty had continued under the Protectorate, by a judgment of the International Court of Justice (ICJ) in 1952, and so an extension of that reasoning would suggest that its continuing sovereignty would extend to its former limits. The reasoning was tenuous, but as long as it related to territories still under colonial control it could be advanced in the name of decolonization. But 1958 was the year of sudden change. In French West Africa, the colonies faced a referendum, already prepared in the framework law of 1956, to choose association in the French Community or independence, and in Algeria the war for independence was in its fourth year. So as Morocco laid its claim for further retrocession, the neighboring states were preparing for their own sovereignty.

The most distant area of the irredentist claim was northern Mali, which became independent through the breakup of the Mali Federation in 1960. Mali then joined Ghana and Guinea, already independent in 1957 and 1958, respectively, in the Union of African States (UAS) that became a major player in the process of diplomatically sorting out the newly independent African states in the early 1960s.[5] The next step in the more radical states' diplomatic coordination was a meeting hosted by Morocco in 1962, which brought Algeria and Egypt into a group with the UAS. With the formation of the Casablanca Group, Morocco dropped its claims over Malian territory.

A major part of Morocco's foreign policy activity in the early years of its independence related to the Algerian nationalist struggle, where Morocco was torn between two policy goals. On the one hand, Morocco gave solid support to the National Liberation Front (FLN), providing sanctuary for the National Liberation Army (ALN) and diplomatic engagement for the Provisional Government of the Algerian Republic (GPRA). The most specific basis of distinction between the Casablanca and the rival moderate Monrovia Group was the type of support to be given to the Algerian struggle. On the other hand, Morocco had its border claim. Mohammed V agreed not to press it during the Algerian war but got a promise from Ferhat Abbas and Benyoussef Ben Khedda, president of the GPRA, to discuss the border question after independence. The north–south border was delimited by the 1845 Treaty of Lalla Maghnia between France and Morocco from the Mediterranean to the Figuig oasis (in Morocco) but the rest of the line to the west was undefined because, as the Treaty stated (art. 6), further delimitation would be "superfluous" because it was uninhabitable desert. Upon Algerian independence, the focus of Morocco's Saharan policy was directed toward the "superfluous" border between the two neighbors. Morocco pressed for an implementation of Abbas' and Ben Khedda's promise to talk, but newly elected Algerian president Ahmed Ben Bella declined and the border situation became tense.

The earliest international recognition of Morocco's claims came from the Arab League, which published a booklet in 1960 endorsing the Moroccan position.[6] The league was the only international organization from which Morocco could gain support at the time, and no neighboring states were as yet members to contest the claim. However, by 1963 the competition between the Casablanca and Monrovia groups was bridged at a meeting called by the latter in Addis Ababa to set up a regional organization for all of Africa. The founding resolution of the resulting Organization of African Unity (OAU) clearly supported the notion of *uti possedetis*, recognizing colonial boundaries as permanent and legitimate, but Morocco (and Somalia, which also had undefined boundaries) demurred, and joined the organization with reservations. The test of the OAU came five months after the organization's establishment, when war broke out along the border as Morocco pushed for consideration of its claims. When the Royal Armed Forces (FAR) quickly surrounded Tindouf, which it claimed, the National People's Army (ANP) gave the same treatment to Figuig, which was not contested, and the war bogged down in a mutually hurting stalemate. Ethiopian Emperor Haile Selassie and Malian President Modiba Keita seized the ripe moment to negotiate a cease-fire and move the conflict into an ad hoc OAU committee. Tunisian President Habib Bourguiba brought Hassan II and Ben Bella together at the OAU summit in Cairo in July 1964 and then at Saidia in April 1965, where Ben Bella finally picked up the previous Algerian promise to negotiate. The promise, after the ANP's frustrated efforts, was one of the reasons for Ben Bella's overthrow by the army the following year.

The years after 1965 were difficult times for the monarchy. The experiment in constitutional and parliamentary government fell apart as the parties rushed into a balance of power system and Hassan II, recently in power, reacted, dismissing parliament and the parties. Morocco went into a five-year state of emergency with parliament suspended after 1965, redefined its political rules in two successive constitutions in 1970 and 1972, and underwent political tremors in the attempted military coups in 1971 and 1972 and a radical left-wing opposition harbored in Algeria in 1973. In this situation, the wisest policy was to mend fences with Algeria and the best fence to mend was the common border.[7] The king made his first trip to Algiers for the OAU Summit in September 1968 and President Houari Boumedienne returned the visit to Ifrane to sign the Treaty of

Solidarity and Cooperation with Morocco on January 15, 1969. They then met in Tlemcen four months later to coordinate Saharan strategy and work on the common border; on May 27, 1970, producing the border treaty of June 15, 1972, signed at the OAU Summit in Rabat. Hassan reported to the OAU that the Saharan issue with Algeria was settled. The border treaty was not submitted to the Moroccan parliament because there was no parliament at the time, as the king pointed out later on, but the king's signature was all that was necessary in the monarchy for entry into force.[8] The Algerian National People's Assembly (APN) ratified the treaty on May 17, 1973. As part of the reconciliation policy, Morocco recognized Mauritania in 1969, and Boumedienne at the OAU Summit told Mauritanian President Mokhtar ould Daddah to patch up with Morocco. Ostensibly two aspects of the Saharan question were resolved.

The roughly east–west boundary established in 1972 from Figuig to the Tarfaya (Southern Spanish Protectorate) border is similar to the Varnier Line proposed sixty years earlier and running along the hamada escarpment on the south side of the Draa River Valley;[9] it is clearly delineated but has yet to be demarcated because of remaining tensions. Morocco has made a major tactical error in not showing the border as settled in official documents and maps (including a large wall map in the Foreign Ministry). The treaty marks the end of Moroccan claims over Tindouf and western Algeria and supports evacuation of iron from the Gara Jebilet mines through Moroccan ports;[10] in exchange Morocco gained Algerian support for Moroccan claims over the remaining portion of Morocco's *irredenta*, the Spanish Sahara.

The campaign for the decolonization of the two Spanish provinces of the Sahara began in 1965 with a United Nations General Assembly (UNGA) Resolution calling for negotiations, but the UNGA annual resolutions thereafter backed Algeria's call for self-determination by referendum. Under the continuing pressure of UNGA Resolutions, Spain announced its intention in 1973 to comply and hold its referendum in 1975. Morocco pressed its claims on the territory, as did Mauritania, but after Moroccan recognition of Mauritania, the three states bordering the Spanish colony moved to coordinate their policy focusing on Spanish withdrawal. Presumably, the territory was then to be split along the twenty-sixth parallel into its two components, Rio de Oro going to Mauritania and Saqiet el-Hamra to Morocco; Boumedienne blessed the solution at an Arab League summit in Rabat on October 29, 1974, as did his Foreign Minister, Abdulaziz Bouteflika, in July 1975. The process was too slow and the outcome too uncertain for the claimants, and so Morocco and Mauritanian sponsored a UNGA resolution calling on the ICJ to issue an advisory opinion on the precolonial legal ties of the territory to the Sherifian Empire and to a Mauritanian entity. Algeria appeared before the court as a party contesting the claims. With this maneuver to leap to a conclusion, the Maghribi tripartite coordination fell apart.

The court's opinion, issued in October 1975, recognized such legal ties but judged them insufficient for current claims of territorial sovereignty; self-determination, not history or society, was the only acceptable basis for territorial decolonization, as UN Resolutions had declared since 1966 and as stipulated in the original UN Resolution 1514 (XV) of 1960.[11] Morocco seized on the first part of the opinion, declared justification, and massed 350,000 civilians with a military guard on its hitherto southern border for a "Green March" into the territory. Under the continuing pressure from Morocco, with Generalissimo Franco on his deathbed, Spain agreed to negotiate. Morocco called off the Green March, its pressure on Spain and its popular rally behind the king and the irredentist cause having been accomplished, and the three countries soon arrived at the Tripartite Agreement of November 14, 1975, transferring administration of the territories to Morocco and Mauritania. Morocco bought Mauritania into support by further limiting its irredenta and giving Mauritania a third of the territory, along a southeast–northwest diagonal line, in a partitioning agreement of April 14, 1976, and the FAR moved in to take control.

Much of the decolonization of Africa to date had been accomplished by a territorial assembly elected under colonial rule, which then declared independence (after negotiations) by legislative act. Morocco worked to complement its decolonization agreement with Spain by obtaining a similar vote from the legislative assembly of Spanish Sahara, the *yemaa* (*jema'a*) in Hispano-Arabic; it had been instituted in 1967 and reelected in 1971 with thirty-six directly elected seats and forty-six tribal chiefs, with membership increased by twenty in 1973 to 102. On December 22, 1975, seventy-two members of the *yemaa* endorsed the Tripartite Agreement in writing and on February 28, 1976, sixty-five of them met in Laâyoune to reaffirm their support. However, on November 28, 1975, sixty-seven members (including forty who would later meet at Laâyoune to support Morocco) met at Guelta Zemour to support independence and then to dissolve their body. Yet to Morocco, the issue was never one of decolonization but of reconstitution of a dismembered state, with the doctrine of territorial integrity taking precedence over self-determination in international law.[12]

The takeover of Western Sahara in 1975–1976 consummated Moroccan territorial claims, trading off a reduction in territory for an imperfectly legal handover from the colonial authority and the territorial assembly, and losing the support of Algeria in the process. The evolution of the process was integral to the challenges of Moroccan domestic affairs, as the reign of Hassan II entered into a critical period.[13] Ridding himself of parliament and parties, the king found himself alone with the army, who then twice tried to remove him. Hassan needed some basic support from civil society, and so had to revive the parties, make a pact with them, gain popular support, and give the army something patriotic to do. The Saharan issue served the purpose admirably, with the whole irredentist claim concentrated in one territory under the internationally attractive label of decolonization.

The only problem was that an even more attractive label for the international community was a national liberation movement bent on self-determination.[14] There had always been a good deal of Sahrawi opposition to Spanish colonial rule, but the most notable beginnings came from a group of conservative Muslim Sahrawi students in Rabat who organized a Saharan Liberation Front in 1968. In retrospect, it was a fatal mistake for Morocco not to court the group, but their type of decolonization—and activity as students—did not fit the tactics of the palace. Joining up with local students, the Rabat group fled to Mauritania and organized themselves as the Popular Front for the Liberation of Saqiet el-Hamra and Rio de Oro (Polisario Front) in May 1973, launching guerrilla attacks on the Spanish troops; they then shifted their base to Algeria, who offered them encampments, sanctuary, and supplies in the Tindouf area, plus diplomatic support. The Polisario made three early strategic decisions that shaped the future conflict: they organized nomads, local populations harassed by the "liberating" Moroccan army, native auxiliaries from the Spanish army, and unemployed Saharans from neighboring countries, and herded them into the camps at Tindouf; they turned the focus of the military activity on Mauritania; and they declared a Sahrawi Arab Democratic Republic (SADR) on February 26, 1976, which Algeria supported in the OAU and elsewhere. Just when it thought it had won the cause, Morocco was immediately thrown on the defensive.

DEFENSIVE CONFIRMING

Once in the territory, Morocco adopted a complex strategy based on military, sociopolitical, and diplomatic tactics. By the mid-1980s, it had won on the first two but lost on the third, a situation that remains through many turns three decades later. During this time, the Saharan issue had risen to the point where it was on a par with recognition of the monarchy as the linchpin of acceptance into the Moroccan political system. By the same token, to those inside that system, it was a symbol of pride and identity, and so served the king in his reassertion of control and coherence over the system. Thus the issue was enormously important to stability in Morocco, and the king was as much nailed to its success as were his people: he had to deliver.

On the military front, Morocco sent in nearly 50,000 troops, including 9,000 in Mauritania, and engaged in a roving campaign against the mobile Polisario. The FAR held up well but after June 1976, the Polisario adopted a clever new strategy, focusing its attacks on Mauritania, wearing it down until the government collapsed in mid-1978 and a year later gave in, renouncing its claims on the Western Sahara. To this turn, Morocco adopted a double strategy, attempting to take over the regime in Nouakchott itself, against competition from similar attempts from Algeria and Libya, and moving in to occupy the whole territory of the Western Sahara. Major campaigns in 1979 and 1980 took the initiative away from the Polisario to regain territorial control. Until then, the occupation continued to be tactically beleaguered: When the FAR camped at night it built a defensive sand wall around itself and so was surrounded. In 1980, the idea came to open the circles and join the defense walls, containing first the "useful triangle" of Saqiet el-Hamra and then by 1987, 80 percent of the territory, leaving only the eastern fringes (and western Algerian bases) to the Polisario. The ground war ended for all intents and purposes in 1984, with the FAR in control behind its defenses.

Sociopolitically, the early military campaign was accompanied by collecting the remaining population in the territory and providing for their sedentarization behind army lines, along with large numbers of Sahrawis who had fled to Morocco following French and Spanish campaigns in the 1950s and 1960s. Morocco provided millions of dollars in development programs, continually augmented through the coming years, bringing impressive economic growth but also internal social conflict between original natives and "carpetbaggers" (see the discussion in the articles by Khadija Finan and Anouar Bouhkars). A corollary of this policy was the encouragement of "transfuges" or "deserters" from the Polisario returning to Morocco. The policy had worked to some effect toward Mauritania in the 1960s when a number of notable Mauritanians came to Morocco and were rewarded with good, often high, positions. A similar campaign toward Western Saharans provided some notable "returns," particularly in the late 1980s and early 1990s, but also succeeded in the long run in concentrating power within a small group in the Polisario and in justifying their paranoia.

The diplomatic strategy was less successful. King Hassan felt that the same years of the early 1980s were the most promising for a direct agreement with Algeria.[15] Instead, every time some mediatory gesture by a third party brought the two parties physically together—if only for a handshake—the raised hopes were dashed even lower by some counter-incident. A series of small events led to a meeting between Hassan and Boumedienne's successor, Gen Chadli Bendjedid, at the border village of Akid Lotfi (Algerian name) or Zouj Bghal (Moroccan name) in February 1983 to arrange some steps toward a solution (including autonomy). But in March and April Algeria made a Peace and Friendship Treaty with Tunisia and Mauritania, isolating Morocco and Libya, who unexpectedly but quite naturally, made their own "African Union" in July. The OAU's downward spiral then ensued. (Morocco correctly perceived that the period of Algerian weakness during the Islamist attacks of the early 1990s was highly unpropitious for any agreement, since parties tend to make tough concessions during times of strength, not weakness.)

Faced with an assiduous campaign by Algeria and Libya (including financial inducements) to promote the recognition of the SADR by African states and its admission into the OAU, Morocco shifted its strategy in 1981 from clear recognition of its claims to organization of a referendum (discussed in greater detail in Antonin Tisseron's chapter). Turning itself into an Implementing Committee of the OAU, the Committee of Wisemen seemed to provide the sought-for solution, and in the OAU Summit at Nairobi in June 1981, King Hassan declared his support for a "referendum of confirmation" or a referendum "*contrôlé*." All the details were in place until the committee chair, Nigeria, changed to recognition of the SADR following a military coup in Lagos. In 1982 when the outgoing OAU administrative secretary general declared the SADR an OAU member, the OAU was frozen for sixteen months and stalled for another sixteen months, until the twentieth summit in Addis Ababa in November 1984 when the SADR was fully admitted to the OAU and Morocco left, never to return. With a good prospect of Moroccan success through referendum, the Polisario and its supporters bolted to immediate recognition, thereby killing any future role of peacemaker for the OAU and even its successor, the African Union (AU), after 2000. In 1991, the OAU handed the conflict over to the UN and begged out.

Morocco's policy remained unchanged: press for a referendum but refuse the direct contact with the Polisario called for in UNGA Resolutions. In that view, the road to the first while avoiding the second ran through Algeria, and the path to Algeria was marked by mediators. There was no contact between the two countries between January 1985 and May 1987, when Saudi Arabia brought the two leaders back to Zouj Bghal/Akid Lofi again, on May 16, 1988, bringing a detailed agreement for a referendum without direct contact, plus the renewal of open relations and economic cooperation. At the end of August 1988 Morocco and the Polisario accepted a more detailed proposal for the referendum, including the possibility of a third choice of autonomy. Soon after, on February 17, 1989, the five members of the two opposing alliances met in Marrakesh to create an Arab Maghreb Union (UMA) even before the Saharan issue was fully resolved. Morocco pressed for these developments and continually took their progress as an indication of Algerian good faith in moving toward a Saharan solution as well.

But the same pitfalls of disillusion and distrust lay in wait for the rising hopes of the 1980s. To Morocco, progress was betrayed by Algerian missteps; the same impression was held on the other side, and there is no way to establish which side made the bigger false step first and which answered inappropriately next and so on. The UMA lasted seven summits through 1994, making some institutional decisions but implementing none, but then Morocco "froze" it for inappropriate conduct by Algeria in blocking a UN plan for a referendum. Morocco later complained of terrorist infiltration, in the explosion in Marrakesh in 1994; Algeria closed the border and has kept it closed ever since.[16]

Morocco has not always shown diplomatic finesse in its defensive confirming strategies, but it did come close on a number of occasions in the 1980s to a realization of its goal of holding a confirming referendum. It succeeded in avoiding the UN-mandated direct talks, which it felt would give the Polisario equal standing, but it did not succeed in keeping Algeria on track toward an outcome-oriented process. Discussions never got to the details that would sink the referendum preparations in the next phase, although on some occasions they did produce credible moves and plans of action. Observers feel that King Hassan and his Interior Minister Driss Basri felt confident about referendum results during this period, but that the king wanted to win big, with no margin for error, and so was very careful about the conditions of the referendum. Algeria continued to press for direct contacts and direct recognition whenever possible, leaving Morocco feeling betrayed in the progress it felt it was making toward a "referendum of confirmation," the same kind of referendum as Algeria had had in 1962, but for its independence.

The third segment of this phase began officially in 1991 when the UN mediated a cease-fire (although fire had already ceased for all practical purposes since 1984). The UN Secretariat began its interest as early as 1986, in cooperation with the OAU president that year, Senegalese President Abdou Diouf. UN Secretary-General Javier Pérez de Cuéllar began a process of proximity talks with Morocco and the Polisario and then put UN Undersecretary-General for Special Political and Decolonization Affairs Abderrahim Fares on the case. Pérez de Cuéllar favored a status of autonomy as a means of breaking the integration-independence deadlock.[17] Morocco was interested, but technical progress achieved by the Secretariat was hobbled by the Moroccan-Algerian hurdle. Further proposals from the UN and the OAU were accepted by both parties in August 1988, and the Security Council (Resolution 658 [1990]) approved a report from the secretary-general providing for a cease-fire and the organization of a referendum, with the appointment of a Special Representative of the Secretary-General (SRSG) and then (Resolution 690 [1991]) the creation of a United Nations Mission for the Referendum in Western Sahara (MINURSO).

Morocco's strategy continued to back the referendum, with the tactics shifting to make sure that Morocco would win when the referendum took place.[18] Hassan's referendum policy since the beginning of the 1980s had two conditions: a plebiscite confirming Moroccan sovereignty, with no option for independence, and an electorate deemed likely to support the sovereignty option. The Polisario tactics were the same but exactly opposite of course: independence and a favorable electorate. The original resolution foresaw a referendum in February 1992, but the Identification

Commission (IDC) went to work only in August 1994, and ran into the predicted difficulties. Over the following decade, whenever a voters' list was established that appeared to favor one side, the other objected, adding criteria that would provide a list favoring its side, upon which the first side objected, and so on. In so doing, both sides acted rationally within their own needs.

The king wanted to expand voter eligibility beyond the 1974 census at the end of Spanish colonization and their families (i.e., demographic growth over two decades), plus their historic families over five generations going back to the beginning of the Spanish colonization and refugees who had fled to Morocco in the 1950s. With these criteria in place (except for the historic condition, limited to only one generation, and for the identity to be expressed in terms of tribal subfraction rather than the broader tribe), the king appeared satisfied about an acceptable outcome and agreed to UN Secretary-General Boutros Boutros Ghali's proposal in June 1993. It was a slogging process once begun in August 1994 and it broke down at the end of the following year. In mid-March 1997, Secretary-General Kofi Annan appointed former US Secretary of State James Baker III as his Personal Envoy (PESG). Baker accepted because he saw a challenge worthy of his talents and he proposed a negotiated political solution; instead the parties both insisted on sticking to a referendum. The eligibility battle then turned to three remaining subfractions favored by Morocco and contested by the Polisario. Baker mediated the Houston Accords defining conditions for the referendum in mid-September, including procedures for appeal. Two years later and at the beginning of 2000 the IDC published its two Provisional Voters Lists (PVLs) of 86,412 eligible voters out of 250,000 names proposed; in February 131,000 appeals were launched, mainly by Morocco, and the process ground to a halt.

Morocco's defensive confirming policy under King Hassan moved from the second element—the plebiscite—to the first—the electorate. As the chances of a confirming referendum slipped, the policy became one of blocking an independence vote by insisting, within the agreed rules, on a friendly voters' list (or none at all). Morocco worked on other fronts during the same period. It convinced a number of African states to withdraw their recognition of the SADR (discussed in Tisseron's chapter), although still not quite enough to remove it from AU membership. It developed its repopulation and sedentarization policy in the territory, although the result has been heightened tensions among the different populations. The explanation for the impasse lies in the existence of a classical soft, stable, self-serving stalemate in which each side prefers the impasse to the dangerous alternative posed by the other side, and is entrapped by its policies.[19] That preference is hardened by the fact that both sides consider the issue as existential. For Morocco, it is the basis of legitimacy and identity for the regime, not only for the current incumbents but for the entire political system—"a war that it cannot win but cannot afford to lose."[20] For the Polisario, of course, it is their existence. And Algeria washes its hands of it.

OFFENSIVE BARGAINING

The 2000s saw a shift in policy along with a new monarchy. Mohammed VI remains strongly attached to the maintenance of Moroccan sovereignty over the area, but more flexible about the means to assure it. In an interview with *Time* magazine soon after his accession to the throne, Mohammed indicated that his biggest wish was to end the Saharan conflict. Clearly he has felt that a new tack is necessary, a higher moral ground, and that opportunity was offered by the UN mediators. The deadlock over a referendum had to be either officially recognized or authoritatively broken by an imposed solution. Such was the report (S/2002/178) of Baker on February 16, 2002; as at Houston, the parties preferred to remain comfortably in the impasse and the UNSC urged more talks. Baker then proposed a three-year delay (S/2003/565, May 23, 2003) in the referendum, during which time a provisional administration elected by Sahrawis on the PVLs plus all who had lived in the territory since 1999 (Baker Plan II). Polisario accepted with reservations, Morocco submitted a counterproposal for a "Saharan Autonomous Region" in December,[21] and rejected the transition idea and, finally, clearly, in April 2004, the option of independence.

The idea of autonomy had been floating around for a while, as noted.[22] Baker I (S/2201/613 of June 20, 2001) proposed integration within Morocco with a degree of autonomy; Morocco accepted and of course the Polisario rejected it. Pérez de Cuéllar, Boutros Ghali, and, eventually, Kofi Annan considered autonomy to be the optimal solution, between two extremes. Unfortunately, autonomy was dogged by two images as a transition to something else: Baker II as transition to referendum and the Camp David I agreement between Israel and Egypt as a transition to independence (or, in Israeli eyes, to integration). After Baker resigned, disillusioned, in June 2004, he was succeeded by Alvaro deSoto as PESG and Peter van Walsum a year later, who also backed autonomy four years afterward when he left office.

When Morocco rejected Baker II, it did so in the name of "autonomy within the framework of Moroccan sovereignty. Thus, the population would be expected to manage its own local affairs"; it was the autonomy option that precluded the independence option (S/2004/325/enclosure). The first announcement of an autonomy option by Mohammed VI came on the thirtieth anniversary of the Green March in 2005. The king then, in March 2006, announced the revival of a 140 member Royal Advisory Council for Saharan Affairs (CORCAS) to make proposals on autonomy, which it did in December. Then on April 11, 2007, under pressure from Washington, Paris, London and Madrid, Morocco issued its "Initiative for Negotiating an Autonomy Status for the Sahara." The initiative was specifically not a final fleshed-out proposal but rather an invitation to negotiation. As a result, the UNSC dropped the fifty-year campaign for a referendum and called on the parties to engage in direct talks "in good faith and without preconditions" for a political solution. In the four talks in Manhasset under van Walsum, the Polisario refused to discuss autonomy or anything else but independence. His successor, Christopher Ross, tried a new track of discussing confidence-building measures and asked that the referendum option be retained, producing no results until finally in June 2012 Morocco declared its lack of confidence in Ross. In fact, in the talks, the two parties stuck to their positions: Polisario to independence and Morocco to its new position of autonomy. Ross's strategy of an indirect approach focused on visits of divided families but failed to produce any movement toward a final status agreement. Observers from all sides tend to agree that an agreement will come only from a meeting of the two heads of state—Morocco and Algeria—that may have to await the 2014 Algerian elections at best.[23]

The autonomy proposal was the first attempt ever made by one of the parties to strike a compromise between their two extreme positions. As such it had inevitable strategic vulnerabilities. When one side moves toward the middle, it is easy for the other side to say, "So that's your new position; let's then seek a middle ground between it and my [unchanged] position." Furthermore, Morocco, proud of its autonomy demarche, refers to it as "The Moroccan Initiative," whereas it would have to be discussed without attribution to be acceptable to the other side. While presented as a framework to be filled in by negotiation, it is vulnerable to criticisms for being imprecise; yet if presented in detail, it would be criticized for being inflexible. If Morocco were to take its rebuff as an incitation to go ahead on its own and implement the autonomy idea, it could change facts on the ground but not make them any more acceptable to the Polisario. Yet the proposal stands as an invitation to negotiation "in good faith" to give it enabling details, a challenge to be taken up by the UNSC friends of Morocco plus Spain even if not by the other side.[24]

The autonomy proposal had a significant relation to important Moroccan domestic developments that is not often recognized. As is typical of the kingdom, it was unveiled after a lengthy process of discussions with all players within the body politic. A question frequently met was whether it was compatible with the Moroccan constitution; the initiative could be a royal decision but its institutionalization needs to fit within constitutional structures. On this and on other subjects, the topic of constitutional reform was much discussed, even before Mohammed VI's accession to the throne in 1999. The idea of regionalization, combining devolution, deconcentration, and delegation,[25] had also been a subject of discussion in political circles, with the objection that any measure that applied to the Saharan south would risk inciting separatism in the Riffan north. A year after the Autonomy Initiative, on the thirty-third anniversary of the Green March, the king announced a plan for regionalization, and the following year, on November 6, 2009, on the thirty-fourth anniversary, and again on January 3, 2010, he announced the formation of an Advisory Committee for Regionalization, to report at the end of the year. But regionalization was impossible without constitutional reform, so when the deconcentration report was given, the king created an Advisory Committee on Constitutional Reform, composed mainly of the same membership as the previous committee. Thus, when the Arab Spring hit Morocco, on February 20, 2011, the process of constitutional revision was already in course, allowing for the royal introduction of a new constitutional draft on March 6 that was approved on July 1, 2001. More and in different ways than anticipated, the Sahara has had a defining impact on Moroccan politics since the king has indicated that the decentralization/regionalization reforms would begin in the "southern provinces" and be extended throughout the country The magnitude of this latest effort is clearly evident in the recommendations for regionalization crafted by the Environmental, Social, and Economic Council (CESE), tasked by theking bo both assess and develop the "new development model for the kingdom's southern provinces." Its recommendations have significant implications for local governance and economic growth, and it was publicly launched in November 2013 with a budget of US$18 billion over the next ten years.

CONCLUSION

Moroccan policy toward the Western Sahara has been a success in the sense that it has not been a failure. Yet it has been a failure in the sense that after four decades it still has not been able to consummate the physical possession of the territory with a legal possession, and the Moroccan arguments for its claim have not been accepted by the international community or its individual members. Only its administrative control has been recognized, and a significant number of states, primarily in Africa, have recognized the counterclaim of sovereignty by the SADR. The ensuing diplomatic stalemate has been held firmly in place as much by the Polisario's unwillingness to budge as by Morocco's steadfastness. Even Morocco's attempt to break the positional deadlock with its autonomy proposal has not weakened the opponent's unwillingness.

Morocco is left with the alternative of waving its proposal before an unresponsive audience or filling in its own details and implementing them unilaterally. The latter would indeed change the situation, since it would give occasion for a formalization of the restiveness already in evidence among the Saharan population, even if the Polisario pouted outside the wall, as discussed in the Boukhars and Finan chapters. Whether under autonomy or not, the current situation poses an internal challenge to Morocco, since any repression of disturbances creates its own problems, whether warranted or not. The former alternative, of continued unproductive deadlock, also carries its own dangers, as much for the international community as for Morocco. An explosive incident, unforeseeable at the moment, could cause the tense relations within the region to snap and draw in interested states outside. That danger in itself provides Morocco with a policy opportunity to bring in those states to take up the offer to negotiate autonomy's details and recognize the outcome. The challenge for Moroccan policy lies in making the interested states, such as France, Britain, Spain, and the United States, interested enough to take their own initiative in a world, and specifically a region, that holds more pressing challenges for the international community.

NOTES

1. Four comprehensive works on the topic are John Damis, *Conflict in Northwest Africa* (Stanford, CA: Hoover Institution Press, 1983); I. William Zartman, "Conflict in the Sahara," in *Ripe for Resolution: Conflict and Intervention in Africa* (New York: Oxford University Press, 1989); Khadija Mohsen-Finan, *Sahara Occidental: Les Enjeux d'un Conflit Regional* (Paris: CNRS, 1997); Hugh Roberts, "Western Sahara: The Cost of the Conflict," *International Crisis Group*, Middle East/North Africa Report no. 65 (June 1, 2007). See also Hugh Roberts, "Out of the Impasse," *International Crisis Group*, Middle East/North Africa Report no. 66 (June 11, 2007).
2. Fernando Moran, *El Proceso de Autodeterminacion del Sahara* (Valencia: Fernando-Torres, 1982).
3. F. E. Trout, *Morocco's Saharan Frontiers* (Geneva: Droz, 1969).
4. Robert Rézette, *Le Sahara Occidental et les Frontières Marocaines* (Paris: Nouvelles Editions Latines, 1975), 35–50.
5. I. William Zartman, "Party State and Alliance," in *International Relations in the New Africa* (Lanham, MD: University Presses of America, 1987).
6. Jamal Sa'd, *The Problem of Mauritania* (New York: Arab Information Office, 1960).
7. I. William Zartman, "Conflict in the Sahara," in *Ripe for Resolution*, 19–82.
8. Ratification, announced by the king in April 1973, was cut short by the discovery of an Algerian-supported plot against Hassan, possibly the "real reason" to go along with the above-noted "good reason." Hassan stated on June 1, 1981, that the treaty stood and the border conflict was over.
9. Ian Brownlie, *African Boundaries* (Berkeley: University of California Press, 1979), 55–83.
10. On the Gara Jebilet issue, see Tony Hodges, *Western Sahara: The Roots of a Desert War* (Westport, CT: Lawrence Hill, 1983), 114, 194; it is doubtful if it is available as a bargaining chip with Algeria any longer, but "settled" issues are not settled until they are actually settled!
11. International Court of Justice, *Western Sahara Advisory Opinion* (October 16, 1975), www.icj-cij.org/docket/files/61/6195.pdf.
12. John Damis, "King Hassan and the Western Sahara," *The Maghreb Review* 25, no. 1–2 (2000): 20; Roberts, "Out of the Impasse," 9–10.

13. I. William Zartman, "King Hassan's New Morocco," in *The Political Economy of Morocco*, ed. I. William Zartman (New York: Praeger, 1987).

14. Ahmed Baba Miské, *Front Polisario: l'Âme d'un Peuple* (Paris: Rupture, 1978). See also Hodges, *Western Sahara: The Roots of a Desert War*, chap. 14, chap. 15, and chap. 30.

15. Zartman, *Ripe for Resolution*, 60.

16. I. William Zartman, "The Ups and Downs of Maghrib Unity," in *Middle East Dilemma: The Politics and Economics of Arab Integration*, ed. Michael Hudson (New York: Columbia University Press, 1999).

17. Pérez de Cuéllar received a positive response from Hassan and Bendjedid to the idea that autonomy was the preferable outcome, and the king asked Pérez de Cuéllar to ask the Algerian president to approach the Polisario, with no indicated result. *Memoires*, cited in Anna Theofilopoulou, "The United Nations and Western Sahara: A Never-ending Affair," *United States Institute of Peace*, Special Report 166 (July 2006): 166.

18. The story was current in Morocco that a Central American country was holding an election and the dictator wanted to be sure to win. "Call Basri," an assistant suggested, and Driss Basri was summoned from Morocco. The election was held and when the results came in, the dictator asked anxiously, "How did it turn out?" "Well," the assistant replied nervously, "It was great: we got 96 percent. Only they all voted for King Hassan."

19. I. William Zartman, "Analyzing Intractability," in *Grasping the Nettle*, eds. Chester Crocker, Fen Osler Hampson, and Pamela Aall (Washington, DC: United States Institute of Peace, 2005); Karin von Hippel, "Sunk in the Sahara: The Applicability of the Sunk Cost Effect to Irredentist Disputes," *Journal of North African Studies* 1, no. 1 (1996): 95–116; Remy Leveau and Khadja Mohsen-Finan, "L'Affaire du Sahara Occidental," *Etudes*, January 2000.

20. Damis, "King Hassan and the Western Sahara," 30.

21. I have often suggested that Morocco call it the Saharan Autonomous Development Region or SADR to take the acronym away from the Polisario.

22. Abdelhamid El Ouali, *Saharan Conflict: Towards a Territorial Autonomy* (London: Stacey, 2008).

23. Leveau and Mohsen-Finan, "L'Affaire du Sahara Occidental," 11–23.

24. "Why the Maghreb Matters," *Potomac Institute for Policy Studies and the Conflict Management Program of the School of Advanced International Studies*, March 2009, www.whythemaghrebmatters.org/NorthAfricaPolicyPaper032509.pdf.

25. Yossef Ben-Meir, "Morocco's Regionalization 'Roadmap' and the Western Sahara," *International Journal on World Peace* 27, no. 2 (June 2010): 63–85.

FOUR
The Emergence and Politics of the Polisario Front

Stephen J. King

This chapter traces the emergence and evolution of the Polisario Front (*Frente Popular de Liberación de Saguía el Hamra y Río de Oro*). Primarily, it argues that early in the military conflict with Mauritania and especially Morocco, the Polisario Front determined that it could not win a military conflict and the mainstay of its politics became efforts to advance its cause on the regional (African Union [AU]) and international (UN) diplomatic stages. Secondarily it sketches out the evolving nature of Saharawi nationalism, which began, to an extent, as part of a Moroccan push for national independence from France and Spain. Once the early Polisario determined that it would seek a national state apart from Morocco rather than as part of it, the international forum and the principle of self-determination provided resources that helped compensate for its military inferiority vis-à-vis Morocco.

The roots of the Polisario Front can be found in indigenous resistance to Spanish and French colonial rule in Northwest Africa. Part of this resistance turned into a nationalist movement of the Sahrawi people seeking an independent, modern nation-state in the Spanish or Western Sahara. The Polisario Front has been the main organizational manifestation of Sahrawi nationalism. Chronologically, the evolution of the Polisario Front can be divided into the origins of Sahrawi nationalism, the war against Mauritania and Morocco, and a decades-long military and diplomatic struggle between the Polisario Front and the Moroccan government over competing claims to the same territory. Throughout the conflict, the Polisario Front has been constructing what it considers to be the political, economic, and social foundations of its future nation-state in the Sahrawi refugee camps located in the southwestern Algerian Sahara desert.

THE ORIGINS OF SAHRAWI NATIONALISM

The Sahrawis of Western Sahara are descendants of Moors, or *beidan* (whites) an ethnic group that was a fusion of Sanhaja Berbers, Beni Hassan Arabs (migrants from Yemen), and black Africans.[1] Fusion led to the adoption of the Hassaniya dialect of Arabic at the expense of the Sanhaja language. Sahrawis were camel-herding nomads known for their military and political independence.[2] The Sahrawis share this broad cultural identity with the Moors of Mauritania. Their distinctive way of life and Hassaniya Arabic marks them off from the Tashelhit Berbers in southern Morocco.[3]

Nomadic, independent, and masters of the desert, Sahrawis across the centuries, with few exceptions, paid little heed to attempts at supra-tribal organization.[4] Still, they reportedly always viewed themselves as coming from a fairly well-defined area of northwest Africa — that is south of the River Draa in Morocco and north of central Mauritania; closer to the Atlantic Ocean than other populations in the region.[5] This general sense of self and place would not turn into modern nationalism until the latter part of Spanish colonial rule when it was sparked by profound socioeconomic and political changes within Western Sahara.[6]

An intensification of Spanish colonialism and socioeconomic changes including mining activities, the growth of urban employment, trade, and educational opportunities led to the widespread abandonment of the nomadic way of life in the Western Sahara in the 1950s.[7] Sedentarization brought the Sahrawis into much more direct contact with the Spanish and spurred a growing sense of their own group identity. Additionally, in the late 1950s, the Spanish began to view the Spanish, later the Western, Sahara as a coherent territorial political entity, rather than as an adjunct to other Spanish holdings in northwest Africa (Ifni in southern Morocco, the Canary Islands, Ceuta and Melilla in northern Morocco). Western Sahara was placed under the rule of its own Spanish governor general in 1958.[8] In the early 1960s, provincial and municipal councils were established creating, for the first time, a structured political system for Western Sahara, albeit as a province of Spain.[9] The socioeconomic and administrative changes in Western Sahara in the 1950s and early 1960s contributed to the sense of Western Sahara as a distinct and autonomous political entity.[10] These changes set up a typical colonial dialectic in which processes of domination forge identities: a Western Saharan identity emerged to counteract Spain's imperialist ambitions in their new province.[11]

Anticolonial movements against Spanish and French rule in northwest Africa as a whole also contributed to the development of Sahrawi nationalism. However, this dimension of nationalist fermentation and awakening in Western Sahara was more a part of Moroccan nationalism as it fought for independence from France and Spain in the 1950s, than a desire and push for a separate Western Sahara identity and nation-state. Western Sahara scholars point to the pivotal role of the Army of Liberation, which was constituted in 1955 in northern Morocco to fight for Moroccan independence.[12] This well-organized and highly motivated guerrilla army was composed of both Moroccans and Saharans.[13] They fought to end French and Spanish rule in Morocco. They also fought against Spain's presence in Western Sahara and French rule in Mauritania. The successes of the guerrilla army—it drove the Spanish army out of most interior locations in Western Sahara and attracted a great deal of popular support—led the Spanish and French to form a joint counterinsurgency campaign, Operation Ouragon.[14]

In 1956, the Army of Liberation extended its activities to southern Morocco, often staging attacks from Spanish Sahara against the Spanish forces and their French allies.[15] Thousands of Sahrawis joined the Army of Liberation.[16] Moroccan independence, granted for most of the territory in 1956, and the participation of Sahrawi combatants in the Army of Liberation inspired nationalist feelings among the Sahrawis. It is in a sense ironic that these first organized demands for a separate national identity possibly had its roots as part of Moroccan nationalism. The leaders of the Army of Liberation were Moroccans while Sahrawi nomads made up most of the guerrilla group's strength.[17]

The shifting or evolving nature of Sahrawi nationalism was also present in the other main precursor organization to the Polisario Front, the Basiri-led independence movement. European colonialism in Africa and Asia began its final decline after the end of World War II. The Spanish held on to the Western Sahara longer than most. Domestically, during the late 1960s, an overt indigenous nationalist independence movement coalesced in the Spanish Sahara. It was led by Mohammed Sidi Ibrahim Basiri. Basiri was born in Spanish southern Morocco near Tan Tan, then moved farther south during the Army of Liberation's military campaign in the area.[18] Like other emerging leaders in the region he had a formal education, partly in Moroccan universities. In 1967, Basiri took up residence within Western Sahara and recruited a nucleus of an underground anticolonial movement, the *Harakat Tahrir* (Independence Movement).[19] Harakat Tahrir sought internal autonomy, an agreement from the Spanish government fixing a time limit for independence, and no exploitation of the country's mineral resources without the organization's consent.[20] Their drive for independence was largely silent about the competing Moroccan and Mauritanian claims to Western Sahara.[21] Some analysts assert that Basiri hoped for a Western Sahara integration into Morocco. He had studied in Morocco and briefly in 1966 he published a periodical in Morocco called *Al-Shihab* (The Torch) which espoused Moroccan claims to Western Sahara.[22]

Harakat Tahrir was crushed by the Spanish in late 1970. Basiri was arrested and presumably murdered by his Spanish captors.[23] The Polisario Front later claimed that he was tortured to death in jail in the Canary Islands. He became their movement's first martyr, symbolizing their belief that Harakat Tahrir sought an independent, autonomous nation-state apart from Morocco.

After demolishing Harakat Tahrir, Spain backed the formation of a political party in the then Spanish Sahara that would support Spanish interests even as domestic and international pressures signaled the near end of Spanish domination. The Partido De La Union Nacional Saharaui (PUNS) sought to attain Saharan independence, economic and social development, and preserve cooperation with Spain in every field.[24] For Spain, PUNS offered the possibility of limited Western Saharan autonomy under continued Spanish rule. PUNS leaders were the traditionalist minded *Chioukh* who had collaborated with the Spanish and served on its governing assembly in the colony, the *Djemma*.[25] Compromised by its ambivalent position on Spanish domination and subsidized by colonial authorities, PUNS was temporarily able to generate support from Sahrawis (in 1974–1975), but it collapsed when faced with competition from the growing strength of the more independent and progressive Polisario Front.

The creation of the Polisario Front (The Popular Front for the Liberation of Saguia El Hamra and Rio de Oro), and its military wing, the Sahrawi Peoples Liberation Army (SPLA) became the next major step in Sahrawi nationalism. The initiative came from another Moroccan-educated Sahrawi nationalist, El-Ouali Mustapha Sayed. El-Ouali and other Sahrawi students in Morocco began to meet in the early 1970s to discuss ways to end Spanish rule in Spanish Sahara. Initially, they sought alliances among Moroccan political parties and did not advocate the establishment of an independent Western Saharan state.[26] However, impatient with the limited support they were receiving from Moroccan political parties, the group began to consider itself a more autonomous unit and the notion of a Sahrawi state separate from Morocco took hold among them.[27] As they connected with others in the Sahrawi Diaspora and also made increasing contact with Sahrawis within Spanish/Western Sahara their nationalistic outlook solidified, especially after Morocco began repressing anti-Spanish demonstrations within Morocco.[28]

The Polisario Front was formally constituted on May 10, 1973, with the express intention of militarily forcing an end to Spanish colonization in Western Sahara.[29] Elected as the general secretary of the Polisario, El Ouali appointed an executive committee, which issued a manifesto announcing that the front had been founded as the "unique expression of the masses, opting for revolutionary violence and the armed struggle as the means by which the Sahrawi Arab African people can recover its total liberty and foil the maneuvers of Spanish colonialism."[30]

It is ironic, as one prominent Western Sahara scholar asserts, that if the Army of Liberation had succeeded in driving the Spanish from Western Sahara at the end of the 1950s, the territory would have been integrated into Morocco and a separate Sahrawi nationalism would not have emerged as a political force since European powers—France and Spain— had arbitrarily drawn the lines in the desert that we know as the borders of Western Sahara.[31] Instead the Army of Liberation was crushed in 1958. Once Spain began the process of decolonization in the 1970s, the stage was set for the current conflict between Moroccan and the Polisario Front's claim to represent Sahrawi nationalism. These competing narratives of identity and territorial control dominated the transition from Spanish rule.

In 1974, facing a military insurgency, international pressure, and domestic upheaval, Spain announced plans to decolonize Western Sahara within a year and undertake a referendum to decide its future status.[32] However, Spain never conducted the referendum. Instead, in late 1975, Spain handed over administrative control of Western Sahara to Morocco and Mauritania. The Polisario Front, which by then had become a tested guerrilla force with material support and territorial sanctuary provided by Algeria, was forced to directly confront two new rival claimants to what it considered to be its national homeland. It did so both militarily and diplomatically.[33]

THE POLISARIO FRONT'S MILITARY AND DIPLOMATIC WARS OF INDEPENDENCE

Polisario Front revolutionaries seeking to overturn the Moroccan and Mauritanian occupation of the former Spanish Sahara were constrained by military weakness vis-à-vis Morocco and to an extent, Mauritania (despite Algerian support for the Polisario). To compensate for this weakness, the liberation party sought its ultimate goal of an independent state by supplementing its military efforts with extensive and largely effective diplomatic means that enable them to achieve early support from other newly liberated countries in Africa. The Polisario Front used the principle of self-determination to gain allies in the international arena and to isolate its adversaries, especially Morocco.[34]

On the warfront, the Polisario realized that Mauritania's army was far weaker than Morocco's and it attacked there first. Within two years, with Algerian backing, the Polisario was able to reach Mauritania's capital, disable the country's economy, and precipitate a coup.[35] In 1979, a Mauritanian-Polisario peace agreement was signed and Mauritania withdrew from the Western Sahara. The Polisario also had significant victories against the Moroccan army in the late 1970s and early 1980s, extending its attacks hundreds of miles past the northwestern Saharan border established by the Spanish and the French.[36] By 1981, the Polisario had reduced Morocco's control over the territory to a triangular-shaped region in the far northwest corner around the capital Laâyoune, the phosphates mines of Burka', and the area surrounding the coastal town of Dakhla in the south.[37]

The Polisario's early military victories and possibly its very existence would not have been possible without the strong backing of Algeria. Algerian patronage had provided an alternative when early Polisario leaders began to question their alliance with Morocco due to tepid Moroccan support for their uprising against Spanish domination in Western Sahara. This Algerian military, financial, and diplomatic support for the Polisario Front, that continues today, deserves some discussion here as many in Moroccan quarters question the pivotal insertion of the role of Algerian military power into a conflict in which it is not directly involved.

Analysts suggest that Algeria's motivation for backing Polisario, that is, its stake in the Western Sahara conflict, has both idealistic and regional balance of power dimensions.[38] In terms of ideals, forged as a state during a horrific war of independence in which more than a million Algerians lost their lives, post-independence Algerian regimes have held a strong belief in the principles of nationalism and self-determination. From the beginning, they claimed that there were parallels between the Polisario struggles against Morocco and their War of Independence against France.

Algeria's involvement in the Western Sahara conflict has also been part of Algeria's struggle to become and remain the regional hegemony in North Africa.[39] Since they achieved independence in the 1950s and 1960s, Morocco and Algeria have been competing with each other to become the dominant power in northwest Africa. Their conflicts included a brief border war in 1963 and sharp ideological divisions between a conservative monarchy and an Arab socialist regime. By absorbing the Western Sahara, Morocco threatened to challenge Algeria's advantage in natural resources and bolster Morocco's claim to historical sovereignty over parts of southwestern Algeria. Depriving Morocco of Western Sahara and bleeding its treasury dry in a decades-long dispute against the Polisario has helped Algeria's regional hegemonic aims. A robust pro-Polisario policy also has offered Algeria the possibility of greater access to the Atlantic Ocean if a satellite state or at least a sympathetic Polisario regime is established in the whole of Western Sahara.

Despite Algeria's military support, in the 1980s the military tide turned against the Polisario Front in its war against what they considered to be Moroccan occupation of its national homeland. With the financial and diplomatic backing of France, the United States, and Saudi Arabia, Morocco managed to expand its control over the Western Sahara.[40] To do this, it used primarily a series of concentrically constructed defensive barriers—a wall with mines and troops strategically placed along it. By 1991, the war in the Western Sahara had essentially ended in a military stalemate. The Polisario could not gain and hold territory or hope to win a war of attrition; Morocco had gained control over most of the territory but could not destroy the Polisario without crossing the Algerian border (risking war with Algeria) and attacking the Polisario's base camps.[41]

In the diplomatic wars that have overlapped the military efforts to attain an independent West Saharan state, the Polisario Front has focused on garnering support from the international system through the UN and International Court of Justice (ICJ), the Organization of African Unity (OAU), the backing of its main patron, Algeria, and other nation-states. Throughout the long conflict, there have been incidents of direct or indirect diplomatic engagement between the Polisario Front and Morocco.

In the 1960s, the UN became involved in the decolonization process in the Western Sahara urging Spain to decolonize based on the principle of self-determination. Spain resisted the pressure longer than most European colonial powers, holding on well into the 1970s. Nineteen seventy-five was a pivotal year in the modern diplomatic history of Western Sahara.[42] The Madrid Agreement, transferring administrative control of the Spanish Sahara to Morocco and Mauritania, was signed in 1975. Operating at cross purposes to the Madrid Agreement, in 1975 a UN observation team in Western Sahara found overwhelming support within the territory for independence under the leadership of the Polisario.[43] Fearing such an outcome, that same year the Moroccan government requested an opinion from the ICJ on its historical claim to the territory.[44]

Morocco argued that the structure of the Moroccan state or Sherifian state was one founded on the common religious bond of Islam and on the allegiance of various tribes to the sultan, through their *caids* or *sheikhs*, rather than on the notion of territory. Furthermore, it stated that the Moroccan state has historically had two expressions, and local authorities in both accepted the Sherifian state's central power. In the *Bled Makhzen*, effective and continuous display of state activities from the central power were more dominant than in the *Bled Siba*, areas that the Moroccan government claimed were areas of indirect rule, in which the local *caids*, while having more authority than in the *Bled Makhzen*, were still largely appointed by the Moroccan sultans and demonstrated allegiance to them.

The Moroccan government submitted to the ICJ evidence of internal sovereignty and external or international acts, which demonstrated Moroccan sovereignty over the whole or part of Western Sahara. Evidence of internal sovereignty included Dahirs (royal decrees) and other documents concerning the appointment of *caids*, the imposition of Qu'ranic and other taxes, and acts of military resistance to foreign penetration of the territory. International acts included Moroccan treaties concluded with Spain, the United States, and Great Britain in the eighteenth and nineteenth centuries, which dealt, in part, with the safety of persons in Western Sahara. Diplomatic correspondences between Morocco and Spain and Morocco with Germany in the early twentieth century were asserted to show that both countries considered Moroccan sovereignty to reach deep into the Sahara.

The court's 1975 opinion declared that native Western Saharans' right to self-determination was paramount over Morocco's limited historical title to the land (similar Mauritania's claims were also dismissed). Within hours, Morocco's King Hassan II announced that 350,000 Moroccan civilians would walk, in what became known as the Green March, into Western Sahara to claim the territory as part of the kingdom.[45] The annexation of Western Sahara quickly led to the proclamation by the Polisario Front of its own nation-state.[46]

The Polisario Front announced the creation of the Sahrawi Arab Democratic Republic (SADR) on February 27, 1976. The Provincial National Council would be its legislative body. Through the SADR, the Polisario Front sought to internationalize the Western Sahara conflict in its favor by becoming a recognized nation-state in the international community.[47] Internationalizing the conflict in this manner helped a weaker military power challenge Morocco and Mauritania by utilizing international norms to exert pressure on its adversaries.[48]

By internationalizing the conflict, the Polisario Front sought to shift perceptions of the conflict away from the claims of Morocco and Mauritania, which sought to portray the war as one between established nation-states battling guerrilla insurgencies within their legitimate historical borders.[49] And it also aimed to counter the Moroccan government's implication that instead of being an independent actor, the Polisario insurgents were proxies for the Algerian government seeking to claim the Western Sahara for itself.[50]

In 1976, at a ceremony in front of thousands of Sahrawi guerrillas and refugees and a few dozen foreign journalists, Provincial National Council President Muhammad Ould Zion announced "the birth of a free, independent, sovereign state, ruled by an Arab, national, democratic system of unionist, progressive orientation and of Muslim religion, named the Saharan Arab Democratic Republic."[51] In an effort to create this democratic, egalitarian, and new Muslim state, the Polisario Front created a government, mainly in exile, complete with a bureaucracy and diplomatic corps. The government was formally established in the Polisario refugee camps in Tindouf, southwest Algeria, created when tens of thousands of Sahrawis fled or were coerced to leave the Western Sahara during the Moroccan and Mauritanian initial occupation and fighting.

In addition to the Provincial National Council, the first constitution of the SADR created a twenty-one-member political bureau, including a nine-member (later seven) executive committee.[52] The constitution also provided for Primary Popular Congresses at the local level, which elected members to the congress of the *Wilaya* or state level. General congresses of the putative nation-state were to be held yearly. According to most analysts, members of the executive committee held day-to-day control over political and military matters and immense decision-making capacity rested at the top, not at the bottom of the new political system.[53] Still, Polisario leaders described a more populist, egalitarian, and democratic political process in their emerging nation-state:

> One month before the [General] Congress, Primary Popular Congresses were held in every local area. Everyone, including old women and young people, came to discuss the political and military situations, social and economic problems, ideological issues, all in a mature way. Finally, they elected representatives, who went on to meet at the Congress of the Wilaya, the next level. And finally all went on to the General Congress.[54]

In policy and academic circles, the early Polisario's ideological orientation was generally perceived to be Third World Communist, largely due to the Polisario Front's Algerian tutelage, Libyan supplied Soviet arms, and close relations with other Third World Communist regimes.[55] Some analysts, however, disputed this characterization. They pointed out the Polisario Front's refusal to identify itself as Marxist, its disavowal of the notion of a vanguard party, and its focus on nation-building and national liberation, meaning that the Polisario Front's ideological, class, ethnic, and tribal tent had to be big enough to include Western Saharans of any background.[56]

Unsurprisingly, as it is the case in many political organizations and institutions, the internal workings of the Polisario/SADR in theory have seldom been congruent with the organizations' activities in practice. Notably, there has been dissension among the leadership with several defections to Morocco and elsewhere. Omar Hadrami, one of the founders of the Polisario, member of the executive committee of Polisario's military arm, early organizer of the Tindouf refugee camps, and former SADR foreign minister defected to Morocco in 1989. He claimed that the Polisario was rife with "tribalism" favoring his own Rgaybat. He came to view the Polisario as a highly authoritarian organization that repressed uprisings in the Tindouf refugee camps, and deemed its efforts at independence unrealistic.[57] In terms of authoritarianism, many note that the third and current leader of the Polisario Front, General Secretary Mohamed Abdelaziz, who is also president of the SADR, has been in power since 1976.

Ibrahim Hakim, a former ambassador for the SADR in Algeria, defected to Morocco in 1992. He claimed that even Algeria no longer believed in the struggle for Western Sahara. He reported that he was told by one of Algeria's top military leaders, Khaled Nezzar, that: "[Polisario] should stop dreaming about a state in the Sahara because the establishment of such a state is not in Algeria's interest and against its wishes."[58] Ayob Lahbib, a founder of the Polisario Front, member of the Polisario's Executive Ministry, Minister of the Occupied Territories, and military leader revered for many military victories early in the conflict, defected to Morocco in 2002. He blamed his disaffection from the Polisario Front on the Algerian intelligence agencies' control over the Polisario.[59]

Former Polisario diplomat, ex-ambassador to Canada, Baba Sayed (brother of Polisario's revered first leader and Polisario martyr lost in war at the outset of hostilities in Western Sahara, El Ouali Mustapha Sayyed), followed a circular path from seeking and attaining political asylum in Canada, strongly criticizing the Polisario/SADR in a number of published articles, to a return to the Polisario/SADR fold in 2007. He had sought asylum for what he claimed was political persecution within Polisario, an organization he deemed poorly led by Mohamed Abdelaziz. Sayyed criticized the gap between official discourse and prevalent practices in Polisario/SADR dominated by clientelism, tribalism, and ostracism of leaders daring internal criticism of the organization, including numerous political arrests. Notably, Sayyed was also highly critical of Morocco during his asylum. Upon his return to the Tindouf refugee camps in 2007, he claimed that he heard that Morocco was preparing an attack to destroy the Polisario Front and that Morocco was and has always been the real enemy.[60]

Life in the Tindouf refugee camps—nominally populist, democratic, and egalitarian with an emphasis on a total end to slavery (still practiced in areas of the Sahara), and gender equality—also has not always lived up to its ideals. While many refugee scholars and humanitarian reports praise the camps for effective self-management and use of aid, democratic practices, and an egalitarian ethos, others see an authoritarian top-down rentier state and rampant tribalism and corruption in the refugee camps under the dictatorship of Mohamed Abdelaziz.[61]

Despite the gaps between the Polisario/SADR in theory and in practice, once established, the SADR government often successfully utilized diplomacy to advance their case for an independent state in the former Spanish Sahara. As mentioned earlier, the diplomatic struggle with the Polisario's main foe, Morocco, began at the start of the conflict when Spain decided to withdraw from the territory and Morocco sought to prevent a referendum on self-determination by appealing to the ICJ to rule that Western Sahara was historically part of Morocco before Spanish and French forces colonized northwest Africa.

As mentioned earlier, in its advisory opinion the ICJ decided that there were legal ties between Western Sahara and Morocco at the time of the Spanish occupation, including ties of allegiance between the sultan and some of the tribes living in the interior. However, the court concluded that the materials and information submitted by Morocco did not establish any tie of territorial sovereignty, and that the principle of self-determination through a referendum should be applied in the Western Sahara.

The Polisario/SADR's other early major diplomatic success was achieved with Algeria. From its founding, Algeria took a particularly active diplomatic and military stance supporting a fully independent SADR, consistently arguing in international forums that the Sahrawi nationalist group was the sole legitimate representative of the native population.[62] In 1977, the UN conflict resolution operations meekly attempted to end the conflict over Western Sahara. The UNGA passed a resolution (32/22, November 1977) reaffirming the right of all Western Saharans to self-determination but did not take steps to achieve this goal.[63] In 1978, within the UN, the Polisario Front's patron, Algeria, sought to advance the efforts to legitimize the SADR in the international arena.[64] This created tensions and confrontations with Morocco within the UN.[65] In 1979, Morocco and Algeria continued to clash over what the UN declared to be the unresolved issue of decolonization in Western Sahara.[66] Within the world body, Algeria continued to press the case for the self-determination demands of SADR diplomats, while Rabat accused Algeria of sending mercenaries into Western Sahara.[67]

By the latter 1970s, representatives of the UN's conflict resolution apparatus began to believe that the OAU offered the best opportunity to bring about a peaceful resolution of the dispute over Western Sahara.[68] The UN spent the late 1970s and early 1980s supporting OAU attempts to resolve the conflict.[69] The OAU led peacemaking efforts [in Western Sahara] from 1976 to 1984. In 1979 the continental body proposed a ceasefire followed by a referendum on independence or integration with Morocco. Convinced that native Western Saharans favored independence, Polisario has always accepted the idea of a referendum to resolve the conflict. King Hassan agreed in 1981, but would not work toward its implementation. With no other means of pressure, the OAU decided in 1984 to recognize the Polisario-led SADR as the legitimate government of Western Sahara. Deeply offended, Morocco left the organization and a boycott of the OAU's successor organization, the AU, continues.[70]

The conflict between Morocco and the Polisario Front placed a major strain on the OAU/AU. The young organization was better equipped to deal with self-determination claims made by African countries against European countries than similar conflicts between fellow African states.[71] While the OAU/AU had Moroccan and Mauritanian supporters in the conflict over Western Sahara, they were in the minority. The Polisario Front/SADR could press a diplomatic advantage because the annexation of Western Sahara "transgressed two of the OAU's holiest principles— the right of colonial peoples to self-determination and acceptance of the frontiers inherited from the European powers."[72]

By the mid-1980s confidence in the OAU's ability to resolve the conflict had waned and the UN ratcheted up its own efforts. In 1986, UNSG Javier Pérez de Cuéllar organized "proximity talks" between Morocco and Polisario Front/SADR representatives.[73] These "direct negotiations" (long resisted by Morocco which still considered the Polisario Front to be a guerrilla organization operating in its territory or Algerian proxies), were viewed as precursors to a self-determination referendum including initial discussions on who would vote among the traditionally nomadic Sahrawi people.[74] Gradually, in the latter part of the 1980s, momentum built for the UN to send a peacekeeping and administrative force to Western Sahara to pursue a comprehensive peace and organize a free and fair referendum to resolve the conflict.

In September 1991, the UN established a mission to bring about a peaceful end to the strife in Western Sahara. The establishment of the *Mission des Nations Unies pour l'Organisation d'un Referendum au Sahara Occidental* (MINURSO) was meant to facilitate a 1992 referendum on the status of the Western Sahara. UN monitors verified the continued observance of the cease-fire and identify and register qualified voters for the referendum. Deciding on who would be able to vote became the crucial sticking point that bedeviled negotiations throughout the 1990s. A particular stumbling block in negotiations leading up to the planned MINURSO-supervised referendum was the so-called contested tribes. As the Western Sahara had never existed as a *de facto* independent state, the composition of the electorate for the referendum was by no means clear.

The Polisario Front/SADR favored voting based on the 1974 Spanish colonial census of the territory. A report from March 1998 indicates that a referendum held under this logic would have covered an electorate of roughly 74,000 Sahrawis.[75] Morocco, while agreeing to the referendum in principal, demanded that a number of tribal groupings—the "Chorfa," "Tribes of the North," and "Coastal and Southern" tribes—be included as "genuine" Sahrawis as well. Moroccan negotiators argued that these groups had fled into southern Morocco in the face of Spanish repression, and should thus have a say in the fate of their putative homeland. Including all these groups would have added an additional 50,000–70,000 voters to the referendum. The general assumption during the 1990s was that these "contested tribes," having lived in Morocco under Moroccan protection and largesse, would support integration, while the uncontested tribes would vote overwhelmingly for independence. This conflict over the electorate was thus crucial, as the outcome of the referendum was believed to hinge on the manner in which it was defined.

As discussed elsewhere in this volume, this conflict over who could vote and what options would be included in the referendum would ultimately torpedo this initiative. Even reaching a preliminary determination of who could vote created a number of diplomatic impasses. Some in the UN held little hope that a referendum would actually take place, but did hope that progress in the identification process could create an opening for bilateral dialogue between Morocco and Polisario in which "an understanding on something between integration and independence" could be reached. No such agreement was forthcoming, as Polisario and Morocco remained far apart on the possibility of full independence, on which the former insisted and at which the latter continued to balk. The identification and referendum preparation process completely broke down in 1996, to be revived by the 1997 Houston Agreement after the intervention of former US Secretary of State and UN envoy James Baker.[76]

The Houston Agreement was supposed to lead to a referendum in 1998, but the two sides remained too far apart and international actors did little to move the referendum forward. In 1999, King Hassan II died bringing to power a young ruler, Mohammed VI, who was as concerned as his father about a vote that might lead to Western Saharan independence. Within the Security Council, the United States and France also felt that the political situation in Morocco was too dangerous for a referendum.[77]

At the turn of the millennium, the conflict remained stalemated. After nearly a decade of cease-fire, neither side was willing to budge on core issues. Polisario continued to operate out of large refugee camps in Tindouf, Algeria, where it had created something of a functioning government. It had maintained the steadfast backing of Algeria, even through that country's devastating civil war during the 1990s, and was neither under sufficient pressure for major compromises with Rabat, nor in possession of sufficient leverage to wrest them from Rabat.

As discussed in the following paragraphs, in the next decade leading up to date, the international system that provided a strategic advantage to the Polisario Front early on no longer seems to be in its favor as its support began to wane and the international community gradually moved away from a referendum in favor of a negotiated settlement. Regionally, despite backing the Polisario Front, the AU proved to be impotent at changing Morocco's policy of opposition to a referendum option between independence and integration. The UN's MINURSO has largely prevented military warfare but so far has failed at completing a comprehensive peace through diplomatic means. The UN seems unwilling to exert significant pressure on Morocco to accept the referendum option and has opted for promoting a negotiated political settlement. Its powerful backers in the international system, the United States and France, provide the Moroccan government with considerable leverage in the international arena to resist anything that compromises Moroccan sovereignty and territorial integrity.

In the 2000s, the United States, more than ever, supported Morocco.[78] France too supported Rabat.[79] The Polisario Front/SADR had little consequential international backing outside of Algeria, apart from occasional sympathy from Spain. It was in this context that James Baker attempted further proposals to break the impasse. As indicated in a companion essay, the initial proposal put forward by James Baker, acting as the UN personal envoy of the secretary-general (PESG), started from the premise that a true referendum was now a dead option. His plan would allow Moroccan rule for five years after which there would be a final status referendum held, but with one year of residency in the territory being the only criteria for participation. This would include Morocco-sponsored settlers, and presumably encourage a Morocco-friendly outcome.[80]

This proposed solution and a second proposed by Baker foundered on referendum proposals with a choice of one of three options—independence, integration, or some form of affiliation with Morocco—in which case Morocco believed that independence would win with a minority of the votes cast despite adding Moroccan residents of the Western Sahara to the voter rolls of the referendum.[81] However, the Polisario, with the encouragement of Algeria, accepted the latter plan as a basis for negotiations. This raised Polisario's esteem in the eyes of some previously skeptical observers, and led to international frustration with Morocco:

> Polisario's surprise acceptance of the 2003 Peace Plan, after months of studying Morocco's cold reaction to it, and with some nudging from Algiers, was a diplomatic coup for the liberation front. For three years Polisario had been on the defensive, but former guerrillas turned the tables on Morocco to stunning effect. This meant that they now had much more sympathy from the US government vis-a-vis Baker. Morocco's stern refusal to even consider the 2003 Baker Plan, which allowed all Moroccan settlers in Western Sahara to vote in the final status referendum, caused great confusion. The only logical conclusion was that Rabat did not trust its own citizens, they might actually vote for independence with Polisario.[82]

However, just as it appeared that Algeria and Polisario were becoming more accommodating, Morocco was becoming more insistent in its opposition to a referendum, and international events made pressure on Rabat more difficult. In 2003, the largest terrorist attack in Moroccan history occurred in Casablanca, and numerous Moroccans were involved in the Madrid bombings in 2004, raising the profile Moroccans involved in transnational terrorist activities. France and the Security Council were reluctant to pressure Morocco to accept Baker's second plan while it faced such volatility.[83]

While international forces stalled in movement toward a settlement strategy, Morocco worked during this period to undercut the Polisario claim to be the sole representatives of the Sahrawi people. In 2005, King Mohammed VI re-created the Royal Advisory Council for Saharan Affairs (CORCAS) as the Baker Plan collapsed. The council has 141 members drawn from Moroccan and Sahrawi society, with Khelli Henna Ould

Rachid (the former Sahrawi head of the late Spanish era PUNS party) as its chairman. It became the leading body for discussing an autonomy plan for the Western Sahara. The autonomy plan CORCAS gradually developed along with other key players in Morocco became the proposal presented to the UNSC in 2007. Its plan is in many ways similar to that attempted by Spain near the end of the colonial period,[84] which provides for Sahrawi autonomy under Moroccan sovereignty, which Rabat presented and has been noted as the "only realistic and feasible solution" to the conflict.[85]

The impasse at the UN regarding a way forward continued until UNSC Resolution 1754 (2007), which called on Morocco and Polisario to negotiate a solution without preconditions. Both the Polisario and Morocco submitted proposals that were to serve as initial points of discussion in the negotiations. The Polisario position restated its demands for an independence referendum to satisfy the demands for self-determination; while the Moroccan proposal offered autonomy as the realistic way forward for achieving self-determination in the Western Sahara. This process has been underway since then, most recently under the aegis of former US Ambassador Christopher Ross, who was named PESG in 2009; but little concrete progress has been made.[86]

In response to international response, Morocco did not wait for the UN process. In addition to tabling the autonomy proposal for negotiations at the UN, Morocco also sought to normalize the status of the Western Sahara in the context of 2011 constitutional revisions that ostensibly provide for regional devolution of power across Morocco. This "regionalization" policy is meant to provide a large measure of local control over most domestic affairs to Morocco's provinces, beginning with the Western Sahara. It is anticipated that the organic law on regionalization called for in the 2011 Constitution will be drafted sometime before 2014.

Meanwhile, the Polisario Front, while reserving the right and (in theory) capacity to revert to armed struggle, has little leverage. Few think that support for further fighting would be forthcoming from Algeria, and such support would be surely necessary against the 100,000 troops that Morocco continues to deploy in the territory.[87] Some in the Sahrawi community have grown frustrated with the Polisario's lack of progress in its international diplomatic strategy and its loss of influence among supporters in Africa and elsewhere. In 2004, an organization called Khat al-Shahid (the Way of the Martyr) was formed among Sahrawi refugees, deeply critical of alleged corruption and purported compromises that Polisario has made around key sovereignty issues (statements by Polisario leaders that could be read as open to autonomy arrangements have been vociferously criticized by this group).[88] Mahjjoub Salek, one of the original founders of Polisario, heads the movement. He has urged a boycott of the 2011 Polisario Congress, accused Polisario's current leadership of "getting profit from the status quo" and thus not seeking a permanent solution to the conflict, and denounced Sahrawi President Mohamed Abdelaziz as a "tyrant with absolute powers" whose government is based on "corruption, bribery and lies."[89] Apart from a change in leadership and a desire to resume bilateral negotiations, it is unclear what, if any, dramatic shifts in strategy this splinter organization advocates.

The situation among Sahrawis under Moroccan control has not been entirely quiescent either. Popular protests including hunger strikes and street demonstrations roiled urban areas of Western Sahara throughout the fall of 1999. Protesters demonstrated against the Moroccan occupation and, as the demonstrations escalated, so too the brutality with which security forces responded.[90] In 2005, wider pro-independence demonstrations took place throughout the year, reaching a peak in May and June and triggering solidarity protests in Morocco proper.[91] "The El-Aaiun Intifada," as it is sometimes called, triggered a large crackdown and led to the arrests of many Sahrawi human rights and independence activists.[92]

Again in the fall of 2010, protesters gathered around the capital of Laâyoune, setting up a large tent city outside the capital. The initial demands were less overtly political, and the protest reportedly focused more on economic and social inequities faced by the Sahrawis under Moroccan rule.[93] When the Moroccan government believed that the demonstrations were being co-opted by radical pro-independence militants, the security response was intense. Hundreds were beaten and detained and Moroccan security services joined settler civilians in retaliatory attacks against the Sahrawi populace.[94]

As of summer 2012, Morocco continues its control over the vast majority of Western Saharan territory. The Polisario Front seems unable to execute effective diplomatic or military strategies that will end the Western Sahara conflict in favor of their vision of an independent SADR. The diplomatic wars continue in a variety of arenas. The Polisario has engaged in a sophisticated media strategy to challenge Morocco's exploitation of the natural resources on and off shore of the Western Sahara; it has recruited international movie stars to attend annual conferences and festivals to highlight their cause; its representatives have been successful in building support among some European publics, particularly in the Nordic countries, for its insistence on a referendum for self-determination; and the Polisario continues to seek broad international recognition as the sole legitimate representatives of the Sahrawi people. And yet, with three generations of refugees in the Tindouf camps, the Polisario seems further from a resolution for an independent state than at any time in their struggle. Despite continued international scrutiny of Morocco's treatment of pro-independence Sahrawis in the Western Sahara and routine reports of human rights violations there, Morocco has managed to portray the Polisario as a closed, autocratic, militant group that takes advantage of the Sahrawi refugees for the benefit of the leadership.

Today, the nature of Sahrawi nationalism as exemplified by the Polisario is under siege due to growing unrest among the younger generations in the camps, the proximity of terrorist and criminal elements that recruit people from the camps to join in illicit and illegal activities, and the diplomatic stalemate that seems devoid of any strategic alternatives. What was once a quasi-socialist freedom movement seems mired in the politics of the larger region and especially the troubled relationship between Morocco and Algeria. The Arab Spring brought a semblance of reforms to Morocco and some stirrings are also evident in Algeria. Yet SADR remains caught up in a revolutionary vision that may no longer be viable given international concerns with stability and security in the region and beyond. How the Polisario reasserts and redefines itself within the context of the challenges of the *realpolitik* emerging out of the Arab Spring and the increasingly critical attention being paid to failed and failing states in the Sahel and elsewhere in Africa will largely determine its survival and the sustainability of Sahrawi nationalism.

NOTES

1. Tony Hodges, "The Origins of Saharawi Nationalism," *Third World Quarterly* 5, no. 1 (1983): 30.
2. Hodges, "The Origins of Saharawi Nationalism," 30.
3. Hodges, "The Origins of Saharawi Nationalism," 30.
4. Hodges, "The Origins of Saharawi Nationalism," 30.
5. "Western Sahara: Who Is Polisario?" *Africa Confidential* 22, no. 1 (1981): 2–5.
6. Hodges, "The Origins of Saharawi Nationalism."
7. Hodges, "The Origins of Saharawi Nationalism," 34–36.
8. Hodges, "The Origins of Saharawi Nationalism," 34–36.
9. Hodges, "The Origins of Saharawi Nationalism," 36–37.
10. "Western Sahara: Who Is Polisario?" 2–5.
11. Stephen Zunes and Jacob Mundy, *Western Sahara: War, Nationalism, and Conflict Irresolution* (Syracuse, NY: Syracuse University Press, 2010), 91–92.
12. Zunes and Mundy, *Western Sahara*.
13. Anthony G. Pazzanita, *Historical Dictionary of Western Sahara*, 3rd ed. (Lanham, MD: Scarecrow Press, 2006), 31.
14. Pazzanita, *Historical Dictionary of Western Sahara*, 31.
15. Pazzanita, *Historical Dictionary of Western Sahara*, 31.
16. Tony Hodges, *Western Sahara: The Roots of a Desert War* (Westport, CT: Lawrence Hill, 1983), 150.
17. Pazzanita, *Historical Dictionary of Western Sahara*.
18. Hodges, *Western Sahara*, 153.
19. Hodges, *Western Sahara*, 153.
20. Hodges, *Western Sahara*, 154.
21. Pazzanita, *Historical Dictionary of Western Sahara*, 186.
22. Stephen O. Hughes, *Morocco under King Hassan* (Ithaca, NY: Garnet and Ithaca Press, 2001), 246.
23. Hughes, *Morocco under King Hassan*, 155.
24. Pazzanita, *Historical Dictionary of Western Sahara*, 329.
25. Pazzanita, *Historical Dictionary of Western Sahara*, 151.
26. Pazzanita, *Historical Dictionary of Western Sahara*, 158.
27. Pazzanita, *Historical Dictionary of Western Sahara*, 159.

28. Pazzanita, *Historical Dictionary of Western Sahara*, 159.
29. Pazzanita, *Historical Dictionary of Western Sahara*, 160–61.
30. Pazzanita, *Historical Dictionary of Western Sahara*, 160–61.
31. Pazzanita, *Historical Dictionary of Western Sahara*, 160–61.
32. Zunes and Mundy, *Western Sahara*, xxviii.
33. Zunes and Mundy, *Western Sahara*, xxviii.
34. Jeffrey M. Schulman, "Wars of Liberation and the International System: Western Sahara—A Case in Point," in *Studies of Power and Class in Africa*, ed. Irving Leonard Markovits (New York: Oxford University Press, 1987).
35. Zunes and Mundy, *Western Sahara*, xxix.
36. Zunes and Mundy, *Western Sahara*, xxix.
37. Zunes and Mundy, *Western Sahara*, xxix.
38. Jacob Mundy, "Algeria and the Western Sahara Dispute," *Maghreb Center Journal*, no. 1 (2010).
39. Mundy, "Algeria and the Western Sahara Dispute," 3.
40. Zunes and Mundy, *Western Sahara*.
41. Zunes and Mundy, *Western Sahara*.
42. "The Question of Western Sahara," *United Nations Yearbook* (1975): 175–90, 798–804.
43. Zunes and Mundy, *Western Sahara*.
44. Zunes and Mundy, *Western Sahara*.
45. Zunes and Mundy, *Western Sahara*.
46. Zunes and Mundy, *Western Sahara*.
47. Zunes and Mundy, *Western Sahara*, 67.
48. Schulman, "Wars of Liberation and the International System," 68.
49. Schulman, "Wars of Liberation and the International System," 68.
50. David Lynn Price, "Morocco and the Sahara: Conflict and Development," *Conflict Studies*, no. 88 (1977).
51. Quoted in Hodges, *Western Sahara*, 238.
52. Zunes and Mundy, *Western Sahara*, 116.
53. Zunes and Mundy, *Western Sahara*, 116.
54. Polisario Head of Communication, Mohammed Salem Ould Salek, quoted in Zunes and Mundy, *Western Sahara*, 116.
55. Polisario Head of Communication, Mohammed Salem Ould Salek, quoted in Zunes and Mundy, *Western Sahara*, 115.
56. Polisario Head of Communication, Mohammed Salem Ould Salek, quoted in Zunes and Mundy, *Western Sahara*, 115. See also Stephen Zunes, "Nationalism and Non-Alignment: The Non-Ideology of the Polisario," *Africa Today* 34 (1987): 33–46; "Western Sahara: Who Is Polisario?"
57. See *Western Sahara Weekly News* 28, no. 6 (1998); "Que Sont-Ils Devenues?" *Jeune Afrique*, September 2010; Zunes and Mundy, *Western Sahara*, 118.
58. Quoted in Zunes and Mundy, *Western Sahara*, 120.
59. Pazzanita, *Historical Dictionary of Western Sahara*, 38–40; "Que Sont-Ils Devenues?"
60. "Que Sont-Ils Devenues?"; Baba M. Sayed, "Rompre avec la Mentalite Marrakchie," *Jeune Afrique*, October 10, 2012, www.arso.org/opinions/BabaSayed47.htm; "Le Makhzen Marocain Est et Reste Toujours, L'Ennemie!!" *Jeune Afrique*, October 10, 2012, www.arso.org/opinions/BabaSayed48.htm.
61. Elena Fiddian-Qasmiyehm "Representing Sahrawi Refugees," *Journal of Refugee Studies* no. 3 (2009): 533–47; Elena Fiddian-Qasmiyehm, "Ideal Refugee Women and Gender Equality Mainstreaming in the Sahrawi Refugee Camps: Goof Practice for Whom?" *Refugee Survey Quarterly* 29, no. 2 (2010): 64–84; Elena Fiddian-Qasmiyya, "The Pragmatics of Performance: Putting Faith in Aid in the Sahrawi Refugee Camps," *Journal of Refugee Studies* 24, no. 3 (2011): 533–47.
62. "Western Sahara," *United Nations Yearbook* (1977): 737–40.
63. "Western Sahara," *United Nations Yearbook* (1977): 880–83.

64. "Western Sahara," *United Nations Yearbook* (1978): 861–63.
65. "Western Sahara," *United Nations Yearbook* (1978): 861–63.
66. "Western Sahara," *United Nations Yearbook* (1979): 1046–51.
67. "Western Sahara," *United Nations Yearbook* (1979): 1046–51.
68. "Western Sahara," *United Nations Yearbook* (1978).
69. "Western Sahara," *United Nations Yearbook* (1978).
70. Jacob Mundy, "Autonomy and Intifadah: New Horizons in Western Saharan Nationalism," *Review of African Political Economy* 33, no. 108 (2006): 255–67.
71. Hodges, *Western Sahara*, 307–32.
72. Hodges, *Western Sahara*, 307.
73. "Western Sahara," *United Nations Yearbook* (1986): 964–66. See also "Who Should Vote," *Africa*, no. 178 (1986): 28.
74. Dede-Esi Amanor, *Africa Events (London)* (September 1988): 8–9.
75. Research Directorate, "Morocco: Whether Saharawis Who Refuse to Join the Polisario Are Perceived as Supporters of the Moroccan Government; Whether Saharawis in General Are Perceived as Members of the Polisario by the Moroccan Authorities; and Situation of the Lahalaleef Tribe," *Immigration and Refugee Board (Canada)*, 2000, www.unhcr.org/refworld/topic,463af2212,469f2e912,3ae6ad6974,0,IRBC.html.
76. Mundy, "Autonomy and Intifadah," 255–67.
77. Mundy, "Autonomy and Intifadah," 255-67.
78. Zunes and Mundy, *Western Sahara*, 59–91.
79. Zunes and Mundy, *Western Sahara*, 59–91.
80. Alexis Arieff, "Western Sahara," *Congressional Research Service*, Report RS20962 (2013), www.fas.org/sgp/crs/row/RS20962.pdf.
81. Toby Shelley, "Behind the Baker Plan for Western Sahara," *The Middle East Research and Information Project* 229 (2003).
82. Mundy, "Autonomy and Intifadah," 255–67.
83. Mundy, "Autonomy and Intifadah," 255–67.
84. Malainin Lakhal, Ahmed Khalil, and Pablo San Martin, "Moroccan Autonomy for the Western Sahara: A Solution to a Decolonisation Conflict or a Prelude to the Dismantling of a Kingdom?" *Review of African Political Economy* 33, no. 108 (2006): 336–41.
85. "Sahara Issue—CORCAS Urged Polisario Leadership to Return to Morocco," Moroccan Embassy Australia-New Zealand-Pacific Islands, December 18, 2007, www.moroccoembassy.org.au/?q=sahara-issue-corcas-urged-polisario-leadership-return-morocco.
86. Arieff, "Western Sahara."
87. Arieff, "Western Sahara."
88. Way of the Martyr, "Opinion: Appel à Tous les Nationalistes Sahraoui(e)s [founding manifesto]," July 4, 2004, www.arso.org/opinions/FPelualifr.htm.
89. "Sahrawis Awake to Government Opposition," *Afrol News*, October 2012, www.afrol.com/articles/36743.
90. "Western Sahara; Sahara Weekly News Update," *Africa News*, October 1999.
91. "Western Sahara Protests to Continue Despite Moroccan Crackdown: Polisario," *Agence France Presse*, June 2005.
92. "Sahrawis Talk of New Intifada in Al Aaiun," *Afrol News*, May 2012, www.afrol.com/articles/16424.
93. "Diplomacy over the Western Sahara: Morocco v. Algeria," *The Economist*, November 4, 2010, www.economist.com/node/17421589.
94. "Western Sahara: Beatings, Abuse by Moroccan Security Forces," *Human Rights Watch*, November 26, 2010, www.hrw.org/news/2010/11/26/western-sahara-beatings-abuse-moroccan-security-forces.

FIVE

The Algerian Foreign Policy on Western Sahara

Laurence Aïda Ammour

When Algeria's minister of Maghreb and African affairs, Abdelkader Messahel, declared in March 2010, "I have consulted geography books and have found no indication that Morocco had a border with the Sahel," he was merely reaffirming Algeria's long-standing belief that it has preeminence over the Sahara and the Sahel.[1]

Reflecting the territorial imbalances that undergird rivalries in the Maghreb, these words illustrate the regional diplomacy that Algeria has forged in opposition to its near enemy Morocco and in a confrontational logic still dominated by the Western Sahara issue. The minister's statement also contains two implicit reminders of Algeria's core assumptions:

1. Western Sahara is not, and never will be, part of Moroccan territory.
2. Security in the Sahel remains the prerogative of Algeria, which—unlike Morocco—does have Saharan borders along the Sahel.

Border stabilization continues to be one of the biggest concerns throughout the Maghreb. In fact, border disputes still weigh so heavily on Maghreb affairs that they impede all prospects for unity and cooperation. These land disputes are rooted in a fundamental problem: the geographic inequality among Algeria, Morocco, and Tunisia that resulted from their emergence from French control. The Western Sahara conflict is part of the broader issue of the territorial makeup of the Maghreb countries, where sharp territorial inequalities dominate geopolitics.

The nationalistic and militaristic political culture forged by Algerian leaders during the country's war of independence has left its mark on domestic and foreign policy, which are inextricably linked. It explains Algiers' unwavering position on this conflict, which successive governments have exploited for four decades, despite changes in international relations, the emergence of a multipolar world, and the recent upheavals caused by the "Arab Spring." Algiers' management of the conflict has resulted in intense diplomatic and strategic competition and a race for regional hegemony with Rabat. The pursuit of geopolitical balance, a prerequisite for any fairly orderly multilateral relationship, remains central to the Maghreb issue.

Unlike Morocco, Algeria's political boundaries preceded the emergence of the state. This forced Algeria to exercise its authority within a preexisting territorial framework in the postcolonial historical context, where national territories were still in flux. Later on, Algeria's methodical creation of a near enemy motivated by what Algiers perceived as threats to its territorial integrity resulted in a tense diplomacy. Algeria became preoccupied with thwarting any attempt to modify the geopolitical framework it acquired at independence, attempts that Algeria interpreted as a strategy to surround and attack the nation.

Algerian diplomacy was born out of the struggle against colonial occupation and has therefore been overly focused on territorial issues, leading its representatives to pursue a strategy that is both hegemonic and systematically opposed to Morocco's strategy.

A clear illustration of how this conflict has been transcribed into Algerian foreign policy is in Algiers' military, logistic, political, and financial support for the Polisario Front.

MAKING LAND AN ISSUE OF SOVEREIGNTY

The Sahara was undeniably an asset for Algerian power. With its independence on July 5, 1962, Algeria's position in the region was fundamentally transformed. In the process of achieving territorial integrity and building national unity in Algeria, integrating the Sahara into the nascent nation was a major objective. Thus, the Algerian Sahara helped in part to crystallize the state-building process.

The Algerian government's relationship with its desert—one that mixes the strategic imperative of land acquisition with the strategic need to develop energy resources—has resulted in a rather distinct form of land appropriation based on the financial windfall from hydrocarbons, the country's main source of revenue. Algeria's geopolitical appetite cannot simply be summarized as a quest for land. Rather, it is fixated on this portion of land as an attribute of economic, military, and even political power.

Knowing that its land is rich and vast, Algeria has been guided by a fundamental belief of territorial hegemony in its future position vis-à-vis the Sahara as a whole, and Western Sahara in particular. Its advantageous geographic position led the newly created state to overestimate the value of the Saharan territory, both ideologically and politically.

Although the French government treated the *départements* (Algeria) more favorably than the protectorates (Morocco and Tunisia), Algeria's independence should have resulted in a more equitable distribution of land.[2] The Moroccans and Tunisians were well aware that Algeria had acquired its regional dominance at their expense and wanted Algeria to settle what they considered a debt owed to them. Attempting to renegotiate the borderlines as a form of compensation, they encountered blunt refusal on the part of Algeria, the only country that shares a border with Mauritania, Western Sahara, Morocco, Tunisia, and Libya. Having acquired an advantageous land base, Algerian diplomacy abandoned the priority of anticolonialism and took up a territorial policy that would end up penalizing its neighbors. To this day, the issue of geopolitical imbalance continues to permeate inter-Maghreb relations.

The Battle for the Sahara

The subsequent expansion of the Maghreb toward the Sahara occurred over a period of several years. Algeria perceived several developments as threats to its preeminence.

Algeria was the biggest beneficiary of the colonial division of land, which it has never questioned. On the contrary, it has tried to consolidate this territory and has pursued a strategy of sovereignty over the Sahara that has been contested by its two neighbors. Algeria's Western Sahara policy has been central to its strategy of maintaining the status quo. Emblematic of local border disputes, this conflict is one of the arenas where the region's two main countries, Morocco and Algeria, openly express their historic antagonism. Consequently, a major portion of Algeria's strategy in the Sahara and the Sahel has focused on ousting, or at least containing, Morocco (and Libya prior to that) from the southern zone of influence.

The Border Issue

Since gaining independence, the North African states have been involved in cross-border geopolitical projects that vary in form but are all based on the common issue of the intra-Saharan borders. Several of these borders are still not demarcated, and stances on their location vary depending on whether relations between the countries are warm or cool. The advantage of maintaining fluctuating borders with contested or incomplete lines is that a dispute can be reactivated at any time. Depending on the needs of domestic policy, pressure can be exerted on neighboring countries or doubt cast on the conduct and intentions of the actors involved. Borders, therefore, are frontlines.[3] But if a constant degree of tension is maintained, a border can also be a deterrence tool to contain disputes within boundaries that preclude a return to armed conflict, or to defuse any urge to engage in conflict. Based on this assumption, borders can also be an element of stability since they regulate relations between states in the context of a cold peace, especially when they are supposed to separate two states of unequal status. Thus for Algeria,

> The danger is not within its borders. It lies beyond the boundary, without being clearly pinpointed. Here, this boundary is the limit of the Algerian government's claim of sovereignty, which it has continued to push farther and farther south since its independence. This conception recalls the analogy (or is reminiscent of) with the [Roman] notion of "limes." Consequently, it is impossible on a practical level for the Algerian government to dissociate its portion of the Sahara from that of its neighbors to the south.[4]

Direct, interstate rivalries also serve to push back spheres of influence in a battle over the Sahara featuring Algeria and Morocco as the main actors. These relations are characterized by strong suspicion coupled with uncertainty over the neighboring country's conduct. In each of these countries, the central governments (and capital cities) are far-removed from the desert border regions where they struggle to assert their sovereignty. This is why they are forced to cooperate with itinerant communities that find themselves in "nationalized" territories of different countries.

A Road-Paving Policy to Further a Pipeline Policy

Algeria has used the road as an instrument of national sovereignty and influence, a channel for riches, and an element of military power and political influence. It has helped the government not only take ownership of the territory acquired by the newly formed state at independence but also to inscribe its political legitimacy there *a posteriori*. Roads have also served to expand the government's influence to marginalized border regions in neighboring countries, such as northern Mali and the Tuareg zone, that have always been the subject of Algerian-Libyan rivalries. Its road-paving policy has also been used to further its "pipeline policy." It was evident in the construction of the Trans-Sahara Highway (also called the "African Unity Highway") that stopped at Tamanrasset in 1978 rather than continuing through to West Africa as originally planned.[5] Next was a north–west connection along the border with the Cherifian Kingdom in the 1980s (Saoura and Tindouf). That stretch sent a strong signal to Morocco, which has claimed historical ownership of this zone, despite its incorporation into Algeria by the French colonial government.

The additional expanse of strategic land Algeria acquired when it incorporated the Sahara in 1961 could have represented true regional hegemony. However, the authorities did not capitalize on this territory and failed to take advantage of the opportunity to strike a balance between a Mediterranean orientation and an African orientation. Despite strong Pan-African ideology in the 1960s–1970s, Algeria's actions toward the Sahara were primarily based on its oil power through and on behalf of the north, and on a somewhat effective fluctuating policy of influence over pivotal border zones.

Over time, this shortcoming sharpened Algiers' hostility toward its recalcitrant neighbors and fueled an increasingly declaratory hegemonic rhetoric, especially at a time when the security context in Algeria and in the Saharan-Sahel region had deteriorated considerably.[6] This strategic failure explains the contradictions in Algeria's policy toward its southern region. Paradoxically, in seeking to assert and consolidate its desire to project power, the Algerian government ended up becoming the instigator of the Sahrawi cause.

To understand the rationales at work, a brief overview of the historical and geographic motives for this projection of power to the south is first necessary.

THE SPACE-TIME ANTINOMY

On July 5, 1962, Moroccan and Tunisian troops launched an attempt to take over the disputed border posts evacuated by the French army. The attempt failed, but these two countries were particularly eager to lay claim to this territory since their territorial ambitions had been so long suppressed. In 1967, Tunisia was forced to soften its position because the Algerians wanted their border validated as a prerequisite to any future agreement. On January 6, 1970, more than seven years after independence, the Algerian government logged its first success with the definitive demarcation of its eastern border.

On its western flank, Algeria sought to avoid having its territory further reduced by the Common Organization of the Sahara Regions (OCRS)[7] and decided to sign an agreement with Morocco on July 6, 1961, in appreciation for Morocco not participating in French attempts to divide the Sahara.[8] Even so, the seeds of tension did not disappear with this newfound peace and would soon reemerge. Algeria encountered unexpected resistance from Morocco and had to grant it economic advantages and make a relatively clear commitment on the devolution of the Spanish Sahara. Facing challenges from its neighbors, Algeria got them to recognize the borders it had inherited from France. Its position progressively hardened into total intransigence. Sensing that its policy of retrocession for land consolidation risked being compromised, Morocco continued to maintain its claims to the Tindouf and Béchar regions. This lead to the "Sand War" in October 1963, in which Royal Armed Forces (FAR) had the advantage over the National Popular Army (ANP). The Organization of African Unity (OAU) intervened to end the conflict, but the border with Morocco between Figuig and Béchar remained intact.

Following its military defeat in 1964 (a defeat that caused lasting resentment), Algeria got the OAU to adopt the principle of inviolability of colonial borders. It also refused to negotiate with Morocco over relinquishing part of its territory bordering Morocco, pursuant to their 1961 bilateral agreement. Similarly, the 1972 Algerian-Moroccan agreement stipulated that Morocco would agree to relinquish its claims to Algerian territory in exchange for regaining Western Sahara. In an effort to prevent its neighbor from expanding its reach into the Sahara, Algeria placed responsibility for the conflict squarely on Rabat's shoulders by framing the Saharan problem as an issue of decolonization and the Sahrawis' right to self-determination and by presenting the Polisario Front as the legitimate and sole representative of the Sahrawis.

In October 1974, Morocco and Mauritania banded together and advanced the argument that the decolonization of Western Sahara needed to be understood in the context of their territorial integrity, which had been dismembered under colonization. They agreed to share the land that was to be recovered. President Houari Boumediene did not object because Spain had promised him the creation of an independent state in the Sahara. Instead, he argued at The Hague in favor of a referendum in the Sahara and recognition of the Polisario Front as a representative group. This about-face allowed Algeria to align its revolutionary legacy and the principle of peoples' right to self-determination with a third-world diplomacy in keeping with its national interests.[9] In January 1976, a direct confrontation between the FAR and the ANP in Amgala ("Amgala 1") ended in a victory for Morocco and a withdrawal of the Polisario from the zone. The following month ("Amgala 2"), the Moroccan army took control of the region.

However, when Rabat and Nouakchott negotiated the terms of Spanish withdrawal with Spain (1975 Madrid Accords), and after the "Green March" (November 14, 1975), Algeria refused to go along with any solution devised without its input. Since the Madrid Accords had been signed against its will, Algeria tried to thwart their implementation by allying with Libya in December 1975. It then recognized the Sahrawi Arab Democratic Republic (SADR) that the Polisario Front proclaimed on February 27, 1967. As a result, diplomatic ties with Morocco and Mauritania were broken. Algeria supplied arms to the Polisario Front, provided a safe haven, and took in 50,000 refugees near Tindouf. It opposed its adversaries while being careful not to engage in an open war, challenged the idea of a bilateral Algerian-Moroccan dispute, and advocated direct negotiations between Moroccans and Sahrawis.

Systematic recourse to instruments of international law is another facet of Algeria's political influence in the region. Algeria's ambitions for leadership drive it to hold key positions in numerous institutions where alternative strategies and reform plans are developed, for example: the UN, the OAU, which became the African Union (AU) in 2002, the New Partnership for Africa's Development (NEPAD), the Organization of Petroleum Exporting Countries (OPEC), the Arab League, the Organization of the Islamic Conference. Algeria's presence in these international organizations—privileged forums for its diplomatic action—enabled it to defend its interests, even before gaining independence, as well as promote its vision for international affairs ("the new international order"), and develop its regional and international strategies and tactics.

> During the Soummam Congress in 1956 where the first FLN [National Liberation Front] doctrinal platform was developed, an international strategy was defined with the outlines of a position vis-à-vis international organizations. Given that France wanted to treat the Algerian issue as a domestic matter outside the scope of international forums, particularly the UN, the FLN believed, on the contrary, that these forums were important and developed an entire policy to this effect that included: establishing external delegations, appointing the most active and skilled activists to these international organizations, using aid from ally countries to gain access to all the forums where it could defend the Algerian revolution, and making the connection between domestic activities (strikes, popular demonstrations, increase in military operations) and debate at the UN. This strategy enabled Algeria, very early on, to have an effective diplomatic machine and a coherent foreign policy that served the purposes of the new state.[10]

Anxious to resolve African conflicts without foreign intervention on the continent, such as the UN intervention proposed by Morocco to settle its dispute with Algiers, the OAU responded to the Algerian-Moroccan border conflict in 1963 by establishing an ad hoc commission.

When the SADR joined the OAU in 1982, the Cherifian Kingdom of Morocco, one of the founding members in 1963, withdrew from the organization in 1984 as a sign of protest. Morocco's absence helped Algeria assert the historic legitimacy of its position in the Western Sahara conflict. But time is definitely not on the SADR's side. After being formally recognized by more than sixty countries in the 1980s, it suffered a series of setbacks when several states withdrew formal recognition.[11] During the 18th African Union Summit held in Addis Ababa, January 29–30, 2012, several African heads of state and heads of government recognized that Morocco's absence was an anomaly and that Morocco would return to the organization only if the SADR were excluded. This condition was difficult to meet given both Algeria and South Africa's support for the SADR.

With the recent resolutions adopted by the UN (December 17, 2009) and by the AU (July 3, 2009) criminalizing the payment of ransom to kidnappers and the more recent law on preventing and combating terrorism presented at the African Center for Studies and Research on Terrorism (ACSRT)[12] meeting on December 16, 2010, Algeria gained new means of applying pressure on its immediate neighbors (particularly in the Sahel) and on western countries affected by kidnappings. The legal argument underpinning its principled position on Western Sahara allows Algeria to assert its positions under the guise of diplomacy and to sidestep the thorny issue of the Polisario's involvement in criminal activities.

Western Sahara: A Telltale Sign of Inequalities in Territorial Makeup

It is evident that each state is seeking to base its legitimacy on criteria taken from different periods in its history—an indication of a disagreement on the very principles of international relations—producing two conflicting rationales: historic rights versus the inviolability of colonial borders.

History's influence on foreign policy has always helped shape perceptions of reality.[13] This explains why perceptions play such a preponderant role in Algerian-Moroccan relations. History, the past, and historic legitimacies—all extremely meaningful—are heavily used in "fabricating" the enemy, as seen in the "war of words" that runs rampant in the press in both countries whenever it comes to the Western Sahara conflict. In both cases, the press attributes bellicose intentions to its neighbor and echoes the increasingly radical official position of the leaders.

These constructs, projected into the countries' respective diplomacies, are first and foremost the result of two very different historical experiences. They also help to create and maintain a negative image of the other country. The military's role and status in these societies make these images appear even more threatening since the army's role is precisely to deal with threats. Finally, the lack of a common vision of a just and legitimate order, like the absence of community input in economic choices, reinforces the perception of the neighboring country as being distant and alien.

States assess each other's intentions on the basis of portrayals, national constructs, the influence of history, and how it is interpreted. Thus, the way that threats are designated in the political rhetoric clearly illustrates how governments perceive the near enemy and how, in turn, the effects of these perceptions influence their attitudes. Designating an enemy is also part of the political legitimization process. Whether real or imaginary, "if people say a threat is real, even though there is nothing in reality to justify this opinion, then this threat has real consequences."[14] The

Western Sahara issue, therefore, is not only part of a body of representations that make up national identity, but also part of the close relationship between domestic politics and foreign politics in Algeria.

ALGERIAN DIPLOMACY: A LEGACY OF WAR

The Algerian diplomacy that preceded the birth of the state[15] was born out of war, which explains its military and ideological nature during the first few decades and the emergence of a political culture of belligerence structured around the army. On the international and regional levels, this is seen in the historic monopoly on the formulating and executing foreign policy that the military has held through its "*maquis* power."[16]

Algerian officers, heirs of the anticolonial struggle,[17] are deeply immersed in the nationalist culture that envisions a centralizing state and a keen sense of territorial sovereignty. The significance of these values is seen in the ongoing hostility toward Morocco, hostility that dates back to the 1963 defeat by the FAR. The military believes it is the only true heritor of the country and sees itself as the only guarantor of the nation-state.

The organic link between the military and Algerian nationalism dates back so far that any president who tries to break away from the system of generals dictating political decisions is discretely but firmly dismissed. Nationalism and the narrative of a nation that belongs exclusively to the military realm rule out any possibility for an alternative narrative and prevent any deviation from the roadmap imposed by the military hierarchy. When President Chadli Bendjedid sought to establish better relations with Morocco in 1985, the army thwarted his efforts on the Western Sahara issue and the border dispute. In 1992, Khaled Nezzar[18] rallied against Mohamed Boudiaf's conciliatory attitude toward Rabat, which was perceived as ceding sovereignty.

The Algerian Army: A State within a State

From the start, the ANP has played a central role in building the Algerian state. This has resulted in the creation of a security state in which public order, the law, coercion, and law enforcement measures prevailed over representative institutions. This military-over-civilian predominance is rooted in the failure of the Soummam Congress principles. From the outset, it positioned the ANP as the main political actor: the guardian of the revolutionary acquisitions and values, as well as territorial integrity, whose main mission was to defend the borders during the "Sand War" against Morocco (1963), a country considered to be pro-Western.

Today, the army's apparent withdrawal from politics shields it from responsibility for abuses the civilian government may commit. By ruling but not governing,[19] high-ranking officers protect themselves from the risks of daily governance. The pseudo-democratic institutions, set up after the fierce crackdown on the 1988 riots (and the establishment of a multiparty system under the 1989 Constitution), serve to maintain the stability of the regime. This configuration gives the military establishment a lot of leeway to return to the forefront of politics whenever it deems it necessary. For example, in the 1992 coup d'état, the generals took back power for several years through the *Haut Conseil de Sécurité* (High Security Council)[20] and the military-security apparatus tightened its grip on the state and on managing the country. In this "bunker state,"[21] at a time when Algeria was nearly bankrupt, the International Monetary Fund (IMF) structural adjustment measures put in place in 1994 enabled the members of the military enclave to become private actors. Debt rescheduling freed up additional resources for the armed forces during the war on radical Islamism. This deregulation generated new sources of revenue for the military establishment and its civilian allies through a monopoly on the newly privatized state-owned companies and imports of select goods (medicines, construction materials, etc.).[22]

The timid attempt to "demilitarize politics" in the 2000s was particularly important in that it concerned both top government leaders and a society decimated by the civil war. The Algerian army tolerated this formal political liberalization in exchange for significant additional compensation through privileged access to new economic sectors and oil income. Given that this partial liberalization was not accompanied by the establishment of a true market economy, only one class of entrepreneurs and business people—those whose fortunes were closely tied to the state— prospered. This pseudo-democratization also expanded the circle of clientelism to a few repentant Islamists. The army continued to intervene politically through the state intelligence service (the *Département du Renseignement et de la Sécurité*, or DRS[23]), which was tasked with regulating the political field for the regime in spite of the infighting between factions that rocked the government at regular intervals. As one Algerian researcher noted, the DRS acted like "a clandestine party, [. . .] the only true political party with resources, objectives, and a coherent strategy."[24]

The military systems Algeria has put in place reflect the government's concerns and its desire to be a regional power. They show which means of sovereignty the government has used most to establish its claims. This system and its territorial manifestation resulted in a considerable increase in military spending starting in the 2000s. Algiers allocates 3.3 percent of its GDP to defense. According to the SIPRI Yearbook 2011, after several years of successive increases, the Algerian military budget jumped 44 percent in 2011 with 1.9 billion Euros in expenditure (US$2.5 billion), surpassing South Africa on the African continent.[25]

Russia is Algeria's biggest partner. The two countries signed a strategic partnership agreement in 2001. In 2006, Algeria purchased US$7.5 billion in equipment from Moscow in exchange for cancellation of its $4.7 billion debt, and in 2010, it signed an agreement to purchase sixteen fighter jets. In 2012, it also bought Russian tanks at a total value of $400 million. Just recently, the Algerian government decided to purchase US$5 billion in electronic surveillance devices (radars and optronic sensors) and early warning equipment to establish a security zone along its southern border. It also purchased a total of $400 million in Russian tanks.

After the United States lifted restrictions on arms purchases at the end of 2002, Algeria purchased British vehicles and light equipment (£7.2 million) via Qatar. Although Morocco is still the United States' privileged ally, US military aid to Algiers nearly quadrupled between 2001 and 2008, reaching US$800 million.

The Gradual Decline of Algerian Diplomacy

Algerian foreign policy has undergone several phases over the past four decades:

- diminishing influence and isolation due to the civil war in the 1980s–1990s
- through its participation in the "global war on terrorism" (GWOT) at the beginning of the 2000s
- at present, an unexpected wait-and-see policy, which confirms its loss of influence

Despite these upheavals, the army is still a player in politics and regional diplomacy and continues to maintain an unwavering position on the Western Sahara issue, even in the absence of any direct or indirect political benefit. This position is essentially motivated by a refusal to see its rival attain its territorial claims and thereby gain a larger portion of the Sahara. Pro-Sahrawi activism was a burden on independent Algeria's diplomacy for its first twenty years. Not only was Algeria's place in the regional and international arenas viewed through the lens of this conflict, but Algeria's discourse touting itself as a unifier was at odds with its "cold war" with its neighbor. This forced Algiers to scale back its diplomatic ambitions starting in the 1980s, while continuing to unconditionally support the Polisario Front.

When Algeria found itself isolated on the world scene during the "black decade," Morocco seized the opportunity to tip the balance of diplomatic power back in its favor and proposed its autonomy plan for the "southern provinces." This shift would weaken Algiers' position on the Saharan issue for a long time to come. In an effort to restore his country's international image starting in 1999, President Bouteflika successfully revived a diplomacy of mediation and integration on the

African continent (Eritrea-Ethiopia Peace Agreement in 2000, NEPAD project in 2001, 2006 Algiers Accord on the Tuareg issue), but he was unable to restore the "golden years" of the past,[26] despite the benefits he gained through his involvement in GWOT efforts.

The new security problem caused by the events of September 11, 2001, offered the Algerian government renewed international legitimacy and enabled it to transform its foreign policy into a new source of legitimacy for its domestic policy. Algeria's regional diplomacy now seems very uncertain and overcautious at the very least. It appears to be paralyzed by the unprecedented context of extreme volatility stemming from the political upheavals of the "Arab Spring," particularly in Libya and Tunisia. Even so, exploiting nationalism to implement foreign policy on Western Sahara remains a historic privilege and domestic political tool for Algerian generals and leaders.

Foreign and Defense Policy: Exclusive Domain of the Military

The army and security services share a set of common interests in defense and foreign policy. Despite the suspicions that have shrouded and continue to shroud the more-than-ambiguous role the armed forces played during the civil war, the military has managed to maintain a potentially strong influence on politics, to boost its public image, and to cultivate a reputation of efficiency in maintaining law and order and providing security.

The "national reconciliation" process has only reinforced the military's influence and primacy in security policies. The *"Rahma"* (forgiveness or mercy) provided immunity for a large portion of the security forces and officers' corps, as well as certain violent Islamists who took up arms, and shielded them from prosecution for acts of violence committed during the civil war.[27] This political potential has been reinforced considerably since 9/11 when the United States gave the regime a blank check. Algeria's support for the GWOT has thus provided it leverage in restoring the army's standards and capacities and rebuilding Algeria's diplomacy.

To understand Algeria's pressing need to take advantage of the new alignments offered by the GWOT, it is necessary to understand the central role that the army and intelligence services (i.e., DRS) play in the state apparatus and in foreign and defense policy.

Restoring Algeria's International Image via the GWOT

After ten years of internal violence that caused Algeria to be erased from the international scene, the country is attempting to emerge from its diplomatic isolation through a rapprochement with the United States on the security and economic level. This approach illustrates the Algerian authorities' desire to be firmly integrated into the new dynamic and the north-south security system.[28] The results have undoubtedly been beneficial for Algiers, which has now become a new partner for Washington in the region, resulting in a new American perception of Algeria. Once the ideological antagonism with the United States was toned down, Algiers could play the role of "proxy state"—a conduit for US penetration in the region, especially in the Sahara and the Sahel. In December 2009, for example, Algeria authorized US planes to fly over its air space to conduct reconnaissance of the border zone with Mali and Mauritania, particularly the Tindouf region.

The strengthening of ties with Washington has also resulted in a flurry of visits to Algiers by US officials and regular invitations to the White House for Algerian ministers and President Abdelaziz Bouteflika. On the security level, there has been an increase in the number of joint operations and initiatives. The FBI has opened a field office in Algiers, ANP officers have been trained in the United States, and there has been a series of joint intelligence missions between high-ranking DRS officers and their US counterparts. The two countries have therefore established relations that are primarily focused on the security issue, with Washington formulating and determining the principles, methods, and strategies.

In a game of dual détente that integrates foreign and domestic interests, the interpretation of what constitutes terrorism and the execution of "the fight against terror" are both captive to the interests of Western partners and convergent with the interests of Algerian soldiers, who subscribe to them in order to ensure their own survival: the opportunity to negotiate the allocation of aid without any conditionality.

Despite a persistently high level of violence (1,102 attacks and bombings since 2001, versus nine in Morocco, twenty-seven in Mauritania, thirty-eight in Niger, and forty-nine in Mali),[29] Algeria continues to project its exact same vision of threat to the south. With military capabilities superior to those of the Sahel states, Algeria feels that it has *de facto* security expertise (and therefore authority), thanks to the aid provided by the United States and other northern countries. It also sees itself as a relay between its creditors and Western partners and the Sahel and as the guarantor of their military interests in the region. Backed by Western military capabilities and systems, it seeks to convince its neighbors to the south of the soundness of its strategy, to influence their position, and to dictate the rules and time of engagement. By urging the other states to adopt Algeria's definition of the threat and support its assessment of the threat and, thus, its priorities, Algerian decision makers are trying to incorporate these countries into their own security process, while ruling out all other analyses of the situation.

Herein lays the greatest paradox of Algeria's security policy: by fueling state violence, it confirms the government's lack of legitimacy and its weakening sovereignty. The ever-widening gap between rhetoric and reality highlights the failure of the military strategy and the disproportionate importance attached to military-based governance. This contributes to undermining the government's credibility to act, since it must continually justify its actions both at home and abroad. Consequently, although Algeria appears to be a strong state because it is authoritarian and dominated by the military, it is actually a weak state struggling to control its territory, protect its borders, safeguard its citizens, and resolve social issues that have been manifest throughout the country during the past decade. Finally, the ongoing tensions within the government between opposing civil-military factions thwart any possibility for regime change and severely limit the implementation of a regional integration policy. "There is no opposition in Algeria, except for power struggles between clans. [. . .] The executive branch is the true arena for political representation through secret networks, given that the Parliament does not have any real power and society is not represented. Society represents itself through direct action, through riots."[30]

Regional Security as a Means of Circumventing Morocco

Abdelkader Messahel's statement finds its full meaning in the context of growing instability in the Sahel. Algiers denies any correlation between regional security issues and the Western Sahara conflict and excludes the Polisario Front from the regional security problem. However, for the past three years, the Western Sahara political issue has been aggravated by security issues related to the Polisario Front: its members' involvement in kidnappings and weapons and drug trafficking, and the fact that its camps have become recruitment centers for Al-Qaeda in the Islamic Maghreb (AQIM), the Movement for Unity and Jihad in West Africa (MUJWA), and other criminal groups. The Polisario Front's gradual weakening and political decline, along with Mauritania's proximity to Western Sahara, have created a vacuum that members of this organization exploit for money through arms and cigarette trafficking and smuggling illegal immigrants to the Atlantic coast of Western Sahara to Morocco. The Sahrawis know the area well and are able to cross the landmine zone known as "PK55," which gives them know-how sought out by criminal and terrorist networks.[31]

This is evidenced by the following:

- The December 2010 arrests in Mali and Mauritania of several Polisario leaders involved in one of the biggest drug-trafficking networks.
- The dismantling of a twenty-seven-person terrorist cell in January 2011 and the discovery of caches of Russian-made arms by Moroccan security services near Amgala in the "buffer zone."[32]

- The kidnapping of three European humanitarian workers in Rabouni (Tindouf) in October 2011[33] by the MUJWA, which suggests accomplices within the camp.

The latter episode is particularly significant in that it also highlights shortcomings in monitoring the zone, which officially falls under the jurisdiction of both the Polisario Front and the Algerian army. From a diplomatic point of view, these events place the Algerian government in a position that is uncomfortable at the very least, especially the military intelligence unit, which has blocked the Western Sahara issue since the 1990s. A diplomatic cable in March 2008 indicated that Abdelaziz Bouteflika had approached David Welch, US assistant secretary of state for Middle Eastern affairs, seeking an exit plan for the crisis that above all would allow Algeria to "save face."[34] In other words, he sought a plan that would pull Algeria out of its increasingly untenable position and promote a civilian-diplomatic solution. Aware of the growing damage that the Polisario's involvement in criminal activities could inflict on it, Algeria recently decided to purge its ranks. The Front's minister of defense, Mohamed Lamine Ould Bouhali, an Algerian national who has held this position since the 1980s, was dismissed on the grounds of his alleged involvement in drug trafficking and kidnappings.[35]

In August 2012, after paying a fifteen million euro ransom for the release of Spanish nationals kidnapped in Rabouni, Madrid decided to pull all its humanitarian workers out of the Sahrawi refugee camps in Algeria. This was a major setback for Algiers, which had been trying to reign in the Polisario Front amid a deteriorating domestic situation and the criminalization of a growing number of young Sahrawi castoffs. It was also a setback for the Polisario Front as several of its missions were shut down in Spain.

Even more illegitimate in the Tindouf camps, the Polisario is increasingly challenged by Sahrawi youth. After a large number of high-ranking Polisario members defected and returned to Morocco and northern Mauritania,[36] there was an internal split in 2004 that broke the Polisario's monopoly on representation. The main reasons behind this dissidence are the issues of refugee rights and living conditions and the corruption of the leaders. Concerning the Tindouf camps, for example, Polisario leaders claim that the number of refugees has remained unchanged for several years: 155,430 people. The United Nations High Commissioner for Refugees (UNHRC) estimates the number between 70,000 and 90,000. The Polisario Front has two reasons for inflating this number. First, it reinforces its legitimacy as a party to the conflict and to the referendum. Second, it profits from the humanitarian aid, which is distributed in proportion to the number of refugees, by selling a portion of it off elsewhere. *Khat al-Shahid* (Line of the Martyr), the splinter group that resulted from this division, asked the UN to treat it "as a representative of a part of

Sahrawi public opinion domestically and abroad." The emergence of separatist claims starting in May 2005 exemplifies the Polisario Front's inability to attract the younger generations. Recent actions led by the "Sahrawi Revolutionary Youth" movement to protest the reelection of Mohamed Abdelaziz, who has been in office for thirty-six years, illustrate the rise of a generation that no longer relates to the old guard. The slogan "*Erhal*" (clear off) chanted by protestors is a sign of the Arab Spring's impact on a generation of youth demanding social justice and rebelling against the leaders' tribalism.

The porosity of the Tindouf camps, as evidenced by the presence of Polisario members in the Malian town of Gao (headquarters of the MUJAO, whose spokesperson is Adnan Abou Oualid Sahraoui), and the regular clashes between rival criminal gangs (such as the one between two groups of traffickers in the Amtierat region at the end of August 2012) have placed the zone on near constant high alert. The Algerian police have had to beef up surveillance through increased patrols and checkpoints.

Some experts are now calling for a resolution of the Western Sahara crisis "which is inhibiting both security and economic cooperation in the Maghreb and Sahel, and is driving a wedge between two of the region's most influential nations—Morocco and Algeria," and recommending a "shut down [of] the refugee camps run by the Polisario near Tindouf, Algeria, because they are a recruiting ground for terrorists, traffickers, and other criminal enterprises" targeting idle young Sahrawis.[37]

Exploiting the "Terrorist Threat" and Projecting Power

Despite its reputation for counterterrorism expertise, Algeria is not militarily active in the Sahara. The weak security in the zone is evidenced by the June 30, 2010, attack on Algerian security forces in Tamanrasset, which killed eleven gendarmes and border guards; the kidnapping of an Italian tourist on February 2, 2011, by Abou Zeid's *katiba* in the Djanet region; the kidnapping of the prefect of Illizi on January 17, 2012, by youth who handed him over to AQIM in Libya; the March 2012 bombing of a gendarmerie barrack in Tamanrasset, followed by the Ouargla bombing in June 2012; and, finally, the April 5, 2012, kidnapping of the Algerian consul (who was assassinated at the beginning of September) and six other staff from the consulate in Gao by the MUJAO for a fifteen million euro ransom. Like its Sahelian neighbors, the Algerian government struggles to maintain control over its entire territory.

Whether in January 2010 or in July 2012, security measures have been limited to closing borders and increasing troop deployments in these regions. These measures included assigning an additional 3,000 soldiers to the border guard unit (*Groupement des gardes-frontières*, or GCF); declaring the border zones with Mali (1,200 km), Niger (700 km), and Mauritania (500 km) to be military zones; and requiring a *laissez-passer* for nomadic populations.

Besides the regional power imbalances and the competition for leadership among the Maghreb countries, Algeria's feeble action in its part of the Sahara may help explain why counterterrorism cooperation among the neighboring countries has not moved past the declaratory stage.

In the presence of a country with hegemonic ambitions like Algeria, which views its territory as extending beyond its actual political borders, the Saharan region serves as a backyard, a more or less privileged place to exercise foreign policy. The disparities between the partners involved force the countries of the Sahel to exploit the rivalries between the countries in the north and to play them off each other to oppose their contradictory, divergent, and competing claims. This results in fluctuating geopolitical alliances, with or without Algeria, depending on conditions and each state's interests.

The current state of regional cooperation is also the product of low levels of confidence. The Saharan-Sahelian and Maghreb countries' distrust of Algiers springs from suspicions surrounding the role played by the DRS in infiltrating the Armed Islamic Group (GIA) and the Salafist Group for Preaching and Combat (GSPC) and in exporting Algerian terrorism to their territories. In June 2008, the Malian president accused Bouteflika of failing to control his security service, which is playing its own game in the Sahel by stirring up tensions, particularly through the Tuareg rebellion. Both Bamako and Nouakchott blame the growing insecurity on the Algerian government's inability to defeat the Islamist *maquis* on its own soil and for spreading insecurity into the Sahel by pushing Algerian jihadists toward the south. Algiers is nonetheless pursuing its activism like a bridgehead in the counterterrorism fight through a series of initiatives aimed at centralizing the "fight against terror" in the Sahara and the Sahel.

The reality on the ground contradicts the government's claims of military and technical superiority and seniority in terms of its expertise, operational experience, and counterterrorism intelligence. The United States has also expressed doubt about Algeria's ability to secure its own territory. In a diplomatic cable dated December 2007 (a few days before the attack on the UNHCR (United Nations) office and the Constitutional Court headquarters in Algiers), the former US ambassador observed that Algerian authorities "were not happy about fighting AQIM" and no longer only fighting "the old Algerian terrorist group GSPC from the end of the 1990s."[38]

In a contradictory manner, Algeria is seeking to recast itself strategically through its involvement in the GWOT, while still displaying a testy sense of sovereignty and invoking the nationalist narrative to legitimize its diplomatic and security choices. It knows what it stands to gain from the United States' strategic reorientation in Africa: closer relations with

Washington will henceforth enable it to compete with its neighbors in strategies it considers to be "win-win."

THE WAY FORWARD

What can be done to break the stalemate and to normalize the situation in a context of widespread, acute crisis?

Urgency of the Threat Puts Unilateral, Regional Initiatives in an Awkward Position

Regional initiatives are frequently compromised by Algeria, which is opposed to its partners operating independently, to the detriment of Algiers. Rather than encourage these initiatives, Algiers looks unfavorably on the establishment of regional alliances that do not include it.[39] Eager to keep Rabat out of any regional security mechanism, Algiers has undertaken a series of initiatives intended to centralize the "fight against terror" in the Sahara and Sahel.

Two joint, French-Mauritanian operations in July and September 2010 led Algiers to fear the establishment of a Nouakchott-Bamako axis that would exclude it, especially since Mauritanian-Moroccan relations had greatly improved since the election of President Mohamed "Aziz" Abdelaziz in July 2009. The French-Niger operation in February 2011 against the kidnappers of two young French citizens was also ill-received by Algerian leaders.

In April 2009, a General Staff Joint Operations Committee (CEMOC) was set up in Tamanrasset at Algeria's instigation. It excluded Morocco and included "countries from the field," namely, Mali, Mauritania, and Niger. This structure was supposed to implement a new plan for regional security with a force strength that would triple by 2011 (from 25,000 to 75,000 including 5,000 Tuaregs), but in reality it has never organized any joint operations. One year later, the Fusion and Liaison Unit (FLU) was established. This is a coalition of intelligence services from seven countries: Algeria, Mali, Mauritania, Niger, Libya, Burkina Faso, and Chad, plus Nigeria, which joined at the end of 2011. This unit holds technical meetings periodically to assess the situation and, above all, "to analyze security intelligence concerning the region."[40]

Algeria also refused to take part in the G8 meeting of experts held in Bamako on October 13, 2010, with Morocco's participation. It continued to reiterate its opposition to any decision made without its input. In April 2011, Algiers hosted a regional security conference for the foreign affairs ministers from Mauritania, Niger, and Mali, along with experts from the European Union (EU) and representatives from member states of the UNSC, but it did not invite Morocco. To compensate for being excluded and to retake control of African affairs, Morocco decided to revive the Community of Sahel-Saharan States (CEN-SAD), which had been inactive since Gaddafi's death, by holding a meeting of the CEN-SAD Executive Council in Rabat in June 2012. Unlike other countries in the Maghreb, Algeria is not a member of this organization.[41] The council examined two draft agreements on security cooperation and on conflict prevention mechanisms. If this global economic union—which is based on investments in the agricultural, industrial, energy, social, and cultural sectors—becomes active, it could be a powerful lever for influence on the continent, given the variety of member countries, including those from West Africa.

Tactical Rapprochement

With Mauritania

In an effort to consolidate its strategy of gaining a stronghold in the Saharan west, Algiers recently established closer ties with Nouakchott, which is still neutral on the Western Sahara issue. The opening of the Nouakchott-Nouadhibou road had caused deterioration in Algerian-Mauritanian relations, since this road provided a land link with Morocco, whose borders with Algeria had been closed since 1994. Morocco's borders with Mauritania had been closed off by the Western Sahara "berm," but Mauritanian-Moroccan relations began to warm when President Ould Abdel Aziz came to power. The new Mauritanian president, who had attended the Royal Military Academy in Meknes and had family ties to Morocco, was perceived by Algiers as being "Rabat's man." Algiers worked with "Aziz" in December 2011 to revive the Algerian-Mauritanian project to build a road from Tindouf to Choum, which would allow Algeria to have direct access to the Atlantic Ocean, bypassing Morocco to the south, and position itself closer to Western Sahara.[42]

With Morocco

Current challenges from threats in the Sahel and the deteriorating regional security situation, which resulted from a power vacuum within the old geopolitical framework, have direct repercussions—both domestic and transnational—on the entire Maghreb and Sahel regions. With the Libyan crisis, whose impact reached well beyond the Sahara-Sahel territory, it is increasingly difficult for Algeria to continue excluding its Moroccan neighbor from regional security policies. Now that the EU is strongly encouraging intra-Maghreb cooperation with Morocco, Algeria can no longer ignore the need to include Rabat in any credible initiative in this area. Already, some EU countries are offering counterterrorism training programs for security officers and judges from the Maghreb.

Algiers would like to use this opportunity to subcontract the security of refugee camps by expanding the European training program to members of the Polisario Front, against Morocco's advice.

At the Maghreb level, Algiers and Rabat were forced into a rapprochement in January 2012 because of the urgency of the situation at hand. However, there should be no illusions. As the Moroccan minister of foreign affairs stated, "The current indicators, while they convey Morocco and Algeria's desire to establish bilateral relations on the whole, do not, nevertheless, predict an imminent normalization of relations between the countries."[43] His Algerian counterpart, Mourad Medelci, clearly indicated that the question of opening the border was not on the agenda.[44] The two countries appear to have opted to separate out the most hotly disputed issues, such as Western Sahara and reopening the borders, and to leave them in the care of international bodies. Thus, the disputes remain deadlocked, with each party fully aware that no progress is possible for the time being. As one Algerian general, speaking on condition of anonymity, said, "Until Morocco apologizes to Algeria for having accused it of being behind the 1994 attack we will not give in on opening our common border."[45]

The tentative warming has forced Algiers and Rabat to sit together at the table, such as during the Arab Maghreb Union meeting of foreign affairs ministers in Algiers at the beginning of June 2012[46] and the meeting of the Council of Foreign Affairs Ministers held in Rabat on February 18, 2012, which was attended by the Algerian minister-delegate for Maghreb and African affairs, Abdelkader Messahel.

Regional Behind-the-Scenes Diplomacy

Toward Northern Mali

When northern Mali was in the midst of secession and Libya in an uncertain transition, Algeria appeared unwilling to assume the responsibilities that the hegemonic status of a pivotal nation would demand. Refusing to consider any joint strategy, as seen in its position on the Malian crisis, Algeria has once again succumbed to the fear of encirclement that characterized its policies in the 1970s. Behind this refusal, there is also the desire to maintain its position as a key country in regional security matters while conducting a wait-and-see diplomacy, which many observers and regional leaders have deemed incomprehensible.

Internal power struggles at the highest levels of government have without a doubt permeated Algeria's policy vis-à-vis the Malian crisis, hampering Algiers' ability to act regionally and weakening its position as a regional leader. In other words, the current lack of commitment could in fact be the result of conflicting positions and divergent interests within the regime and of the lack of transparency in decision making. These factors are crippling its diplomatic power.

Preferring to keep a low profile, it would seem that Algeria is waiting to see how the regional situation plays out before making any decision and leaving the risks of resolving the crisis to others. This is illustrated in two conflicting visions and strategies: Morocco wants to elevate the Malian crisis to the international level, while Algeria is advocating a "peaceful solution" and is doing everything possible to negotiate and coordinate a solution on its own—behind closed doors and without any outside intervention, especially from France.

The rote use of past mediation strategies that helped bolster Algeria's position as a leader (such as the 2006 Algiers Accords on the Tuareg issue) seems to have outlived its usefulness. The parties to the conflict— with whom Algiers had discretely met in the summer of 2012—ended up turning to other actors deemed more "neutral" or more representative (among others, Burkina Faso and ECOWAS,to which Algeria does not belong).[47] In fact, in July 2012, Bouteflika met in utmost secrecy with emissaries from the terrorist organization Ansar Eddine, representatives of the MNLA, and even envoys from the MUJAO, which was responsible for kidnapping the Algerian consul in Gao.[48] In parallel, that same month, the Algerian government sent supply trucks and three military vehicles carrying soldiers and intelligence officers to the Ansar Eddine-controlled city of Kidal. A second convoy carrying food aid was sent to MUJAO-controlled Gao. The two Islamic terrorist organizations were in charge of distributing the supplies from the Algerian government.

Members of the Malian interim government also traveled to Algeria and the French minister of foreign affairs, who met with Algerian leaders in Algiers on July 15, noted the divergent points of view between Algiers and Paris:

> Algerian leaders, who have always been suspicious of French and Western motives, reject foreign "meddling" in the affairs of the region and have repeatedly backed diplomacy. France openly favors intervention against Islamists and is pressing Algiers to accept a military option in Mali. This divergence in approaches for now represents the natural limit of security cooperation between the two countries.[49]

Toward Libya

At the time of the Libyan crisis, the Algerian government, caught off guard by the Arab uprisings, adopted an ambiguous position toward Colonel Muammar Gadaffi. Its stance only further isolated the country and proved that the cultural matrix of Algiers' diplomacy had not changed. After all, President Abdelaziz Bouteflika was from the same era of political struggle as the Libyan leader. Given this background, this is probably why Algiers sent military equipment and mercenaries to Tripoli in 2011, both by land and by sea, in violation of UN Resolutions 1970 and 1973. Algiers was also strongly criticized within the AU, particularly by its ally South Africa, for not recognizing Libya's National Transition Council (NCT). "While it has been proven that hundreds of Polisario Front members fought alongside Gaddafi forces in Libya, it is certain that they would not have been able to do so without the help of the Algerian authorities."[50] Thus, in this context of growing uncertainty, the Western Sahara issue has been transformed from a stumbling block into a source of Maghreb unity. It has become a national security issue for both sides, because of how it is perceived and exploited.

CONCLUSION

Algerian leaders have had difficulty adapting to the new realities of international relations and to new regional alignments—a necessary condition to formulating a clear geostrategic vision and a realistic foreign policy. The archaic management of diplomacy by aging leaders who are heirs to Cold War–influenced thinking can no longer be limited to an exercise in volunteerism to influence regional geopolitics.

The decline of Algeria's regional diplomacy and its lack of transparency—which have been even more blatant since the "Arab Spring"—are related to several factors:

- the loss of legitimacy during the popular uprisings in North Africa and the Middle East, when Algiers firmly supported the dictators, thereby diplomatically isolating the countries of the region
- its weak African policy and the lack of a strategic vision for the subregion and the continent
- its obduracy concerning the true humanitarian and security conditions in the Tindouf refugee camps
- its support for the Polisario Front, a true political burden, which has become counterproductive now that the organization's involvement in criminal activities (trafficking and kidnapping) has been proven
- its distrust of its neighbors in the Sahel and the protagonists in the Malian crisis, which undermines its leadership in resolving the regional conflict and stabilizing the zone
- the need to compromise with its Moroccan neighbor to revive the Arab Maghreb Union (AMU) and to cooperate in the context of regional and international security mechanisms.

Despite this unfavorable context, two recent events confirm that a shift in Algeria's position is still inconceivable:

- The appointment of General Othman Tartag, a.k.a. "Bachir,"[51] to the Homeland Security Service (*Direction de la Sécurité Intérieure*, or

DSI), the backbone of the DRS, on December 21, 2011. Tartag, who advocates a hard line against Morocco and is strongly opposed to opening the border with Morocco, is said to become (or is to be lined up to be) the successor to Mohamed Médiène, a.k.a. "Tewfik," head of the DRS.

- The reinforcement of the army's security approach, which favors the DRS to the detriment of the general staff, to better control the state apparatus and society.

Similarly, the fact that a new generation of high-ranking officers, who lack the historic legitimacy gained from serving in the national liberation war, was promoted within the ANP three times in four years (in 2008, then in the summer of 2011 and 2012) indicates that Algeria will not change its position on Western Sahara. These officers remain vigilant "vis-à-vis Morocco, which is still the main adversary in the eyes of the military-security apparatus and executive branch, thereby justifying the need to maintain a balance of power in Western Sahara."[52]

For many regional and international actors, the possible emergence of a new "failed" state is an unacceptable risk, especially in the context of state proliferation illustrated by the secession of northern Mali. Until now, in the absence of any strategic benefits, Algeria has deemed the status quo to be preferable and far more convenient than any poorly negotiated or hasty attempt to overcome the crisis, which would add to the current uncertainty.

In the dual context of globalization and regionalization, it should be easy for Algeria to embrace a perspective that extends beyond its short-term interests to definitively resolve this historic, but not unavoidable, rift that is penalizing the entire Maghreb—a transition necessary to address the security and development challenges of the twenty-first century.

AFTERWORD

Since this chapter was written in late 2012, a great deal has transpired to text the conclusions above, yet the reality remains that Algeria has not yet moved to develop a more timely strategic vision vis-à-vis security issues in the region or its relationship with Morocco. The prolonged absence of President Bouteflika due to sickness, then his return and subsequent changes he is making with in the military and intelligence oligarchy and the diplomatic personnel only serve to reinforce the image of a national leadership motivated by domestic considerations that define its foreign policy primarily caught in a "cold war" consciousness. Algerian actions during the hostage crisis at In Amenas, its handling of growing security threats across the Tunisian and Libyan borders, strengthening the closed border with Morocco to combat the "terrorism" of drug and other smuggling, its vacillating security posture toward Mali and the Sahelian states, and its continued lack of transparency in dealing with regional security issues indicate an inability to comprehend the shifting demands and constraints in its self-defined role as the regional hegemon. While muddling along may, for now, suffice to secure its borders, it will not enable Algeria to recapture its former role of international leadership, it most desired prize.

NOTES

1. Cherif Ouazani, "Union sacrée contre Al-Qaïda," *Jeune Afrique*, March 29, 2010, www.jeuneafrique.com/Article/ARTJAJA2567p040-044.xml0/. The General Staff Joint Operations Committee (CEMOC), which brings together four countries (Algeria, Mali, Mauritania, and Niger), meets in Tamanrasset and is chaired by Ahmed Gaïd Salah, chief of staff of the Algerian army. Some observers are surprised by the absence of Morocco, Libya, and Chad. However, as soon as the Malian delegation expressed the desire to enlarge the counterterrorism coalition to other states in the subregion, particularly Morocco, Algeria vetoed the idea, and Messahel made this statement. Abdelkader Messahel was part of the Military Security (*Sécurité Militaire* or SM) team in charge of the Polisario issue in the 1970s. Other members of the team were Kasdi Merbab (first head of the SM after independence) and Noureddine Zerhouni, who worked at the SM for his entire career until 1997.

2. In keeping with the promise that Ferhat Abbas, president of the Provisional Government of the Algerian Republic (GPRA), made to Hassan II in July 1961.

3. Michel Foucher, *Fronts et frontières. Un tour du monde géopolitique* (Paris: Fayard, 1991).

4. Louis Blin, *L'Algérie du Sahara au Sahel. Route Transsaharienne, Economie Pétrolière et Construction de l'Etat* (Paris: L'Harmattan, 1990), 178–79.

5. Thirty-six years later, the completion of this road was put back on the agenda. Construction began on two sections of the road toward the Malian border (Tamanrasset-Timiaouine and Tamanrasset-Tin Zaouatine) and is scheduled to be completed in 2014. The 2,000-kilometer section leading to Lagos, Nigeria, was discussed again at the last meeting of the Trans-Saharan Highway Liaison Committee in Algiers in April 2012.

6. See Laurence Aïda Ammour, "Regional Security Cooperation in the Maghreb and Sahel: Algeria's Pivotal Ambivalence," *Africa Security Brief* no. 18 (February 2012).

7. The OCRS (1957–1963) was established by France to consolidate the economic expansion of the Saharan zones under French domination, in other words, to continue developing the Sahara's mineral resources, including hydrocarbons.

8. Foucher, *Fronts et frontières*, supra note 3.

9. Algerian independence was also the fruit of a self-determination referendum that was held July 1, 1962, pursuant to the Évian Accords signed on March 18, 1962.

10. Ahmed Mahiou, "L'Algérie et les Organisations Internationales," *Annuaire Français de Droit International* 28 (1982): 127–45.

11. The SADR was not recognized by the United States, China, Russia, or any European state.

12. African Center for Studies and Research on Terrorism was established in Algiers in 2004 under the aegis of the AU.

13. See Valérie Rosoux, "Les usages du passé dans le cadre de la politique étrangère" (paper, Université Paris I, September 2003).

14. Lewis A. Coser, *Les Fonctions du Conflit Social* (Paris: Presses universitaires de France, 1982), 79.

15. Since the start of the armed struggle, FLN leaders have integrated a political-diplomatic dimension into their strategy to give more weight to the anticolonial liberation struggle. See Matthew Connelly, *A Diplomatic Revolution: Algeria's Fight for Independence and the Origins of the Post–Cold War Era* (New York: Oxford University Press, 2002); Nicole Grimaud, *La Politique extérieure de l'Algérie* (Paris: Karthala, 1984).

16. Term used by Hugh Roberts in *The Battlefield, Algeria 1988–2002: Studies in a Broken Polity* (London: Verso, 2003). The author notes that after 1962, "the men of the *maquis* [Resistance] became men in the shadows. This was the beginning of covert power, the hidden tip of the iceberg. The confrontations, battles for influence, and behind-the-scene dealings that preceded any major decision happened far from the public eye, not in formal political institutions, but in the shadows," p. 9.

17. The fact that Algerian leaders still use war names is indicative of this culture of secrecy.

18. Commander of the army in 1986, he was promoted to Chief of Staff, then Minister of Defense from 1990 to July 1993. From January 1992 to January 1994, he was one of the five members of the *Haut Comité d'État* [High State Council, or HCE], a five-member military junta that replaced the president-elect. He is currently being prosecuted by the Swiss courts for having "ordered, authorized, and incited soldiers and civil service agents to commit acts of torture, murder, extrajudicial executions, forced disappearances, and other serious violations of international humanitarian law."

19. Steven A. Cook, *Ruling but Not Governing: The Military and Political Development in Egypt, Algeria and Turkey* (Baltimore, MD: Johns Hopkins University Press, 2007).

20. William B. Quandt, *Between Ballots and Bullets: Algeria's Transition from Authoritarianism* (Washington, DC: Brookings Institution, 1998).

21. Concept used by Clement Moore Henry and Robert Springborg in *Globalization and the Politics in the Middle East*, 2nd ed. (New York: Cambridge University Press, 2010), 113–61. According to the authors, Algeria, Iraq, Yemen, Egypt, and Syria are weak states in which economic operators are part of a system of clientelism and are excluded from decision making. Economic freedom is absent and the economy is primarily based on imports with the money supply residing outside the formal banking system. In these countries, the main barriers to development are, above all, political in nature.

22. Bradford L. Dillman, *State and Private Sector in Algeria: The Politics of Rent-Seeking and Failed Development* (Boulder, CO: Westview Press, 2000).

23. The *Département du Renseignement et de la Sécurité* (Department of Intelligence and Security, or DRS) is the successor to the *Direction Centrale de la Sécurité Militaire* (commonly referred to as the *Sécurité militaire*, or SM) that was established at independence with the help of the KGB. The SM's structures and methods were heavily inspired by the KGB. Created in 1990, the DRS played the role of a true political police, exercising tight control over the media, the economy, chancelleries, and Algerians living abroad.

24. Lahouari Addi, "L'armée, l'Etat, la Nation," *El Watan*, March 30, 2012.

25. The SIPRI figures do not include a 2.2 billion euro order placed in Germany for corvette ships.

26. See Akram Belkaïd, "La diplomatie algérienne à la recherche de son âge d'or," *Politique Etrangère* 2, no. 74 (2009).

27. The referendum on the "Charter for Peace and National Reconciliation" plan (August 14, 2005) initiated by President Abdelaziz Bouteflika was preceded a few years prior by the "Civil Concord" (July 13, 1999) approved by referendum on September 16, 1999. The Charter offered exemption from punishment, the possibility of probation, or sentence reduction for "persons involved or having been involved in acts of terrorism or subversion who sincerely express their desire to cease their criminal activities" (Articles 1 and 3). In 2000, the benefits of the Civil Concord Law were extended to combatants from the Islamic Salvation Army (AIS), most of whom were granted amnesty through a legislative decree on January 10, 2000. "Thus, government agents or those acting with the approval of the government (soldiers, gendarmes,

police officers, patriots, etc.) were never affected by these measures. Today, the excesses committed by government agents during the ten years of conflict are officially recognized by the highest authorities. It therefore seems logical that there should be a general amnesty to exonerate these agents." In the end, the Civil Concord did not convince the majority of the violent extremists to surrender their arms and restore civil peace. The suicide attacks on December 11, 2007, were committed by two men who had received official amnesty. A sustainable political solution to the Islamic-military conflict has not been found. See Laurence Aïda Ammour, "The Legislative Environment of the Algerian Civil Society," in *Governing the Public Sphere: Civil Society Regulation in North Africa*, ed. Bhekinkosi Moyo (Dakar: Trustafrica in cooperation with the European Foundation Centre and the African Grant Makers Network, 2012).

28. Algeria joined NATO's Mediterranean Dialogue in 2000, six years after its creation, and participated in the United States' Pan-Sahel Initiative (2002), which became the Trans-Sahara Counterterrorism Initiative (TSCTI). Algeria is also one of the founder members of the Global Counterterrorism Forum (GCTF) launched in New York in September 2011. On November 16 and 17, 2011, Algiers organized a regional task force on capacity-building in the Sahel. A meeting was held in Algiers from April 18–19, 2012, on the issue of paying ransom to terrorist groups for the release of hostages, and in June 2012, Algeria and Canada co-presided over a ministerial-level meeting of the Sahel Working Group in Istanbul.

29. According to Britain's Maplecroft Terrorism Risk Index, Algeria is ranked as an "extreme risk" country, along with Colombia and Somalia. For more details on the number of terrorist attacks, see Yonah Alexander, "Special Update Report—Terrorism in North, West, and Central Africa: From 9/11 to the Arab Spring," *Potomac Institute for Policy Studies/ International Center for Terrorism Studies*, January 2012. The bombing of the gendarmerie barracks in Tamanrasset at the beginning of March 2012 and the Ouargla attack committed in January 2012 by the Movement for Unity and Jihad in West Africa (MUJWA) are not included in these statistics. See also Andrew Lebovich, "AQIM returns in force in Northern Algeria," *CTC Sentinel*, September 26, 2011.

30. Roberts, *The Battlefield*, supra note 16. See also, "Le pouvoir exécutif est le véritable lieu de représentation politique par des réseaux occultés," *El Watan*, July 9, 2012.

31. Interview with a security officer based in Nouakchott in December 2009. For further details, see Laurence Aïda Ammour, "Flux, réseaux et circuits de la criminalité organisée au Sahara-Sahel et en Afrique de l'ouest," *Centre d'Etudes et de Recherches de l'Ecole Militaire*, Cahier spécial Sahel, no. 13 (December 2009). On the Polisario's political decline, see Laurence Aïda Ammour, "The Frozen Conflict of Western Sahara: Who Benefits?/A qui profite le gel du conflit du Sahara occidental?" *NATO Defense College (Rome)*, Research Paper 30 (November 2006).

32. Already in December 2007, the DRS was looking into the disappearance of a batch of weapons that Algiers had supplied to the Polisario. In January 2010, the DRS arrested Sidi Mohamed Mahjoub, a Polisario imam, and seized twenty kilograms of explosives at his home along with his correspondence with the Algerian emir of the Kabylie *maquis*, Abdelmalek Droukdel. By October 2010, the imam was back home.

33. Released in July 2012 in exchange for a fifteen million euro ransom.

34. Ford, "Algerian Leadership Tows Western Sahara Line," *U.S. Embassy Algiers*, March 3, 2003, 08ALGIERS261, http://wikileaks.org/cable/2008/03/08ALGIERS261.html.

35. In an interview with the Spanish newspaper *ABC*, Bouhali admitted that approximately thirty people in the Tindouf camps had ties to AQIM and MUJWA. In 1982, Bouhali had embezzled light weapons supplied to the Polisario by Algeria to give them to Algerian Tuareg rebels. See Luis de Vega, "El Polisario reconoce qua hay saharauis alistados en Al Qaida del Maghreb," *ABC*, August 11, 2012.

36. The most recent being Haj Ahmed Barikallah, SADR minister of cooperation, who resigned his position after discovering in Spain how much money his predecessor, Salek Baba Hassana, had been embezzling from Spanish NGO funds sent to refugee camps, with the complicity of Prime Minister Abdelkader Taleb Omar.

37. Yonah Alexander, "Special Update Report," supra note 29, 7.
38. Diplomatic Cable, U.S. Embassy Algiers, December 19, 2007, A.ALGIERS1704, no. 135031.
39. See Laurence Aïda Ammour, "Regional Security Cooperation," supra note 6.
40. See Tahar Fattani, "Réunion des chefs de services de renseignement des pays du Sahel à Alger. Sept pays forment une 'Union de liaison'," L'Expression (Algeria), October 2, 2010. "Citing Malian sources, AFP reported that the intelligence chiefs did not come to an agreement on including Morocco in this union, notably because of 'the Western Sahara dispute.' According to Algiers, the region's problems should concern only the countries of the region. Morocco is hardly concerned by this problem. Algeria's position on including Morocco in this alliance has nothing to do with the Western Sahara issue. It is therefore entirely clear that the Western Sahara issue is in no way related to the problems in the Sahel. As highlighted in previous editions, the Sahel issue is neither politically, nor geographically relevant to the Cherifian Kingdom. Geographically, Morocco does not share a border with this turbulent zone. Politically, it is not a member of the African Union," p. 2.
41. Established in 1998 in Tripoli at the instigation of the Libyan leader, the original founding members were Sahel states: Burkina Faso, Chad, Libya, Mali, Niger, and Sudan. Over the next two years, this original group was joined by Central African Republic, Eritrea, Djibouti (in 1999), Gambia, and Senegal. Sixteen other countries joined the organization later: Benin, Comoros, Côte d'Ivoire, Egypt, Ghana, Guinea, Guinea Bissau, Kenya, Liberia, Mauritania, Morocco, Nigeria, Sao Tome and Principe, Sierra Leone, Togo, and Tunisia.
42. This project, which has been suspended since 2006, will cover 1,200 kilometers, including an eighty-kilometer stretch in Algerian territory that has already been built.
43. Boualem Alami, "Le Maroc sceptique sur une rapide normalisation entre Alger et Rabat." Maghreb Emergent, March 28, 2012.
44. "Mourad Medelci. L'ouverture de la frontière 'n'est pas à l'ordre du jour'," El Watan, February 4, 2012.
45. Interview on February 10, 2012.
46. This meeting, known as "Algiers 1," was the first of its kind and was intended to establish a framework for security cooperation among the countries of the Maghreb, the Sahel, and the Sahara. There are plans for a follow-up meeting, "Algiers 2," on partnerships, security, and development in the Sahel. A meeting of AMU interior ministers is also scheduled to be held in Morocco prior to the next AMU Summit in Tunis.
47. On September 16, 2012, the ECOWAS defense ministers declared that they would seek the support of nonmember countries such as Algeria and Mauritania, both of which are opposed to deploying the West African force to northern Mali.
48. On June 20, Ansar Dine indicated that it had sent a delegation to Algiers at the same time that the group was holding talks in Ouagadougou. Algiers never officially admitted to this meeting, but Abdelkader Messahel did confirm having been in contact with all the parties, at their request. The MNLA rebelled against the fact that wounded Tuaregs had been turned away at the Algerian border and accused the DRS of trying to infiltrate its ranks.
49. Laurence Aïda Ammour, "France, Algeria Diverge on Regional Security," Global Insider: World Politics Review, July 23, 2012.
50. Lahouari Addi, "Les mercenaires du polisario n'ont pas pu se rendre en Libye sans l'aide d'Alger," El Watan, August 29, 2011.
51. Between 1990 and 2001, Othman Tartag (then commander) headed up the Centre Principal Militaire d'Investigation (Main Military Investigation Center, or CPMI in Algiers), one of the main centers where opponents were tortured and killed, which was under a branch of the DRS (army central intelligence unit).
52. Flavien Bourrat, "L'armée algérienne: un Etat dans l'Etat?" in La place et le rôle des armées dans le monde arabe contemporain, ed. Revue Les Champs de Mars (Paris: Institut de Recherche Stratégique de l'Ecole Militaire, Winter 2011), 36.

SIX

The Evolving Role of the United Nations

The Impossible Dual Track?

Jacques Roussellier

> One never goes so far as when one doesn't know where one is going.—
> J. W. von Goethe

The UN involvement with the Western Sahara issue, often fraught with shifting ground, secrecy, coded words and diplomatic opacity, has gone through four distinct, yet at times overlapping phases (statutory, norm setting, crisis management, and conflict resolution). This evolution demonstrates the depth and complexity of the UN's role in addressing the conflict. The UN was first asked to look at the Western Sahara dispute as part of its decolonization mandate. This initial period we refer to as *statutory* involvement (i.e., defining the legal and institutional framework of the conflict) from the time the UN decided to designate the former Spanish colony as non-self-governing territory (1963) and ending with the Moroccan Green March and subsequent International Court of Justice (ICJ) Advisory Opinion in 1975. Based on the positions of the main parties involved and the ICJ ruling, the UN has pursued a more creative approach in defining the legal and political parameters for the future status of Western Sahara. By setting norms and processes that are relevant to the territory (decolonization, self-determination, and independent statehood), the UN exercised an effective, *normative* role through UN General Assembly (UNGA) Resolutions that lay the ground for future settlement plans while simultaneously provided limited *crisis management* through the UN Security Council (UNSC). The UN also deferred the issue to the Organization of African Unity (OAU) for further critical guidelines as the armed conflict took hold (1974–1984). With diplomatic failure at the OAU, the UN resumed a more proactive stand which eventually led to the UN secretary-general's (UNSG) personal mediation efforts to secure a cease-fire and a lasting settlement (1985–1991).

The UN Settlement Plan of June 1990 defines broad parameters for the UN's *conflict resolution* mandate and tasks, leading to stalemate and search for new plans. The UN's approach to the Western Sahara dispute demonstrated a remarkable conceptual evolution and institutional division of labor. In general, the UNGA—supported more ambiguously by the ICJ—had a leading role in framing the statutory and normative perspective on the conflict; the UNSC only stepped in when the dispute reached a regional security crisis dimension and when it eventually required peacemaking efforts, thus leaving at times the UNGA as a default forum.

At the conceptual level of the UN's perspective, the initial decolonization paradigm under the statutory phase gave way to normative and crisis management efforts. At the same time, the concurrent emergence of *realpolitik* with key UN members' concern for the internal stabilization of Morocco ushers in a complex and conflicting dual track approach by the UN, blending—with varying degrees of success—the self-determination paradigm and the political settlement option. This in turn reflects the tension between integrating international legal principles and political reality.

STATUTORY: THE DECOLONIZATION PARADIGM

International pressures for the decolonization of the Western Sahara territory built up throughout the 1960s. As fighting broke out between Moroccan and Algerian forces in the Tindouf region (southwestern Algeria) in September 1963, the newly created OAU responded by establishing a stand-by mediation process to deal with African disputes. A joint Ethiopian-Malian mediation recommended an *ad hoc* commission to apportion responsibility in the Western Sahara conflict and devise proposals for settlement. As the commission's work proved fruitless, Morocco and Algeria were left to negotiate directly. The OAU's early involvement in the Western Sahara dispute was motivated principally by its concern for the legitimacy and intangibility of borders inherited from colonial past and the precedent that an armed conflict on recognized frontiers might entail for the whole continent.[1] It was at Morocco's request in 1962 that the UN initiated consideration of the Western Sahara issue. In 1965 the UNGA issued a resolution approving the provisions of a resolution dated October 16, 1964, of the UN "Special Committee on the Situation with regard to the Implementation of the Declaration of the Granting of Independence to Colonial Countries and Peoples relating to Ifni and Spanish Sahara," which essentially asked Spain to free these territories "from colonial domination and, to this end, to enter into negotiations on the problems relating to sovereignty presented by these two territories."[2] A 1966 UNGA Resolution added similar decolonization language calling for "the return of exiles and the free exercise by the indigenous population of its right to self-determination" and for "the holding of a referendum under United Nations auspices with a view to enabling the indigenous population of the Territory to exercise freely its right to self-determination." Ifni was held to a different decolonization process (albeit sharing with Western Sahara the same UN non-self-governing territory under Spanish Trust) as the resolution requested Spain "to determine with the Government of Morocco, *bearing in mind the aspirations of the indigenous population* (emphasis added), procedures for the transfer of powers in accordance with the provision of General Assembly 1514."[3] Subsequent annual UNGA Resolutions from 1967 to 1974 (with a gap in 1971) did not add any new or substantive language (except in 1972) but reinforced previous calls "to take all the necessary steps to ensure that *only* the indigenous people of the Territory participate in the referendum";[4] the Resolutions also indirectly call on states to refrain from economic exploitation of the Territory and its peoples, including new investment.[5] The 1970 UNGA broadened the scope of the self-determination process by including the need for Spain to consult "with the Governments of Mauritania and Morocco and any other interested party, the procedures for the holding of a referendum under United Nations auspices with a view to enabling the indigenous population of the Sahara to exercise freely its right to self-determination." It also explicitly invited states to refrain from making investment in the Territory "in order to speed the achievement of self-determination by the people of the Sahara."[6] The 1972 UNGA resolution went a step further in linking right to self-determination and right to independence, thus providing for "the procedures for the holding of a referendum under United Nations auspices with a view to enabling the indigenous population of the Sahara to exercise freely its right to self-determination and independence . . ;" it further urged Spain "to take all the necessary steps to ensure that only the indigenous inhabitants exercise their right to self-determination *and independence*, with a view to the decolonization of the Territory."[7]

In the dual track approach that the UN has built over the years on its settlement attempts of the Western Sahara dispute, the decolonization narrative has laid the ground for a historically embedded and ideologically rooted interpretation of the dispute. In the postcolonial, Cold War context of the 1960s and 1970s, the UNGA articulated principle-defined processes and named parties to the dispute: the Western Sahara territory has a defined indigenous population; the indigenous inhabitants of the Territory have an exclusive right to self-determination and independence, and that right can only be achieved through a self-determination referendum, whose outcome is already and implicitly decided by the right to independence; both entitlements (self-determination and independence) define the achievement of the decolonization process.

NORMATIVE: FRAMING ISSUES, ACTORS, AND PROCESSES

The UN moved from establishing the legal framework of the conflict in the 1960s and early 1970s to a more active crisis management approach by the Security Council which included presenting options for solving the crisis. Though the council was not involved in the actual resolution of the Western Sahara dispute, its crisis prevention and management record has set a new and lasting paradigm for future UN's dispute settlement efforts.

External events and political factors also played a role in shaping and intensifying the UN's and ICJ's respective approach to resolving the conflict. In addition, the rapid collapse of the Portuguese colonial possessions in Africa (1974–1975) prompted Spain to renew its commitment to holding a plebiscite under UN supervision with a view to determining the future status of the territory. Spain's unexpected move clearly caught Morocco off guard, as Rabat always favored diplomatic negotiations to secure its sovereignty over the territory out of concern that, with rising nationalist sentiment in the Western Sahara, the population of the territory would fail to overwhelmingly opt to join the Moroccan kingdom.

On December 13, 1974, as a legal controversy arose over the status of Western Sahara between Morocco and Mauritania, the UNGA, under Morocco's initiative, requested an advisory opinion from the ICJ on the legal status of Western Sahara before Spanish colonization. Namely, the UNGA asked the ICJ to answer two questions: (1) Was Western Sahara (Rio de Oro and Sakiet El Hamra) at the time of colonization by Spain a territory belonging to no one (terra nullius)? (2) What were the legal ties between this Territory and the Kingdom of Morocco and the Mauritanian entity?

At the same time, the UNGA urged Spain to postpone the planned referendum to allow the Court to reach an opinion. The 1974 UNGA resolution also for the first time linked the persistence of the dispute to stability in the northwest African region and specifically referred to statements made by Algeria alongside Morocco, Mauritania, and Spain. The UNGA resolution raised the stakes in the Western Sahara dispute, thus paving the way for the UNSC to seize the matter. It also effectively, though indirectly, acknowledged Algeria's stake in the dispute while simultaneously describing Morocco and Mauritania as "interested parties" (para. 2). In addition, the UNGA failed to mention the right to independence as it was repeatedly included in all previous resolutions since 1972, perhaps out of concern for the ICJ's opinion which maintains the validity of the more inclusive decolonization process and principles rather than a straightforward granting of independence. In doing so, the UNGA effectively "de-politicized" the request to the ICJ by keeping the standard UN decolonization language to the "right of the population of the Spanish Sahara to self-determination."[8]

On October 16, 1975, the ICJ rendered its opinion: by unanimous decision it found that the Territory was not *terra nullius* at the time of Spain's colonization and that there were (a) legal ties of allegiance between the Moroccan sultan and some tribes, and (b) rights, including some land rights, which constituted legal ties between the Mauritanian entity and the territory. The court, however, observed that these legal ties did not entail territorial sovereignty between the territory and Morocco or the "Mauritanian entity." The court concluded that there were no legal ties that might impede the right of the population of the Western Sahara to exercise self-determination through the free and genuine expression of the will of the peoples of the territory, as called for by various UNGA Resolutions. In diplomatic terms, the ICJ advisory opinion was hailed as a shrewd compromise between, on the one hand, the sanctity of the right of self-determination, and effective legal ties between Morocco (and Mauritania) and the Western Sahara territory, on the other hand.[9]

The ICJ's advisory opinion reset the contours of a future resolution in several important ways. First, it recognized Morocco's and Mauritania's historical and legal ties to Western Sahara. Second, it acknowledged Algeria's role in the dispute. Third, it broadened the scope of the UN's initial characterization of the dispute as the right to self-determination and independence. Thus the ICJ Advisory Opinion essentially redefined the framework for a future resolution by transforming it from a decolonization question to a political dispute with a number of interested countries, namely, Morocco, Mauritania, and Algeria. On December 10, 1975, the UNGA took note "with appreciation" of the ICJ Advisory Opinion and endorsed the conclusion of the UN Visiting Mission sent by the UNSG to the Western Sahara[10] "that measures should be taken to enable all Saharans originating in the Territory to decide on their future in complete freedom and in an atmosphere of peace and security."[11] The UNGA resolution did not relay the findings of the UN Visiting Mission that "there was an overwhelming consensus among Saharans within the territory in favor of independence and opposing integration with any neighboring country," and there was no mention either of the mission witnessing "mass demonstrations of support for one movement, the Frente Polisario."[12]

CRISIS MANAGEMENT: THE REALIST PARADIGM

Despite setbacks in seeking broad support for Morocco's claims, a politically weakened King Hassan II of Morocco interpreted the ICJ opinion as a vindication of his kingdom's claim. The king, motivated by a precarious domestic and international political standing, exploited nationalist demands at home about the integration of Western Sahara and launched a massive peaceful march of 350,000 civilians into the Western Sahara Territory.

The Green March, as it came to be known, sent off alarm bells in Spain, which petitioned the UNSC to take action, using a language that refers expressively to UNSC actions under chapter VI of the UN Charter. The UNSC for the first time took up the question of Western Sahara in the wake of Morocco's preparations for the Green March. The council, mindful of the impending ICJ Advisory Opinion as well as "negotiations that the parties concerned and interested might undertake," called on "the parties concerned and interested to exercise restraint and moderation and to enable the mission of the Secretary-General to be undertaken in satisfactory conditions." Based on UNGA Resolution 3292 (XXIX) of December 13, 1974, "parties concerned and interested" would refer to Morocco/Mauritania and Algeria, respectively.[13] During the council's debate, a draft resolution presented by Costa Rica asking Morocco to renounce the proposed march was turned down.

In this context, UNSG Waldheim visited Madrid, Rabat, Algiers, and Nouakchott, October 25–28, 1975, but consultations yielded no results beyond Madrid's acknowledgment of trilateral talks with Morocco and Mauritania and support for a solution within a UN framework.[14] The UNSG report also indicated that the UN could provide a temporary administration of the territory "until the wishes of the population could be ascertained."[15] In a meeting with US ambassador to the UN Moynihan on October 29, Waldheim referred to a possible breakthrough on the basis of the West Irian precedent[16] and to Morocco's cancellation of the march, which would be followed by Spain's withdrawal from Western Sahara. An interim UN administration would then organize a self-determination referendum, which the UNSG reportedly described later as a manipulation to hand over the territory to Morocco and Mauritania. Waldheim reportedly confirmed Spain and Algeria's acquiescence but doubted King Hassan could agree on a voting formula for the self-determination referendum, let alone on calling off the march.[17]

Amid reports of Moroccan army's clashes with Polisario forces in the northeastern corner of the territory, on November 2 the Security Council issued a resolution that appeared retrospectively as an "interim" warning that the situation was escalating and that all parties should exercise restraint so as to allow the UNSG to continue his consultations.[18] Madrid initially requested an emergency meeting to convince Morocco to cancel the proposed march. Following a second mission to the region by UNSG's spokesman (November 4–6, 1975), the UNSG reported that Morocco rejected his initial proposals for a temporary UN administration and organization of referendum (the Waldheim Plan). Spain stated it was open to a transfer of sovereignty to the UN with a UN temporary administration but kept the option of a trilateral agreement as a viable alternative.[19]

The United States meanwhile proceeded cautiously in espousing any policy toward the crisis. In a White House meeting on the morning of November 3, Secretary of State Henry Kissinger briefed President Gerald Ford who was accompanied by National Security Adviser Brent Scowcroft. Kissinger analyzed the situation in regional and economic terms, pointing out that Algeria's interests in the Western Sahara's phosphate mines and access to the Atlantic Ocean impelled Madrid to change its initial plan while Algiers threatened to reciprocate on the Middle East conflict. Kissinger was intent on avoiding any US entanglement in a conflict where he saw no positive outcomes either way. Kissinger's preference was to turn the problem over to the UN; he even referred to the Western Irian precedent, suggesting that the UN could manage a speedy turnover to Morocco with a dubious popular consultation.[20]

On the eve of the march (November 5), Spain, looking for a dignified exit, hinted that Morocco could have the Sahara if only it could call off the Green March. At that point, however, it would have been political suicide for King Hassan to cancel the march. In this context, Kissinger concluded that the best option was to turn the Western Sahara dispute to the UN with the understanding that Morocco would eventually get it, as the very survival and stability of the Moroccan kingdom were at stake.[21] On the ground, however, US support for a deal between Madrid and Rabat elicited concerns about Algeria's reactions as well as the depth and intrusiveness of the UN's involvement in the process. Despite these concerns, the United States continued using the Waldheim Plan as a cover for its own diplomatic efforts. Kissinger also understood that King Hassan's failure to secure the Sahara could undermine the very survival of his regime. This was an added reason to shift the resolution of the dispute to the UN and ensure that Morocco's pulling back from the Western Sahara was only temporary. Kissinger hoped for a rigged UN vote that would hand over the Western Sahara to Morocco. Instead the tripartite Madrid Accord put these expectations on a long hold.

The Green March went ahead on November 6, 1975. The president of the UNSC, at the behest of Spain and as authorized by the council, urged the King of Morocco to end the march. The Security Council passed a strongly worded resolution on November 6, which "deplored" the Green March, calling on Morocco "immediately to withdraw from the territory of Western Sahara all the participants in the march." Without specifying military personnel, the council also asked all parties to cooperate fully with the secretary-general's consultations.[22]

The resolution was the last words uttered by the Security Council on the Western Sahara issue until 1988. On November 14, 1975, Spain agreed to transfer the administration of the territory (though not sovereignty) to a temporary tripartite administration made of Spain, Morocco, and Mauritania. On February 26, 1976, Madrid informed the UNSG that it had terminated its presence in Western Sahara and relinquished its responsibilities, though it maintained in a separate communication that it had not transferred sovereignty to Morocco. The transfer of administrative authority did not affect the status of Western Sahara as a non-self-governing territory.

The legality of Spain's relinquishing its status and duty as administering power is debatable. In light of the ICJ Advisory Opinion of June 21, 1971, *Legal Consequences for States of the Continued Presence of South Africa in Namibia (South West Africa)*,[23] it is clear that the UNGA has the exclusive power to terminate a UN Trust Mandate.[24] In the case Namibia/South West Africa, as the Court noted,

> The General Assembly adopted resolution 2145 (XXI) on the termination of the Mandate for South West Africa. Subsequently the Security Council adopted Resolution 276 (1970), which declared the continued presence of South Africa in Namibia to be illegal and called upon States to act accordingly.[25]

As far as Western Sahara is concerned, the UNGA has indicated repeatedly and consistently, including in 1990 at the start of the implementation of the UN Settlement Plan, that the question of Western Sahara was a question of "decolonization." The resolution stated that the process "remained to be completed on the basis of the exercise by the people of Western Sahara of their inalienable right to self-determination and independence."[26] This could be interpreted as inferring that Spain should still be considered legally as administering power—or at least that the issue was in abeyance—in the absence of either a formal termination by the UNGA and a corresponding presidential statement or resolution by the UNSC.

Unlike UNGA, the council's pronouncements, though not addressing explicitly the substance of the Western Sahara dispute, are important indications of a qualitatively different approach to the understanding of a future or possible settlement. In effect, the council's rather cautious and relatively conservative reaction to the Green March was indicative of deeper concerns on the part of the US and Western allies about Morocco's internal regime stability as well as parties' failure to reach a deal on an interim plan under the UN auspices. The UNSG's conflict prevention efforts in contrast went beyond calling for restraint but confined themselves to a tactical cooling off period rather than offering serious steps toward self-determination. Not only did the UN provide cover for the US diplomatically cautious position but it showed no hesitancy in ignoring long-held principles of decolonization and popular referendum on self-determination by embracing a process it knew would not meet some basic democratic requirements. It set the tone for a future UN transition role: without agreement on how to conduct the referendum, its interim intervention was never intended to lead to lasting settlement but to facilitate political accord on sovereignty. Kissinger's conveniently selective interpretation of the Western Sahara ICJ Advisory Opinion (sovereignty shared between Morocco and Mauritania) seems benign compared to Waldheim's sobering readiness to trample consistent norms of self-determination in the name of political *realpolitik*.

As of 1976, the Western Sahara issue reverted to the UNGA marking a supportive and rather symbolic role for the OAU's parallel efforts at finding a lasting settlement. The UNGA, as the default UN lead institution on the Western Sahara issue, used its annual resolution on conflict to (a) reaffirm decolonization and self-determination principles, including a right to independence; (b) express concerns about the situation on the ground; (c) reiterate appreciation for the OAU-led search for a settlement; and (d) add its voice to persuade parties to accept the OAU mediation efforts. In 1980, the UNGA went further in calling on Morocco (a) to withdraw from the territory ("terminate its occupation"); (b) to enter into negotiations (which it later described as "direct")[27] with Polisario on a lasting settlement; and (c) to agree on a cease-fire and organization of a self-determination referendum.[28]

In 1983, in a landmark resolution, the UNGA endorsed the OAU Resolution 104 in which the organization offered for the first time some basic outlines of a settlement plan:

> 2. Urges the parties to the conflict, the Kingdom of Morocco and the POLISARIO Front, to undertake direct negotiations with a view to bringing about a cease fire to create the necessary conditions for a peaceful and fair referendum for self-determination of the people of Western Sahara, a referendum without any administrative or military constraints, under the auspices of the OAU and the United Nations, and calls on the Implementation Committee to ensure the observance of the cease fire....
> 4. Requests the United Nations in conjunction with the OAU to provide a Peace Keeping Force to be stationed in Western Sahara to ensure peace and security during the organization and conduct of the Referendum.[29]

The following year, the UNGA reappropriated the OAU package, without mentioning a peacekeeping force, mindful perhaps of the UNSC's prerogative in this regard, in what would remain its standard position until the UN Settlement Plan. In essence, the UNGA requested:

the parties to the conflict, the Kingdom of Morocco and the Frente Popular para la Liberacion de Saguia el Hamra y de Rio de Oro, to undertake direct negotiation with a view to bringing about a cease-fire to create the necessary conditions for a peaceful and fair referendum without any administrative or military constraints, under the auspices of the Organization of African Unity and the United Nations.[30]

The OAU plan as well as other previous statements and resolutions (1979–1981) provided for the withdrawal of Morocco's and Polisario's forces from the Territory, a cease-fire, neutral, interim government and a self-determination referendum allowing voters to decide on independence or integration with Morocco. With Polisario/SADR taking its seat at the OAU in 1964, Morocco pulled out of the organization, and the OAU credibility in taking the lead with the implementation of the plan was questioned.[31]

In 1985, as the parties (Morocco and Polisario) to the armed conflict increasingly realized their failure to achieve political gains and shifted attention to direct negotiations,[32] the UNGA stepped up pressure on parties, calling directly on the OAU chairman and UNSG to persuade Morocco and Polisario to "negotiate, in the shortest possible time and in conformity with resolution AHG/Res.104 (XIX) and the present resolution, the terms of a cease-fire and the modalities for organizing the said referendum."[33] The resolution provided a broad mandate for the UNSG Perez de Cuellar contacts and facilitation efforts with the parties, which took place in 1985 and early 1986 resulting in proximity talks held in New York in April 1986. A few months later, the UNGA "noted with appreciation the joint good offices process" initiated on April 9 by the OAU and UN on the implementation of relevant OAU and UN Resolutions, which called for parties to enter into direct negotiations with a view to organizing a self-determination referendum.[34] Subsequent UNGA Resolutions in 1987, 1988, and 1989 repeated expression of support for these good offices efforts.

CONFLICT RESOLUTION: THE IMPOSSIBLE DUAL PARADIGM

Following the UNSG's extensive consultations and the report of a UN technical mission on the ground, the diplomatic climate in northwest Africa improved significantly. Algeria and Morocco resumed diplomatic relations, while the UNSG outlined several settlement proposals which included the appointment of a special representative in charge of an interim administration and peacekeeping forces. More importantly, the provisions led to a cease-fire, confinement of troops, exchange of prisoners or war, and a census of the Western Sahara population, which posed the option of a self-determination referendum on independence or integration with Morocco. Both parties, Morocco and Polisario, agreed to abide by the outcome of the referendum and to cooperate with the UN in supervising the cease-fire and in organizing the referendum.

The UNSC "taking note of the agreement in principle" asked the UNSG to appoint a Special Representative and report back to the council as soon as possible "on the holding of a referendum for self-determination of the people of Western Sahara and on ways and means to ensure the organization and supervision of such a referendum by the United Nations in cooperation with the Organization of the African Unity."[35] By UN parlance, this represents the weakest form of referring to an agreement in principle that was not signed but accepted separately by parties. The council's focus on the organization and supervision of the self-determination process indicates deep anxiety as to the chance and practicality of a possible accord on voter definition and referendum result.

The council waited almost two years before it finally approved the UN Settlement Proposals as contained in the UNSG's report and "as accepted by the parties on 30 August 1988"; it also fully supported the UNSG's good offices.[36] Incidentally, the UNSC confirmed Morocco and Polisario as parties to the conflict, without including Algeria explicitly. Despite two technical missions and with the UN distracted by the Iraq's invasion of Kuwait, no agreement could be reached on such critical issues as voter registration for the referendum and confinement of troops. As UNSG Pérez de Cuéllar confided in his memoirs, Morocco and Polisario had conflicting expectations about the role of the UN during the interim period. Meanwhile, at the UN, the task force charged with drafting the implementation plan did not communicate with the UNSG and his close aide who were deeply involved in negotiations with the parties. Pérez de Cuéllar even admitted that while working on the settlement plan he had discussed the possibility of autonomy for Western Sahara within Morocco, which King Hassan and the Algerian president reportedly endorsed.[37] Thus UNSC's anxious support for the settlement may have been less candid and wholehearted than some council members might have wished. In fact the settlement plan could benefit from the council's support for two contradictory reasons. Some members, attached to the decolonization and self-determination track, wanted the plan to go ahead, providing sufficient guarantees for Polisario and independence prospect. Others thought the plan was only instrumental in bringing parties (1) to acknowledge the impossibility of an agreement on who should qualify for the referendum and (2) to explore the possibility of a political agreement, which essentially meant autonomous status within Morocco sovereignty.

On the contentious issue of the right to vote in the self-determinantion referedum, the Settlement Plan included a fairly sketchy agreement: "All Saharans counted in the 1974 census taken by the Spanish authorities and aged 18 years or over will have the right to vote in the referendum,"[38] and that the United Nations High Commissioner for Refugees (UNHCR) will assist in providing a census of Saharan refugees living outside the Territory, while the UNSG is asked to "set up, in consultation with the current Chairman of OAU, an identification commission responsible for carefully and scrupulously reviewing the 1974 census and updating it."[39] The voting was to be by secret ballot and the people of Western Sahara were to "choose, freely and democratically, between independence and integration with Morocco."[40] In this regard, the Western Sahara Settlement Plan stands in sharp contrast with South West Africa/Namibia and East Timor, both former UN non-self-governing territories that have achieved self-determination through independence.

In the case of South West Africa/Namibia, the transition to independence was initially framed by UNSC Resolution 435 (1978), which included a Settlement Plan that provided for universal and secret ballot for the election of the Constituent Assembly. In 1982, the Contact Group on South West African/Namibia and parties to the conflict agreed on supplementary principles for the Constitutional Assembly elections. The December 1988 accord among Angola, Cuba, and South Africa paved the way for the transition period and the successful organization of elections.[41]

For East Timor, the agreement signed by Indonesia and Portugal on May 5, 1999, mandated the UN to organize and conduct a popular consultation on accepting or rejecting a constitutional framework that provided for a special autonomy within Indonesia for East Timor. The parties agreed that the popular consultation was to be run on the basis of direct, secret, and universal ballot; the parties also agreed on who should be eligible to vote.[42]

Notwithstanding the fact that neither of these self-determination processes included the three options as required by UNGA Resolution 1514 (XV) of December 14, 1960, the transition and settlement plans in Namibia and East Timor were predicated on one or several political agreements. These agreements included critically definition of voter eligibility and referendum questions. In this context and in hindsight, it is obvious that the UN Settlement Plan for the Western Sahara had a different intent: lacking fundamental agreement on principles and processes for the envisaged self-determination referendum, the plan was expected to assist the parties in finding common ground on voter eligibility and voter lists. In fact, such an agreement should have been secured prior to the start of the transition process. Thus the Settlement Plan was a misnomer, as it only delayed and effectively deferred the resolution of one essential element of a putative peace accord. For members of the UNSC that supported a decolonization process, the prospect of reaching a compromise among the parties on the organization of a self-determination referendum may have been seriously entertained, while other countries in the council expected the Settlement Plan to induce parties to a stalemate, which would then pave the way for a political agreement on the future status of Western Sahara.

From 1992 to 1996 the UN settlement process faced tremendous challenges in particular on identification of voters for the referendum. This was the cornerstone of the UNSC biannual resolutions—except in 1992, where the council did not take up the question of Western Sahara, and 1996, when it issued four resolutions—taking a supportive stand on the UNSG's efforts at finding solutions and compromises on voter eligibility and other settlement plan implementation issues, and calling for the parties full cooperation with the UN Mission on the ground. The United Nations Mission for the Referendum in Western Sahara (MINURSO) was established by Security Council resolution 690 of April 29, 1991, in accordance with settlement proposals accepted on August 30, 1988, by Morocco and the Polisario Front. The last two resolutions in 1996 included requests by the council to seek "alternative steps, in the framework of the Settlement Plan, should there be no meaningful progress towards removing the obstacles to the implementation of the Plan,"[43] which echoes the previous resolution's call on the parties "to consider additional ways to create confidence between themselves to remove obstacles to implementation of the Settlement Plan."[44]

While these elliptic appeals stop short of calling for alternative solutions, they are significant in acknowledging impasses in the plan and seeking alternative means while remaining within the Settlement Plan framework. In fact they should be construed as coded language for direct talks between Morocco and Polisario. In his report to the UNSC dated May 9, 1996, the UNSG recommended the suspension of the work of the UN Mission's Identification Commission together with reduction in civilian police and military personnel, but retained a rather rhetorical search for solution with voter identification. He also proposed to retain a political office in Western Sahara, which "will maintain a dialogue with the parties and the two neighboring countries (Algeria and Mauritania) and will facilitate any other effort that could help set the parties on the course towards an agreed formula for the resolution of their differences."[45] Incidentally, the offer of dialogue sets a format that will remain to-date: Morocco and Polisario as parties to the conflict, and Algeria/Mauritania as neighboring states (in fact, interested parties). In his previous report, the UNSG, taking note of the stalemate on voter identification, stated that he "remained at the full disposal of the parties, should they agree to hold talks in whatever format, in order to facilitate a settlement of their conflict."[46] Both comments by the UNSG are indicative of the Settlement Plan stalemate on reaching ripeness for direct talks, though the UNSC found a formula that reintegrated the idea with an ambiguous reference to settlement framework, which the UNSG reports did not contain. Hence the role of the UNSC should be assessed as both supportive of the

Settlement Plan and its technical implementation as well as being open to negotiations outside of the plan's narrow parameters.

The new UNSG Kofi Annan commissioned a policy review which took stock of the Western Sahara impasse and the parties' responsiveness to reduced UN involvement on the ground. The appointment of former US Secretary of State James A. Baker III as UNSG's Personal Envoy for Western Sahara created a new dynamic that allowed for the resumption of voter identification in December 1997 and the resolution of their contentious issues (code of conduct for the referendum campaign, confinement of Polisario troops, reduction of Moroccan troops, refugees, prisoners of war and political prisoners) under the Houston Agreements adopted in September 1997. In this context the UNSC took a backseat approach, supporting and endorsing Baker's efforts, though the renewed process was only breathing space for yet another deadlock on voter identification to occur later. The UN was again forced to propose technical solutions to the problems raised by Morocco regarding the identification of some 65,000 Moroccan applicants from contested groupings. The "package" of measures, which dealt with the identification of the contested groupings, the appeals process and other issues for the transitional period, was finally but conditionally accepted in 1999. The UNSC confirmed *expressis verbis* an earlier assessment by the UNSG,[47] expressing "concern that the problems posed by the current number of candidates who have exercised their right of appeal and the opposing positions taken by the parties on the issue of admissibility seem to allow little possibility of holding the referendum before 2002 or even beyond" (UNSC Resolution 1282 of December 14, 1999, para. 2).

The completion of the identification process at the end of 1999 found 86,412 applicants eligible and 131,038 appeals to be processed. The following UNSG's report, in a sweeping and candid review of nine years of UN operations in Western Sahara, made three critical observations. On the issue of the voter identification process, it concluded that "throughout the identification process, the cooperation of one or the other party with MINURSO has been predicated upon its perception of how the results might be favouring the other side." On the question of appeals, it commented that "[t]he respective positions of the two parties do not augur well for an early resolution of the issue of admissibility of appeals for hearings. Under these circumstances, the timetable envisaged is no longer valid, as indicated in my previous report, and the date of the referendum, which has been repeatedly postponed since 1991, can still not be set with certainty at this juncture."[48] The report further noted that "experience has shown that each time the United Nations has proposed a technical solution to bridge the parties' differing interpretation of a given provision of the settlement plan, a new difficulty, requiring yet another round of protracted consultations, arises."[49] The UNSG then requested his Personal Envoy to "consult with the parties and, taking into account existing and potential obstacles, to explore ways and means to achieve an early, durable and agreed resolution of their dispute, which would define their respective obligations."[50] This was asking the UNSC for a clear mandate for negotiation on a political agreement. On February 29, the UNSC, "Noting the concern expressed in the report about the possibility of achieving a smooth and consensual implementation of the Settlement Plan and agreements adopted by the parties," supported the UNSG's intention to "ask his Personal Envoy to consult the parties and, taking into account existing and potential obstacles, to explore ways and means to achieve an early, durable and agreed resolution of their dispute."[51] This was a balanced statement in which the council urged parties to cooperate and achieve a lasting solution to their disagreement over the Settlement Plan but concurrently mandated the search for a negotiated agreement on the Western Sahara dispute. This was vintage UNSC approach to the Western Sahara dispute: leveraging the expected failure of the self-determination referendum process with a view to securing greater commitment to a negotiated solution. If the resolution's language was ambiguous, the following UNSC resolution left no doubt as to the "fundamental differences between the parties over the interpretation of the main provisions of the Settlement Plan remain to be resolved" and gave Baker a dual mandate "to try to resolve the multiple problems relating to the implementation of the Settlement Plan and to try to agree upon a mutually acceptable political solution to their dispute over Western Sahara."[52] However, UNSC Resolution 1342 of February 27, 2001, in addition to reiterating the same expectations about the Settlement Plan and mutually acceptable solution, contained stronger language on the need to continue support for the implementation of the settlement, including "a free, fair and impartial referendum," though it also noted that "fundamental differences between the parties over the interpretation of the main provisions of the Settlement Plan remain to be resolved."[53]

In September 2000, Morocco had made its first offer to discuss with the Polisario Front a solution of the dispute outside the Settlement Plan (i.e., process leading to self-determination referendum). It also informed the UNSC of its intention to grant autonomy to Western Sahara, but failed to follow up with concrete proposals. As a result, in June 2001, Baker shared with the UNSC the draft Framework Agreement on the Status of Western Sahara (FA), which he had already presented to the parties. The FA outlined a possible political solution involving devolution of authority to the inhabitants of the territory with final status to be determined by a referendum five years later. In contrast with the Settlement Plan, the FA envisioned a referendum about the status of Western Sahara (and not about independence). Morocco supported the draft framework, but Polisario and Algeria expressed strong reservations, sending proposals on overcoming obstacles to the implementation of the Settlement Plan and memorandum on the status of Western Sahara, respectively. The contentious issue was not so much about the extent of exclusive local competences as the fact the FA only envisioned a referendum on the status of Western Sahara, and not independence. The UNSC's reaction was to remain noncommittal, acknowledging all four options on the table: MINURSO and the 1990 Settlement Plan, recent proposals from the Polisario and Algeria, and the FA. The council noted, however, that the latter provided "for a substantial devolution of authority, which does not foreclose self-determination, and which indeed provides for it."[54] Only the FA elicited such a substantive comment from the council. The council eventually encouraged "parties to discuss the draft FA and negotiate any specific changes they would like to see in this proposal, as well as to discuss any other proposal for a political solution, which may be put forward by the parties, to arrive at a mutually acceptable agreement."[55] It also added that these discussions should consider Polisario's proposals.

In February 2002, the secretary-general presented to the Security Council four options to resolve the current impasse on a nonnegotiable basis: (1) continue with the Settlement Plan; (2) revise the draft FA; (3) explore division of the Western Sahara territory; and (4) terminate the UN mission in the Western Sahara. Morocco, only under duress, supported option two; Polisario predictably supported option one; and Algeria favored option three. All parties however agreed that MINURSO should not be terminated. As to the council itself, its response was to reiterate its determination to "secure a just, lasting and mutually acceptable political solution which will provide for the self-determination of the people of Western Sahara in the context of arrangements consistent with the principles and purposes of the Charter of the United Nations." The council also underlined "the validity of the Settlement Plan, while noting the fundamental differences between the parties in implementing the Plan." Finally, the council invited Baker to pursue his efforts to find a political solution and expressed "its readiness to consider any approach that would provide for self-determination."[56] This was again vintage UN approach in neither supporting nor abandoning the self-determination referendum option while hoping for progress on a political and negotiated solution. The council suggested that a political solution would only be acceptable if it included a self-determination referendum, thus putting tremendous pressure on Morocco, which favored a negotiated solution without a referendum on independence.

In January 2003, Baker presented to the parties a revised draft FA: the Peace Plan for the Self-Determination of the People of Western Sahara. The plan provided for a referendum on the final status of the territory for *bona fide* residents of the territory that would ask three questions: independence, integration with Morocco, and self-government or autonomy. The proposed voter list included three overlapping voter rolls: (1) MINURSO's provisional list of voters of December 1999; (2) the UNHCR repatriation list of October 2000; and (3) those persons who have resided continuously in the territory since December 30, 1999, as determined by the UN, despite initial attempts to reinstate the Settlement Plan. Polisario officially accepted the plan in July 2003. Morocco could not accept that the final referendum included the independence option; it officially rejected the plan in April 2004. Algeria adopted a supportive stand. On July 31, 2003, the UNSC unanimously adopted Resolution 1495, which supported "the Peace Plan for self-determination of the people of Western Sahara as an optimum political solution on the basis of agreement between the two parties."[57] For the first time the UNSC resolution failed to mention or refer to the Settlement Plan, though the resolution and all future resolutions reiterated the 2002 language about "mutually acceptable political solution, which will provide for the self-determination of the people of Western Sahara in the context of arrangements consistent with the principles and purposes of the Charter of the United Nations." The Settlement Plan was effectively replaced by the 2003 Baker Peace Plan, to which the Resolution added the 2002 introductory paragraph containing explicit references to self-determination and decolonization principles.

On April 29, 2004, the Security Council adopted resolution 1541. While expressing support for the Peace Plan, it also "reaffirms its strong support for the efforts of the Secretary-General and his Personal Envoy in order to achieve a mutually acceptable political solution to the dispute over Western Sahara"; thus effectively modifying its early and exclusive endorsement of the Peace Plan. Reflecting Morocco's rejection of the plan and some key council members' concerns, the resolution "recycled" an operative paragraph the 2002 language contained in the resolution's introduction ("mutually acceptable solution"), without reference to self-determination. The council thus implied support for a political agreement without provision for self-determination referendum. The following UNSC Resolution 1598 (2005) referred to "political solution" in one of its perambulatory paragraphs only.

With the resignation of UNSG's Personal Envoy James Baker in June 2005, the UN and US mediation efforts came to an abrupt end. Morocco's offer of its autonomy plan for Western Sahara on April 11, 2007—one day after Polisario presented its own proposal—relaunched the process, albeit on shifty ground, owing to changing diplomatic and political context. On April 30, 2007, UN Security Council Resolution 1754 "took note" of the Moroccan and Polisario proposals, "welcoming serious and credible Moroccan efforts to move the process forward towards resolution," which should not be interpreted *stricto sensu* as meaning the council viewed the Moroccan autonomy plan as "serious and credible." In addition, the council asked parties to start negotiations without preconditions "with a view to achieving a just, lasting and mutually acceptable political solution, which will provide for the self-determination of the people of Western Sahara." This operative paragraph remains highly ambiguous as it combined reference to the Moroccan autonomy plan, which considers that a final vote on the plan would constitute the free exercise by the Western Sahara populations of their right to self-determination; and the Peace Plan, which provides for a final referendum with the independence option. Meanwhile the UNGA, which has reiterated since December 2003 and until 2007 "its support of the peace plan for self-determination of the people of Western Sahara as an optimum political solution on the basis of agreement between the two parties,"[58] urged parties to start negotiations without preconditions "with a view to achieving a just, lasting and mutually acceptable political solution, which will provide for the self-determination of the people of Western Sahara."[59]

What has then been achieved with the 2001 FA and the 2003 Peace Plan? The net impact remains ambiguous: on the one hand, the 1990 Settlement Plan is now obsolete (though it is still provides the mandate for MINURSO—the UN Mission in Western Sahara) but stalemate among the two parties has shifted from voter registration and eligibility to the scope of the referendum (political agreement or/and independence). On the other hand, depending on one's perspective, it could be seen either as a regression from the 1990 Settlement Plan process or progress toward a political accord. The UN's dual track approach has not yet converged to re-reconciling international law principles and political reality. This actually begs the question of achievement of self-determination through referendum or political agreement. Staying with the UN and looking at UN (formerly League of Nations) trust territories, which, together with other non-self-governing territories, were deemed by the UN to have achieved self-determination, the overall picture is less than convincing. In fact, none of the eleven trust territories which have achieved self-determination, as decided by the UN, had had a referendum or plebiscite on the three options of independence, free association, or integration/status quo, though six of them had had a plebiscite or referendum that directly or indirectly entails a vote on independence. In all instances of actual plebiscite/referendum, (1) a prior political agreement on free association (Nauru, Pacific Islands), (2) a draft constitution or constitutional amendment amounting to independence (Togoland-French, Cameroon-French, and Western Samoa), or (3) a decision to join neighboring countries as a way to gain independence (Togoland-British, Cameroon-British, Papua-New Guinea, Somaliland) is submitted for approval. In all other cases, independence was granted directly by the Administering Authority or the UNGA without a referendum (Somaliland),[60] or as a result of a political agreement between the Administering Authority and the non-self-governing territory (Tanganyika, Papua-New Guinea, and Nauru). It is thus worth noting that there is no case of plebiscite or referendum held on a political agreement that stipulates independence. In none of these instances, where no referendum took place, even on the political accord, or in the case of Ruanda-Urundi and Somaliland, where independence was granted, did the UNGA or the UNSC object to the lack of popular consultation. Only with regard to Nauru did the UNGA specify that the United Kingdom, as "Administering Authority has complied with the request of the representatives of the Nauruan people for full and unqualified independence."[61] Furthermore, the UN did not criticize the holding of referendums on independence for failing to include the alternative options nor did it challenge referendums on free association for lack of providing a vote on independence and integration (Pacific Islands). It is thus clear that, on the basis of self-determination practice for these eleven UN trust territories, the UN has never required a three-option referendum; it did not even ask for a referendum when independence was the expected outcome, whether independence was borne out of constitutional or territorial changes or directly awarded by colonial powers or the UNGA. When free association compacts were approved for three of the US trust territories of the Pacific Islands (with a US territory status for the Commonwealth of the Northern Mariana Islands), no alternative status was offered.

The UNSC noted that it was:

> *Satisfied* that the peoples of the Federated States of Micronesia, the Marshall Islands and the Northern Mariana Islands have freely exercised their right to self-determination in approving their respective new status agreements in plebiscites observed by visiting missions of the Trusteeship Council and that, in addition to these plebiscites, the duly constituted legislatures of these entities have adopted resolutions approving the respective new status agreements, thereby freely expressing their wish to terminate the status of these entities as parts of the Trust Territory.[62]

Similar language was used by the council when it endorsed the conclusion of a Compact of Free Association in the case of Palau four years later.[63] Thus the UNSC has formulated a new self-determination paradigm: (a) a plebiscite on a political agreement must take place, (b) the plebiscite has to be observed and validated by UN missions, and (c) the new status agreement has to be approved by legitimate legislatures (elected assemblies).[64]

In this context, it might be worth revisiting the 1975 Western Sahara ICJ Advisory Opinion's comments that:

> The validity of the principle of self-determination, defined as the need to pay regard to the freely expressed will of peoples, is not affected by the fact that in certain cases the General Assembly has dispensed with the requirement of consulting the inhabitants of a given territory. Those instances were based either on the consideration that a certain population did not constitute a "people" entitled to self-determination or on the conviction that a consultation was totally unnecessary, in view of special circumstances.[65]

If there is no possible agreement on who the people of Western Sahara is, shouldn't the court then be asked to establish whether a political agreement on the future status of Western Sahara—as agreed by the parties and approved freely and democratically by the people of Western Sahara—could be considered by the UNGA as sufficient evidence of achievement of self-determination? The answer to the question would help to determine the validity of the current Moroccan autonomy proposal or sustain the mandatory inclusion of self-determination referendum on independence in any future political accord.

NOTES

1. Tony Hodges and Anthony G. Pazzanita, *Historical Dictionary of the Western Sahara*, 2nd ed. (Metuchen, NJ: Scarecrow, 1994); John Damis, "The O.A.U. and Western Sahara," in *The OAU After Twenty Years*, eds. Yassin el-Ayouti and I. William Zartman (New York: Praeger, 1984), 286–95.

2. United Nations General Assembly, "Resolution 2072 (XX) (December 16, 1965)."

3. United Nations General Assembly, "Resolution 2229 (XXI) (December 20, 1966)."

4. United Nations General Assembly, "Resolution 2428 (XXIII) (December 18, 1968)" (emphasis added).

5. United Nations General Assembly, "Resolution 2591 (XXIV) (December 16, 1969)," para. (c).

6. United Nations General Assembly, "Resolution 2711 (XXV) (December 14, 1970)," para. 6–7.

7. United Nations General Assembly, "Resolution 2983 (XXVII) (December 14, 1972)," para. 5, 5(b) (emphasis added).

8. Reference to "right to independence" did not appear in subsequent UNGA Resolutions in 1975, 1976, and 1977, but resurfaced in 1978 with the much strongly worded UNGA Resolution 33/31 of December 13, 1978; United Nations General Assembly, Resolution 3292 (XXIX) (December 13, 1974).

9. Tony Hodges, *Western Sahara: The Roots of a Desert War* (Westport, CT: Lawrence Hill, 1983).

10. Not to be confused with the visiting mission that the General Assembly has been trying to dispatch to the territory since 1966, as stated in UNGA Resolution 2229 (XXI) of December 20, 1966.

11. United Nations General Assembly, "Resolution 3458 (XXX) (December 10, 1975)," para. 5."

12. Hodges and Pazzanita, *Historical Dictionary of the Western Sahara*.

13. United Nations Security Council, "Resolution 377 (October 22, 1975)," S/RES/377.

14. *United Nations Yearbook*, 1975.

15. Hodges and Pazzanita, *Historical Dictionary of the Western Sahara*.

16. In the case of the decolonization of West Irian (West New Guinea), which opposed the Netherlands as administering power, and Indonesia from 1954 to 1969, an agreement was reached and approved by the UNGA that provided for the transfer of West Irian to Indonesia in 1963, followed by a popular consultation in 1969. However, the 1969 consultation involved a vote by regional councils only on remaining with Indonesia or severing ties. Thus, "the integration of West Irian into Indonesia amounted to a substantial denial of self-determination." Antonio Cassese, *Self-Determination of Peoples: A Legal Reappraisal* (Cambridge, UK: Cambridge University Press, 1995).

17. Jacob Mundy, "Neutrality or Complicity? The United States and the 1975 Moroccan Takeover of the Spanish Sahara," *Journal of North African Studies* 11, no. 3 (2006): 275–305.
18. United Nations Security Council, "Resolution 379 (November 2, 1975)," S/RES/379.
19. Hodges and Pazzanita, *Historical Dictionary of the Western Sahara.*
20. Mundy, "Neutrality or Complicity?"
21. Mundy, "Neutrality or Complicity?"; Robert Parker, *North Africa: Regional Tensions and Strategic Concerns* (New York: Praeger, 1987).
22. United Nations Security Council, "Resolution 380 (November 6, 1975)," S/RES/380.
23. International Court of Justice, *Advisory Opinion: Legal Consequences for States of the Continued Presence of South Africa in Namibia (South West Africa) Notwithstanding Security Council Resolution 276 (1970)* (June 21, 1971).
24. Ralph Wilde, *International Territorial Administration: How Trusteeship and the Civilizing Mission Went Away* (Oxford, UK: Oxford University Press, 2008), 143–90; John Dugard, *The SWA/Namibia Dispute: Documents and Scholarly Writings on the Controversy between South Africa and the United Nations* (Berkeley: University of California Press, 1973), 376–446.
25. International Court of Justice, *Western Sahara Advisory Opinion* (October 16, 1975), para. 86.
26. United Nations General Assembly, "Resolution 45/21 (November 20, 1990)," A/RES/45/21.
27. United Nations General Assembly, "Resolution 38/40 (December 7, 1983)," A/RES/38/40.
28. United Nations General Assembly, "Resolution 35/19 (November 11, 1980)," A/RES/65/19.
29. United Nations General Assembly, "Resolution 38/40 (December 7, 1983)," A/RES/38/40.
30. United Nations General Assembly, "Resolution 39/40 (December 5, 1984)," A/RES/39/40, para. 3.
31. John Damis, "The O.A.U. and Western Sahara"; Yahia H. Zoubir and Daniel Voltman, eds., *International Dimensions of the Western Sahara Conflict* (Westport, CT: Praeger, 1993).
32. I. William Zartman, *Ripe for Resolution: Conflict and Intervention in Africa* (New York: Oxford University Press, 1985).
33. United Nations General Assembly, "Resolution 40/50 (December 2, 1985), A/RES/40/50, para. 5.
34. United Nations General Assembly, "Resolution 41/16 (October 31, 1986)," A/RES/41/16.
35. United Nations Security Council, "Resolution 621 (September 20, 1988)," S/RES/621, para. 2.
36. United Nations Security Council, "Resolution 658 (June 27, 1990)," S/RES/658, para. 1–2.
37. Anna Theofilopoulou, "The United Nations and Western Sahara: A Never-ending Affair," *United States Institute of Peace*, Special Report 166 (July 2006): 4–8.
38. United Nations Security Council, *Report of the Secretary General on the Situation Concerning Western Sahara* (June 18, 1990), S/21360, para. 24.
39. United Nations Security Council, *Report of the Secretary General on the Situation Concerning Western Sahara* (June 18, 1990), para. 25.
40. United Nations Security Council, *Report of the Secretary General on the Situation Concerning Western Sahara* (June 18, 1990), para. 31.
41. National Democratic Institute for International Affairs, *Nation-Building: The UN and Namibia* (Washington, DC: National Democratic Institute for international Affairs, 1990); Chester A. Crocker, *High Noon in Southern Africa: Making Peace in a Rough Neighborhood* (Johannesburg: Johnathan Ball Publishers, 1993).

140   Chapter 6

42. United Nations Security Council, *Report of the Secretary General on the Question of East Timor* (May 5, 1999), S/1999/513.
43. United Nations Security Council, "Resolution 1084 (November 27, 1996)," S/RES/1084, para. 8.
44. United Nations Security Council, "Resolution 1056 (May 29, 1996)," S/RES/1056, para. 9.
45. United Nations Security Council, *Report of the Secretary General on the Situation Concerning Western Sahara* (May 8, 1996), S/1996/343, para. 36.
46. United Nations Security Council, *Report of the Secretary General on the Situation Concerning Western Sahara* (May 8, 1996), para. 31.
47. United Nations Security Council, *Report of the Secretary General on the Situation Concerning Western Sahara* (December 6, 1999), S/1999/1219, para. 28.
48. United Nations Security Council, *Report of the Secretary General on the Situation Concerning Western Sahara* (February 17, 2000), S/2000/, para. 33–34.
49. United Nations Security Council, *Report of the Secretary General on the Situation Concerning Western Sahara* (February 17, 2000), para. 35.
50. United Nations Security Council, *Report of the Secretary General on the Situation Concerning Western Sahara* (February 17, 2000), para. 37.
51. United Nations Security Council, "Resolution 1292 (February 29, 2000)," S/RES/1292, para. 2.
52. United Nations Security Council, "Resolution 1309 (July 25, 2000)," S/RES/1309, para. 1.
53. United Nation Security Council, "Resolution 1342 (February 27, 2001)," S/RES/1342.
54. United Nations Security Council, "Resolution 1359 (June 29, 2001)," S/RES/1359.
55. United Nations Security Council, "Resolution 1359 (June 29, 2001)," para. 2–3.
56. United Nations Security Council, "Resolution 1429 (July 30, 2002)," S/RES/1429.
57. United Nations Security Council, Resolution 1495 (July 31, 2003)," S/RES/1492, para. 1.
58. United Nations General Assembly, "Resolution 58/109 (December 9, 2003)," A/RES/58/109.
59. United Nations General Assembly, "Resolution 62/116 (December 17, 2007)," A/RES/62/116.
60. British Somaliland was first granted independence by the United Kingdom, followed a few days later by Italy bestowing independence on Italian Somalia (June 26 and July 1, 1960, respectively). In 1961, the independence of Ruanda-Urundi was approved by constitutional referendum.
61. United Nations General Assembly, "Resolution 2347 (XXII) (December 19, 1967)."
62. United Nations Security Council, "Resolution 683 (December 22, 1990)," S/RES/683.
63. United Nations Security Council, "Resolution 956 (November 10, 1994)," S/RES/956.
64. Arnold Leibowitz, *Defining Status: A Comprehensive Analysis of United States Territorial Relations* (The Hague: Kluwer Law International, 1989), 485–637; Stanley K. Laughlin, *The Law of United States Territories and Affiliated Jurisdictions* (Rochester, NY: Lawyers Cooperative Publishing, 1995).
65. International Court of Justice, *Western Sahara Advisory Opinion* (October 16, 1975), para. 59.

SEVEN

Diplomatic Struggle in Africa and Europe over the Western Sahara Conflict

Antonin Tisseron

On August 30, 1988, the UN's proposed peace plan for the Western Sahara region was approved by Morocco and Polisario. It took an additional three years of military confrontation before a cease-fire agreement was signed. However, despite the signing of this agreement in September 1991, the conflict has not ended but has entered into a new phase.

Rather than engaging in any real negotiations, Morocco, the Polisario Front and its ally Algeria continue the fight in diplomatic venues. Diplomatic quarrels have taken place mainly over the conditions for holding a referendum, originally scheduled in January 1992.[1] Although the UN is at the center of the diplomatic conflict between the three main stakeholders (Morocco, Polisario, and Algeria), the international organization is not the only place of confrontation. Indeed, Africa and Europe are themselves additional battlefields as proponents of the various positions search for intermediaries that may have an impact on the conflict to promote their interests. Although no longer a member within the former Organization of African Unity (OAU)—now African Union (AU)—Morocco pursues efforts to expel the Sahrawi Arab Democratic Republic (SADR) from the organization and obtain official recognition of its sovereignty over Western Sahara. For their part, those favoring Saharan independence insist that those people have the freedom to exercise their right to self-determination and ask the AU and the European Union (EU) to take tough actions against Morocco. They want to force Morocco to hold a referendum on terms favorable to them.

This internationalization of the conflict in Western Sahara did not start with the 1991 cease-fire. The strategies used by the protagonists to gain international support are well known and developments of the last twenty years illustrate this as both are seeking allies to their cause. From the early days of armed conflict, to the hit and run raids that drove Mauritania out of the equation, and Morocco's erection of a berm to limit Polisario access to the territory, the lines of contention shifted from warfare during the first two decades after the end of the Cold War to the diplomatic arena. Over time, the results of these diplomatic offensives have had mixed results. On the one hand, Morocco is less isolated on the African continent and the Polisario Front's self-proclaimed government—SADR—has lost the support of a number of states. Nevertheless, African and European states remain strongly divided about the conflict, which contributes to a lack of resolution on the international scene.

This article examines the ramifications in Africa and Europe of the conflict over the Western Sahara. It examines three interrelated areas of analysis. First of all, it describes the strategies that the protagonists to the conflict have adopted in order to obtain international support; it then questions those strategies by examining their impact on the main African and European states engaged on the issue; and finally, it puts into perspective the current impasse of the dynamics of the conflict. The first part deals with the diplomatic power struggles within the OAU and the AU, while the second part focuses on the European continent and especially the role of France and Spain, the former colonial powers.

POLICY DIVISIONS ON THE AFRICAN CONTINENT

The period from 1991 until now has been punctuated by several events that changed the nature of the parties' diplomatic efforts to resolve the conflict. In 1999, King Hassan II, who orchestrated the Green March in 1975 and had ruled Morocco for nearly four decades, died at the age of seventy. His son, King Mohammed VI, who ascended the throne, brought new ideas and policies regarding the Sahara. Among them was Morocco's proposal to find a "third way" based on Saharan autonomy within the kingdom (2007). However, even if the diplomatic effort by Morocco since 1990 is to delegitimize the SADR, the continent remains divided and the overall situation frozen.

The SADR in the OAU: The Original Breakdown

The regional impact of the Western Sahara conflict on the African political scene took place long before the cease-fire of 1991. Since the 1970s, the claims of the Polisario Front were discussed in the OAU Council of Ministers as well as the Conference of Heads of State and Governments of Africa. Also, several attempts at good offices or mediation were undertaken. In October 1977, Colonel Gaddafi suggested the formation of a Maghreb confederation to allow for the joint operation of Saharan resources. A few weeks later, on November 25, Hosni Mubarak, then Vice-President of Egypt, traveled to Algiers, Rabat, and Nouakchott to try to reach an agreement between the parties—without success.

To support the Polisario Front's claims to represent the Sahrawi people, the Algerian authorities challenged the Moroccan position by calling for it to be handled within the framework of the OAU. The UN supported this position and decided to refer the Saharan issue to the African organization pursuant to articles 33 and 52 of the UN Charter.[2] Following the agreement signed between Mauritania and the Polisario Front in 1976, and at the same time fearing the SADR's admission to the OAU, which had been narrowly avoided in 1980, Hassan II returned to the negotiating table. Although from his point of view the Saharan issue had been closed by the Green March, he announced at the Nairobi Summit in June 1981 that he agreed to hold a referendum.[3]

Hassan II's announcement did not immediately put an end to the deadlock since the Polisario Front was hostile to the king's change in policy for two reasons: First, it was not the first time the Sahrawi independence movement would have been the subject of a referendum. Spain had previously promised to hold one—but did not fulfill its promises. The UN had also recommended a referendum but lacked the necessary resources to implement it. In both cases, the refusal of Morocco was a key factor preventing the holding of the referendum. With this in mind, Morocco's renewed interest in this solution in Western Sahara was regarded as a rather dishonest maneuver.[4] Second, the direct consequences of King Hassan II's initiative, i.e., the creation by the OAU of an implementation committee[5] to enforce the cease-fire and organize the referendum, appeared to be a way of ensuring that the referendum would not be held in accordance with the Polisario's demand for outright independence, and also posed a danger to the Polisario's diplomatic offensive, since the OAU admission procedure to enable the Polisario Front to join the organization was now set aside.

Two other meetings held in the Kenyan capital in August 1981 (Nairobi II) and in February 1982 (Nairobi III) form part of the evolving scenario. During these meetings, the Polisario and Morocco again failed to find common ground. However, during the Thirtieth Ordinary Session of the Council of Ministers of the OAU, held in Addis Ababa on February 22, 1982, the Secretary-General Edem Kodjo, who was favorable to the Algerian position, invited the SADR to join the OAU by notifying to member states of its membership request. Although no African country had recognized the SADR at the time of the summits in Nairobi, and in contradiction to the resolutions of the OAU and Article 4 of the Charter of African Unity, Edem Kodjo treated SADR's membership as an administrative matter under his exclusive jurisdiction that could be resolved quickly. This decision put an end to the admission discussions. Morocco protested against this procedure, which it considered tarnished with illegalities. The SADR voluntarily refrained from sitting at the 19th OAU Summit, held in Addis Ababa from June 6–12, 1983. Algeria meanwhile obtained recognition of the SADR from twenty-six African countries—seventeen alone in 1979 as a result of the peace agreement signed between Mauritania and the Polisario.[6] On the eve of the Nairobi III Summit, it presented its independence arguments, in particular advocating direct negotiations between Morocco and the Polisario Front.[7]

During the 20th OAU Summit held in November 1984, the Heads of State ratified the secretary-general's decision. Algiers had achieved its objective,[8] but not without relying on the support of the heads of emerging African states. With black African elites wary of any pan-Arabism, Moroccan politics was fueling discontent. On the one hand, the Moroccan territorial claims on Mauritania were raising the disapproval of the other members of the Francophone countries. On the other hand, the War of Sand against Algeria (1963) reinforced the image of an expansionist Morocco in opposition to the philosophy of the African Unity. In 1959, the Guinean President Sékou Touré said in the German magazine *Der Spiegel*: "We are not back in the North or North-East Arab-Muslim world. . . . Africa is not the living space of any expansion; it will be not colonized, exploited nor populated by Asians, Europeans, nor the Arabs. Africa belongs to Africans."[9] As stressed by Khadija Mohsen-Finan in 1997, it has been in Black Africa that Morocco's Saharan politics was the most harshly judged insofar as the annexation of Western Sahara was going against two important principles for the OAU, that is, the peoples' right to self-determination and the acceptance of borders inherited from colonialism.[10]

Putting an End to Morocco's Isolation

For Morocco, the membership of the SADR in the OAU in 1982 was a failure of its diplomacy. Its strategy based on the preservation of its acquired right to the Western Sahara as a result of the Green March was defeated. In response to the OAU's decision, Morocco left the OAU on November 12, 1984. This departure led to a political crisis within the organization and denied the kingdom a forum for debate while isolating it on the African scene. King Hassan II responded by launching a new diplomatic initiative to rebuild Morocco's relationships with African countries, which continues today under King Mohammed VI.

Hassan II and the Reform of Morocco's African Policies

To regain its key role on the continent, Morocco reformed its policy toward Africa in 1985 with the aim of gaining greater policy flexibility. Morocco reactivated relationships with countries with which it had good diplomatic relations such as Chad, Niger, and the Congo. Morocco also approached countries with which it had ceased all ties because of the nature of their political systems. The monarchy entered into relationships with Angola in 1985, Cape Verde in 1987, and Benin in 1991, as well as with Togo and Mozambique. During the same period, Morocco formed the Moroccan Agency for International Cooperation, under the control of the Foreign Affairs Department, initially created to deal with foreign grants as well as cultural exchanges. Since its inception, the agency has annually provided between 1,500 and 2,000 state scholarships to graduate African students. Furthermore, Casablanca hosted the 15th Franco-African Summit in 1988 in an effort to strengthen Morocco's diplomatic role within the Francophone zone.

It took a decade of efforts for Hassan II's attempts to put an end to Morocco's isolation following its departure from the OAU to begin reaping any diplomatic benefits. In 1996, six African heads of state[11] visited Morocco, compared with just one the previous year. Morocco also played host to the presidents and ministers of the National Assemblies of Côte d'Ivoire and Benin. Twenty cooperation agreements were signed with sub-Saharan Africa countries in 1996 alone, whereas only eighty-eight were drawn up between 1972 and 1985.[12] Faced with the blockade of the realization of the Arab Maghreb Union (AMU), Morocco developed a rapprochement strategy toward Africa based on bilateral cooperation and economic incentives. Morocco's efforts to reconnect with Africa during the second half of the 1990s was helped by three external developments: the UN's unsuccessful bid to hold a referendum in Western Sahara; Algeria's focus on its internal problems and civil war, which made it less willing to proactively support the Polisario; and the shift by many African governments away from Marxist-Leninist political economic principles in favor of economic liberalization and efforts to attract foreign investment to rebuild their economies.[13]

Continuity and Change under Mohammed VI

When Mohammed VI came to power following the death of his father in 1999, he maintained the country's Africa policy, albeit with some changes. Whereas relationships with African countries were mainly bilateral and based on personal connections during Hassan II's presidency, King Mohammed had a different approach. He increased efforts to make Morocco's voice heard in international and regional fora. Moreover, he advocated on behalf of countries in debt and promoted greater Moroccan economic cooperation and integration with West Africa.

Morocco's economic cooperation in West Africa has been an important policy. First, Morocco undertook to establish a solid axis with Nouakchott and Dakar through cooperation agreements and investments in Mauritanian and Senegalese companies. Then, it expanded this approach on a larger scale throughout West Africa, especially with several of its regional organizations. The most striking example is the West African Economic and Monetary Union (UEMOA), which represents a single currency zone. In October 2000, Morocco signed a preferential trade and investment agreement with the eight members of that organization. One year later, Morocco joined Community of Sahel-Saharan States (CEN-SAD). At that time, CEN-SAD consisted of sixteen countries bordering the Sahara, which has since expanded to neighboring states. Its aims were to fight against poverty in its member states, promote economic development, establish a common market for agricultural products, and to act as a mediator in regional conflicts. Due to Muammar Gaddafi's activism in the group, however, the CEN-SAD became perceived as an instrument of Libyan politics and an element of Gaddafi's Pan-Africanism. This created obstacles for Morocco to build strong ties with the organization.[14] Lastly, Morocco began to diversify its African policy by focusing on its role as an Atlantic state. In August 2009, the ministers of the African states bordering the Atlantic met in Rabat to tackle security issues and to attempt to coordinate efforts against common threats, particularly networks of organized crime and drug trafficking.

By 2011, Morocco had a total of twenty-five diplomatic missions on the African continent. The king's official visits signaled the importance of Morocco's Africa policy. From a commercial point of view, Moroccan trade with Africa increased from $533 million in 1998 to nearly $3 billion in 2008.[15] Despite the increase, a report by the Moroccan Department of Economic Studies and Financial Forecast (DEPF) published in 2012 showed that Morocco's share in the sub-Saharan African market represented just 0.26 percent of the total in 2010, whereas South Africa and Nigeria held, respectively, 4.2 percent and 2.8 percent.[16] Although Morocco's push to fight diplomatic isolation within Africa was not the only motivation to expand its presence in sub-Saharan Africa, it remains a priority.

DEADLOCK IN THE AU

Under pressure from the Moroccan diplomacy and the redistribution of power resulting from the collapse of the USSR, African support for the SADR weakened since the mid-1990s. Ten countries,[17] including six French-speaking countries, cancelled their recognition following the example of Equatorial Guinea, which had done so in 1980. A benchmark of this evolution was the first attempt by Morocco to exclude the SADR from the OAU at the 33rd Summit of the regional organization in June 1997. However, due to the lack of support from the host country, Zimbabwe, and because of the role of the SADR as vice president of the OAU and on the "Committee of the OAU responsible for the prevention and settlement of conflicts in Africa," the maneuver was postponed for one year. In 1998 at the 34th Summit in Ouagadougou, Senegal, Gabon, and Burkina Faso suggested suspending SADR's participation until the referendum on self-determination scheduled by the UN. The debate and vote were put to the Ministerial Council at the beginning of 1999 but most member countries renewed their support of the SADR and of the UN's efforts.[18]

Despite these setbacks, Morocco's diplomatic efforts continued. Following Morocco's autonomy proposal for the Western Sahara in April 2007, additional countries rallied in support of Morocco and broke off contact with the SADR. Burundi, Cape Verde, Guinea-Bissau, Kenya, Madagascar, and Malawi decided to withdraw their support for SADR between 2000 and 2010.[19] However, while Morocco attempted to rally support for its cause, Algeria was acting to do the same for its position. Its influence within the organization was considerable, mainly due to its financial commitment and its activist diplomacy. Algeria was one of the main African financial contributors to the AU in the 2000s alongside Egypt, South Africa, Nigeria, and Libya.[20] Moreover, several prominent Algerian diplomats had an important influence on the continent since 1991: Mohamed Sahnoun, UN special representative to Somalia in 1992; Lakhdar Brahimi, former Algerian Minister for Foreign Affairs and Under-Secretary-General for Special Assignments in Support of the Secretary-General's Preventive and Peacemaking Efforts who chaired the panel on peace operations, which published the "Brahimi report"[21] in 2000; and even President Bouteflika himself, who acted as mediator during the Eritrean-Ethiopian conflict.[22] As a sign of this importance, Algerian diplomats took the lead as representatives of all three organizations in negotiations with the Mauritanian junta, shortly after the coup d'état led by General Ould Abdel Aziz in August 2008.

Algeria is also using its vast hydrocarbon wealth to exert its influence throughout Africa, along with its leadership on the regional counterterrorism agenda in the Sahel and Sahara regions. First, as explained by Chakib Khelil on February 25, 2008, then Algerian Minister of Energy and Mines, Algeria has a large presence in Mali, Mauritania, Niger, and Libya. The proportion of hydrocarbons in the volume of trade between Algeria and African countries in 2007 shows their importance in Algerian regional politics: of $835 million in Algerian exports, $751 million were attributable to oil.[23] More generally and according to Algerian Customs, hydrocarbons represented 97.19 percent of total Algerian exports[24] in

2011, offering considerable opportunities to Algiers for funding diplomatic efforts and to provide assistance to its African partners. Second, over the last few years, the fight against terrorism has gradually emerged as a second vector of the Algerian counterinfluence to Morocco, including obstructing the links between Rabat and Nouakchott after the election of General Abdel Aziz in July 2009. In April 2010, a joint terrorism operational committee based in Tamanrasset was set up among Mauritania, Algeria, Mali, and Niger. Five months later, fearing marginalization by France and keen to regain control over regional cooperation and planning, Algiers called an urgent meeting among the heads of the four countries, which resulted in the implementation of a central information Committee for the Saharo-Sahelian countries headquartered in the Algerian capital.

Although Algeria is the main and historical African supporter of the Polisario Front,[25] SADR also enjoys support from other continental powers. According to the author of an American diplomatic telegram written in 2009, the region's main powers—Algeria, South Africa, Nigeria, and Ethiopia—recognized or even offered support to the SADR.[26] For Ethiopia and Nigeria, recognition took place in 1979 and 1984, respectively. For Nigeria, it was a gesture of opposition to the Moroccan refusal to sit alongside representatives of the Polisario in the Implementation Committee despite requests of the president of the OAU and other members of the committee, and although criticized by other states such as Mauritania and even Senegal. South Africa's recognition is more recent, although it reflects the political legacies and foreign policy of Hassan II. Indeed, during the Cold War, Morocco had supported the UNITA of Jonas Savimbi in Angola, and had established relationships with the apartheid regime in Pretoria. Algeria and the Polisario, meanwhile, were supporting the African National Congress (ANC). So, in 1994, after coming to power, Nelson Mandela made a written commitment to Mohamed Abdelaziz to recognize the Sahrawi entity immediately and explained that he authorized the Polisario Front to open an office in Pretoria due to previous Moroccan policies. Despite this solidarity with the Polisario, South Africa offered to mediate the conflict. In 2000, Minister Nkosazana Dlamini-Zuma informed Morocco that her country was prepared to act as mediator between the kingdom and the SADR, and suggested holding direct negotiations. At that time, direct negotiations were unacceptable for Morocco. Nonetheless, Morocco did not want to offend South Africa and agreed to a preliminary meeting that would be held in Pretoria in September 2004. The meeting went badly, and a second appointment was proposed for a few days later at the same location. However, arguing that it was busy with the visit of UN special representative Alvaro de Soto to the Sahara, the Moroccans declined, which angered President Thabo Mbeki. He took advantage over the Pan-African parliament meeting to make the break official, claiming that Morocco had rejected the Baker plan.

In looking at the overall impact of the Sahara crisis on the AU, it is clear that the AU's position on SADR extends beyond political and diplomatic concerns. The Charter of the AU is clear: it is not possible to exclude a member after accepting admission. Indeed, Article 31 of the Constitutive Act of the AU does not make provision for exclusion but only for a procedure to renounce membership. There is no provision for the case of a state that will no longer be recognized by the majority of members. The only legal way to exclude the SADR is voting an amendment or the revision of the Constitution by virtue of Article 33. But to do this, it should meet some requirements: (1) an application must be filed with the president of the Commission; (2) other members shall be notified; (3) the Conference of the Union should consider the proposition following an advisory opinion on the proposed amendment by the Executive Council; and (4) the amendment must be approved by at least two-thirds of the member states. Despite growing support for Morocco, the effort challenging SADR's membership remains blocked, while the AU, particularly Algeria and South Africa, continue to support the Polisario Front.

EUROPE AND THE SAHRAWI QUESTION

The African continent and the AU are only one arena for the rivalries and tensions around the Western Sahara conflict. The conflict extends to the other side of the Mediterranean, starting in Spain, the former colonial power in Western Sahara and a historic and strategic actor in the region. Even if the Spanish position has changed significantly since the 1975 Green March, Madrid maintains an ambivalent position. Conversely, Paris has chosen to support Morocco consistently, pushing the Polisario Front to work within European institutions to prevent the French position from influencing other European states and agencies.

The Spanish Balancing Game

In Spain, the position on the Western Sahara conflict has changed significantly since the signing of the Madrid Agreement (1975), which marked the transfer of the territory to Morocco and Mauritania. Morocco's neighbor across the Mediterranean, although closer to Rabat than to the Western Sahara, continues to have an ambivalent attitude on the issue. Right after the Madrid Agreement, Spain faced pressure from the Polisario and Algeria, which rejected the pact as contrary to previous commitments. Algiers had two strong counterpoints to the Spanish position. First was its energy weapon of concern to the Spanish authorities, which received a significant supply of gas from Algeria. Second, Algeria

Table 7.1. African States that Recognize the SADR (unofficial list)

States	Date of the Recognition	Withdrawal of the Recognition
Algeria	March 6, 1976 (embassy)	
Angola	March 11, 1976 (embassy)	
Benin	March 11, 1976	March 21, 1997
Botswana	May 14, 1980	
Burkina Faso	March 4, 1984	June 5, 1996
Burundi	March 1, 1976	June 2005, reestablished June 17, 2008, canceled October 2010
Cape Verde	July 4, 1979	Frozen July 2007
Chad	July 4, 1980	May 9, 1997, relations reestablished, canceled March 17, 2006
Congo	June 3, 1978	September 13, 1996
Ethiopia	February 24, 1979 (embassy)	
Equatorial Guinea	November 3, 1978	May 1980
Ghana	August 24, 1979	Frozen May 2001?
Guinea-Bissau	March 15, 1976	April 2, 1997, embassy reopened, canceled April 2010
Kenya	June 25, 2005	Frozen October 19, 2006
Lesotho	October 9, 1979	
Liberia	July 31, 1985	September 5, 1997
Libya	April 15, 1980	
Madagascar	February 28, 1976	June 2005
Malawi	November 19, 1994	June 2001, reestablished February 1, 2008, canceled September 16, 2008
Mali	July 4, 1980	
Mauritania	February 27, 1984	
Mozambique	March 13, 1976 (embassy)	
Namibia	June 11, 1990	
Nigeria	November 12, 1984 (embassy, September 2000)	
Rwanda	April 1, 1976	
Sao Toma and Principe	June 22, 1978	October 23, 1996

Seychelles	October 25, 1977	March 17, 2008
Sierra Leone	March 27, 1980	Frozen July 2003?
South Africa	September 15, 2004 (embassy)	
Swaziland	April 28, 1980	July 4, 1997
Tanzania	November 9, 1978 (embassy)	
Togo	March 17, 1976	June 18, 1997
Uganda	September 6, 1979	
Zambia	October 12, 1979 (embassy July 2005)	April 2, 2011
Zimbabwe	July 3, 1980	

Source: www.arso.org (pro-Sahrawi site) and news articles.

decided to host and support a movement that called for the independence of the Canary Islands, which are ruled by Spain. Algiers even included the territory on the agenda of the Liberation Committee of the OAU as an African territory still·colonized. For its part, the Polisario repeatedly attack Spanish fishing vessels, taking hostages who were released only after a Spanish declaration in favor of Sahrawi independence. As a consequence, the Spanish government decided in December 1977 to suspend arms deliveries to Morocco. Then a high-ranking Spanish official attended the Fourth Congress of the Polisario in September 1978. In some of their official statements, Spanish politicians even claimed that Spain had not transferred the sovereignty over the territory in 1975, but only its administration.[27]

In this context, the accession to power in Spain of the *Partido Socialista Obrero Espanol* (PSOE) in the elections of October 1982 worried the Moroccan government since on March 12, 1977, this coalition of the Socialists and the Communist Party had published a statement asking for the revocation of the Madrid Agreement. However, pragmatism prevailed and the Socialists refuted their past commitments favoring the independence position. On November 30, 1982, Fernando Moran, who was going to become Minister of Foreign Affairs of the Socialist government a few days later, declared: "Not only we will do nothing to destabilize Morocco, but we will do everything in our power to maintain its stability."[28] The first official overseas visit of Prime Minister Felipe Gonzalez was to Rabat. A key element in this relationship is economic. In 1977, the Moroccan government did not submit to Parliament the fisheries agreement with Spain, which allows Spanish vessels to fish off the coast of Morocco, including Western Sahara. To avoid critics, the Spanish government only talked about "water under Moroccan jurisdiction," and not under Moroccan sovereignty.[29] Then the Moroccan government simply signed an interim agreement extended every six months, while regularly restating its claims to the Spanish enclaves of Ceuta and Melilla, which are on the north coast of Morocco.

Since the signing of a friendship and cooperation treaty between Spain and Morocco[30] in 1991, links between the two countries have grown considerably closer. On February 5–6, 1996, then Head of Government Felipe Gonzalez signed an agreement granting the Kingdom of Morocco $1.2 billion worth of loans over four years to facilitate trade relations between the two countries. Three and a half months later, the new head of government, José Maria Aznar chose Morocco for his first foreign visit. However, despite this rapprochement, relations between the two countries remain complicated and potentially conflicting, as demonstrated by the deterioration of bilateral relations between the two neighbors in 2000. Tension began with Morocco's refusal to renew the fishing agreement with the EU, which expired in December 1999. Numbers of Andalusian fishermen were laid off and a general anti-Moroccan climate developed in the country. In response, Morocco reiterated its demands for a return of the Spanish enclaves of Ceuta, Melilla, and nearby islands. In response to a statement by the Head of Spanish diplomacy Abel Matutes on February 21, 2000, in which he rejected the description of the Spanish presence in the two enclaves as "colonial," the Moroccan Ministry of Foreign Affairs published a press release reaffirming "the inalienable rights of Morocco to those territories still under Spanish rule."[31]

The Parsley Island crisis during the summer 2002 fits into this context: on July 11, Moroccan soldiers occupied this uninhabited rock of thirteen hectares, causing a Spanish military intervention to expel them. The case of Parsley Island seems not entirely foreign to the Western Sahara conflict. Indeed, it could even be a way for Morocco to remind Spain that it was a territorial dispute still unresolved between their two countries. "By reopening dramatically the Spanish colonization file," wrote the French journalist Jean-Pierre Tuquoi, "Morocco probably had another goal in mind: to have a card to force Madrid to change their attitude on another capital issue, that one of Western Sahara."[32] Indeed, in 2001, Prime Minister José Maria Aznar did not hesitate to exploit the Western Sahara as a pressure point on Morocco by refusing to support the agreement presented by the secretary-general of the UN and then declaring his position for self-determination for the Sahrawi people.[33]

When the Socialist coalition again came to power in 2004, more and more bilateral partnerships were formed and the Spanish government grew significantly closer to Morocco on the subject of Western Sahara. Its position is that, in the absence of a UN resolution offering a solution to the Western Saharan conflict, Moroccan laws apply[34]—tacit recognition of Moroccan sovereignty over the Sahara. The Socialist-led government made an active commitment alongside Rabat to promote a "third way."

On December 15, 2010, Foreign Minister Trinidad Jimenez had to explain her department's policy regarding an autonomy plan for Western Sahara to her Congress following the publication of American diplomatic cables that revealed that Spain—through its ambassador to Rabat in 2006—had encouraged and helped Morocco to form an autonomy plan using Catalonia as an example.[35] But despite the PSOE's commitment to an autonomy plan, Spanish policy on Western Sahara is marked by a refusal to make an overly explicit commitment to any of the main stakeholders. Officially for Madrid, the definitive status of Western Sahara must be the result of negotiations between the different parties and of the free exercise of the right to self-determination of the Sahrawi people under the auspices of the UN, that is, a referendum. Spain believes that it should not take a position supporting any side explicitly, but rather stand behind the UN, EU, or the United States.[36]

In fact, Spanish governments do not want to affect their relationship with Algeria or take the risk of coming up against public opinion, which is more sympathetic to the SADR position. First of all, although Morocco is an important economic and strategic partner for Spain—not only in military terms[37] —trade between Algiers and Madrid doubled between 2007 and 2010, Spain became Algeria's third largest trade partner and a bilateral cooperation treaty was signed in October 2008. Second, there is a section of the Spanish public opinion that has expressed strong feelings of solidarity with the Sahrawi people. This is due to the impression that Spain is directly responsible for the fate of its former colony and these ties bind the Spanish with the Sahrawi people. The latter mostly speak Spanish in addition to their Arab dialect, and exchanges between the two peoples are common. For instance, between 7,000 and 10,000 Saharawi children are welcomed by Spanish families since 1988 each year, in a program managed by the *Union de Juventud de Saguia el Hamra y Rio de Oro* (the Polisario's youth organization) with three hundred Spanish mutual aid associations.[38] The fact that public opinion is attentive to the fate of the Sahrawi people is shown by the strong Spanish presence in the Tindouf camps providing humanitarian aid. Two Spanish aid workers were kidnapped in October 2011 as well as an Italian colleague. As for the Spanish press, it usually adopts a highly critical tone toward Morocco. When, for example, Moroccan security forces forcibly dismantled a camp near Laâyoune in November 2010, several newspapers erroneously published the photo of a Palestine child to make their case against Morocco's alleged use of indiscriminate force, claiming that the child came from Western Sahara.[39] This was a huge embarrassment for several dailies, as it proved the Moroccan claim that Spanish media were biased against Morocco.

France's Choice in Favor of Morocco

Among foreign powers, France is the only country that has never really tried to hide its opposition to the independence of Western Sahara. Officially, Paris is said to be neutral in the conflict and supports a negotiated political solution—wishing to neither fuel existing tensions nor force Morocco to resolve the Western Sahara issue, nor jeopardize its relationships with Algiers—yet French leaders are clearly in favor of Morocco's position.[40]

By virtue of defense agreements signed with Mauritania, President Valéry Giscard d'Estaing agreed to provide Breguet-Atlantic surveillance aircraft as well as Jaguar attack aircraft for use against the Sahrawi People's Liberation Army in late 1977 and early 1978.[41] Subsequently, during the two seven-year terms of François Mitterrand, there was a slight decline in Franco-Moroccan relationship, including the opening of a Polisario Front representation in Paris. However, the pro-Morocco French attitude on Western Sahara returned and was even strengthened during Jacques Chirac's two terms of office (1995–2007). Chirac was staunchly pro-Moroccan, and made his first official presidential visit to Morocco. French policy remained largely consistent during Nicolas Sarkozy's presidency (2007–2012). France objected to the extension by the UNSC of the MINURSO mandate to include human rights monitoring in the Western Sahara, causing bitterness among Sahrawi supporters, especially since the nongovernmental organization (NGO) Human Rights Watch had attempted to draw the international community's attention to the situation in Western Sahara and the Tindouf camps.[42]

Although France is a loyal advocate for Morocco, the Polisario Front attempted to sway French policy. On January 25, 1996, AFP reported that the independence movement reproached France, as a leading Mediterranean power, for being too "caught up" in its relationships with Rabat and Algiers. "If France was considering Western Sahara outside the context of its relations with Morocco and Algeria," says the Polisario's leader Bachir Moustafa Sayed, "its position would be with fewer complexes and much fairer."[43] Two years later, in April 1998, the study group on Western Sahara of the French National Assembly, formed and chaired by MP Daniel Paul, held its first meeting. The group had two aims: to organize meetings between politicians of every affiliation and Sahrawi authorities and associations and to draw the government's attention to the conflict. In particular, Mohammed Abdelaziz was a guest of the study group on May 10–15, 1998, which enabled the SADR president to meet French politicians.

However, for French leaders, the relationship between France and Morocco was too tight and dense for the conflict to jeopardize their connection. What is more, the pro-Moroccan lobby in mainland France is institutionalized in the "Circle of Franco-Moroccan friendship," created in 1991 by a Moroccan painter living in France, Mehdi Qotbi, in reaction to the publication in 1990 of a book by Gilles Perrault criticizing Hassan II *Our Friend the King*.[44] France was Morocco's second biggest creditor after the World Bank in the 1990s; and, in 2011, France was its main trading partner with a volume of trade of $9.9 billion and a market share of 14 percent.[45] Approximately, six hundred French companies are currently employing 70,000 people in Morocco, and nearly 40,000 French are living in the kingdom.[46] As far as personal relationships are concerned, a high proportion of the French political class (both left and right wings) has also close connections with the Kingdom of Morocco. Nicolas Sarkozy, Dominique Strauss-Kahn, and Hubert Védrine visit Marrakesh regularly. In this context, François Hollande's accession to presidency will probably not change French policy. In March 2012, First Socialist party Secretary Martine Aubry said to Mohammed VI that Hollande was supporting the Moroccan Autonomy plan and, after the election, the king was the first head of state to be welcomed at the Elysée palace.

Debates in the EU

To bypass the support in Paris and Madrid for the Moroccan Autonomy plan, the Polisario attempts to influence Europe around the issue of natural resources exploitation and other relationships between the EU and Morocco. However, there is a distinction to make between the European Commission and the European Parliament. The first one, due to its scope of expertise and functions, is not affected by the problem of Western Sahara. Although the new neighborhood policy initiated during summer 2011 places more focus on democratization and human rights, the European Commission emphasizes economic cooperation with Maghreb countries as well as the creation of a free trade area in the Mediterranean. It is the European Parliament that takes the leading positions on the Western Sahara conflict.

The European Parliament's interest in the Polisario cause goes back to the early 1980s. Until 1981, this institution rushed through resolutions favorable to the Moroccan position. Following the strategy of the Polisario to obtain the support of mainly left-wing political parties, associations, and trade unions, an inter-parliamentary group for the Sahrawi question was created in 1982 with the aim of changing the position of the European Parliament to support the Sahrawi right to self-determination.[47] Its members and supporters, who consider Western Sahara as the last African colony, have three objectives: (1) to "counter the Moroccan influence in Brussels,"[48] in the words of Régine Villemont, General Secretary of the French Association of Friends of the SADR; (2) to raise awareness about the issue of Western Sahara alongside the SADR representative in Brussels and national inter-parliamentary groups; and (3) to encourage the UN, European leaders, and European institutions to take on an active role in promoting a self-determination referendum, reinforcing respect for human rights in the Moroccan Sahara, and increasing humanitarian help for the Saharawi populations.

Concretely, Parliament's position in favor of the Polisario resulted in two steps. First, the Parliament has adopted annual resolutions such as the one of October 24, 2005, which said that the Parliament "supports a fair and definitive solution about the conflict in Western Sahara based on the law and international legality" but is concerned "by reports of violations of human rights in Western Sahara, including on freedom of speech and freedom of movement" and "asks for the protection of the Sahrawi people, the respect of their fundamental rights of which freedom of expression and freedom of movement."[49] Second, Parliament has sent delegations on the ground to investigate the situation. A delegation was created in late 2001 under the direction of Catherine Lalumière, then vice president of the European Parliament. The delegation has undertaken visits in late 2001 and early 2002: Algiers and Tindouf (October 28, 2001, to November 2, 2001), Laâyoune and Rabat (February 11–15, 2002). The conclusions of the report submitted by the delegation described the Sahrawi problem as "anachronistic and unresolved colonialism remnant," and asked for the EU to become more involved in finding a solution to the conflict while considering that the UN "had failed in its mission" and that there was a need "to find an acceptable compromise for both parties."[50]

For the independence movement, each agreement signed between the EU and Morocco is an occasion to reaffirm through the media its opposition to Morocco's presence as well as attempting to influence European policy, which it regards as being too slanted in favor of Morocco and dismissive of Sahrawi concerns. Following a parliamentary resolution regarding the Western Sahara, Mohamed Sidati, then Minister-Counselor to the SADR president and representative in Brussels, declared in 1999 that it was time for the EU to use its influence over the Moroccan government to make it stop applying "double standards" and "to persuade it to apply all the suggestions made by UN General Secretary."[51]

The Polisario's efforts against the EU-Morocco Fishing Agreement illustrate its strategy of opposing Moroccan interests within European institutions. In March 2011, SADR President Mohamed Abdelaziz, criticized the decision made by the Coreper (Committee of Permanent Representatives in the EU) to allow the European Commission to negotiate a one-year extension to the Fishing Agreement between the EU and Morocco. He declared that, by virtue of international law, exploiting the wealth of a colonized country without the latter's permission was illegal, particularly in a territory recognized as nonautonomous by the UN and awaiting decolonization via a self-determination referendum, and especially since the territory in question was part of the AU.[52] The Polisario Front's protests against the Fishing Agreement between Morocco and the EU are nothing new. In 1995, the leader of the SADR criticized an agreement that he claimed did not make allowance for the international borders of Western Sahara.[53] Similarly, on January 22, 2009, the Polisario Front announced the existence of an exclusive economic area for Western Sahara that would stretch two hundred nautical miles from the territorial coast and asked the EU to suspend the application of the Fishing Agreement signed with Morocco in 2005.

For the supporters of the Sahrawi cause in the corridors of the European Parliament, there is a feeling that their audience is growing. For Spanish MEP Raül Romeva, the initial rejection of the extension of the Fishing Agreement between the EU and Morocco at the end of 2011 revealed an awareness of the Sahrawi issue in the European Parliament; statements leaning toward the Sahrawi cause are starting to take shape elsewhere as well.[54] However, there are other groups outside of the members of the Intergroup Peace for the Sahrawi People who are taking positions on these issues. In the case of the Agricultural Agreement between Morocco and the EU approved by the Parliament on February 16, 2012, the farm lobby, especially Spanish and French, were campaigning for a "no" vote, fearing competition for their produce. Similarly, in regard to the Fishing Agreement, environmental groups have opposed the agreement based on concerns for damage due to overfishing and pollution.

Yet, despite the actions of the Polisario and its supporters, the position of the Parliamentary Assembly of the Union remains ambivalent. Indeed, as in the EU Commission, the Parliament is concerned about the economic interests of Europe and therefore promotes cooperation with Morocco. Pro-Polisario positions are primarily focused on ideological and declarative statements. On June 5, 1996, the Association Agreement between Morocco and the EU was adopted by 263 votes against 65 with eight abstentions. In May 2006, the European Parliament ratified the Fishing Agreement with Morocco. On October 13, 2008, Morocco was granted advanced status[55] and was the first beneficiary of the European Neighborhood and Partnership Instrument. The Initiatives Program for 2007–2013 awarded the country €1234.5 million.[56]

CONCLUSION

With regard to Africa (OAU/AU), the Western Sahara conflict has become less central even before the cease-fire of 1991. Even if, on the diplomatic front and thanks to the commitment of Algeria, the Polisario seems at this moment to have strong support within the AU, Morocco succeeded in 1980 and 2000, with other African states, to adopt a pragmatic approach to their relationships and since then has gradually intensified its presence on the continent. However, due to support for SADR from several key African regional powers and the AU's rigid constitution, the Moroccan kingdom failed to expel the SADR from the AU. Thus, the AU majority position still regards the SADR as the representatives of the Sahrawi people and Morocco as a colonial power.

The same deadlock repeats itself on the European continent, but for different reasons. In bilateral relationships, France supports the autonomy solution proposed in 2007 and does not want to force Morocco's hand on the Western Sahara issue. Spain is more ambivalent, partly because of the historic attachments to the region, its guilt over its former colonial role, but also because of the importance of other issues that impact Spain's Sahara policy, chiefly the territorial disputes around Ceuta and Melilla. Second, at the EU level, the commission has chosen to support tight relationships between Europe and Maghreb and refuses to make any political commitment in a conflict in which there is no consensus between European countries. With the strengthening of Parliament's authority in foreign policy and the entry in the EU of countries as Sweden and Finland in 1995, the Polisario has gained new supporters to strengthen its voice. Northern European countries are indeed very sensitive to human rights concerns and voice respect for the principle of self-determination, which impact their relations with Morocco. In 2006, the Fishing Agreement between Morocco and the EU came up against opposition from Sweden, Denmark, Finland, and the United Kingdom. Five years later in February 2011, while most permanent representatives of Member States supported the commission's proposal on Fishing Agreement with Morocco, the Swedish minister of fishing still expressed his opposition.

In the coming years, it is unlikely that there will be any major changes in the relationships between Morocco and the EU. On the one hand, Polisario's supporters remain a minority. On the other hand, EU remains a community of states with a cult of national sovereignty in foreign and defense policies. The creation of a European External Action Service does not alter limitations of a Europe that is challenged in developing a role for weighing in on the resolution of conflicts. This new service is merely an implementation tool for relaying policies in support of member states' diplomacies and not for defining policies. Moreover, Parliament's role is ever limited. With the Lisbon Treaty, it plays an increasing role in European politics and contributes to the development of community legislation on an equal footing with the council. The co-decision procedure is also enshrined as "ordinary legislative procedure," and its field of skills has been extended significantly. Agriculture, fishing, freedom, security, and justice as well as common trade policy—among other things—are now jointly managed by the commission and the Parliament. However, the European assembly can only vote on the commission's proposals by simple majority, thereby limiting the impact of supporters of the Polisario in the community institution, which generally is content to follow the Security Council by calling for respect for international law.[57]

In this way, within the AU and the EU, the deadlock of the Western Sahara conflict is likely to continue, due to the persistence of differences, the ability of stakeholders to neutralize each other, and most important, the concern of states which have interests in one or another camp to not harm allies. The lines of force have moved but the absence of consensus, and the interests of countries that lead camps on the two continents, block any resolution being imposed on the parties.

NOTES

1. Khadija Mohsen-Finan, "Sahara Occidental: Le Maintien du Statu Quo," *CERI* (May 2004), www.sciencespo.fr/ceri/sites/sciencespo.fr.ceri/files/artkm.pdf (accessed July 22, 2012); International Crisis Group, "Western Sahara: Out of the Impasse", Middle East/North Africa Report no. 66 (June 11, 2007), www.crisisgroup.org/~/media/Files/Middle%20East%20North%20Africa/North%20Africa/Western%20Sahara/66_western_sahara___out_of_the_impasse.pdf (accessed July 18, 2012).

2. Pierre Vellas, "La Diplomatie Marocaine dans l'Affaire du Sahara Occidental," *Politique Etrangère* 4 (1978): 425–26; United Nations, *Charter of the United Nations* (October 24, 1945), www.un.org/en/documents/charter/index.shtml (accessed August 20, 2012).
"Article 33: 1. The parties to any dispute, the continuance of which is likely to endanger the maintenance of international peace and security, shall, first of all, seek a solution by negotiation, enquiry, mediation, conciliation, arbitration, judicial settlement, resort to regional agencies or arrangements, or other peaceful means of their own choice. 2. The Security Council shall, when it deems necessary, call upon the parties to settle their dispute by such means.
"Article 52: 1. Nothing in the present Charter precludes the existence of regional arrangements or agencies for dealing with such matters relating to the maintenance of international peace and security as are appropriate for regional action provided that such arrangements or agencies and their activities are consistent with the Purposes and Principles of the United Nations. 2. The Members of the United Nations entering into such arrangements or constituting such agencies shall make every effort to achieve pacific settlement of local disputes through such regional arrangements or by such regional agencies before referring them to the Security Council. 3. The Security Council shall encourage the development of pacific settlement of local disputes through such regional arrangements or by such regional agencies either on the initiative of the states concerned or by reference from the Security Council. 4. This Article in no way impairs the application of Articles 34 and 35."

3. Maurice Barbier, *Le Conflit du Sahara Occidental* (Paris: L'Harmattan, 1982), 335–43.

4. Olivier Vergniot, "La Question du Sahara Occidental: 1981–1982," Chronology and Annex, in *Annuaire de l'Afrique du Nord*, eds. Hubert Michel and Maurice Flory (Paris: Éditions du CNRS, 1984), 333.

5. The Implementation Committee was composed of Guinea, Mali, Nigeria, Sierra Leone, Sudan, Tanzania, and Kenya.

6. The twenty-six African countries, in alphabetical order, are: Algeria, Angola, Benin, Botswana, Burundi, Cape Verde, Chad, Congo, Ethiopia, Ghana, Guinea-Bissau, Lesotho, Libya, Madagascar, Mali, Mozambique, Rwanda, Sao Tomé and Principe, the Seychelles, Sierra Leone, Swaziland, Tanzania, Togo, Uganda, Zambia, and Zimbabwe. Following Mr. Kodjo's decision, however, several countries close to Morocco made it clear to the secretary that he had shown a lack of courtesy (Sudan, Senegal, Guinea, the Comoros) in failing to inform the other states. Morocco, on the

other hand, enjoyed the support of eighteen countries: Cameroon, Côte d'Ivoire, Guinea, Central African Republic, Senegal, Sudan, Zaire, Djibouti, Niger, Mauritius, Equatorial Guinea, Gambia, Somalia, Comoros, Gabon, Tunisia, Republic of Upper Volta (future Burkina Faso), and Liberia.

7. Barbier, *Le Conflit du Sahara Occidental*, 339–40; Abdelkhaleq Berramdane, *Le Sahara Occidental, Enjeu Maghrébin* (Paris: Karthala, 1992), 69–71, 92.

8. Algeria included the Polisario Front's representative on the diplomatic list drawn up by the Department of Foreign Affairs for the first time in February 1981.

9. Philippe Decraene, *Le Panafricanisme* (Paris: Presses Universitaires de France, 1976), 106.

10. Khadija Mohsen-Finan, *Sahara Occidental: Les Enjeux d'un Conflit Régional* (Paris: Éditions du CNRS, 1997), 66.

11. The African heads of state that went to Morocco in 1996 were: Alpha Oumar Konaré (Mali), Joaquim Chissano (Mozambique), Blaise Compaoré (Burkina Faso), Abdou Diouf (Senegal), Théodore Obiang Nguema (Equatorial Guinea), and Lansana Comté (Guinea).

12. Laurence Aïda Ammour, "Stratégies d'Influence et Projection de Puissance des Pays Maghrébins sur les Territoires Sahéliens à la Lumière des Enjeux de Sécurité Régionaux," *GéopoliSudconsultance* no. 4 (September, 16, 2011), www.geopolisudconsult.com/papers/PRESENTATION_CODESRIA_16SEPT2011.pdf (accessed August 20, 2012; Alain Antil, "Le Royaume du Maroc et sa Politique Envers l'Afrique Subsaharienne," *Institut Français des Relations Internationales* (November 2003): 37. Most of the cooperation agreements signed between 1972 and 1985 were with French-speaking countries as Senegal (fifteen agreements), Gabon (fourteen), Zaire (ten), Guinea (eight), and Mali (eight).

13. Antil, "Le Royaume du Maroc," 33, 39. Morocco's African policy was no less fragile, not least as a result of its lack of consistency. For certain analysts, Morocco's African diplomacy at the end of the 1990s and early 2000s was like sending emissaries in the nineteenth century, in successive waves. The king endorses an idea, the services in question react energetically before running out of steam more or less rapidly, until the next impetus.

14. Antil, "Le Royaume du Maroc," 46.

15. Ammour, "Stratégies d'Influence et Projection," 5.

16. Mohamed Mounjid, "Le Maroc-Afrique à Bout de Souffle," *Le Soir (Morocco)*, April 10, 2012.

17. These ten countries were Benin, Togo, Burkina Faso, Congo, Liberia, Madagascar, Malawi, Sao Tomé and Príncipe, Swaziland, and Chad.

18. Albert Bourqi, "Voyage à l'Intérieur de l'OUA," *Politique Etrangère* 4 (1998): 781; Thomas de Saint-Maurice, *Sahara Occidental 1991–1999: L'Enjeu du Référendum d'Autodétermination* (Paris: L'Harmattan, 2000), 136.

19. "30 Pays Ont Retiré Leur 'Reconnaissance' à la RASD Depuis 2000," *Afrique Avenir*, November 5, 2010.

20. It should be pointed out that 75 percent of the organization's funding is from foreign partners.

21. This report analyses peacekeeping operations and makes political, strategic, and organizational recommendations.

22. Pierre Berthelot, "Les Relations Entre les États de l'Union du Maghreb Arabe et l'Union Africaine: Coopération ou Confrontation?" *Géostratégiques* 32 (2011): 119–28.

23. Nezha Alaoui, "La Projection Economique des Pays du Maghreb sur l'Afrique Subsaharienne," *Institut Français des Relations Internationales*, 2010, www.ifri.org/downloads/noteocpalaouidef.pdf (accessed December 18, 2012).

24. "Statistiques du Commerce Extérieur de l'Algérie (2011)," *Customs Department of Algeria,* www.douane.gov.dz/pdf/r_periodique/ANNEE%202011.(DEF).pdf (accessed December 18, 2012).

25. Barbier, *Le Conflit du Sahara Occidental*, 292. Recognition of the SADR in the years 1970–1980 is often purely symbolic. Generally, relation is provided by the foreign ambassador in Algiers, also considered as the representative with the SADR

26. American diplomatic cable from Embassy Rabat published in Wikileaks, July 14, 2008.

27. Azedine Hannoun, "L'Ambivalence des Stratégies Marocaines sur le Problème du Sahara Occidental" (PhD dissertation, University of Perpignan, 2006), 240.

28. Berramdane, *Le Sahara Occidental: Enjeu Maghrébin*, 220.

29. Barbier, *Le Conflit du Sahara Occidental*, 246.

30. High-level annual meetings were to be held according to the treaty, but it was not respected due to discord between Morocco and Spain on the subject of fishing.

31. Hannoun, "L'Ambivalence des Stratégies Marocaines," 359–60.

32. Jean-Pierre Tuquoi, "L'Îlot du Persil Provoque une Grave Crise entre le Maroc et l'Espagne," *Le Monde*, July 19, 2002.

33. Hannoun, "L'Ambivalence des Stratégies Marocaines," 362.

34. Bill introduced by the PSOE in mid-December 2009 regarding government policy.

35. "WikiLeaks: L'Espagne Conseille au Maroc le Modèle Catalan," *Maghreb Intelligence*, December 15, 2010, www.maghreb-intelligence.com/articles-gratuits/420-wikileaks-lespagne-conseille-au-maroc-le-modele-catalan.html (accessed August 10, 2012).

36. Laurence Aïda Ammour, "L'intégration régionale au Maghreb à l'Epreuve du Conflit Gelé du Sahara Occidental," *The Maghreb Center*, February 10, 2010. www.geopolisudconsult.com/papers/FINAL_LONGAmmourSAHARA_PDF08102010.pdf (accessed July 20, 2012); Louisa Dris-Aït-Hamadouche and Chérif Dris, "Algérie-Espagne: Relations à Géométrie Variable," *Barcelona Centre for International Affairs*, 2007, http://dialnet.unirioja.es/servlet/articulo?codigo=2554513&orden=150522&info=link (accessed July 20, 2012).

37. Rabah Beldjenna, "Contrat d'Armement entre l'Espagne et le Maroc," *El Watan*, February 10, 2007. In February 2007, the Algerian newspaper *El Watan* devoted its front page to an arms deal signed between Spain and Morocco. The contract was signed in November 2006 by the Moroccan national authorities and Spanish companies in Galicia. It comprised 1,200 armored vehicles, 800 military trucks, and 10 war frigates worth a total of 200 million euros.

38. Gina Crivello, Elena Fiddian, and Dawn Chatty, "Des Vacances en Paix: Des Enfants Sahraoui Visitent l'Espagne," *Forced Migrations Review* 25 (May 2006): 59, www.fmreview.org/sites/fmr/files/FMRdownloads/fr/pdf/MFR25/34.pdf (accessed December 19, 2012).

39. Antonin Tisseron, "Violences et Tempête Médiatique Autour du Sahara Occidental: La Région A Besoin d'Apaisement," *Institut Thomas More*, November 29, 2010, www.institut-thomas-more.org/upload/media/artatisseron-nov2010-2-fr.pdf.

40. Saint-Maurice, *Sahara Occidental 1991–1999*, 152–56.

41. Berramdane, *Sahara Occidental*, 62–65.

42. Philippe Bolopion, "Sahara Occidental: la France Contre les Droits de l'Homme?" *Le Monde.fr*, December 22, 2010. In December 2010, Philipe Bolopion, UN Director of Human Rights Watch, pleaded with France in the online edition of the newspaper *Le Monde* to convince Morocco to improve the living conditions of the Saharawi in Western Sahara.

43. Quoted by Saint-Maurice, *Sahara Occidental 1991–1999*, 152.

44. Jean-Pierre Tuquoi, *Majesté, Je Dois Beaucoup à Votre Père; France-Maroc: Une Affaire de Famille* (Paris: Albin Michel, 2006).

45. French Foreign Ministry, "La France et le Maroc," www.diplomatie.gouv.fr/fr/pays-zones-geo/maroc/la-france-et-le-maroc/#sommaire_2 (accessed January 21, 2013).

46. Ammour, "L'Intégration Régionale au Maghreb," 4.

47. Naissance du Groupe Inter-parlementaire: 'Paix pour le Peuple Sahraoui'— Parlement Européen," *Le Temps d'Algérie*, February 25, 2010. In 2010, following the

2009 European elections, this *Intergroup Peace for the Saharawi People* regrouped approximately 70 MPs—from a total of 754, presided over by German politician Norbert Neuser from the Progressive Alliance of Socialists and Democrats Group.

48. Régine Villemont, *Avec les Sahraouis. Une Histoire Solidaire de 1975 à Nos Jours* (Paris: L'Harmattan, 2009).

49. European Parliament conference paper B6-0561/2005 (October 24, 2005), quoted in Hannoun, "L'Ambivalence des Stratégies Marocaines," 364.

50. Hannoun, "L'Ambivalence des Stratégies Marocaines," 364.

51. Quoted in Saint-Maurice, *Sahara Occidental 1991–1999*, 179.

52. Quoted in Y. M., "L'Union Européenne Complique le Problème Sahraoui," *Le Post.fr*, March 13, 2011, http://archives-lepost.huffingtonpost.fr/article/2011/03/13/2432949_l-union-europeenne-complique-le-probleme-sahraoui.html (accessed June 25, 2012).

53. Saint-Maurice, *Sahara Occidental 1991–1999*, 176.

54. "Sahara Occidental: Cesser de Privilégier le Maroc (Eurodéputés)," *Algeria Press Service*, May 30, 2012.

55. The advanced status roadmap was adopted on October 13, 2008. Its objectives were to strengthen political dialogue and economic and social cooperation in parliamentary, security, and judicial areas and in various fields, in particular agriculture, transport, energy, and the environment as well as progressive integration of Morocco in the common internal market and legislative and regulatory convergence.

56. "Commission sur le Financement du Codéveloppement en Méditerranée—Rapport au Président de la République," May 15, 2010, www.elysee.fr/president/root/bank_objects/rapportfinal.pdf (accessed July 5, 2012).

57. Hannoun, "L'Ambivalence des Stratégies Marocaines," 364.

EIGHT

The Evolution of US and Moroccan Policy on Western Sahara

From Conflict to Cooperation

Ambassador Edward M. Gabriel
and Robert M. Holley[1]

On the margins of an international meeting in Morocco on November 3, 2009, Secretary of State Hillary Clinton addressed the Western Sahara conflict directly in response to a question from the media covering the event. In her remarks, which had obviously been prepared in advance, Secretary Clinton spoke out clearly and without ambiguity in saying that US policy supporting Morocco's 2007 initiative to offer a broad autonomy for the Western Sahara under Moroccan sovereignty to resolve this more than thirty-five-year-old conflict was "a plan that originated in the Clinton Administration. It was reaffirmed in the Bush Administration and it remains the policy of the United States in the Obama Administration. . . . I don't want anyone in the region or elsewhere to have any doubt about our policy, which remains the same."[2] In two subsequent public statements, the first in Washington and the second in Rabat in 2011 and 2012, respectively, Secretary Clinton again referred to the Moroccan autonomy initiative as "serious, credible and realistic."[3] This was the US description of the initiative originally made public during the previous Bush administration to which Secretary Clinton eventually, and usefully, added the word "realistic."

However, a cooperative and mutually supportive policy stance on Western Sahara had not always been the defining feature of US-Moroccan relations. Indeed, throughout the first Clinton administration, Western Sahara had become an increasingly serious point of contention in US-Moroccan relations.

The evolution of US and Moroccan policy on the Western Sahara is the subject of this chapter. It is a history that involves initially successful efforts by both parties to overcome years of inertia and entrenched resistance to new approaches in both countries. It is also a history of how even good intentions and sound policy choices can slowly unravel unless governments commit themselves firmly to their choices in both word and deed.

Much of the information contained in this chapter has never been made public before and reflects the authors' firsthand knowledge of events and their roles as active participants in the process as well as their subsequent and continuing efforts to support a solution to the Sahara question based on the policies that were forged at that time. The continuing discussion of current US policy on the Western Sahara, at the time of this writing, often overlooks that this policy and the mostly cooperative support by the United States of Morocco's initiative on the Western Sahara, however imperfect that cooperation might seem today, nevertheless represented a substantial shift in position in Washington beginning in early 1999 and a subsequent major policy adjustment in Morocco that began to quietly take shape the following year. That shift in Moroccan policy first became publicly visible, under the new leadership of King Mohammed VI, when Morocco agreed in the spring of 2001 to negotiate a solution based on a sovereignty/autonomy trade-off formula in what former UN Personal Envoy James Baker originally referred to as his "Framework Agreement." The United States had endorsed this approach earlier. As a matter of fact, Baker's original proposal for this kind of compromise political solution was itself a product of the 1999 shift in US policy and the subsequent Moroccan willingness to accept new US policy approaches to resolve the conflict. In Morocco, the policy shift was ultimately solidified in Morocco's 2007 presentation to the UN Security Council (UNSC) of its own autonomy initiative for the region. An examination of the evolution of policy in both the United States and Morocco, and the eventual embrace by the international community of the need for a fundamental political compromise, is essential to any understanding of how this problem might eventually be resolved.

This chapter addresses some of the most important factors underlying the evolution of US and Moroccan policy on Western Sahara and some of the obstacles to that shift, and concludes with critical commentary and recommendations on current efforts to find a reasonable compromise political solution to this longstanding issue. Much of the shift in policy in both Washington and Rabat was originally undertaken through internal policy reviews by both governments and through equally quiet diplomatic discussions between the two countries. The eventual shape of these new policies, and the eventual Security Council embrace of the need for fundamental compromise, only gradually became apparent to a larger audience.

END OF THE SPANISH OCCUPATION, THE UN CEASE-FIRE, A FAILED REFERENDUM ATTEMPT

In 1991, with the Cold War over and what appeared to many perhaps overly optimistic observers of international affairs as "the end of history" and the beginning of a new, more orderly process of global transformation, the UN was able finally to broker a cease-fire in the war over the Western Sahara. The war had begun in 1975 between Morocco and the Algerian backed Polisario Front after Spain withdrew from its nearly century-long colonial domination of the region, then called "Spanish Sahara." Hopes for a quick resolution of this Cold War legacy were widespread. A UN peacekeeping mission for the region, United Nations Mission for the Referendum in Western Sahara (MINURSO), supported by the United States, was charged with organizing a referendum on the future of the territory. The vote, as originally proposed, would have involved a choice between full integration of the territory into Morocco or total independence and the establishment of a new state. In the beginning, Morocco and the Polisario Front agreed to support this UN-led and US-backed process. However, what was unforeseen at the time, and what ultimately led to serious conflict in the US-Moroccan relationship on the question, was that Morocco and the Polisario Front would adopt radically different views as to who should be qualified to vote in the referendum. This issue may have been innocent enough given the optimism of the day about prospects for a new, less contentious world order, but clearly the United States and the UN failed to appreciate the depth of discord between Morocco and Algeria surrounding this problem in particular, and the Moroccan-Algerian relationship more generally. Its Cold War dimension may have been swept into the dustbin of history, but its more compelling local antecedents remained very much alive and well.

However hopeful some may have been for a speedy resolution, the core conflict that would eventually scuttle any prospects of a referendum on the needlessly stark choice of either full integration or full independence became quickly apparent to all. The Polisario Front sought to restrict the voter list to only those adult members of the various Sahrawi tribes who had been physically resident in the former Spanish Sahara, and who had been included in a flawed and politically motivated 1974 Spanish census of the territory.[4] However, from Morocco's perspective, since the referendum was to be a definitive vote on the future of the region, it argued for a more inclusive and democratic voter list—one including all Sahrawis, regardless of their 1974 whereabouts—who had their tribal origins in the former Spanish Sahara. Morocco insisted that those Sahrawi tribes and individuals who had been driven out of the territory, or who had fled the region to escape Spanish colonial oppression, should not be penalized and denied the right to vote on the future of what was their own homeland.[5]

From 1991 until late 1998, the Sahara question generated vigorous and frequent debate at the UNSC over various proposals to bridge the difference between Morocco and the Polisario Front on a commonly agreed voter list. The UNSC mandate for the UN peacekeeping mission, MINURSO, was often renewed on a very short leash (sometimes for as little as thirty days) with the idea of keeping the pressure on the parties to compromise, but more often simply further exacerbating tensions between Morocco and the United States.[6] Unfortunately, after a fruitless and frustrating eight-year effort to resolve the mutually exclusive approaches, the UN ended the voter registration process in late 1998 with roughly 130,000 appeals still pending and no agreed method to adjudicate the cases. This period was marked by increasingly strained and contentious diplomatic conversations between the United States and Morocco as the United States sought to persuade its longtime friend and ally and close Cold War partner to make ever more concessions on the voter registration process in order to reach a compromise on an agreed voter list. Similar conversations with the Polisario Front's leadership proved no more fruitful and no less contentious in the search for compromise, one that both sides viewed as decisive to the outcome of any potential future vote.

REGIONAL STABILITY CONCERNS, TENSION IN THE US-MOROCCO BILATERAL RELATIONSHIP ULTIMATELY DRIVE CLINTON POLICY CHANGE

Despite the failure of the referendum option by late 1998, the foreign policy community in Washington was nevertheless reluctant to take new decisions concerning Western Sahara that many feared might damage regional security and further aggravate the already problematic nature of relations between Morocco and Algeria. There was some concern in Washington that any dramatic departure from the status quo could potentially lead to renewed hostilities between Morocco and the Polisario Front that might also threaten more open conflict with Algeria. Despite some lessening of internal strife in Algeria by the late 1990s, there was still serious concern about potential instability there from the continuing violence following Algeria's failed 1991 elections and the subsequent outbreak of what was virtually a civil war in the country that eventually claimed more than 250,000 casualties. Questions about Algeria's stability remained open. Nevertheless, there was also a growing awareness that the Western Sahara was driving ever deeper wedges in the US-Morocco relationship that needed attention without risking greater instability in the region. Exacerbating those concerns was mounting pressure from a conservative US Congress to curtail US support for global peacekeeping missions that appeared unproductive. MINURSO's mission appeared to many members to be an example of everything wrong with the UN in general and peacekeeping operations in particular. As a consequence, there was at the time serious concern within some circles at the State Department that Congress would seek to end US participation in UN peacekeeping missions globally. US funding for MINURSO was indeed eventually suspended, and US military forces that had long been an important element of the peacekeeping mission were withdrawn.

Throughout much of 1998, the pressure on the State Department from Congress led to ever shorter renewals of the MINURSO mandate and increasing pressure by US diplomacy to urge ever more compromise on the parties to overcome the issues and "bridge the gap" on voter registration for the long-stalled referendum. As is often the case with our friends in asymmetrical power relations, the US government leaned more heavily on Morocco to compromise rather than on the Polisario or Algeria. The Polisario Front remained intransigent on the issue with backing from Algeria. Despite long years of friendship and close cooperation throughout much of the Cold War, as well as important collaboration on such high priority US foreign policy goals as the Middle East Peace Process, US-Moroccan diplomatic exchanges on the Western Sahara became increasingly contentious. Morocco refused to budge from its position that any vote would have to be as inclusive as possible and this meant not excluding what Morocco insisted were legitimate voters with a serious existential stake in the outcome of any referendum.

Throughout these circumstances, it had been the US Embassy in Rabat that had been obliged to carry out most of the increasingly difficult diplomatic exchanges on the subject, not only with Morocco, but with the Polisario Front as well. At that time, it had principal responsibility for diplomatic exchanges with the leadership of the Polisario Front in the person of the embassy's Counselor for Political Affairs.

By the time the authors of this chapter arrived in Rabat in 1998, tensions in the US-Morocco bilateral relationship had already become seriously strained over the Western Sahara. This occurred despite general goodwill in Washington for progress on political development issues in Morocco following the 1998 inauguration of a newly elected Moroccan government—a government composed largely of former opposition political leaders and an accompanying opening of the political space in Morocco for civil society advocacy groups focused on a wide variety of social reform issues. The US Embassy in Rabat was more keenly aware of the increasing dangers to the bilateral relationship than senior US foreign policy officials in Washington more removed from the matter and more focused on moving the referendum forward and avoiding mounting threats to larger US foreign policy goals on global peacekeeping capabilities emanating from a conservative Congress. As a consequence, the embassy led an effort to sensitize senior officials at the State Department of the need to focus constructive attention to remedy the growing schism between Morocco and the United States over Western Sahara. This effort, suggesting a new US approach to the problem, eventually culminated in January 1999 in a formal US interagency policy review in Washington.

At that review, an interagency policy group assembled by the State Department, concluded that the referendum approach had reached a dead end. Further, they agreed that even if a resolution to the issue of voter registration could be found, which they believed unlikely, holding such a vote was neither in the interest of the United States nor of the Maghreb region. Any winner-takes-all formula, they concluded—such as an up or down vote in a referendum on either independence or integration—was bound to be rejected by the loser and certain to perpetuate the problem, deepening the conflict further and increasing the risk of renewed hostilities. The State Department policy group agreed instead to promote a balanced political compromise that would require fundamental concessions from both parties, but would also offer both the essential elements of what they needed to resolve the conflict. It was determined that Morocco needed to retain its sovereignty over what it referred to as its "southern provinces" as essential to national stability. From the moment it recovered its independence, Morocco has always defined the Western Sahara conflict as an existential issue intimately tied to its efforts to reassert its territorial integrity over all precolonial Moroccan territories occupied by France and Spain. Given the ethnic and cultural identity of the region, it was also clear that a substantial degree of self-governance was required to satisfy the local demand for some legitimate form of self-determination and to meet the commitment of the international community that this principle be protected in any eventual resolution.

Despite this awareness among members of the policy group, it appeared that there was considerable skepticism among other senior officers at the State Department regarding the complex historical, societal, and political factors defining Morocco's perception that it needed to retain sovereignty over the Western Sahara. From Morocco's point of view, the territory is critical to its national unity, territorial integrity, stability, and the legitimacy of its political institutions.[7] Yet doubts remained among some at the State Department about Morocco's desire to resolve the problem. They argued then, and some continue to argue today, that Morocco was essentially content, or should be content, with a status quo that left them in charge of the territory with little prospect that either the Polisario or the international community would be willing or able to force them to abandon the region. "Do no harm" was an expression heard in Washington and the international policy community in assuming that Morocco was more or less content with the status quo. Morocco's actions however suggest otherwise. With the solemnly pledged support of the United States, Morocco chose to seek a compromise political solution rather than accept the status quo, even though any compromise would require it to abandon its original intent of fully integrating the territory. Instead, with US encouragement, it embraced a new approach, despite its uncertainties, so that it could resolve this issue and move on to larger domestic and regional matters. In fact, Morocco has repeatedly signaled, privately and publicly, that it views a solution to the Western Sahara as critical to regional efforts to build a more coherent and integrated Maghreb that better serves the region's economic and security interests.

Viewing the Western Sahara in the context of larger regional issues was a key factor in Morocco's increasing frustration with the lack of progress in the UN process and was one of the principal factors leading to its May 2012 public declaration of "no-confidence" in the work of former US Ambassador Christopher Ross, the current UN Personal Envoy for Western Sahara. Nine rounds and more than three years of "informal meetings" have produced no progress on the core issue of finding a fundamental political compromise.[8] This despite yearly Security Council encouragements to the parties to seek a "mutually acceptable political solution" and repeated endorsements by the United States and some other permanent members of the UNSC of Morocco's autonomy initiative as "serious, credible and realistic." Instead, the diversion of the UN process away from the original mandate into nonpriority issues led, in Morocco's view, to a process that was failing to focus on the core issue of a mutually acceptable political solution.

The current ambivalence among some State Department bureaucrats for proactively supporting a policy to advance a sovereignty/autonomy trade-off solution is based on a kind of flawed reasoning that overestimates the sustainability of the status quo as "good enough." Unfortunately, "good enough" is rapidly becoming worse as the region evidently accelerates into increasingly dangerous uncertainties. One only needs to consider the deterioration in regional security in the aftermath of the Arab uprisings, the Libyan civil war, and the instability in northern Mali and the Sahel to understand Morocco's insistence that resolving the Western Sahara issue will contribute to the stability of the region and provide for a more cohesive and effective counterterrorism strategy involving all key players.[9]

At the 1999 US interagency policy review, the negative consequences of continuing to promote a winner-take-all solution were seriously assessed as the recognition of the damage being done to the US-Moroccan relationship over the increasingly contentious nature of pursuing an up or down referendum. Additionally, some senior State Department officials, concerned with the increasingly critical attention being given the issue by some influential members of Congress, believed that a policy shift to resolving the Western Sahara conflict through the UN process was a reasonable approach. In the end, some at the State Department viewed the proposed policy shift as a strategic move promising a possible resolution to the problem, while others viewed the shift as a tactical move designed to end the contentious aspects of the issue between the United States and Morocco and provide better opportunities to manage not only the bilateral relationship but the difficult conversation with some in Congress about global peacekeeping issues more generally. In the end, the arguments in favor of moving away from a referendum and toward a political compromise based on a sovereignty/autonomy trade off carried the day. Following a formal decision made by then Secretary of State Madeleine Albright, Morocco was officially approached by the United States to explain its new policy on the Western Sahara and seek its cooperation. The US Embassy was also charged with informing other US friends in the international diplomatic community in Rabat that such a policy adjustment was necessary to avoid further dangers to regional stability and more likely to produce a sustainable resolution to the conflict.

Following the shift in American policy, this political compromise formula was first publicly advanced, with US support, in the spring of 2001 by former Secretary of State James Baker, then serving as the Personal Envoy of the UN Secretary General for the Western Sahara. The core element of this first Baker proposal, which came to be known as "The Framework Agreement," was designed to allow Morocco to continue its sovereignty in the region, but would also have established a significant degree of autonomous self-government for the region, consistent with international standards and the principle of self-determination.[10] The details of the arrangement were left to the parties to negotiate directly. This was critically important because policy makers understood at the time that any agreement that did not have the buy-in of the parties themselves was unlikely to be sustainable. Any attempt to impose such a compromise was likely to run the same risk of simply aggravating tensions rather than resolving them. It was essential that the parties willingly embrace the need for such a compromise and find fair-minded ways through direct negotiations to agree on the particulars of this kind of power-sharing arrangement. The proposal also called for the establishment of a process or mechanism to seek popular approval of any final agreement that might emerge from direct negotiations among the parties. While there is no requirement in international law that such negotiated agreements be put to a popular vote, the common view then, as now, was that it was important to allow such a referendum in the interest of establishing both the legitimacy of the solution as well as its sustainability. As it had been agreed in consultations with the United States, and with former Secretary Baker, Morocco also publicly acknowledged in the spring of 2001 that it was prepared to negotiate a solution to the conflict according to the framework laid out in James Baker's initial proposal. However, very few in the US government appreciated that support for the Framework Agreement had not come easily for Morocco. On the other hand, the Polisario Front rejected Baker's proposal outright and Algeria backed the Polisario position.

In 2002, amid rumors that he would resign if the Security Council did not give him a stronger mandate, Baker attempted, with support from the Clinton administration, to move the Framework Agreement forward by suggesting that the Security Council choose among four options: (1) proceed with the (failed) referendum process; (2) advance negotiations uniquely on the basis of the Framework Agreement; (3) partition the territory; or (4) abandon the UN effort and withdraw the MINURSO peacekeeping mission.[11] The Security Council was divided over an open and exclusive endorsement of the Framework Agreement, even though it largely recognized that the other options were all dead ends. Instead, it renewed MINURSO's mandate and urged the parties to cooperate fully with the Personal Envoy to achieve "a mutually acceptable political solution."[12] This shift away from the established course of continuing to pursue the referendum option was subtle at the outset, but it was complete. From this point forward, the emphasis of the Security Council would focus increasingly on a mutually acceptable political solution that respected the principle of self-determination, but references to any up or down referendum would gradually disappear. It had become clear that other options were simply not viable and that the only reasonable way forward would have to be grounded in a fundamental political compromise that would deny both parties their optimal goals. This approach would allow each party enough of what it needed to resolve the problem and protect the core interests of all parties, including the international community's interest in support for the principle of self-determination.

SHIFTING POLICY APPROACHES AND RESERVATIONS IN MOROCCO

The policy shift in Morocco for supporting this compromise approach was every bit as difficult as the shift had been in Washington. In the first instance, many in Morocco were genuinely persuaded that if the voter registration issue could be resolved in its favor it would win the vote. Many senior Moroccan government officials, most importantly then Minister of Interior Driss Basri, were firmly committed to pursuing the referendum which he often insisted Morocco would win. This strong opinion of Minister Basri carried substantial weight in Moroccan political circles. The government had taken a strong and very public stand during the period 1991–1998 in favor of the referendum and had argued vigorously in favor of conducting a vote that it deemed was fair to all those Sahrawis whom it believed were legitimate stakeholders. And while there were those who were skeptical that this process would eventually produce a fair vote, there were also many among Morocco's political elites who were convinced that this was the best approach and that Morocco should stay the course with the referendum. However, despite this seemingly widespread consensus in Morocco, there was also periodic press commentary and private exchanges about the need to pursue what was then referred to in a kind of coded fashion as "the third way" between independence and full integration. Nevertheless, in Morocco these were clearly minority voices in the late 1990s.

A further obstacle to shifting policy was the simple fact that Morocco's commitment to the referendum had been a decision of King Hassan II and, over the years since that original policy choice, a consensus among the political class of the nation had formed around this "sovereign" position. There had been only limited discussion among the political elites about other options as Morocco had pressed forward with great energy to justify its stance on voter registration.

There was also at the time substantial concern in Morocco about the use of the term "autonomy" as an element of any alternative political solution because of the prevailing view that the Arabic translation of this term conveyed a sense of full independence for the territory. A further issue of some consequence at the time was widespread concern among many senior Moroccan policy makers and opinion leaders that granting Western Sahara any kind of special status, such as autonomy, might provoke similar demands from other regions in Morocco that could prove destabilizing to national unity and the country's long effort to reestablish its full territorial integrity and a coherent, even if culturally diverse, national identity.

As a further impediment, there was also a deep skepticism in Morocco over the willingness of either Algeria or the Polisario Front to accept any kind of compromise that did not guarantee them their ultimate objective—independence for the territory. Most Moroccans, then as now, believed the Polisario Front represented little more than a tool of Algeria in its regional contest with Morocco over Maghreb leadership.[13] Few Moroccan political leaders were persuaded that Algeria would come to the bargaining table in a spirit of goodwill and compromise to settle the issue. And finally, and of equal importance, there was also a common concern among many Moroccans as to whether Morocco's friends in the West, especially the United States, could be relied upon to remain steadfast in pursuit of the kind of compromise political solution they were advocating. In these circumstances, many believed that it was impolitic for Morocco to abandon its original position of support for a fairly arranged referendum that, while it may not produce a solution in the short term, nevertheless sustained the peace and allowed the dispute to be managed forward in a way that avoided significant risks. These misgivings in Morocco about striking out on a new approach, an "adventure" some called it, to find a "political solution" should not be underestimated. Given the lack of progress toward a mutually agreed political solution in the years since, and the sometimes ambiguous and ambivalent backing by Morocco's partners in this effort, many of those who were skeptical from the beginning are increasingly frustrated today.

Following the shift in Washington policy, a series of high-level meetings took place, some led by assistant secretary for Near East Asian Affairs, Martin Indyk, in an attempt to explain the reasoning behind the shift in US policy away from the referendum and in favor of a compromise political solution and to explain why the United States thought such an approach was also in the best interest of Morocco and the region. Initially, these consultations ran afoul of the reservations explained earlier, but Morocco made it clear that it was open-minded about new proposals and was willing to continue the discussions. Just prior to his death, in July 1999, King Hassan II indicated his desire to find a political solution followed by a confirmatory referendum.

Following the death of King Hassan II and the accession to the throne of King Mohammed VI, these meetings culminated some months later in direct talks between senior Moroccan officials and James Baker to determine whether it was possible to reach agreement on a formula for autonomy under Moroccan sovereignty that would protect Morocco's basic interests in the region and its national unity and territorial integrity. It was these talks, supported by the US government that eventually culminated in Baker's original Framework Agreement and Morocco's public agreement to negotiate a solution based on the basic terms of the proposal. The Framework Agreement was welcomed in Washington and became the basis of US diplomacy at the time to persuade the parties and others in the international community to embrace this promising new beginning in the search for a realistic and sustainable settlement, despite the initial rejection by the Polisario Front and Algeria.[14]

SUBSEQUENT DEVELOPMENTS THROUGH THE ELECTION OF THE BUSH ADMINISTRATION

Efforts continued throughout the remainder of the second Clinton administration to bring Algeria and the Polisario Front to agree to negotiate under the terms of the Framework Agreement and to build support within the Security Council and the international community for this compromise political approach. Yet, both Algeria and the Polisario Front remained intransigent in their rejection of any solution other than the original proposal for a winner-take-all referendum on the terms they preferred with respect to voter eligibility.

The election of the Bush administration was marked initially by a lack of attention to the Western Sahara question. The new US administration tended to refer questions about the conflict to James Baker who continued to serve as UN Personal Envoy. For reasons that have never been publicly explained, nor fully understood by the authors, James Baker eventually decided to rework his original proposal and submit to the Security Council a new version of a political settlement which he referred to as "the Peace Plan" for Western Sahara.[15] This new and unexpected proposal differed radically from the terms of the Framework Agreement and was viewed in Morocco as a major departure from the original proposal and a fundamental threat to Moroccan interests in the issue.

Initially, the new Baker proposal once again led to increasing tensions in the US-Moroccan bilateral relationship as Morocco assumed that any proposal put forward by James Baker must necessarily have the support of the United States, especially as Baker's close association with the Bush family was well known. This second Baker proposal would have allowed no negotiation or buy-in through the normal give-and-take bargaining process that brings parties to a consensus and enhances prospects for a sustainable solution. Instead, Baker insisted that the parties agree to its terms without modification. The specific terms of the proposal would have obliged Morocco to fully withdraw its military and security forces from Western Sahara without any similar proviso that either Algeria or the Polisario Front demilitarizes the southern border area with Morocco. This, of course, posed a serious potential military threat to Morocco's territorial integrity and national security. The second Baker proposal would have essentially turned control of the territory over to the Polisario Front for a four- or five-year period preceding a vote on autonomy or independence. Under its terms, executive, judicial, and legislative authority would have been vested in new Polisario Front controlled governmental structures that would have allowed the new autonomous government the right to pass local laws without reference to the Moroccan constitution and the protections of Moroccan law for the local population. The dangers inherent in this kind of arrangement were readily apparent to senior Moroccan officials who rejected Baker's proposal, following agreement first by Algeria and then subsequently, and reluctantly, by the Polisario Front as well.

Baker's second proposal came as a shock to Morocco, not only because it deviated so dramatically from the Framework Agreement in its content, but also because Baker seemed so insistent on its implementation without modification or negotiation.[16] What the original proposal indicated should be worked out through negotiations between the parties, the second attempted to impose without discussion. The second proposal essentially handed the Polisario Front what it had previously failed to win on the battlefield or would have had to negotiate under the first proposal. Given that the latter proposal allowed the Polisario a free hand in the territory for four or five years, there was ample room for serious doubt about whether any future vote would ever be held. Morocco's rejection of this offer was predictable. It would have handed Morocco's adversaries an outright victory at the outset and offered little more than a vague prospect of an eventual vote that most agreed would likely never happen. Worse still, from Morocco's perspective, James Baker seemed totally closed to the prospect of even discussing alternatives. For those in Morocco who had been suspicious of this "political" approach from the beginning, it looked like the worst possible outcome was about to be visited upon them by the very partners they had believed were committed to supporting their basic interests in the territory. Suddenly, there was again serious trouble in the bilateral relationship.

Tensions quickly mounted and eventually led to a meeting between King Mohammed VI and President Bush in New York in September 2003. At that meeting, it became clear that Baker's new proposal did not have the support of the Bush administration, which remained committed to a negotiated political compromise within the sovereignty/autonomy formula. Further, the administration remained opposed to any attempt to force Morocco to accept a plan that it opposed as detrimental to its core national interests. It also soon became equally clear that the Security Council had little interest in aggravating regional tension by attempting to impose a solution against the will of any party. James Baker subsequently resigned in April 2004 as Personal Envoy and was replaced by a former Dutch diplomat, Peter van Walsum.

THE BUSH ADMINISTRATION MOVES FORWARD

Following the failure of Baker's second proposal, the Bush administration, as the Clinton administration before it, continued to support a compromise political solution, but also encouraged Morocco to put forward its own initiative. Morocco submitted its own autonomy plan in February 2007.[17] A letter from 173 members of Congress, including nearly the entire Democratic and Republican leadership, was sent to President Bush on April 26, 2007, indicating broad Congressional support for the Moroccan initiative.[18] The Bush administration publicly described this Moroccan autonomy initiative as "serious and credible" and urged the parties to negotiate the details.[19] The Polisario Front rejected the Moroccan initiative and began to openly threaten a return to war unless the Security Council insisted on implementation of the referendum on independence.[20]

Despite its early and persistent rejections and new threats of war, and after submitting a restatement of its demands, the Polisario eventually agreed to enter into direct talks with Morocco without preconditions under UN auspices.[21] However, the subsequent four rounds of formal meetings under van Walsum failed to bring the Polisario Front and their Algerian supporters to accept the need for any kind of fundamental compromise. Peter van Walsum's last report as personal envoy of the secretary-general (PESG) in April 2008 made clear that a compromise was essential and that the notion of either party being able to achieve their maximal demands, including specifically the Polisario Front demands for independence for the territory, was unrealistic.[22] That language elicited an outcry from the Polisario Front and Algeria, which refused to meet further with van Walsum. As a result, van Walsum's mandate as Personal Envoy was not renewed in August 2008. In January 2009, he was replaced by retired American diplomat Ambassador Christopher Ross, who continued to meet with the parties in individual sessions and informal group meetings (nine rounds by the end of 2012). However, these informal sessions under Ross's leadership increasingly focused on ancillary issues and failed to move the Polisario Front any closer to accepting the need for compromise, despite annual urgings from the Security Council to find a mutually acceptable political solution that respects the principle of self-determination. Instead, the Polisario Front continued to insist on a referendum on independence and continued to threaten a return to war.

THE OBAMA ADMINISTRATION EXPRESSES VERBAL SUPPORT

President Obama has made security a key element of his foreign policy. The growth of terrorist activities in the Sahara/Sahel, especially following the mass infusion of weapons from the Libyan civil war and the collapse of governance in northern Mali, reinforced the administration's efforts to promote stability in the region, which some in Congress and elsewhere have insisted also requires a need to resolve the Western Sahara conflict. A letter signed by a bipartisan majority of 233 members of the House of Representatives and sent to President Obama on April 3, 2009, urged him to support the Moroccan initiative in "both words and deeds."[23] In a March 16, 2010, letter to US Secretary of State Hillary Clinton, a bipartisan majority of fifty-four senators joined the House in support of a negotiated settlement of the Western Sahara conflict based on broad autonomy under Moroccan sovereignty.[24] At the end of 2011, further Congressional support for this kind of solution came in the form of the Omnibus Appropriations bill which contained report language urging the Obama administration to use US development assistance mechanisms in the Western Sahara, while expressing Congressional concern about the ongoing dispute, urging action to resolve the crisis.[25]

While international support for a compromise political solution grows, there is also an emerging legal and academic consensus that supports autonomy as a political solution consistent with the principle of self-determination in the postcolonial, post–Cold War environment. This has been evident in the repeated urgings, especially since UNSC Resolution 1541 of April 2004, for a compromise political solution.[26] This view is also clearly reflected in the last report of Peter van Walsum, the previous Personal Envoy, to the secretary-general in April 2008:

> I do not accept the view that taking political reality into account is a concession or surrender, and that it is wrong ever to settle for less than pure legality. The choices to be made are not limited to the dilemma between international legality and political reality. There is also a moral dilemma that comes to light when the virtue of international legality is weighed against the consequences of its pursuit for the people of Western Sahara in real life. The main reason why I find the status quo intolerable is that it is too readily accepted, not only by uncommitted onlookers in distant lands, but also by deeply involved supporters of the Frente Polisario [Polisario Front], who do not live in the camps themselves but are convinced that those who do would rather stay there indefinitely than settle for any negotiated solution that falls short of full independence.[27]

Regional analysts have concluded that without this compromise solution, those in the refugee camps will continue to be subject to increased instability and violence from a growing terrorist threat while tens of thousands of Sahrawi refugees remain condemned to a bleak status quo and denial of freedoms to which they have been subjected for better than three decades.[28] This is the bitter reality of not pursuing autonomy as the vehicle for self-determination for the Sahrawi people.

CURRENT CIRCUMSTANCES

The Obama administration is the third consecutive US administration to support a resolution to this conflict through a political compromise based on sovereignty/autonomy. However, by the end of 2012, the lack of concrete action in support of this policy has provided false hope to the Polisario Front leadership and their supporters that intransigence and a refusal to compromise eventually will lead to a reversal of US policy in their favor. The status quo sustains the humanitarian crisis among the refugees and also raises the risk that, without sufficient attention and cooperation on region-wide counterterrorism efforts, the increasingly dangerous security threats in the region will proliferate beyond the Maghreb, as events in Mali and Algeria in early 2013 would seem to confirm.[29]

In addition to the evidence of the escalating conflict in Mali in early 2013, there have been no less than five reports since 2009 from Washington think tanks that highlight the dangers of the growing security threat in the Sahara/Sahel with specific reference to dangers posed by some associated with the Polisario Front for their involvement in criminal activities in the region.[30] Other reports indicate that the refugees in the Polisario Front controlled camps in southern Algeria are becoming increasingly vulnerable to recruitment by terrorist and criminal enterprises in the region.[31] This situation has been further aggravated by the mass infusion of Libyan weapons and the collapse of governance in northern Mali with the alarming ascendance there of AQIM and other terrorist and criminal gangs intent upon destabilizing the governments of the entire Maghreb region and establishing a new base of operations for global jihadists. This also has, of course, grave humanitarian consequences for the tens and perhaps hundreds of thousands of refugees and internally displaced persons fleeing these conflict zones, further destabilizing an already extremely fragile region.

WHAT CAN BE DONE TO MOVE US POLICY FORWARD

Despite its useful public declarations and urgings from Congress, the first Obama administration did little to implement any concrete actions to support its declared policy backing a compromise sovereignty/autonomy formula as the basis of a "mutually agreed political solution." Likewise, the UNSC, in its annual renewal of the MINURSO mandate, has failed to take a firmer stand on the need for a realistic compromise despite the rise in regional instability. It could more proactively promote options to settle the issue and stop turning a blind eye to the stone-walling of some parties on the need to embrace a fundamental political compromise as the basis of any just and lasting resolution to the conflict.

In the meantime, the refugee population of the camps in southern Algeria are increasingly vulnerable to being drawn ever deeper into growing terrorist and criminal networks thriving in the chaos of the Sahara/Sahel. The UN, through the office of the High Commissioner for Refugees (UNHCR), has failed to promote more durable solutions for the Sahrawi refugees in the Polisario camps despite readily available alternatives. This is deeply worrying since these refugees would at least have the alternative of voluntary repatriation to Morocco, and perhaps elsewhere as well, if the UNHCR, the Security Council, and key state actors would take more concrete action to support such an option. Given events in Mali and the ascendancy of terrorist groups in the region, such alternatives would seem to require some more urgent attention than is presently being given to the status and continued forced existence of the refugees in the Polisario camps.

If the United States is serious about resolving the Western Sahara crisis and contributing in a meaningful way to helping stabilize the Sahara/Sahel region, there are a number of steps that would diminish the security threats to US interests in the region. None of these steps are in the "too hard to do" category and each would help create a better climate for a negotiated solution, as well as help ease larger and increasingly more dangerous tensions in the region.

- Senior US officials, specifically including the US ambassadors in Morocco and Algeria, should be encouraged, indeed required, to visit the Western Sahara and the refugee camps outside Tindouf in Algeria. Such visits are now prohibited by State Department policy. While perhaps arguably useful in the past, today this prohibition conveys the impression that the United States is so unconcerned with the problems in the Sahara/Sahel and the Western Sahara that it does not need the firsthand views of its most senior diplomats to help inform and guide the process of resolving these issues.
- The United States should take every available opportunity to clearly state, in unambiguous terms, its support for a mutually acceptable political solution based on the only reasonable and viable option, that of sovereignty and autonomy. The absence of a clear policy statement only continues to undermine the need for a compromise solution.
- The United States should use its influence in the Security Council to make clear that this option is indeed the only realistic way forward and end restatements of formulas that have already failed.
- The policy decision to restrict US access to the Western Sahara and deny US development assistance funds to the region should be reversed, as Congress has now both authorized and urged. Morocco has invested hundreds of millions of dollars in their southern provinces to improve basic infrastructure and quality of life and would likely welcome US participation in meeting genuine humanitarian and development needs in the area.[32] This kind of engagement would demonstrate through concrete actions that the United States is fully committed to its support for autonomy. Further, it would build confidence among the Sahrawi people to endorse such an outcome. These actions would also help project an image elsewhere in the Sahara/Sahel that there are viable, peaceful alternatives to the chaos being promoted by a rapidly expanding revolutionary jihadist population in the region. Most importantly, funding that leads to improved governance and economic development will aid in stabilizing the region.
- The rest of the State Department should align their internal decision-making criteria vis-à-vis the Western Sahara with Secretary Clinton's verbal statements of support for the Moroccan autonomy initiative. Inside the State Department, there is bureaucratic stalling that inhibits creative approaches and initiatives that could lead to resolution of the conflict. As Zbigniew Brzezinski wrote recently, "As a result [of Obama's priority on domestic political affairs], his grand redefinition of U.S. foreign policy is vulnerable to dilution or

delay by upper-level officials who have the bureaucratic predisposition to favor caution over action and the familiar over the innovative."[33] Nowhere is this more evident than in US policy on Western Sahara where senior officials below the level of Secretary Clinton routinely miss opportunities to support the Moroccan initiative and instead blandly support the "UN process," as though this was somehow a substitute for US national interest or even consistent with what the United States has clearly stated as its policy priority. This kind of ambivalence serves to add confusion to an already difficult situation and perpetuates the problem.

- Existing US foreign assistance programs in Morocco targeting social and economic development should include the inhabitants of the Western Sahara, again as Congress has now specifically authorized, especially those focusing on health, education, entrepreneurship, and similar capacity-building initiatives.
- Continued support for NGO, civil society, and local government programs will enhance the US presence in the region and US support for democratic participation. It will also add much needed US support to the only area in the increasingly volatile Sahara/Sahel region that continues to be an island of stability, security, social and economic progress, and democratic practice.
- The United States should help establish conditions for a successful autonomy arrangement by engaging US agencies including USAID, USTDA, OPIC, and EX-IM Bank in support of enhancing private sector investments in Western Sahara. America's European partners are already investing in key sectors in the region. There is no reason that the United States should not follow suit.
- The United States should recognize the Western Sahara conflict as an impediment to US economic investment and opportunity in North Africa. Once the conflict is resolved, the United States might have better leverage with Algeria by responding to its need to attract US investments in their energy sector, tourism, infrastructure, and a much needed broader diversification of their economy. More importantly, this offers the United States an array of opportunities to promote broader regional economic integration. Expanding Morocco's free trade agreement with the United States to benefit the Maghreb countries will clearly demonstrates the benefits of settling the conflict.
- The UN should implement its mandate to encourage Sahrawi leadership in both the Tindouf camps and Western Sahara region to work together on matters of mutual interest affecting the region. One of the original confidence building measures, this dialogue can help build toward the broader integration of interests on both sides of the berm.

- The United States should urge the UNHCR and the Security Council to urge Algeria to respect its legal obligations under the 1951 Refugee Convention and the 1967 Protocol and reduce the burden associated with maintaining the camps in a hostile physical environment. The UNHCR should immediately begin a public information campaign in the camps to inform the refugees of their rights under international law, including identification, documentation, access to travel documents, and freedom of movement.[34] If the UNHCR carries out a census in the camps, those results, along with freedom of movement that includes voluntary repatriation for the refugees, and more accountability for international food and medical assistance, would drastically change conditions in the camps making them obsolete, thus greatly reducing the humanitarian crisis and the vulnerability of the refugee population to other dangerous enticements.
- In addition to a voluntary repatriation program, the United States should work with the UNHCR and the UNSC to encourage and provide support for any Algerian efforts to allow the refugees to settle elsewhere in Algeria if they choose an option other than repatriation to Morocco.

CONCLUSION

A remnant of the Cold War, the conflict in the Western Sahara historically has not been a priority for US diplomacy. Despite the shift in US policy under President Clinton, the United States has failed thus far to take clearly identifiable actions that make a negotiated solution more attainable. With the existing strong bipartisan Congressional support for the kind of compromise political solution based on the sovereignty/autonomy trade-off, the second Obama administration should take tangible actions now to support its policy and move toward a definitive resolution of the conflict. Circumstances in the region are making this an imperative that needs immediate attention.

Solving the Western Sahara conflict through this kind of fundamental political compromise will provide yet another benchmark for effective conflict resolution strategies that might have broader application in this particular subregion, and that incorporate evolving principles of self-determination, integration of parochial interests through confidence-building measures, and effective external prodding and oversight. As noted, resolving the Western Sahara conflict rests on two core issues: achieving a political compromise based on the sovereignty/autonomy formula that meets the standards for a sustainable solution and recognizing and enforcing the rights of the refugees in the camps.

Autonomy in the Sahara under Moroccan sovereignty remains the only realistic and viable solution to resolve this long-running conflict. Moreover, autonomy addresses key policy concerns for the United States and the international community—providing self-determination for the Sahrawi people and ensuring security and stability for the region. The US government has the support of the majority of the Congress and most of the UNSC to move forward and focus the negotiations on specific steps toward implementing autonomy with international support for the rights and needs of the people living in the region.

Doing less undermines President Obama's call for US foreign policy to "look around the corner" to anticipate where the United States should be active to head off developing threats to America's security. In the Western Sahara, the United States can make a decisive impact on resolving the conflict by implementing its existing policy concretely and helping end the humanitarian crisis for the people of the Sahara.

NOTES

1. The opinions and characterizations in this chapter are those of the authors, and do not necessarily represent official positions of the US government. The coauthors of this article, Ambassador Edward M. Gabriel and Robert M. Holley, were posted at the US Embassy in Morocco at the time of the US policy shift on the Western Sahara issue. They were active participants in the policy review that led to the change in US policy. Edward Gabriel was the US ambassador to Morocco at the time and Robert Holley was Political Counselor at the US Embassy. Currently, Ambassador Gabriel and Mr. Holley advise the Government of Morocco. For more information, please visit the Department of Justice in Washington, DC.

2. Hillary Rodham Clinton, interview with Fouad Arif, *Al-Aoula Television*, November 3, 2009, www.state.gov/secretary/rm/2009a/11/131354.htm.

3. Hillary Rodham Clinton, "Remarks with Moroccan Foreign Minister Taieb Fassi Fihri" (remarks, US Department of State, Washington, DC, March 23, 2011), www.state.gov/secretary/rm/2011/03/158895.htm; Hillary Rodham Clinton, "Remarks with Moroccan Minister of Foreign Affairs Saad-Eddine Al-Othmani after Their Meeting" (remarks, Rabat, Morocco, February 26, 2012), www.state.gov/secretary/rm/2012/02/184667.htm.

4. Erik Jensen, *Western Sahara: Anatomy of a Stalemate?* (Boulder, CO: Lynne Rienner, 2012), 49.

5. Jensen, *Western Sahara: Anatomy of a Stalemate?*, 49–50.

6. United Nations Security Council, "Resolution 690 (April 29, 1991) [on the Western Sahara]," (S/RES/690), http://daccess-dds-ny.un.org/doc/RESOLUTION/GEN/NR0/596/26/IMG/NR059626.pdf?OpenElement;
United Nations Security Council, "Resolution 1198 (September 18, 1998) [on the Western Sahara]," (S/RES/1198), www.un.org/ga/search/view_doc.asp?symbol=S/RES/1198(1998).

7. "Western Sahara: The Cost of the Conflict," *International Crisis Group* Middle East/North Africa Report, no. 65 (June 11, 2007): 2, www.crisisgroup.org/~/media/Files/Middle%20East%20North%20Africa/North%20Africa/Western%20Sahara/65_western_sahara___the_cost_of_the_conflict.

8. "Morocco says it no longer has confidence in UN envoy," *Agence France Presse*, May 17, 2012, www.google.com/hostednews/afp/article/ALeqM5hN8Ygfn_ZxvRnRzXjg-LsQGyEMZw?docId=CNG.737c34631ca379f2d8a2a5ef902157c8.2c1.

9. "Why the Maghreb Matters," *Potomac Institute for Policy Studies and the Conflict Management Program of the School of Advanced International Studies*, March 2009: 13, www.whythemaghrebmatters.org/NorthAfricaPolicyPaper032509.pdf.

10. United Nations Security Council, *Report of the Secretary General on the Situation Concerning Western Sahara* (New York, June 20, 2001), S/2001/613, www.un.org/ga/search/view_doc.asp?symbol=S/2001/613.

11. United Nations Security Council, *Report of the Secretary General on the Situation Concerning Western Sahara* (New York, February 19, 2002), S/2002/178, www.un.org/ga/search/view_doc.asp?symbol=S/2002/178.

12. United Nations Security Council, "Resolution 1394 (February 27, 2002) [on the Western Sahara]," (S/RES/1394), www.un.org/ga/search/view_doc.asp?symbol=S/RES/1394(2002).

13. "Western Sahara: The Cost of the Conflict," 2.

14. Alexis Arieff, "Western Sahara," *Congressional Research Service* (April 5, 2012): 8, www.fas.org/sgp/crs/row/RS20962.pdf.

15. United Nations Security Council, *Report of the Secretary General on the Situation Concerning Western Sahara* (New York, May 23, 2003), S/2003/565, www.un.org/ga/search/view_doc.asp?symbol=S/2003/565.

16. Jensen, *Western Sahara: Anatomy of a Stalemate?*, 100–103.

17. Government of Morocco, *Moroccan Initiative for Negotiating an Autonomy Statute for the Sahara Region*, April 11, 2007, www.maroc.ma/PortailInst/An/Actualites/MOROCCAN+INITIATIVE+FOR+NEGOTIATING+AN+AUTONOMY+STATUTE+FOR+THE+SAHARA+REGION.htm.

18. "173 Members of Congress Take Stand on North Africa," Moroccan American Center for Policy Press Release (Washington DC, April 26, 2007), http://moroccanamericanpolicy.com/documents/173_sig_letter.pdf.

19. Arieff, "Western Sahara," 8.

20. Arieff, "Western Sahara," 8.

21. "Morocco and Polisario Agree to Talk," *Al Jazeera*, May 1, 2007, www.aljazeera.com/news/africa/2007/05/2008525131827899612.html.

22. Peter van Walsum, "Assessment of the Personal Envoy of the Secretary-General for Western Sahara" (report, New York, April 21, 0008), www.corcas.com/Portals/Al/Photos2011/Report-Walsum-1.pdf.

23. Congress of the United States, "Letter to The Honorable Barack Obama" (Washington, DC, April 3, 2009), http://moroccanamericanpolicy.com/wsdocs/233letter.pdf.

24. United States Senate, "Letter to The Honorable Hillary Rodham Clinton" (Washington, DC, March 16, 2012), www.moroccanamericanpolicy.org/SenateLetter.pdf.

25. *Consolidated Appropriations Act of 2012*, Public Law 112–74, 112th Cong., 1st sess., (December 26, 2011).

26. United Nations Security Council, "Resolution 1541 (April 29, 2004) [on the Western Sahara]," (S/RES/1541), www.un.org/ga/search/view_doc.asp?symbol=S/RES/1541(2004).

27. Van Walsum, "Assessment of the Personal Envoy."

28. Anouar Boukhars, "Simmering Discontent in Western Sahara," *Carnegie Endowment for International Peace*, March 2012, http://carnegieendowment.org/2012/03/12/simmering-discontent-in-western-sahara/a2ah; Merrill Smith, "Stonewalling on Refugee Rights: Algeria & the Sahrawi," *United States Committee for Refugees and Immigrants*, 2009, www.uscrirefugees.org/2010Website/3_Our%20Work/3_2_1_3_Morocco/Stonewalling.pdf.

29. "UN envoy warns of risk of new violence in W. Sahara," *Agence France Presse*, November 12, 2012, www.google.com/hostednews/afp/article/ALeqM5htH7sXEM6mE9j-NsimrXas4hWToQ?docId=CNG.714d6206df93e4c0d2493c2c67d87693.311.

30. "Why the Maghreb Matters"; Yonah Alexander, "Addressing the Rising Threat from al-Qaeda and Other Terrorists in North and West/Central Africa," *Potomac Insti-*

tute for Policy Studies, January 2010, www.potomacinstitute.org/attachments/524_Maghreb%20Terrorism%20report.pdf; J. Peter Pham, "Not Another Failed States: Toward a Realistic Solution in the Western Sahara," *The Journal of the Middle East and Africa* no. 1 (2010): 1–24; Boukhars, "Simmering Discontent in Western Sahara"; Yonah Alexander, "Special Update Report—Terrorism in North, West, and Central Africa: From 9/11 to the Arab Spring." *Potomac Institute for Policy Studies*, January 2012, http://moroccoonthemove.files.wordpress.com/2012/02/2012-special-update-report-full-report-terrorism-in-africa-from-9-11-to-arab-spring-icts-potomac-2feb2012.pdf; Wolfram Lacher, "Organized Crime in the Sahel-Sahara Region," *Carnegie Endowment for International Peace*, September 2012, http://carnegieendowment.org/files/sahel_sahara.pdf; "Islamist Extremists Threaten Africa's Rise," *The Soufan Group*, June 27, 2012, http://soufangroup.com/briefs/details/?Article_Id=325.

31. Alison Lake, "Unlikely Bedfellows: Are Some Saharan Marxists Joining Al-Qaida Operations in North Africa?" *Foreign Policy*, January 3, 2011, http://mideast.foreignpolicy.com/posts/2011/01/03/unlikely_bedfellows_are_some_saharan_marxists_joining_al_qaida_operations_in_north_; J. Peter Pham, "Islamist Threat to Africa's Rise in 2012." *Atlantic Council*, January 3, 2012, www.acus.org/new_atlanticist/islamist-threat-africas-rise-2012; Boukhars, "Simmering Discontent in Western Sahara"; "Islamist Extremists Threaten Africa's Rise."

32. Laïla Slimani, "Sahara: l'aménagement des cites du Sud," *Jeune Afrique*, November 30, 2009, www.jeuneafrique.com/Articles/Dossier/ARTJAJA2551p078.xml0/amenagement-du-territoire-infrastructure-sahara-urbanismesahara-l-amenagement-des-cites-du-sud.html.

33. Zbigniew Brzezinski, "From Hope to Audacity: Appraising Obama's Foreign Policy," *Foreign Affairs*, January/February 2010, www.foreignaffairs.com/articles/65720/zbigniew-brzezinski/from-hope-to-audacity.

34. United Nations Conference of Plenipotentiaries on the Status of Refugees and Stateless Persons, *Convention Relating to the Status of Refugees* (Geneva: United Nations, 1951);
United Nations Economic and Social Council, *Protocol Relating to the Status of Refugees* (New York: United Nations, 1967).

Part III

Dynamics of Optimal Solutions

NINE

Dynamics of Intergroup Conflicts in the Western Sahara

Anouar Boukhars

Despite the Moroccan state's efforts to promote economic development and peaceful coexistence, the Western Sahara remains a territory where ethnic cleavages, tribal tensions, and socioeconomic grievances intertwine inextricably. Opposing ethnic groups are increasingly becoming conscious of their separate identity and interests. Such evolution is not so benign as it is marked by the rise of troubling xenophobic sentiments and intergroup hostility. Ethnic cleavages and cultural animosity have become dangerously pronounced, threatening to fuel radicalism, violence, and confrontations. The impact and scars from the violence that engulfed Laâyoune in November 2010 and Dakhla in 2011 are still strongly felt in the streets. Indeed, a growing number of Western Saharans find themselves isolated and frustrated—a precarious development.

This chapter examines how such fissures came into being and how they are creating new divisive forces that threaten the stability of the region. Without immediate adjustments in policy, tensions are bound to escalate and mushroom into dangerous ethnic and tribal divides, worsening cultural prejudices, and deepening a growing clash of identities.

PATTERNS OF ETHNIC TENSION

Since its annexation of the Western Sahara in 1975, Morocco has used threats and incentives to win the support or at least the acquiescence of the indigenous population. But such quest for authority and legitimacy has been contested even as the prospect for the creation of an independent state in the Western Sahara remains impractical. The great powers, including the United States, want the disputed territory to remain Moroccan. Western governments dread the prospect of the creation of a weak state, almost the size of Britain, in an area already afflicted by fragile or failing states, writes Spanish journalist Ignacio Cembrero. "Only a handful of Latin American and African countries hold contrary views," he adds.[1] But despite Western support and the state's own substantial investments in the territory, Morocco, as the late King Hassan II eloquently put it in the late 1980s, struggles to win the hearts and minds of the indigenous population.

The disgruntlement of the local population is attributed to the failure of the Moroccan state to have a "coherent and transparent" approach to modernizing and governing the territory.[2] Morocco deluded itself into believing that the support of local intermediaries, economic development, and international support for its autonomy plan were enough to gain the local's acceptance, refusing to recognize that failure to improve human rights, accountability, and management of resources inflame local tensions and affect its image abroad.[3]

Since 2005, writes Spanish scholar, Bernabé García López, the Algerian-backed Polisario has used the reported violations of human rights in Western Sahara to gain support in international forums and bolster its case for independence. Morocco, he adds, failed to realize that its hardline stance against promoters of independence, refusal to legalize their associations, and dithering in the implementation of the special autonomy plan for the territory was costing it its credibility.

To be fair, Morocco has in recent years become slightly more responsive to international prodding to relax its controls over advocates of independence. The latter are allowed to travel freely from the Moroccan controlled Western Sahara to Algeria and the camps near Tindouf. In the last General Congress held in December 2011 in Tifariti—a no man's land located some ninety kilometers west of Tindouf—a number of Sahrawis from Laâyoune traveled to participate along with 1,600 Polisario representatives in the proceedings that saw Polisario Secretary General Mohamed Abdelaziz reelected by 96 percent of the votes for a record eleventh time.[4] Abdelaziz, born in Marrakesh, has been at the helm of the Polisario for thirty-five years. He left Morocco in 1974, breaking ranks with his own father who served in the Moroccan army and two brothers (one is currently a lawyer in Agadir and the other a doctor in Casablanca).[5]

The local supporters of independence, such as activists Aminatou Haidar and Ali Salem Tamek, still lack the capacity to mobilize their community's discontents in huge numbers. Haidar, for example, who was born outside the disputed territory in Akka in 1966, garners international attention, but her ability to shape the independence discourse and strategy inside the Moroccan-controlled Western Sahara remains limited.[6]

But Morocco's efforts to improve human rights in the Western Sahara have been timid.[7] The April 2013 aborted attempt by the United States to broaden the mandate of UN peacekeepers to include human rights monitoring in the Western Sahara is a dramatic warning to Morocco to quickly act on its promises to improve its management of the territory and expedite its devolution of power to the territory. The politics of complacency threatens to squander the goodwill and sympathy that Morocco's autonomy plan enjoys internationally.

The inability of members of local Polisario sympathizers to fuel a popular revolt against Morocco's rule does not mean that dissent against the Moroccan state is on its last legs. In fact, the fading of the old guard is rapidly giving way to a new and unpredictable generation of protesters. They are less ideological, but more individualistic and violent than their elders. Some are ambivalent unionists, but most are indifferent to both Morocco and the Polisario's independence agenda. This disengaged group has yet to embrace unionism or, ominously for Morocco, independence. This is the generation, to quote a local human rights activist, that has made the region more prone to sudden eruptions of rage and violence.[8] Spontaneous outbursts of discontent among the youth are becoming more frequent, posing a troubling development for the Moroccan government.

The ethnic unrest and violent rampages that twice in 2011 rocked Dakhla, a small city situated at the heart of the Western Sahara long known for its ethnic harmony and calm, was a great shock to the authorities as well as the local population. In each instance, the immediate trigger was a dispute among young men that quickly degenerated into intercommunal violence. The first flare-up occurred in February 2011 when a small group of young Sahrawis brandished the flag of Polisario to capture the attention of the international media present to cover a local festival known as "Sea and Desert." Zealous Moroccan youths saw this as a serious affront to the sovereignty of the nation by conniving provocateurs. The festival was intended to be a showcase of the city's pride in its accelerated development (the Moroccan government invested heavily in the city's infrastructure) and transformation into a hub of cultural tourism and aquatic sports. The festival was also meant to be a beacon of unity and nationalism.[9] But like elsewhere in the Sahara, such events can also be tense, as the majority of the large crowd is intensely nationalistic, chanting pro-Moroccan slogans such as "The Sahara is Moroccan" and waving the Moroccan flag.

Occasional flare-ups between youths are therefore likely, but never before had they degenerated in Dakhla into violence. A spark at the festival on a Friday night on February 24 turned into chaos that spilled over into the next day, forcing the authorities to cancel the last day of the event. It took the intervention of the army to bring an end to the confrontations between the inhabitants of the Sahrawi neighborhood of Oum Tounsi and those who hail from areas populated by nonindigenous Sahrawis.[10]

In September 2011, violence erupted again after verbal altercations between supporters of a local soccer team Mouloudia Dakhla, and those of Chabab Mohammedia, a team from a city near Casablanca, quickly escalated into all-out communal warfare. The clashes lasted three days with a death toll of seven people, including a woman and a teenager crushed by a four-wheel-drive vehicle.[11] The confrontations pitted the indigenous Sahrawi population against the inhabitants of "al-Wahda" (The Union). The latter are referred to contemptuously by the indigenous as "al Wakkala" (the eaters)—that is, migrant "interlopers" and opportunists who reap the benefits of the region's resources at their expense. The "al-Wahda" neighborhood is a residential area populated by thousands of Sahrawis who lived outside the disputed territory before being transplanted into the Western Sahara in 1991 to vote in a referendum on self-determination for the territory that never took place.[12] The state provided them with housing and still supplies them with food subsidies. The perception that government largesse disproportionately benefits nonindigenous Western Saharans has sowed the seeds of anger and hatred within the indigenous community.

Behind the violence and underneath the rage is a mixture of ethnic animosity and resentments tied to long-standing socioeconomic grievances that continue to fuel unrest. Despite Moroccan authorities' claims to the contrary, this ethnic tension and enmity, tinged at times with racism, is real and expressed freely during discussions with a range of actors in Dakhla and Laâyoune. A local Sahrawi activist framed the conflict to this author in terms of group survival in the face of the security threats emanating from the Al Wahda inhabitants and the uncertainty about the Moroccan government's willingness or ability to protect the indigenous community. "They are uncivilized brutes," one bluntly stated. "And the worst of all this," she added, "is that we feel unprotected by the police who suspect our allegiances and see us as profiteers."[13]

For their part, the inhabitants of the al-Wahda attribute the societal tension and violence to the extreme intolerance and hostility of the indigenous population. "They are a widely xenophobic bunch who will do everything possible to make us feel unwelcome, even though we share the same ethnicity and have been living here for decades."[14] Indeed, many of these Sahrawis trace their cultural origins and immediate roots to the Western Sahara. Following the natural ebb and flow of cross-border movements of nomadic populations, several fled conflict and colonialism while others pursued divergent interests and preferences. Today, a non-negligible part of the Sahrawi tribe of Ouled Dlim that dominated Dakhla (though they constitute only half of the population now), for example, still resides in Sidi Kacem, an area north of the center of Morocco to which they relocated during Spanish colonialism.[15] The late General Ahmed Dlimi, once a close associate of King Hassan II and commander of the Moroccan army's southern forces, came from the north of Morocco but his family (Ouled Dlim) came earlier from the Sahara.

Relations between indigenous Western Saharans and non-Sahrawi Moroccans from the north are also tense. The latter are referred to as Dakhilis, a generic term that means people from the center of Morocco and designates anyone who is a non-Sahrawi. That includes military personnel and their families, civil servants, workers (carpenters, mechanics), shopkeepers, and traders. There is deep mistrust between the two communities. In the eyes of the indigenous population, Dakhilis are chauvinistic carpetbaggers who steal jobs. They are referred to in demeaning terms as "Ch'lihat" (little Berbers). Those Dakhilis who occupy menial jobs—work Sahrawis view as beneath them—are degradingly called "hammal" (porter). Dakhilis have their own denigrating designations for Sahrawis, who are usually referred to as lazy, untrustworthy, and ungrateful in spite of government preferential treatment. Other unflattering terms include "m'gamline" (flea-ridden) or "mouskhine" (dirty).[16] This ethnic disharmony and these mutual feelings of antagonism were already laid bare in the November 2010 conflict in the streets of Laâyoune. Insurgent Sahrawis deliberately burned properties owned by northerners; the latter responded in brutal kind. The violence and killings of that day put an end to any semblance of harmonious cohabitation between native Sahrawis and Dakhilis.

It was not supposed to be this way. Dakhla is the least-politicized of all major cities in the Sahara and arguably the place where pro-independence sentiment is the weakest. The tribe of Ouled Dlim takes pride in shielding its "fiefdom" from ethnic nationalist sentiment and corresponding state repression. The tribe, the third largest in the Sahara, has kept its distance from other tribal confederations, especially Rquibate who dominate Laâyoune.[17] Geography served the city well, as the nearest and more populous Laâyoune is 500 kilometers away. Its local economy still thrives almost exclusively on fishing and tourism, providing for a better quality of life and less societal crisis and contention than prevalent in Laâyoune, Boujdour, or Smara.[18] The prime concern of the locals has always been the time frames and regulations imposed by the authorities, which help prevent overfishing but can be disruptive to fish harvest.[19] But like in the rest of the Sahara and indeed throughout Morocco, the distribution of benefits generates resentments and frustrations.

In Dakhla, the locals complain that their proportion of resources is smaller than that of foreign fishing companies and the army generals who are suspected of enriching themselves by illegally grabbing maritime fishing licenses.[20] "There are two Dakhlas," complained an inhabitant of the Sahrawi neighborhood of Oum Tounsi. "Here, Sahrawis have not seen their neighborhood develop and we are all unemployed because we are marginalized."[21] Local authorities, however, counter that jobs are abundant, but skills, personal initiative, and work ethic are lacking.[22]

This perception that the indigenous population is being displaced by outsiders who extract and benefit from local resources is compounded by the city's demographic changes. Since Morocco asserted its control in 1979, the city has become a sanctuary for the military and their families. The last decade has also seen an increase in migratory inflows that naturally accompanied the big surge of investment in infrastructure. The Agency for the Development of the South of Morocco, created in 2002, has devoted more than eight hundred million dollars for the socioeconomic development of the region.[23]

While the desire for independence has few takers in Dakhla, the perception of unfair distribution of benefits and opportunities can become a foundation for intergroup conflict whereby one ethnic community assigns malevolent intent to another and blames it for all its troubles. The city becomes a collection of aggrieved groups, each mobilizing based on parochial ethnic identity. Unless a respected state authority diffuses these simmering antagonisms, the risks for conflagration loom large. It is such fear that has prompted the government to station military units in the different strategic areas of Dakhla to prevent another outburst of violence. Similar deployments can be observed in Laâyoune.

THE ROOTS OF CONFLICT

The growing unrest in the Moroccan administered Western Sahara is the consequence of the far-reaching demographic, social, and economic changes the area has experienced since its annexation by Morocco in 1975. The area experienced four successive waves of migration, each introducing the cleavages that still affect the present state of the region. The annual rate of population growth has been 3 percent, and the natives are no longer the majority.[24]

The first phase began immediately after Spain turned over control of the Western Sahara to Morocco and Mauritania in 1975. Several native Sahrawi tribes, by some estimates nearly half the population, heeded the Polisario's call to flee the territory toward the camps near Tindouf in Algeria. To govern the territory, the state had to rely on the remaining local elites and imported other Sahrawis (mainly Spanish speaking and better educated) from outside the contested zone, especially from the neighboring region of Oued Noun, north of the Western Sahara. The Moroccan southern Saharan cities of Tan Tan, Tarfaya, and Guelmim supplied many of the current elites in the Western Sahara.[25]

Most of these elites belonged to the Saharan tribe of Tekna, whose members extend from the Anti-Atlas to the Western Sahara and all the way to the borders of Mali.[26] This confederation also includes the Ait Ouali Moussa, Ait Oussa, Ait Lahcen, Yaggoute, and Izerguiyine tribes.[27] The latter three have historically been loyal to the Moroccan throne. Its members were prominent in both the region of Saguia el-Hamra in the northern Western Sahara where they were nomadic and in the adjacent Moroccan Saharan region of Tarfaya, Sidi Ifni, and Tan Tan where they were sedentary. "The nomadic Ait Lahssen," as political scientist Abdeslam Maghraoui notes, "are linked to their sedentary brethren Ait Lahssen in the north. These tribes often sought refuge or alliances with other tribes from the area. The Ait Oussa tribe, whose main residence was in Oued Draa in the northern part of Morocco where they held their regional annual fair, also lived in the Hammada plateau, considered today part of the Western Sahara." This is not unusual as there have always been provinces of Morocco (including the Western Sahara) and its northern parts. Even the Reguibat, one of the major tribes in the Sahara, "claims affiliation with a Moroccan saint, Moulay Abdeslam Ben M'chich, who lived in Tetouan, the most northern part of Morocco."[28]

The Tekna confederation, a powerful, loyal, and business-oriented constituency, was naturally seen by King Hassan II as the best support base and intermediary to govern the territory. To retain their allegiance, the monarch rewarded them with significant financial incentives (import licenses and stakes in the exploitation of natural resources, especially fisheries and tourism).[29] To make his adaptive approach more integrated and viable, King Hassan tried to expand privileges and opportunities beyond the Tekna membership. Economic and political incentives accrued to anyone that helped the monarchy administer the territory.[30]

Though this policy was necessary to develop the vast territory that the Spanish left underdeveloped,[31] it began to alter the societal balance of the region and foment the perception that the indigenous Sahrawis were deliberately deprived of positions of authority. In interviews with the original inhabitants of the region, the Sahrawi "transplants" are accused of deliberately marginalizing the indigenous population while enacting policies that favored their ethnic kin. The political influence of the new urban notables created a coalition of opportunistic forces that marginalized the historic Sahrawi notables. The end-goal was to strengthen the position of the Moroccan regime and reaffirm its control over the remaking of the Western Sahara. But the emergence of new forces (neo-urban notables, new urban constituency, embryonic administrative structure, etc.) disrupted the operational links between traditional nomadic society and its social support networks and familiar contexts.[32]

The emerging pillars of Moroccan rule never fully succeeded in providing alternative sources of incentives. As one local activist put it this author: "The old Saharan elite used to protect their tribes. Unfortunately, the state helped destroy these traditional structures of mediation that neither political parties nor associations managed to replace."[33] The events of Dakhla and Laâyoune have exposed the weaknesses of local power institutions and the lack of influence of the existing Saharan elites in society. The inability of tribal leaders and political elites to address catalysts of conflict and mediate crises when they emerge demonstrated the dangerous absence of traditional and political structures for conflict resolution.

SUCCESSIVE PHASES OF MIGRATION

During the first phase of development, hundreds of political appointees, civil servants, skilled workers, and teachers from Morocco were dispatched to assist in governance and to staff lower, intermediate, and senior professional positions in the local administration (justice, health, interior) and schools. These professionals are often described by local Sahrawis as disconnected from local realities and unable to adjust to the local culture and its tribal specificities.

The mid-1980s saw a different wave of migrants enticed by the economic opportunities suddenly made available by the state's aggressive policy of developing the Sahara. As the largest investor and biggest employer, the government provided more generous subsidies, tax exemptions, higher salaries, and low-income housing than in other regions of Morocco. This period also coincided with severe droughts in the kingdom and serious spikes of unemployment. It didn't take much to convince thousands of skilled and unskilled workers to migrate to the dynamic economic centers of the Western Sahara.

This stream of migration increased linearly throughout the decade, creating new cleavages that proved difficult to mend. The new communities remained detached from the indigenous Western Saharans despite efforts by the state to encourage social contact and intermarriage. The consolidation of the communities never really materialized. It is important to note that though the migrants from the north of Morocco represent a majority of the population in the major cities of the Western Sahara, they are severely underrepresented in elected institutions. Indeed, until the late 1990s, they were barred from participating in local elections.

Another dramatic change in the size and demographic composition of the population in the Western Sahara came in 1991, when the UN brokered a cease-fire between Morocco and the Algerian-backed Polisario. Both parties agreed to a peace plan that was supposed to lead to a referendum in January 1992 in which Western Saharans would choose between integration with Morocco and independence. It was at that time that the Moroccan government transported some 120,000 thousand Sahrawis, mainly from the southern towns of Sidi Ifni, Guelmim, and the region of Oued Noun, to the Western Sahara to be registered to vote in the promised referendum. Morocco insisted that these Sahrawis be allowed to vote since they can trace their origins to the Western Sahara. These are the thousands of nomadic Sahrawis, mentioned earlier, who fled conflict and colonialism while others left the Western Sahara to pursue divergent interests.

The Polisario discounted demographic history, common roots, tribal affiliations, and population movements, arguing instead that only the populations who remained in the Western Sahara and were counted in the census of 1974 had the right to vote in the referendum. Only "they" can claim indigeneity based on a common national consciousness that had developed before Spain was forced to leave the territory in 1975. In other words, the Polisario wanted to withhold legitimacy and deny a platform for all those Saharan tribes who happened to be outside the territory by the time of the Spanish census and wished to now articulate their preferences in the referendum on the status of the Western Sahara. But "the fact that many Sahrawis, including several of the Polisario leaders, had been outside Western Sahara at the time of the census, mainly in Morocco, reinforced the (Moroccan) argument," wrote Erik Jensen, former chief of the UN mission in the Western Sahara from 1994 to 1998. "Many had even fought with the Moroccan Army of Liberation," he added, concluding logically "that a decision on the fate of the territory, therefore, could only be taken by Saharans with links to Western Sahara."[34]

The Moroccan government housed these Sahrawis in tent camps in Laâyoune, Smara, Boujdour, and Dakhla. These improvised shelters, dubbed "Al Wahda" (Union), were designed to be temporary, but as the process of identification dragged and stalled, they became permanent. Worse, they were gradually transformed into squatter settlements, where tents were replaced by dilapidated shantytown homes, posing serious sanitary and security problems. The state removed these settlements and provided most residents with newly built housing in the mid-2000s. But up to this day, the state still supplies Al Wahda inhabitants with food subsidies and pays their electricity bills. This has created significant resentment and important fissures in society. The indigenous Western Saharans and non-Sahrawis still complain bitterly about this spoils system and culture of handouts.[35]

In the mid-1990s, a new category of people had been added to the swelling ranks of the welfare system. This new stream of arrivals was greatly prized, as it was made up of Sahrawis who fled the Tindouf camps in Algeria. Moroccan authorities saw vindication of their long-held belief that the misery of the Tindouf camps would ultimately prompt Sahrawis to desert the Polisario and its authoritarian rule. Senior members of the Polisario were rewarded handsomely upon their return to the country with high-level government positions. The most recent example is that of the current Moroccan ambassador to Spain, Ould Souilem. One of the founders of the Polisario Front, Souilem defected to Morocco in July 2009, denouncing a movement he had helped lead after growing increasingly disenchanted with the authoritarianism of Polisario leader Mohamed Abdelaziz and his protectors in Algeria. "The Sahrawi Polisario is dead," he said in an interview with the French weekly *Jeune Afrique*. "Only the Algerian Polisario remains."[36]

Revolutionary romanticism has given way to a militarized organization that has no place for discordant voices, lamented Ould Souilem. Similar discontent was voiced by then police inspector general of the Polisario, Mustapha Salma Ould Sidi Mouloud, who publicly endorsed Morocco's proposal to grant autonomy to Western Sahara in August 2010. "The only remaining possible solution," he told Jennifer Rubin of the *Washington Post* , "is a consensual political solution satisfactory to all parties, which is autonomy—one that is internationally agreed upon and in everyone's interests." That statement led to his imprisonment and then expulsion from the camps. "When I tried to raise my voice about the Polisario and Algeria's disregard for human rights, they expelled me," he said, adding that "anyone who leaves the refugee camps without permission of the Polisario Front is considered a traitor who is committing a crime and, according to the Polisario's penal code, such actions are punishable by ten to twenty years in prison, and this goes for all Sahrawis for the last thirty years." [37]

All returnees from the camps of Tindouf, numbering currently about 8,000 people, were supplied with free housing and a monthly salary. Whole neighborhoods, dubbed "Al Aouda" (Return) were built in the different cities of the Western Sahara to accommodate these new arrivals. Returnees were assigned their residence according to their cities of origin. This generosity of the state was not accompanied by any work requirements or job training. In some cases, the local authorities failed to take advantage of the returnees' experience and skills. "Some of us were teachers, doctors, nurses, and so on in the camps of Tindouf," said two of my interviewees, "but the Moroccan government either deliberately or unintentionally did not hire us in professional positions that match our skills, preferring to condemn us to receiving a meager $160 monthly handout."[38]

It is this frustration with relative deprivation that led many returnees to desert the Polisario in the first place and that is now pushing some to threaten (without ever following through) to go back to Tindouf in protest of the lack of equal opportunities they received upon their return to Morocco. Instead of helping move people from welfare to work, state policies contributed to the development of an entitlement mentality and a dangerous perception that government resources are endless. Worse, these preferential policies did not result in eliciting much goodwill from the beneficiaries of the state's largesse, as they naturally came to expect more benefits.

In talks with this community of former Polisario supporters one easily detects deep malaise and dissatisfaction. Several complained in interviews with the author, especially among the youth, that they fled the camps only to be disappointed by the way the Moroccan authorities treated them. The Polisario leaders might be corrupt, but at least "the collective provides the basic essentials for all," said one of them. Another added that "Life in Tindouf was very hard, but at least it was a shared misery. Here, we witness the unequal sharing of the richness of our territory."[39] This inequality is especially bitter when one remembers that others, especially former top Polisario military and political leaders, have fared very well upon their return to Morocco.

Former Polisario followers expected more material benefits and greater compensation for their years of displacement. They ended up, however, experiencing the same levels of economic and social hardship that their Moroccan counterparts have endured for several decades. The state's failure to help integrate them into the social and economic fabric of society is especially dangerous. Most of these returnees denounce the Polisario as an authoritarian organization, but their views of Morocco's management of the territory is hardly positive. Their disenchantment with their current living conditions can easily degenerate into open revolt against the system.

THE NEW CONFLICT DYNAMICS

There is a growing fear that the state's clientelistic practices and economic mismanagement are contributing to a polarization of society and sharpening tension and competition between and within ethnic groups over the distribution of rent. Since 1976, the problem has always been that many of the resources were not efficiently used and that money was often quickly thrown at socioeconomic challenges to co-opt indigenous Sahrawis and silence dissent.[40] The state has not tried to deal earnestly with the socioeconomic challenges of the region.[41] Thus Morocco's significant investments (nearly three billion dollars in just critical basic infrastructure) have not moved the local economy into a productive stage nor have they fostered sustainable development practices.[42] Worse, they helped cement a traditional spoils system where local tribal leaders, notables, influential Sahrawi refugees who deserted the Polisario, and elected officials scoop up most of the economic and political opportunities.

Frustration with the state for promoting this patronage system was bound to explode, as it did in September 1999 when Laâyoune descended into violence. Indigenous Western Saharans took to the streets to demand social justice (more funding for scholarships, increase in transportation subsidies, compensation for wrongful imprisonment, jobs, housing, and so on). Unfortunately, what started as nonviolent sit-ins degenerated into violent confrontations when the police moved in to break up the protest camp. For thirteen days, the authorities watched nervously as the protests gathered momentum, drawing all sorts of aggrieved Sahrawis, from former political prisoners to phosphate workers.[43] As demands hardened and fears grew that Polisario supporters infiltrated the crowds to manipulate Sahrawi passions, security forces were ordered on the morning of the fourteenth day to forcefully dislodge the protesters, leading to violent confrontations between the police and the demonstrators.[44]

Protests and rioting anywhere in Morocco have typically led to the worst abuses by the authorities. Police brutality and the use of excessive violence were proven practices, referred to in Morocco as "The Basri Violence Norm" in reference to the long-serving interior minister, the late Driss Basri, who was finally fired in November 1999. In this instance, the police used excessive violence, arresting scores of demonstrators and beating some of the detainees. In a dangerous precedent, the authorities, according to a report issued by the US State Department, "reportedly encouraged local thugs to break into, loot, and destroy private shops," owned by Sahrawis.[45]

Pitting Moroccans of the north against indigenous Sahrawis would unfortunately have long-lasting effects. These would have devastating implications on the consolidation of peaceful coexistence between the volatile mixture of populations that populate the Western Sahara. All groups harbor grievances against state authority, but the correspondence between communal identity and conflict was low. In this case, it is the deliberate ethnicization of violence, which pits one ethnic group against another, by the security forces that made the likelihood of a future spiral of violence possible. The events of 1999 spurred mutual antipathies and became a source of ethnic solidarity. More troubling for the state, they managed to homogenize, even if only temporarily, the indigenous Western Saharans and those Sahrawis who were brought to the region in 1991 to vote in the referendum.[46]

Up until the violence of 1999, the two communities did not mingle. As shown earlier, the locals resented them, referring to them initially as the kurds before dubbing them wakkala the eaters). But resentment of the state ended up transcending their mutual antipathies and distrust of each other. The ethnicization of violence and repression served as the immediate trigger for their rapprochement, arousing shared ethnic identification and mutual greater sympathies. During the protests, the "kurds" participated in the demonstrations calling for more state financial aid and support. When violence erupted, they provided shelter and refuge to the indigenous Sahrawis. These dramatic developments showed the extent to which the government policies in the Sahara not only failed to win the hearts and minds of indigenous Sahrawis but that they were alienating even supporters of the country's territorial integrity.

They also created opportunities for the "apostles" of independence to inflame ethnic nationalism and articulate ethnic grievances more vigorously. For the outside world, the grievances become the causes of the revolt. For pro-independence individuals, they become a tool of recruitment, making confrontation with the state almost inevitable. State overreaction leads to more ethnic disaggregation, which confirms mutual suspicions and increases the probability of violence.

The opportunity for violent conflict finally came in May 2005 when state authorities decided to transfer twenty-year-old prisoner Haddi Hamed Mahmoud into a correctional facility in Aït Melloul, twelve kilometers south of Agadir. Mahmoud was classified as a multiple recidivist who made his first appearance before Court when he was twenty. Nicknamed "Al-Kainan" (the man who bites) for his constant fights with the police and disruption of judicial proceedings, he was the subject of several jail stays due to assault, theft, criminal damage of property, and fraud.[47] In 2003, he was sentenced to five years in prison for public intoxication. That prison term would be extended by seven years as a result of new felony convictions: trafficking and distribution of illegal drugs. "At no time during his trial," wrote the French weekly *Jeune Afrique*, "did he make any political statements. "Indeed, adds the magazine, it was not until mid-2004 that he publicly voiced his support for the Polisario and renounced his Moroccan citizenship.[48] His embrace of the cause for independence made him a lightning rod for its advocates and a source of growing trouble to the authorities.

The decision to finally transfer him ignited a cycle of protests and repression. A sit-in organized by the family of Mahmoud—backed by Sahrawi human right activists—to prevent the transfer quickly turned into days of bloody confrontations with the police. The unrest spread to other cities (Dakhla and Smara), including Saharan areas (like Assa) outside the contested zone, and university campuses in Agadir, Marrakech, and Rabat. In all, out of the 180,000 Sahrawis living in the Western Sahara and Morocco, only a few hundred took part in the protests.[49] But contrary to previous demonstrations, the 2005 unrest had separatist connotations. The crowds shouted pro-Polisario slogans and burned (two) Moroccan flags.

Several factors accounted for this agitation. The first issue is pervasive discontent with the government mismanagement of the distribution of resources. The politics of marginality "provide strong incentives for ethno-political mobilization, protest, and rebellion."[50] But the political and social construction of conflict is the creation of charismatic leaders and skilled activists who instill the notion in their distinct community that the road to equality and prosperity is through common struggle for independent statehood.

The success of ethnopolitical action depends on a number of circumstances, including domestic politics, external support, and the international context. The ascent of King Mohammed VI to the throne in July 1999 saw a relaxation of political controls. Sometimes this relaxation was followed by periods of reasserted control (especially after the May 2003 terrorist attacks), but on the whole the country became much less repressive and more open than under the often harsh reign of King Hassan (1961–1999). Prior to the ascent of King Mohammed VI to power, for example, mobile phones had no network coverage in the Sahara.[51]

The Polisario and its local supporters in the Western Sahara took advantage of this opening to pursue their strategies, usually under the guise of human rights activism. The liberalization process also speeded up the growth of cybercafés, providing ideal venues and platforms for disaffected Sahrawis to exchange views with their counterparts in the camps near Tindouf. The Polisario did not have to rely just on its radio and television channels—already widely accessible in Laâyoune—to whip up ethnonational aspirations and exacerbate existing tensions. The arrival of the digital age and the revolutionary cell phone facilitated its information war against Morocco.[52]

Finally, the international context also played a role in contributing to the unrest of 2005. The diplomatic track was deadlocked. The two versions of the Baker plan were rejected, the first by Algeria and the Polisario, the second by Morocco. By 2005, the resolution of the conflict looked as remote as it does today. All these factors combined demonstrated the potential for trouble. It is true that only a small number participated in the protests, but the opportunities and risk factors for ferment were manifold.

After these occasional but deadly outbursts of violence, the state started to realize the mounting gravity of indigenous discontent. The grievances, as articulated in the protests and in dozens of interviews with the author, fall into two broad categories: resource distribution and self-governance. Pro-independence tendencies have always been limited and the Polisario's credibility low, as leaked US State Department cables from Morocco revealed. "Extensive interviews and independent sources in the territory," wrote senior American official Robert P. Jackson in a confidential document in 2009, "suggest that the principal goal of most Sahrawis is more self-government than self-determination."[53]

Nevertheless, Sahrawis' frustration and disappointment with state policies in the Sahara are creating sympathies for the cause of independence. The young are especially susceptible to Polisario's promises of a better and equitable distribution of resources and recognition of their worth and dignity. The local authorities had been oblivious, if not indifferent, to the difficult social and economic conditions weighing upon significant constituencies: high unemployment (estimated at around 20 percent), a permanent dependence on state welfare and social assistance (direct aid programs annually target 34,000 Sahrawis for a budget of US$68 million),[54] an inadequate public health care system, a low-performing school system,[55] and an intractable class system made worse by old tribal rivalries.[56]

The government's preferential policies have exacerbated existing ethnic divides while its noncontingent welfare handouts have promoted a culture of entitlement that is difficult to sustain. The government has directed benefits according to people's tribal and ethnic status as well as strict political considerations. This has heightened ethnic and tribal consciousness instead of strengthening the development of a common identity based on citizenship and democratic rights. For over three decades, the Moroccan government's Saharan policy has failed to develop a system in which every citizen enjoys the same rights and is protected by the same laws.

To address the main drivers of discontent, the government first committed to tackling the housing shortage triggered by steady population growth and the continuing flow of new arrivals. The number of inhabitants went from 74,000 people, according to the Spanish census of 1974, to 507,160 today. In 2008, the authorities designated 20,000 plots of land for distribution to the indigenous Sahrawis. Instead, the land—after the municipal elections of 2009—was allocated based on tribal and electoral calculations. Senior elected officials grabbed public land and handed property deals to their allies and powerful constituencies. More than 5,000 lots destined for inhabitants of Laâyoune disappeared. What is tragic, said Hassana Maoulainine, the head of the Regional Investment Center (the CRI), is that the authorities failed to grasp the seriousness of the situation. Both the elected Istiqlali mayor and the pro-PAM (Party of Authenticity and Modernity) appointed governor were famously not on speaking terms, and both saw the brewing crisis as a political opportunity to undermine and weaken the other. The camps at Igdim Izik, as Boukhars and Amar reported after the violence, were the stage and the theater where all factions and forces came for show and battle: the local Sahrawis versus the outsider northerners, the mayor and the City Council versus the Wali and the central administration, and the Istiqlal Party versus the Party of Authenticity and Modernity.[57]

Intent on keeping influential stakeholders happy, the state and its judicial organs failed to investigate the embezzling of public property for fear that the beneficiaries switch their loyalties to the enemies of the country. "Some leaders exploited this separatist obsession as a means of self-enrichment, acquiring influence and getting closer to the centers of political and economic decision-making within the state and political parties, without really committing themselves to resolving problems in society," said a report by a parliamentary committee tasked with investigating the tragic events of Laâyoune.[58]

The frustration engendered by this gaming of the state's policy to provide free housing for low-income Sahrawi families quickly turned into anger at the system. The social and psychological malaise just became too much to bear, said François Soudan of the French weekly *Jeune Afrique*.[59] In September 2010, thousands of angry Sahrawis began setting up tents outside the city in the now-infamous camp of Agdim Izik on the outskirts of Laâyoune to demand jobs and housing. For three weeks, tensions mounted and protesters' demands hardened, as initial calls for jobs, free housing, and anticorruption measures made way for calls for the immediate resolution of all their socioeconomic grievances. In a predictable sequence, Polisario supporters and notorious traffickers quickly infiltrated the protesters' ranks, helping set up popular committees to administer the camp.[60] Once legitimate social demands became contaminated by politicized and criminal elements, the security services decided to dismantle the camp on November 8, 2010. The whole city would then be paralyzed and areas set ablaze.

Video footage of the riots showed gruesome images of hysterical crowds lynching unarmed security officers. Such frightening carnage, prevalent at the height of the civil war in neighboring Algeria in the 1990s and a trademark of Al-Qaeda in the Islamic Maghreb (AQIM), has always been alien to the Western Sahara. Laâyoune had seen violence and rioting before, but never had the city witnessed such militancy. The sight of masked insurgents marching in the streets of Laâyoune—armed with knives, Molotov cocktails, and stones, setting fires to public buildings, schools, and private property—sent a chilling reminder of the region's vulnerability to destabilization.[61] The violence also demonstrated the deep enmity that has developed between indigenous Western Saharans and communities from the north of Morocco. Never before had the streets of Laâyoune seen clashes between natives and Dakhlis armed with batons, swords, and Molotov cocktails.

Since 1975, important fissures have developed and this naturally created societal tensions, though at restricted levels. But it is only in the last few years that ethnic cleavages and cultural animosity have become dangerously more pronounced. The causes are various and profound, but most centrally they are political.

The native Sahrawi community feels that its views and interests are not represented by its corrupt elected political elites. Some have the impression that the local administration treats them with paternalistic condescension. For their part, inhabitants who hail from northern Morocco complain bitterly that the government usually ignores their concerns, encourages them to maintain a low profile, and avoid disputes with indigenous Western Saharans. In the Sahara, the northerners complain, the supreme law of the land doesn't apply. The common saying is that under the Moroccan state doctrine, the national legal standards don't extend to the region. The legal jurisdiction and authority to hear and apply the law stops south of Tarfaya, the geographical boundary of the Western Sahara. This unwillingness to enforce the law is supposed to keep the peace and avoid antagonizing the natives. In reality, says local activist Abdelmajid Belghzal, it has further undermined the state's authority and trust in its institutions.[62]

THE WAY FORWARD

The Moroccan-controlled Western Sahara is vulnerable to societal tensions and ethnic frictions that seriously threaten to destabilize the area. Ethnic cleavages and cultural animosity threaten to weaken social hierarchies and further exacerbate conflict within groups and the broader communities. The result would be more radicalism, violence, and confrontations.

Heterogeneity is not a risk factor that favors independence. Such sentiment arises from political exclusion, repression, and limited economic opportunity. Most Native West Saharans have been guided by a cost-benefit approach to allegiance to the Moroccan state. As long as the regime delivers law, order, and services, the incentives for independence remain low. The failure of the state to fulfill this unwritten "social contract" inevitably leads this constituent group to reassess the relative benefits and costs of remaining in the union. The perception of economic injustice and political marginalization, precipitated by elite manipulation and corruption, and fueled by ethnic security dilemmas, serve as potent triggers for identity conflict and rebellious action.

So far, conflict and activism for independence have been driven by both grievances and opportunity. The Sahrawi ethnic diaspora and the refugees across the border in Algeria fuel the grievances of their kinsmen in the Moroccan-administered Western Sahara and facilitate the organization of dissent. This is exacerbated by the breakdown of the traditional order and absence of any credible local authority. Legal community-based groups, associations, and intermediary bodies are docile and inactive.[63] The cooptation of these associations and the ethnic Sahrawi elites has severely damaged their reputation and credibility. It has also weakened and discredited the traditional conflict management and mediation mechanisms to resolve local tensions.

One has only to look at the Royal Advisory Council for Saharan Affairs (CORCAS) to see how poorly led and organized are institutions that are supposed to represent the interests of Sahrawis. CORCAS is headed by the controversial Khalihenna Ould Rachid, who once advocated autonomy for the Western Sahara under Spanish rule, then independence through interdependence with Spain. Ould Rachid is strongly criticized by Sahrawis for his disconnect from the locals. His leadership of the CORCAS is also ridiculed by members from within this institution. He is described as a despotic opportunist who lacks both strategic leadership and operational leadership.[64]

Since its restructuring in 2006, the CORCAS has remained undemocratic, its commissions (five in total) have never met, and nearly half of its 144 members don't even live in the Western Sahara. Another drag on the performance of the CORCAS stems from the way its members are selected. The fact that they are appointed by the palace rather than directly elected has deprived it of institutional legitimacy. As Spanish Western Saharan expert, Bernabé García López stated, it has also deprived Morocco of a valuable opportunity to have its autonomy proposal defended by a representative and credible body of Sahrawis.[65] It is therefore necessary for the CORCAS to be restructured in a way that reflects electoral accountability, proximity, and transparency.

Morocco has long believed that a solution to the Western Sahara conflict can only emanate from New York and Algiers. Notwithstanding the recent warming of relations between Morocco and Algeria, no one is under any illusion that the two rivals will soon resolve their differences over the Western Sahara. Given the bleak prospects for successful negotiations, Morocco can no longer dither in preparing the Western Sahara for autonomy.[66] But as political scientist Donald Horowitz cautioned, "states that could benefit from federalism typically come to that realization too late, usually after conflict has intensified."[67]

Morocco has long resisted the idea of instituting an autonomous region in the Western Sahara lest it accentuate the Sahrawis' separate identity and boost their ethnopolitical mobilization. Yet its 2007 proposal for autonomy for the Western Sahara is a good starting point. The July 2011 Moroccan constitution sets into motion a promising decentralization process, whereby effective power is devolved to elected regional councils. This process has great significance for the Western Sahara, as it has the potential to increase participatory development and government responsiveness. It will also meet one of the main demands of the disgruntled inhabitants of the region: the ability to manage their own affairs.

The new constitution provides for cultural inclusiveness as well, specifically guaranteeing Sahrawis their linguistic and cultural rights. And the new Moroccan political pact constitutionalizes the principles of individual rights (freedom of expression, freedom of association, and criminalization of torture and arbitrary detention) and equality for all citizens. For example, the National Council for Human Rights (CNDH) saw its investigative powers enhanced. It now has regional commissions (HRDC) that are responsible for independently monitoring the situation of human rights, investigating complaints, and issuing special or periodic reports. In the Western Sahara alone, three regional commissions CNDH were formed in the summer of 2011.[68] The selection process was transparent, though not all-inclusive. Some activists assert that advocates for independence were sidelined. These efforts by the council to address human rights concerns must be broadened and deepened.

The next step for Morocco is to clearly define the rules and designs for the special territorial arrangement for the Western Sahara. The top priority of the majority of the indigenous people residing in the Moroccan administered Western Sahara remains genuine self-governance, including better access to and management of natural resources.

In the Western Sahara, the authorities must do more to protect freedom of speech, including expressions of independence. Suppressing opposing views does not gain Morocco the sympathy of indigenous Sahrawis. Only democracy can. One has only to look to Spain whose democratic system has withstood the threats of strong separatist groups in Catalonia and Basque regions.

But the challenges ahead are formidable. Without strong and credible Sahrawi interest groups and political elites, it will be impossible for Morocco to advance its transition process for regional autonomy for the Western Sahara. Civil society groups and political parties are weak and the local government is characterized by nepotism and collusion. The relationship between the people and the government is broken. Despite the billions of dollars spent on territory and the significant infrastructural investments, Western Saharans aspirations for good governance, community empowerment and participation, and democracy are still not met.

NOTES

1. Ignacio Cembrero, "Sahara Occidental: Le Maroc a raté une occasion en or," *El Pais*, April 25, 2013, http://blogs.elpais.com/orilla-sur/2013/04/sahara-le-maroc-a-rate-une-occasion-en-or.html.

2. Bernabé López García, "Le Maroc échoue au Sahara," *Lakome*, May 8, 2013, http://fr.lakome.com/index.php/chroniques/738-le-maroc-echoue-au-sahara (accessed May 27, 2013).

3. Human rights defenders in the Western Sahara complain of harassment and intimidation of advocates of independence. Security forces are accused of using excessive force to disperse protests and abusing people in custody. State authorities usually dismiss calls or pressure for investigations as biased and unfair. In the rare occasions when investigations of complaints are launched, they are ineffective. The government and local authorities complain that the reports of some human rights groups and journalists are unbalanced and barely hide their sympathies for those who militate for independence.

4. Interview in the prefecture, Laâyoune, December 28, 2011.

5. François Soudan, "Front Polisario: Mohamed Abdelaziz, jusqu'au dernier Sahraoui," *Jeune Afrique*, January 2, 2012, www.jeuneafrique.com/Article/ARTJA20120102104316/algerie-maroc-mali-electionfront-polisario-mohamed-abdelaziz-jusqu-au-dernier-sahraoui.html (accessed June 20, 2012).

6. Ali Tamek was also born in southern Morocco in Assa in 1973.

7. It is undeniable that that there have been improvements in human rights. The free and open discussions that this author had with a number of local Sahrawis would have been unthinkable during the reign of King Hassan II (1961–1999). Some of my interlocutors did not shy away from criticizing and at times denouncing the local authorities and security services. Such freedom of thought and ability to speak openly and without fear of retribution is welcome. It is also important to point to the vibrant and frank political debates that occur daily in local cafes.

8. Interview with Abdelmajid Belghzal, Laâyoune, December 28, 2011.

9. Constance Desloire, "Émeutes à Dakhla, le Festival Mer et désert annulé," *Jeune Afrique*, February 27, 2011, www.jeuneafrique.com/Article/ARTJAWEB20110227111131 (accessed June 19, 2012).

10. Desloire, "Émeutes à Dakhla, le Festival Mer et désert annulé."

11. Souhail Karam, "Morocco Says 7 Killed in Western Sahara Soccer Clash," *Reuters*, September 27, 2011.

12. The Sahrawis, an ethnic group that shares the same language and social customs, populate an area that encompasses swathes of northern Mauritania, western Algeria, southern Morocco, and the disputed Western Sahara. In the latter, one can find native Western Saharans as well as Sahrawis from the adjacent southern Moroccan provinces.

13. Interview, Dakhla, December 23, 2012.

14. Interview, Dakhla, December 24, 2012.

15. Driss Bennani and Yassine Zizi, "Voyage au sahara: La grande boucle," *Telquel*, July 11, 2003.

16. Driss Bennani, "Sahara. La bombe à retardement," *TelQuel*, November 5, 2011.

17. Rguibate are divided into two main fractions: Rguibat Sahel that populate the Sahara, but also parts of Mauritania. Ouali Mustapha Sayed, founder of the Polisario, belongs to this fraction. The current leader of the Polisario, Abdelaziz, belongs to Rguibat Cherk, dominant in the Eastern Sahara and southeast of Algeria. The biggest tribe is that of Tekna, which extends from the Anti-Atlas to the borders of Mali. In this confederation, we can find the Ait Lahcen, the Ait Ouali Moussa, the Ait Oussa, and the Yaggoute and Izerguiyine.

18. Bennani and Zizi, "Voyage au sahara: La grande boucle."

19. Fisheries represent about 15 percent of the wealth produced in the Western Sahara and 30 percent of employment. See "Évaluation de l'effectivité des droits humains fondamentaux dans les provinces du sud," *Conseil Economique, Social et Environnemental*, March 2013.

20. "Morocco's reforms: Power to Some Other People," *The Economist*, May 17, 2012, www.economist.com/node/21550294 (accessed June 2, 2012).

21. Desloire, "Émeutes à Dakhla, le Festival Mer et désert annulé."

22. Interview, Dakhla.

23. Leïla Slimani, "Dakhla, la perle méconnue du Maroc," *Jeune Afrique*, October 20, 2009, www.jeuneafrique.com/Article/ARTJAJA2546p074-075.xml0/ (accessed May 27, 2012). It is important to note that the agency lacks mechanisms for evaluating whether its investment priorities and strategies promote economic growth, create jobs, and meet the social needs of the population. Several people interviewed decry the high costs and waste of some of the projects created (huge convention center, a conservatory of music that is barely used by the locals). See "Évaluation de l'effectivité des droits humains fondamentaux dans les provinces du sud," *Conseil Economique, Social et Environnemental*, March 2013.

24. Leïla Slimani, "Sahara : après Laâyoune...," *Jeune Afrique*, December 24, 2010, www.jeuneafrique.com/Article/ARTJAJA2605p044-047.xml0/ (accessed May 27, 2012).

25. Bennani, "Sahara. La bombe à retardement."

26. Attilio Gaudio, Les Populations du Sahara. *Occidental* (Karthala, 1993), 97–116.

27. Bennani and Zizi, "Voyage au sahara: La grande boucle."

28. Abdeslam Maghraoui, "Ambiguities of Sovereignty: Morocco , The Hague and the Western. Sahara Dispute," *Mediterranean Politics* 8, no. 1 (2003): 119. See also Gaudio, Les Populations du Sahara *Occidental*. The book displays an extensive knowledge and deep understanding of the tribes of the Western Sahara.

29. Khadija Mohsen-Finan, "Trente ans de conflit au Sahara occidental," *Institut Français des Relations Internationales*, January 2008, http://humansecuritygateway.com/documents/IFRI_SaharaOccidental_30AnsDeConflit.pdf (accessed May 19, 2012).

30. Mohsen-Finan, "Trente ans de conflit au Sahara occidental."

31. Robert Worth and Souad Mekhennet, "Desert Land in Limbo Is Torn Apart," *New York Times*, December 9, 2010, www.nytimes.com/2010/12/09/world/africa/09morocco.html (accessed June 26, 2011). The *New York Times* described it best in 2010 when it wrote that "What was once a Spanish fort and a cluster of tents is now a modern city (Laâyoune) of 300,000, a profitable hub for fishing and phosphate mining

with its own airport. The same applies in other major metropolitan areas of the Western Sahara."
32. Interview with chiouks (tribal leaders), Laâyoune, December 28, 2011.
33. Interview with Abdelmajid Belghzal, Laâyoune, December 25, 2010.
34. Erik Jensen, *Western Sahara: Anatomy of a Stalemate* (Boulder and London: Lynne Riener, 2005), 60.
35. Many of my interlocutors insist that the majority of food aid goes to subsidize the Sahrawi populations of camps El Wahda. This is viewed as discriminatory toward the indigenous Sahrawis. The same criticism is directed toward the state's distribution of direct financial aid, largely reviled as clientelistic and unfair.
36. François Soudan," La longue marche d'Ahmedou Ould Souilem ," *Jeune Afrique*, June 9, 2010, www.jeuneafrique.com/Articles/Dossier/ARTJAJA2577p022-030.xml1/algerie-maroc-ambassadeur-mohammed-vila-longue-marche-d-ahmedou-ould-souilem.html (accessed June 26, 2011).
37. Jennifer Rubin, "Exclusive: Ex-Polisario Front Police Chief Tells His Story," *Washington Post*, January 16, 2011, http://voices.washingtonpost.com/right-turn/2011/01/exclusive_ex-polisario_front_p.html (accessed June 26, 2011).
38. Interview, Laâyoune, December 28, 2011.
39. Interview, Laâyoune, December 27, 2011.
40. The state welfare programs could be optimized by streamlining aid rules and improving delivery mechanisms. So far, the granting for subsidies for food and oil, allocation of land and apartments, scholarships and recruitment in public service are done without coordination, transparency, or determination of their efficiency or impact value on the local populations. The result is that the state's social and economic aid policy does not always reach its intended recipients.
41. There is, for example, no real strategy for creation of jobs. To calm dissent, local authorities devote each year budget allocations to hiring Sahrawis in the public sector. In recent years, some 6,000 positions were created without regard to educational qualifications or other eligibility requirements. Some of those recruited never show up for the jobs. Those that do, have sometimes no official job duties. See "Évaluation de l'effectivité des droits humains fondamentaux dans les provinces du sud," *Conseil Economique, Social et Environnemental*, March 2013.
42. Slimani, "Sahara: après Laâyoune."
43. John Damis, "Sahrawi Demonstrations," *Middle East Report* 218 (2001).
44. This is not the first time that social protests in the Western Sahara degenerated into violence. In 1991, Smara—located only forty kilometers north of the defensive wall (called "berm") built in the mid-1980s to protect against Polisario incursions—saw its share of brutal repression when social demonstrations were broke-up. Activists were persecuted and all forms of sit-ins and peaceful protests were banned. These repressive measures only fueled frustration with the state, especially when economic incentives were not enough to quiet discontent.
45. "Morocco: Country Reports on Human Rights Practices," *US Department of State*, February 23, 2000, www.state.gov/j/drl/rls/hrrpt/1999/422.htm (accessed June 2, 2012).
46. Bennani and Zizi, "Voyage au sahara: La grande boucle."
47. François Soudan, "La guerre des nerfs," *Jeune Afrique*, June 1, 2005, www.jeuneafrique.com/Article/LIN12065laguesfrens0/ (accessed June 12, 2012).
48. Soudan, "La guerre des nerfs."
49. Soudan, "La guerre des nerfs."
50. Ted Robert Gurr, ed., *Peoples Versus States: Minorities at Risk in the New Century* (Washington, DC: United States Institute of Peace Press, 2000), xvi.
51. See Bernabé López García, "Sous le signe du Sahara," *Afkar/Idees* (2010), www.afkar-ideas.com/wp-content/uploads/files/3-25-8-fr.pdf (accessed June 12, 2012).
52. Maria J. Stephan and Jacob Mundy, "A Battlefield Transformed: From Guerilla Resistance to Mass Nonviolent Struggle in the Western Sahara," *Journal of Military and Strategic Studies* 8, no. 3 (2006): 16.

53. Robert P. Jackson, "Western Sahara Realities," *US Embassy Rabat*, August 17, 2009, 09RABAT706, www.wikileaks.ch/cable/2009/08/09RABAT706.html (accessed June 26, 2011).

54. This amount represents half of the national budget aid devoted to the whole of Morocco. It is important to note that the state also devotes annually US$535,467,600 (4.6 billion Moroccan dirhams) to fighting poverty in the Western Sahara. This is done through direct and indirect forms of aid. See "Évaluation de l'effectivité des droits humains fondamentaux dans les provinces du sud," *Conseil Economique, Social et Environnemental*, March 2013.

55. Most Sahrawis complain that there is not one single university in the whole of the Western Sahara. Then there is the problem of education and skills mismatches. There is an undersupply of students who major in science, engineering, and technical fields. Like in the rest of Morocco, Western Sahara suffers from a waste of human capital, as most of the students are ill-prepared and ill-trained for the employment and social development needs of the country.

56. Interview with Abdelmajid Belghzal, Laâyoune, December 28, 2011.

57. Anouar Boukhars and Ali O. Amar, "Trouble in the Western Sahara," *Journal of the Middle East and Africa* 2, no. 2 (2011): 220–34.

58. Siham Ali, "Laâyoune inquiry ends in Morocco," *Magharebia*, January 14, 2011, www.magharebia.com/cocoon/awi/xhtml1/en_GB/features/awi/features/2011/01/14/feature-03 (accessed June 26, 2011).

59. François Soudan, "Sahara: jours de fièvre," *Jeune Afrique*, November 18, 2010, www.jeuneafrique.com/Article/ARTJAJA2601p014-016.xml0/onu-algerie-maroc-genocidesahara-jours-de-fievre.html (accessed June 26, 2011).

60. There was a massive influx of hundreds of young Sahrawis (2,000 in total) who left the camps of Tindouf in the spring of 2010 toward the Moroccan administered Western Sahara. Some of these youths, senior security officials in Laâyoune state, were active in the booming smuggling activity in the region. After Mauritania was forced to tighten its northern border and Morocco its southern flank, a number of Sahrawis, squeezed out by border enforcement, fled the Tindouf camps toward the Western Sahara in search of new opportunity and in hope of finding new ways to replace their lost income from contraband and drug smuggling. The authorities failed to check, as customary, the identities and the backgrounds of the new returnees.

61. Worth and Mekhennet, "Desert Land in Limbo Is Torn Apart."

62. Interview, Laâyoune, December 28, 2011.

63. Civil society actors complain that the local authorities interfere in their internal governance, monitor their activities, and control all funding.

64. Interview with three members of CORCAS, Rabat, January 2, 2012.

65. López García, "Sous le signe du Sahara."

66. Bernabe López García, "Le projet politique du Polisario s'essouffle?" *Telquel*, July 2010.

67. Donald Horowitz, "The Many Uses of Federalism," *Drake Law Review* 55, no. 4 (2007): 953–66.

68. See "Évaluation de l'effectivité des droits humains fondamentaux dans les provinces du sud," *Conseil Economique, Social et Environnemental*, March 2013.

TEN

Self-Determination for Western Sahara

The Evolution of a Concept

Samuel J. Spector[1]

Even before the Arab uprisings commenced in January 2011, most diplomats and policymakers agreed that when it came to resolving the Western Sahara dispute, all options consistent with principles of self-determination under international law ought to be on the table. On February 25, 2010, United Nations Secretary-General (UNSG) Ban Ki-moon remarked that "[i]f the United Nations is to fulfill its obligations in supporting the legitimate aspirations of the peoples of [the world's remaining non-self-governing] ... territories, a pragmatic and realistic approach—taking into account the specific circumstances of each—is most likely to lead to concrete results."[2] The secretary-general's comment reflects a longstanding yet often overlooked reality—namely, that there are lawful options to resolving self-determination disputes that exist in the space *between* the status quo and full independence.

Self-determination is neither synonymous with the outcome of independence for the affected territory nor predicated on a winner-take-all formula for resolution that ignores the interests of other parties to the dispute. Although international law does not offer an exhaustive list of pathways to self-government, General Assembly Resolution 1541, adopted in 1960, sets out three alternatives: (1) emergence as a sovereign independent State, (2) free association with an independent State, or (3) integration with an independent State. General Assembly Resolution 2625, adopted in 1970, builds upon these three alternatives and adds a fourth, namely, "the emergence into any other political status freely determined by a people."[3]

It is within the context of a spectrum of lawful outcomes to disputes over self-determination that the Moroccan government offered its Initiative for Negotiating an Autonomy Statute for the Sahara Region (hereinafter, the "Autonomy Plan") to the UNSG in April 2007 as a formula that could potentially satisfy all the parties to the conflict or, at a minimum, could serve as a new entry point to negotiations and break the longstanding stalemate. The plan provides for the creation of a "Saharan Autonomous Region," presumably—although not explicitly—corresponding to the entire territory of Western Sahara, enjoying broad executive, legislative, and judicial powers apart from Morocco, including control over local administration, the economic sector, infrastructure, social and cultural affairs, and the environment, yet remaining within Morocco's sphere of influence on matters such as defense and foreign affairs.

The Autonomy Plan has been generally well received by the international community. It was greeted in United Nations Security Council (UNSC) Resolutions 1754 and 1871 as a "serious and credible effort to move the process forward towards resolution."[4] It has continued to attract broad international support even after the outbreak of the Arab uprisings in early 2011, a period of tremendous tumult which has arguably strengthened the urgency of examining creative yet realistic compromise solutions settling the Western Sahara dispute. For example, UNSG Ban Ki-moon, in an April 2011 report to the UNSC, acknowledged the importance of the moment, noting that "at this time of protest and contestation throughout the Middle East/North Africa region, the sentiments of the population of Western Sahara, both inside and outside the Territory, with regard to its final status are more central than ever to the search for a settlement that will be just and lasting."[5]

Nevertheless, the Autonomy Plan is not without its potential flaws and in no way offers a sure path to settlement of the conflict. Whereas its strength is that it is attuned to the reality of the broad spectrum of acceptable outcomes under the law of self-determination, its weakness is that it fails to resolve upfront certain core challenges, including the mechanism for obtaining popular consent to a political arrangement—a crucial element in any lawful resolution to the conflict. Unfortunately, criticisms of the plan have generally ignored the diversity of arrangements on the devolution of central power to a newly autonomous territory, including cases of decolonization resulting in free association that have been attempted in recent decades and may even be useful models for the future of Western Sahara.

This chapter assesses the extent to which the Autonomy Plan, as it currently stands, conflicts with and/or conforms to relevant principles of self-determination under international law. It does this by reviewing the legal basis for these principles, actual state practice, and international responses in comparable cases. Various provisions of the Autonomy Plan, including the degree of local autonomy offered, immediate or deferred referenda, and other approaches for the population to make a free and voluntary choice, are examined to assess how they fare in relation to international law and practical implementation in similar situations.

The chapter's selected case studies involve non-self-governing territories (NSGT) and other autonomy arrangements where there has been recognition of the need to substitute a negotiated political status in place of frequently unworkable or unattractive alternatives such as a contentious referendum on independence, open-ended talks, or continued armed conflict. As these cases demonstrate, a negotiated comprehensive political settlement agreed to between the parties may include a referendum that is deferred by a number of years, a high level of autonomy, or even eventual independence for the territory in question.

It is evident from UNSC Resolutions such as 1754 and 1871, as they reflect on the status of negotiations over Western Sahara,[6] that the Autonomy Plan, with certain improvements, can be a viable starting point for negotiations that recognize the centrality of self-determination as a legal framework for resolving the dispute. Modified where needed in light of lessons drawn from comparable cases and employed as a formula for talks, it may free the parties from the current deadlock, while providing helpful guidelines to advance lawful and realistic outcomes to the dispute.

UNDERSTANDING THE LAW OF SELF-DETERMINATION

Self-determination has evolved through a number of conceptual transformations since its emergence into the modern vocabulary of international affairs. Originating as a framework for handling the political aftermath of the First World War and the dissolution of the Ottoman and Austro-Hungarian empires into component nation-states, Wilsonian self-determination was rooted in the belief that every people had the right to select its own form of government, to "choose the sovereignty under which they shall live" and thus be free of alien masters.[7] The UN founding documents intentionally obscured self-determination's definition under international law though it nonetheless set the stage for the period of decolonization. Although not substantially clearing up this definition, a pair of General Assembly Resolutions in 1960 trumpeted self-determination as an immediate and imperative goal for all peoples under Western colonial or alien domination.[8]

The 1975 advisory opinion of the International Court of Justice (ICJ) on Western Sahara must be viewed within this context of unsettled law. The ICJ was asked to weigh in on whether Western Sahara was "at the time of colonization by Spain a territory belonging to no one (*terra nul-*

lius)?" and, "if the answer to the first question is in the negative, (II) What were the legal ties between this territory and the Kingdom of Morocco and the Mauritanian entity?"[9] The court ruled unanimously that at the time of colonization by Spain, Western Sahara was not *terra nullius*.

As for the second question, while acknowledging that its opinion on the question of Morocco's and Mauritania's historic title should in no way be seen as detracting from the fundamental right of self-determination for Western Sahara, the evocation of Morocco's "legal ties" to the territory shifted the terms of the debate, confusing the issue further. By construing "legal ties" as broader than mere ties of territorial sovereignty, and instead calling for an inquiry into the "special characteristics" of the region and its peoples, the court "blurred the line between 'self' and 'territory' arguments that it had drawn by equating the right of self-determination with the free will of the colonial population, and legal ties with pre-colonial claims to territory."[10] Such a finding arguably weakened rather than bolstered the strength and universality of the principle of self-determination.

In addition, the significance of this development was that the "concept of legal ties became a way to recognize relationships other than sovereignty in international law and to tell a more complex legal story about identity in *Western Sahara*."[11] In effect, this opened the door to challenges to the European colonial paradigm that framed the rules on the acquisition of sovereignty over territory under international law at the time, since Morocco and Mauritania were non-European subjects that arguably exercised non-European forms of authority over their respective territories.[12] While weighing in clearly in support of the right of the population of Western Sahara to determine their future political status through their own freely expressed will, the manner in which the pertinent legal issues had been presented and reasoned through by the ICJ, not to mention thoroughly disregarded in the chaotic aftermath of its publication, virtually ensured that the advisory opinion would fail to create clear, enforceable international law guidelines for future state practice.

Since the end of the Cold War, as vestiges of the colonial era have largely faded away, some scholars propose that self-determination has entered a new stage. A healthy debate persists concerning when and how self-determination is to be applied in an era when most disputes over contested sovereignty are no longer colonial in nature, but generally involve ethnonational conflict. In this context, and in the face of newly emerged territorial disputes particularly outside the typical colonial context and ranging from the Balkans to the Caucasus, self-determination is increasingly being reframed by legal scholars as a flexible continuum of rights, minority protections, and negotiated political arrangements conducive to achieving real-world outcomes within existing nation-states. For example, Fox writes that in the post–Cold War era, the right to self-determination as a "vehicle for independent statehood . . . [has] been rendered essentially meaningless."[13] Similarly, Hannum believes that self-determination is best viewed as a "right to autonomy recogniz[ing] the right of minority and indigenous communities to exercise meaningful internal self-determination and control over their own affairs in a manner that is not inconsistent with the ultimate sovereignty . . . of the state."[14]

Despite the fact that several conflicts arising from unresolved decolonization era self-determination claims remain—including that over Western Sahara—the very wisdom of applying to that dispute an understanding of self-determination framed exclusively by decolonization has encountered criticism. White suggests that deadlock in resolving the dispute is to be blamed, at least in part, on an "exclusive focus . . . on independence as the only solution to colonial status";[15] an "all or nothing proposition," as Pomerance terms it.[16] Hanauer contends that "the law of self-determination needs to fade away as an autonomous legal principle and become incorporated into human rights law in order to overcome the obstacles posed by the issues of territorial integrity and state sovereignty."[17] A June 2007 report on Western Sahara by the International Crisis Group (ICG) wonders whether self-determination should remain a legal framework for resolving the dispute, reasoning that the parties are presently inhibited from exploring the possibility of a resolution based on a different principle or set of principles.[18]

White, Pomerance, Hanauer, the ICG, and, most recently, Moroccan legal scholar, El Ouali[19] may very well be correct in their observation that the tendency to view a resolution to the Western Sahara dispute exclusively through the lens of a decolonization-era framework of self-determination has frustrated alternative creative solutions. However, one need not view this legal framework of self-determination as a permanent hindrance to progress. Rather, the body of law and scholarship that has grown around self-determination, as well as its diverse state practice, is surprisingly dynamic and can most likely remain the legal framework for dealing with Western Sahara.

A RANGE OF LEGITIMATE OUTCOMES TO THE DECOLONIZATION PROCESS

The overarching goal of the law, as set out in chapter XI of the UN Charter, which deals with NSGT, is to set them down the path to achieving a "full measure of self-government." That self-government, and not independence per se, is the stated objective for these territories, Falk contends, is the result of a deliberate compromise between the West, including the United States and the former colonial states of Western Europe, and the Soviet and communist bloc of states, which rallied under the banners of anti-imperialism and anticolonialism.[20]

The central aim of chapter XI of the UN Charter—that is, "to develop self-government" for territories that do not presently enjoy it—is expressed in Article 73(b).[21] On the other hand, Article 76(b) of chapter XII, dealing with the International Trusteeship System, anticipates the "advancement of the inhabitants of the trust territories, and their progressive development towards self-government *or* [emphasis added] independence as may be appropriate to the particular circumstance of each territory."[22] Thus, it is evident that the drafters of the UN Charter believed "self-government" and "independence" to be two distinct political statuses, with independence only one of a potential multitude of forms that self-government may take with respect to the exercise of self-determination by a people.

Just who is to serve as the arbiter of when a "full measure of self-government" has been achieved other than through independence? While not expressly set out in the UN Charter, Hillebrink has concluded that the UNGA is competent to decide when a NSGT has attained a full measure of self-government.[23] Musgrave concurs, noting that not only do a majority of states agree that the UNGA possesses jurisdiction to determine whether a territory is self-governing or not, but that the UNGA is the proper judge of when a territory has achieved a sufficient measure of self-government such that the administering state's reporting responsibilities under Article XI terminate.[24]

While the UNGA has recognized legitimate outcomes of the process of decolonization short of full independence, including free association, Principle VII of the Annex to Resolution 1541 sets out a series of additional procedural benchmarks that must be satisfied before international acceptance of such status can be attained. These include, chiefly, that selection of the status of free association should be the result of a "free and voluntary choice by the peoples of the territory concerned expressed through informed and democratic processes." Significantly, Hannum notes that the former New Zealand dependencies of the Cook Islands and Niue are the only examples of decolonization by means of free association to have been formally approved by the UNGA since 1960.[25]

AUTONOMY AND FREE ASSOCIATION

Autonomy is, according to Hannum, a relative term. It is not a term of art or a concept that has a generally accepted definition in international law, and the categories of federal states, internationalized territories, and associated states represent the range of autonomy arrangements that have been recognized or accorded serious consideration under international law.[26] Hannum has identified a core set of powers, most of which, he believes, a "fully autonomous" territory should possess. These include: (1) a locally elected legislative body with some independent legal authority that should not be subject to veto by the principal state unless it exceeds the local legislature's competence as defined in a constituent document; (2) a locally selected chief executive who may have responsibility for the administration of local as well as national laws; and (3) an independent local judiciary with full responsibility for interpreting local laws, and mechanisms for resolving disputes between the autonomous and central governments.[27]

Relative to its alternatives, free association denotes a very high level of autonomy. For a NSGT, it is seen as a self-governing alternative to emergence as a sovereign independent state or full integration with a sovereign state. The specific characteristics of an associated state system will be discussed in depth in the section that follows, although Hannum has offered this brief outline of the concept:

> An associated state ... is an entity that has delegated certain competences (particularly in the areas of foreign affairs and defense) to the principal state, although it retains its international status as a state.... An associated state's control over its internal affairs is unlimited, and it retains the power not only to alter unilaterally its own constitution, but also to sever its relationship with the principal entity.[28]

Along similar lines, Hillebrink has proposed the following as general UN criteria for acceptance of a status of free association for a NSGT:

> [T]he associated state should have full self-government, although it may voluntarily delegate certain tasks to the metropolitan state, especially in the fields of foreign affairs and defense; the association should be embraced by the population in an act of free choice observed by the UN; and the territory should retain the guaranteed right to choose another status in the future.[29]

On the matter of an associated state's right to continuing self-determination, both Hannum and Hillebrink appear to be following the lead of Principle VII of the Annex to Resolution 1541, which retains for the people of an associated state "the freedom to modify the status of that territory through the expression of their will by democratic means and through constitutional processes" at a future point in time. It should be noted that not all scholars concur with this view, as Cassese argues that a people's choice of free association terminates the right to self-determination.[30] The implications of this disagreement for solutions to the Western Sahara dispute will be explored later.

What follows are some actual examples where free association and other forms of autonomy have been arrived at through negotiation of the broad outlines of a comprehensive political settlement. In these cases, open-ended diplomatic discussions, a contentious referendum on independence or armed conflict were all put aside, while agreement on a new political status for the territory as the basis for ending the conflict took priority. These cases include the Cook Islands and Niue (former colonies of New Zealand), Aceh (an autonomous territory within Indonesia), New Caledonia (a colony of France), and Bougainville (an autonomous territory within Papua New Guinea).

CASE STUDIES: OUTCOMES SHORT OF INDEPENDENCE

Cook Islands, Niue

Settling on Free Association

As noted previously, state practice in seeking approval for the status of free association is rather limited; of the three states that have sought UN approval for free association, only the former New Zealand dependencies of the Cook Islands and Niue have been successful and under strikingly similar circumstances. These two cases may be instructive in helping to establish guidelines for decolonizing other NSGTs by means of creative autonomy arrangements within existing states, including through the mechanism of free association.

Located about halfway between New Zealand and Hawaii, the Cook Islands (population: 20,000) and Niue (population: 2,500) were under British protection until they were transferred to New Zealand in 1900 and 1901, respectively.[31] The Cook Islands attained UN recognition for its full self-governing status in 1965, following the gradual development of institutions of self-government, discussions with New Zealand, and active consultation with the UN.[32] Niue's free association arrangement with New Zealand was concluded in 1974, following the establishment of a local legislature and executive authority.[33]

It may prove helpful to evaluate the details of these free association arrangements against the core standards for full autonomy articulated by Hannum. His first factor—the legislative core power—appears to be satisfied in these two cases—as the territories are fully autonomous from New Zealand with regard to their internal affairs. In fact, New Zealand has no legislative power over the Cook Islands on any subject, and in the case of Niue, may only legislate for it if the Niue parliament specifically makes a request, an option the Cook Islands abolished in 1981.[34] In the case of Niue, the assembly "may make laws for the peace, order, and good government . . . [including] the power to repeal or revoke or amend or modify or extend. . . . any law in force in Niue."[35] This power extends even to New Zealand laws applicable to Niue, not least of which are the provisions of their agreement on free association which delegate to New Zealand responsibility for Niue's foreign relations and defense.[36] The arrangement between Niue and New Zealand is so permissive that Niue retains the unilateral right to terminate its relationship of free association with New Zealand at any time, assuming that a two-thirds affirmative vote of the Niue Assembly and a two-thirds vote in a popular referendum can be obtained.[37] The Governor-General, a New Zealand appointee, has no power over the enactment of Niue legislation.[38]

As for Hannum's second and third factors—executive and judicial autonomy—the Cook Islands and Niue cases far exceed the core powers he envisions. In both cases, executive power lies with a cabinet that is appointed by and is responsible only to the parliament.[39] The High Court of Niue has both civil and criminal jurisdiction "as may be necessary to administer the law in force in Niue," and the Niue constitution provides for the right of appeal to the Court of Appeals of New Zealand in three specific instances.[40]

New Zealand may act on behalf of the territories only in matters of foreign affairs or defense.[41] Residents of Niue and the Cook Islands retain their status as British subjects and citizens of New Zealand.[42] New Zealand's view has been that the Cook Islands and Niue retain the option to choose another more permanent form of self-government, including independence or integration, at a later date—a position that seems to have been embraced by UN member states.[43]

Obtaining Popular Consent

Principle VII of Resolution 1541, in requiring that free association "be the result of a free and voluntary choice by the peoples of the territory concerned expressed through informed and democratic processes," essentially places the burden on the principal state to show that the association was the result of a genuinely free choice by the population of the territory. However, significantly, in the case of the Cook Islands, this did not translate into a requirement that the territory hold a UN-supervised referendum. Rather, UN approval for the Cook Islands' free association with New Zealand followed a general election in which political parties that supported that outcome obtained a parliamentary majority.[44]

In contrast, the free association of Niue, which was concluded nine years after the Cook Islands, was approved in a UN-supervised referendum requested by the Niue Island Assembly. These cases may be seen as support for the view that, as for actual state practice, there may be more than one way of consulting a population that is acceptable under international law.

It is important to note that there is no evidence in either the Cook Islands or Niue cases that the populations of the territory in question were given the opportunity to choose between each of the different status options laid out in Resolution 1541: independence, free association, or integration.[45] Rather, in these cases, the terms of the association were determined through negotiations between New Zealand and representatives of the Cook Islands or Niue, after which the result was put to the people either through a referendum in a single "yes or no" vote, as in Niue, or made an issue in a general election, as in the Cook Islands.[46]

The cases which follow, which include both a NSGT (New Caledonia) as well as other territories that recently demanded some degree of self-determination (Aceh and Bougainville), are introduced with the intent of illustrating the diverse diplomatic and political pathways pursued by the parties once a policy decision has been made to end the conflict on the basis of mutually agreeable, broad outlines for a new political status.

Aceh

Getting to Helsinki, and After

Aceh, the westernmost province of Indonesia, was a stronghold of resistance to the Dutch during Indonesia's struggle for independence and experienced demands for autonomy as early as the 1950s.[47] The Free Aceh Movement (GAM) waged an insurgency against the Indonesian government since 1976.[48] The program of democratization under the government of B. J. Habibie helped to give rise to a significant popular movement demanding a referendum to determine Aceh's political future.[49] In August 2001, while East Timor was undergoing its violent process of separation from Indonesia following the August 1999 UN-supervised popular referendum supporting independence, Indonesia enacted a law granting Aceh special autonomy, especially in the fields of education, tradition, and local custom.[50]

The failure of the 2001 Special Autonomy Plan, and the province's regression into a state of martial law imposed by the Indonesian government, has been attributed to the fact that it was devised with minimal reference to popular elements in Aceh that were fueling pressures for secession.[51] Specifically, McGibbon contends that "special autonomy represented a unilateral concession by Jakarta that did not involve separatist leaders or civil society in a process of bargaining and negotiation."[52] As a result, special autonomy enjoyed little popular support and separatist leaders had few political incentives to drop their demand for Acehnese independence.[53]

Most successful autonomy arrangements, according to a study of ethnonational conflicts conducted by Gurr, tend to be the product of a negotiated settlement between a government and a rebel movement.[54] In light of this pattern, McGibbon believes that the Special Autonomy Plan's failure was due to the absence of a comprehensive and "systematic bargaining process . . . link[ing] concessions granted under the laws with a wide-ranging dialogue involving key elements of Acehnese . . . society."[55]

The Memorandum of Understanding (MoU) entered into by representatives of the Indonesian government and GAM on August 15, 2005, in Helsinki, in setting forth the outline of a comprehensive peace settlement—including the broad terms of a new political relationship between Aceh and Indonesia—differs significantly from previous, failed attempts to end the conflict. In this case, a combination of factors, including continuing Indonesian military offensives against GAM and the consequent deterioration of its will to keep up the fight, the destruction wreaked by the December 2004 tsunami, and the subsequent international humanitarian and reconstruction efforts, all gave renewed impetus to earlier overtures by a new Indonesian government to restart the peace process.[56]

Previous agreements had called for cease-fires and demilitarization to be followed by an open-ended dialogue on a resolution to the territorial dispute—a recipe for virtual deadlock given the distance between the parties on the core issue of Aceh's future political status.[57] In contrast, the Helsinki MoU, the result of five rounds of bargaining between January and July 2005, and mediated under the guiding principle that "nothing was agreed until everything was agreed," set as its aim the achievement of a grand compromise on Aceh's political status, to be bolstered by simultaneous agreement on matters of security cooperation, political participation, human rights, the rule of law, economic matters, and the disarmament and reintegration of GAM members into society.[58]

The most notable breakthrough resulting from Helsinki is expressed in the July 17, 2005, joint press statement issued by Indonesia and GAM: "The parties are committed to creating conditions within which the government of the Acehnese people can be manifested through a fair and democratic process within the unitary state and constitution of the Republic of Indonesia."[59] By abandoning its earlier demand for independence, GAM opened the door to key Indonesian concessions.

Autonomy "Within the Unitary State . . . of Indonesia"

The MoU sets out the "principles that will guide the transformation process" toward a comprehensive solution to the conflict in Aceh within the "unitary state and constitution of the Republic of Indonesia."[60] The most pertinent provisions rest in Article 1, mandating that a draft law on the governing of Aceh be promulgated and entered into force by March 31, 2006. However, the Law on the Governing of Aceh (LOGA) was not actually promulgated until August 1, 2006.[61] In Article 1.1.2(a), the MoU makes the following statement as to Aceh's future political relationship vis-à-vis Indonesia:

> Aceh will exercise authority within all sectors of public affairs, which will be administered in conjunction with its civil and judicial administration, except in the fields of foreign affairs, external defense, national security, monetary and fiscal matters, justice and freedom of religion, the policies of which belong to the Government of the Republic of Indonesia in conformity with the Constitution.

As typified in the Cook Islands and Niue free association models discussed earlier—as well as Hannum's core features of full autonomy—foreign and defense affairs were largely delegated to the principal state, in this case, Indonesia. However, unlike in those cases, the principles laid out for Aceh's self-government were relatively narrow and ambiguous. For example, while the MoU grants Aceh "authority" over its public affairs, including its civil and judicial administration, "national security, monetary and fiscal matters, justice and freedom of religion" remain under the control of Indonesia. While aspects of Islamic law will be reintroduced, the MoU holds that Aceh's "independent and impartial court system, including a court of appeals" will remain "within the judicial system of the Republic of Indonesia."

On a number of levels, it is evident that Acehnese authority over its own internal affairs is far from exclusive. Rather, provision is made in the MoU for consultation with and the consent of the legislature of Aceh whenever the Indonesian legislature makes a decision or undertakes any administrative measures affecting it. Clearly, the MoU envisions a continuing, significant governing role for Indonesia in the affairs of post-autonomy Aceh. Also, whereas Article 1.2 of the MoU (Political Participation) discusses the election of a head executive of the Aceh administration and a legislature for Aceh featuring local political parties, the authority to propose, let alone unilaterally carry through on a bid to modify the political relationship at some point in the future between Aceh and Indonesia—as is the case in the free association arrangements in the Cook Islands and Niue—is not envisioned.

While the MoU contains provisions concerning amnesty for former GAM combatants, as well as a substantial monitoring mission and an internationally mediated mechanism in the event of disputes over its implementation, the MoU nonetheless stops short of labeling Aceh's political status within Indonesia as one involving "autonomy" or "self-government," thereby highlighting the ambiguity which remains with regard to Aceh's true political status. Indeed, as late as the lead up to the 2009 parliamentary elections in Aceh, the full implementation of the MoU, not to mention the full implementation of the Law on the Governing of Aceh—which has been termed a "watered down legal embodiment of the [Helsinki] pact"—remained unrealized aims.[62] Disagreement concerning the content of the law's implementing regulations between bureaucrats in Jakarta and political leaders in Aceh was one of the key obstacles.[63]

New Caledonia and Bougainville

Interim Autonomy and Deferred Referendum on Independence: A Happy Medium?

The cases of New Caledonia and Bougainville are both factually and legally diverse—New Caledonia is an overseas, NSGT of France and Bougainville is a region of Papua New Guinea seeking greater autonomy. Yet, from a diplomatic and policy perspective they offer helpful guidelines for the resolution of disputes where the outcomes at the extremes of the self-determination spectrum—immediate, full independence, or the status quo—prove either unattractive or untenable. That is, a process is agreed upon to cast aside armed conflict or a near-term referendum in favor of a comprehensive negotiated settlement between the principal state and the affected region resulting in greater autonomy and a deferred popular referendum down the road.

The case of South Sudan, although itself not a NSGT, deserves brief mention here. Under the Comprehensive Peace Agreement signed in 2005 between the Arab-dominated regime in Khartoum and the largely Christian African peoples of the south, represented by the Sudan People's Liberation Movement, a delayed referendum was held in January 2011 on the unity of Sudan or alternatively the secession of South Sudan. In contrast to the other cases explored in which a deferred referendum on independence remains a future possibility, its outcome uncertain—as in the Cook Islands, Niue, New Caledonia, and Bougainville—as expected, the inhabitants of South Sudan overwhelmingly chose independence, which was declared in July 2011. Notably, an independent South Sudan is no closer today to resolving many of its conflicts with Khartoum than it was pre-independence.

France annexed New Caledonia in 1853, treating it as a *territoire d'outre-mer*, or overseas territory, under the legislative and administrative control of France, until the 1980s.[64] The population at the start of 2001 was approximately 213,000, of which, according to the 1996 census, 44 percent were Melanesian, 34 percent were European, and 22 percent were Polynesian and Asian minorities.[65] As France only minimally cooperated with the UN Decolonization Committee over the decolonization of New Caledonia, and by the late 1940s had stopped transmitting information on it—as required under Article 73(e) of the UN Charter—the General Assembly adopted a resolution in 1986 declaring that New Caledonia remained a NSGT.[66] Yet, international criticism of France's position has diminished since a broad agreement on the future of New Caledonia, the Nouméa Accord, was reached in 1998.

Replacing the referendum on independence originally scheduled for 1998, the Nouméa Accord, signed by France, representatives of the indigenous Kanaks, and the descendants of French settlers, or Caldoches, and approved by a plebiscite in New Caledonia, provides for a negotiated settlement leading to the gradual development toward full independence, free association with France, or maintenance of the status quo, the decision on which is postponed to a later date.[67] The decision as to New Caledonia's future political status—an outcome of the exercise of the population's right to self-determination—is to be determined by popular referendum to be put to New Caledonians between fifteen and twenty years after the inking of the initial agreement, or in the 2014–2019 time frame.[68] In the interim, the Nouméa Accord resulted in constitutional changes to New Caledonia's status within the French republic, creating "shared sovereignty," the election of new political institutions, an "irreversible" transfer of certain administrative powers from Paris to local authorities, and measures to recognize indigenous Kanak culture and identity.[69] Also, France would continue to regulate New Caledonia's external relations, financial matters, law enforcement, secondary and higher education, and penal and private law.[70]

Bougainville, the largest island in the Solomon Islands archipelago and part of Papua New Guinea, has faced significant secessionist pressures since the late 1980s. The Burnham Truce of October 1997 and the cease-fire agreed to in January 1998 set the stage for a political settlement, negotiated by secessionist forces and the government of Papua New Guinea—and overseen by the UN Observer Mission on Bougainville—between June 1999 and August 2001.[71] From the beginning, the peace process was predicated on a consensus among the Bougainville factions that a negotiated settlement, rather than secession by military force from Papua New Guinea, was the key to progress. Similarly, agreement by Bougainville factions to the deferral of a proposed popular referendum on independence, allowing time for reconciliation and providing for a more informed judgment on the sufficiency of autonomy as the basis for ending the conflict, created a vital opening for discussions between the parties.[72]

The comprehensive political settlement outlined in the Bougainville Peace Agreement of August 30, 2001, includes three main elements: (1) a constitutionally guaranteed, but deferred referendum for the people of Bougainville on independence from Papua New Guinea, (2) constitutional arrangements permitting the development of a high degree of autonomy for Bougainville, and (3) a plan for the disposal of weapons by ex-combatants.[73]

A referendum on the future political status of Bougainville is to be held no earlier than ten, but no later than fifteen, years after the election of an autonomous Bougainville government, with the precise date to be agreed upon by the parties in light of progress on the ground in good governance and weapons disposal.[74] As a safeguard for Papua New Guinea's interests, the settlement requires that the outcome of the referendum be subject to the final decision-making authority of the national parliament as well as consultations between the autonomous Bougainville government and the national government.[75]

The autonomy arrangements afforded to Bougainville under the political settlement include development over time of a high degree of freedom to choose its own constitutional structure, the potential to exercise wide powers and functions (including certain aspects of its external relations), and the ability to establish its own public service, police, judiciary, and correctional services.[76] On subjects such as criminal law, human rights, and the regulation of foreign investment—as well as those subjects not expressly enumerated—powers are to be shared between Bougainville and the national government.[77]

This combination of a deferred referendum on independence and high autonomy is probably unprecedented with regard to the resolution of secessionist conflict within independent states.[78] The resolution of the New Caledonia case described previously, while similar in form, is nonetheless different—namely, that of an overseas territory of France seeking self-determination as a matter of decolonization under relevant UN Resolutions. Including retention of the secession option following the deferred referendum on independence "puts pressure on the National Government to ensure that the autonomy arrangements are seen by most Bougainvilleans as a success," Regan recognizes that the political settlement is designed to discourage the push for full independence in favor of solutions including continued autonomy or integration within Papua New Guinea—a dynamic that we might expect to see in other cases, as well.[79]

ASSESSING THE CASES: A DIVERSITY OF OUTCOMES

The preceding cases, while drawing upon both colonial and noncolonial contexts, offer lessons that may be of considerable interest to those committed to novel solutions, consistent with international legal principles, to the negotiation and resolution of colonial-era claims for self-determination such as Western Sahara.

The Cook Islands and Niue are prime examples of the attainment of a full measure of self-government by formerly colonized territories. Under the model of free association, the islands have achieved virtually unlimited executive, legislative, and judicial competence over their own affairs, and easily satisfy Hannum's rough criteria for what constitutes a "fully autonomous" territory. In both cases—and in spite of the failure to hold a direct referendum in the Cook Islands—General Assembly approval was obtained for their respective outcomes. The process by which the principal state sought popular consent to a new political status vis-à-vis New Zealand was successful, at least in part, because at least one of the options available had been seriously worked out in advance with the meaningful participation of opposing sides, and the UN remained actively involved from the very beginning.

In Aceh, a territory that had been under Indonesian sovereignty since independence, some degree of autonomy was attained for the local population, albeit far from a free association arrangement as in the Cook Islands or Niue. While unlikely to satisfy Hannum's minimum threshold of powers exercised by a "fully autonomous" territory and lacking in the clarity exhibited in the preceding cases as to the means by which the popular consent of the affected population was obtained, the parties to the dispute nonetheless managed to devise, through negotiated compromise, the broad outlines of a comprehensive solution to the conflict, including a new political relationship between Aceh and Indonesia.

Progress toward the attainment of a full measure of self-government in the cases of New Caledonia and Bougainville remains ongoing. This is due to the nature of the process adopted in these two cases, which is to gradually devolve power—in line with a mutually agreed upon arrangement—from the central authority with a view toward holding a referendum at a later date on a permanent political status.

It is reasonable to ask to what extent our consideration of these cases relates to the unique factual, territorial, demographic, and historical circumstances of Western Sahara. Specifically, do the cases of small, isolated, underpopulated Pacific islands and regions provide any useful precedent in approaching the dispute over Western Sahara? Hannum notes the General Assembly's concern in addressing the case of Tokelau, another small Pacific island, that "such factors as territorial size, geographical location, size of population and limited natural resources" should not delay its people's exercise of its right to self-determination.[80] Along similar lines, and conceding the unique set of circumstances and challenges facing each case, Hannum reasons that the successful operation of associated statehood for the Cook Islands and Niue "should not be ignored even in non-colonial, non-island contexts."[81]

Overall, international law scholars have come to recognize that perfect legal precedents—and particularly models and the underlying legal principles which are cleanly transferable to new cases—are incredibly rare. Students and practitioners of international law must quite often deal in imperfect case precedents, systematically drawing lessons from composites of different cases, sharing some but not all circumstances in common, as opposed to the perfect matches that too often elude us in real life. While the circumstances surrounding the Cook Islands and Niue may be far removed from those of Western Sahara, a fellow NSGT, certain elements, such as conflicting claims to natural resources and threats ranging from popular unrest to armed insurgency were present, in varying degrees, in Aceh, Bougainville, and New Caledonia. International law is neither too stubborn nor too precise to shun the kind of analytical compromise and innovation required to cope with the vicissitudes of real life conflicts.

ASSESSING THE AUTONOMY PLAN

The Autonomy Plan has attracted criticism from some quarters suggesting that it represents a barely concealed Moroccan attempt to validate its control over the territory, aside from being inconsistent with international legal principles.[82] It has been praised by others as a novel solution to the dispute, reflecting the evolution of international law toward acceptance of "territorial autonomy as a right to democratic self-determination."[83] Even its skeptics acknowledge that the Autonomy Plan "follows a different strategy [from previous Autonomy Plans] . . . it defines the outline and principles governing autonomy, allowing for the proposal 'to be enriched by the other parties during the negotiations phase.'"[84]

It has been noted that the July 2011 Moroccan constitution, with its emphasis on decentralization, including devolution of power to elected regional councils, may present a unique window of opportunity within which to jumpstart the Autonomy Plan.[85] Consequently, are there lessons that can be drawn from the historical cases of free association as well as other recent initiatives toward negotiated high autonomy that can inform analysis of the Autonomy Plan as a formula to restart negotiations in accordance with accepted international legal principles on self-determination?

A Pathway to Free Association?

The preamble to the Autonomy Plan suggests that it be viewed as an effort by Morocco to "set a positive, constructive and dynamic process in motion." It proceeds to identify this effort as working toward "an autonomy proposal for the Sahara, within the framework of the Kingdom's sovereignty and national unity." To provide a less deliberate framework for engaging in serious negotiations, Morocco might consider removing the language "within the framework of the Kingdom's sovereignty and national unity" from the latter half of the preceding sentence while not removing it from its messages on the proffered resolution formula. Although in its eventual form a high degree of autonomy, or free association for Western Sahara within Morocco's overall sovereignty may be the most attractive solution, retaining such language does not help in refuting criticism that the Autonomy Plan is nothing more than a preordained outcome that Morocco seeks to impose on Western Sahara. As a comparison, of the cases studied, only that of Aceh, in speaking of its aim of retaining "the unitary state and constitution of the Republic of Indonesia," expressly excludes the option of independence for the territory.[86]

The Autonomy Plan's preamble also states that "the Sahara populations will themselves run their affairs democratically, through legislative, executive and judicial bodies enjoying exclusive powers." Article II(A)(12), which outlines the powers to be exercised by the Sahara autonomous region, provides that its population:

> shall exercise powers, within the Region's territorial boundaries, mainly over the following:
>
> - Region's local administration, local police force and jurisdictions;
> - In the economic sector; economic development, regional planning, promotion of investment, trade, industry, tourism and agriculture;
> - Region's budget and taxation;
> - Infrastructure: water, hydraulic facilities, electricity, public works and transportation;
> - In the social sector: housing, education, health, employment, sports, social welfare and social security;
> - Cultural affairs, including promotion of the Saharan Hassani cultural heritage;
> - Environment.

While representing a broad range of powers, there remains considerable uncertainty regarding the extent to which these powers are to be exercised exclusively by the autonomous region, whether within the proposed "regionalization" envisioned in the 2011 constitution or as detailed in the UN process.

This chapter's earlier exploration of the Cook Islands and Niue free association arrangements highlighted the importance that the international community attached to the fact that these territories were fully autonomous from New Zealand with regard to their internal affairs, and that New Zealand lacked any veto power, either legislative or executive, against the two. In contrast, in Aceh, the MoU anticipates the Indonesian legislature making decisions affecting Aceh; there, provision is made for consulting with and obtaining the consent of the legislature of Aceh—a far cry from the exclusive powers enjoyed by local legislatures in cases of free association.

El Ouali, in his favorable overview of the Autonomy Plan, contends that executive authority in the Sahara Autonomous Region shall lie with the Head of Government, who, despite being invested by the king and representing the central state, is elected by the local parliament and "only needs answer to this Parliament and, beyond that, to the local population."[87] El Ouali concedes, however, that the Autonomy Plan does not envision the circumstances or procedures under which the dissolution of parliament might take place, noting, simply, that "this kind of question usually comes from the State."[88] Unlike in the Cook Islands and Niue cases, the language of the Autonomy Plan may not address adequately the issue of limitations, if any, on veto powers retained by Morocco with regard to the internal affairs of Western Sahara. This is a detail of considerable significance which Morocco may want to clarify before the parties sit down to negotiate or at least be tabled as part of the negotiations agenda.

In contrast to the powers given to the autonomous region, Article II(A)(14), handling the powers to be retained by Morocco in any autonomy arrangement, refers to areas of *exclusive* jurisdiction over the following:

- The attributes of sovereignty, especially the flag, the national anthem and the currency;
- The attributes stemming from the constitutional and religious prerogatives of the King, as Commander of the Faithful and Guarantor of freedom of worship and of individual and collective freedoms;
- National security, external defense and defense of territorial integrity;
- External relations;
- The Kingdom's juridical order.

It is not altogether surprising that the Autonomy Plan claims control over these competencies, especially as New Zealand retains a limited role in the foreign relations and defense policies of the Cook Islands and Niue, although the reference to "exclusive" jurisdiction appears extreme and begs clarification. In the absence of a more precise delimitation of their scopes, "national security" and "external relations" could be interpreted so broadly as to permit Moroccan interference in otherwise local affairs, especially given the high level of economic dependency that is likely to define any future relationship between Western Sahara and Morocco. Also, Miguel is not entirely unjustified in raising concern about the potential breadth, in practice, of the powers stemming from "the constitutional and religious prerogatives of the King."[89]

Although provision is made in Article II(A)(15) for consultation with Western Sahara whenever exercise of Morocco's responsibilities with respect to external relations "have a direct bearing on the prerogatives of the Region," it is unclear how meaningfully, in practice, this will counterbalance Morocco's otherwise exclusive jurisdiction over such matters. As in the Cook Islands and Niue cases, however, the Autonomy Plan does appear to provide for Western Sahara, as an associated state, the exercise of some degree of international personality, as it allows for it, "in consultation with the Government, [to] establish cooperation relations with foreign Regions to foster inter-regional dialogue and cooperation."

The Autonomy Plan provides that the "Moroccan Constitution shall be amended and the autonomy Statute incorporated into it, in order to guarantee its sustainability and reflect its special place in the country's national judicial architecture," although this falls short of a guarantee against future unilateral constitutional modifications by Morocco. In contrast, even the peace plans for New Caledonia and Bougainville envision the irreversible transfer of certain powers from the central government to the local government as a result of the autonomy arrangement, and institute protections against the principal state's power to unilaterally repeal or alter the terms of the new political relationship. Also, New Zealand's severely constricted freedom of action with regard to the Cook Islands and Niue, as noted earlier, is to be contrasted with the islands' retention of the option to alter unilaterally its internal structure and relationship with the principal state. Therefore, Morocco might consider adding a provision offering assurances that it will not unilaterally modify any arrangement entered into with Western Sahara, although this may have far-reaching implications for its realization of regionalization in other parts of the country.

As it presently stands, Article II(A)(17), in stating that "powers which are not specifically entrusted to a given party shall be exercised by common agreement, on the basis of the principle of subsidiarity," may be perceived as inadequate in enforcing a meaningful separation of powers under free association. It is more probable in any ultimate free association arrangement, that as in the case of Cook Islands and Niue, and to a lesser extent, New Caledonia, where the devolution of centralized French power remains in progress, but in contrast to Aceh or Bougainville, that the legislature of Western Sahara will need to be treated as one possessing general powers, restricted only by *specific* grants of authority to Morocco. On this point, Morocco could expedite the process by bringing its plan in line with that of the other free association cases.

As for the judicial powers to be exercised by Western Sahara, the Autonomy Plan specifies that:

> (22) Courts may be set up by the regional Parliament to give rulings on [local disputes].... These courts shall give their rulings with complete independence, in the name of the King. (23) As the highest jurisdiction of the Sahara Autonomous Region, the high regional court shall give final decisions regarding the interpretation of the Region's legislation, without prejudice to the powers of the Kingdom's Supreme Court or Constitutional Council. (24) Laws, regulations and court rulings issued by the bodies of the Sahara Autonomous Region shall be consistent with the Region's autonomy Statute and with the Kingdom's Constitution.

El Ouali concedes that the Autonomy Plan does not explicitly describe the composition of the High Regional Court or whether it is the responsibility of Morocco or the autonomous region, creating ambiguity as to the judicial independence inherent in the mechanisms for dispute resolution between the parties.[90] Miguel contrasts this unfavorably with an earlier Autonomy Plan, which would have subjected such conflicts to resolution at the hands of the UNSG, a decidedly neutral actor.[91] The present plan also stands in contrast to the Niue case, where the local constitution provides for the right of appeal to the Court of Appeals of New Zealand in certain enumerated instances, and discretionary jurisdiction over appeals in other cases. Without further detail, the judicial powers set out in Articles 23 and 24 appear to more closely reflect the arrangement in Aceh, which stops short of full judicial independence from the principal state of the type that we have seen in cases of free association. Morocco might consider modifying its proposal to extend a heightened level of judicial independence to Western Sahara. It is intriguing to note that the Autonomy Plan, presented in 2007, predates more detailed proposals for the country's regionalization that may provide, as the organic law is elaborated, some guidance for dealing with this and other ambiguous issues.

The Cook Islands and Niue set a very high bar for future aspirants to the status of free association. It is hard to conceive of any internationally acceptable free association arrangement that does not guarantee to Western Sahara at least the same exclusive legislative, executive, and judicial powers that the Cook Islands and Niue presently enjoy, and where only a limited number of fields, as in foreign affairs and defense, are voluntarily delegated to Morocco. Yet, the fact that the Autonomy Plan, as it is presently written, does not mirror, in every detail, the free association arrangements eventually entered into between New Zealand and its former island possessions, need not be a fatal flaw. Rather, with certain improvements, some of which have been suggested in the preceding pages, the Autonomy Plan could serve as a broad formula for resolving the Western Sahara dispute.

OPTIONS AHEAD

The criteria for free association are never satisfied simply by guarantees that certain powers will remain under the exclusive control of a local government. Rather, a key element of free association is that it be subject to an act of free choice by the population of that territory. To that end, the Autonomy Plan envisions that the autonomy statute resulting from negotiations between the parties "shall be submitted to the populations concerned in a free referendum." The plan does not specify a time frame within which the referendum must be carried out, as in a certain number of years following the beginning of talks, as with New Caledonia, Bougainville, or the more recent case of Southern Sudan; neither does it mandate the specific form to be taken by the referendum or the precise status options that it need offer. Rather than providing further detail about its form, the plan pledges to allow for the free exercise of self-determination by the people of Western Sahara, "as per provisions of international legality, the Charter of the United Nations and the Resolutions of the General Assembly and the Security Council." Not directly mentioned by the Autonomy Plan, but implicit in any satisfactory resolution to the dispute under international law, would be the realization of the "free and genuine expression of the will of the peoples of the Territory," as set out in the ICJ's advisory opinion on Western Sahara.[92]

The inability to agree on procedures for obtaining popular consent to an arrangement of free association between Western Sahara and Morocco likely represents one of the greatest obstacles to this plan's success. Aside from the fact that the parties have previously had difficulty agreeing on a list of eligible voters, there remains the issue of continuing self-determination, whether the choice of free association in a free and open referendum terminates a people's right to make another choice in the future. Although Cassese disagrees, there is a general consensus among scholars that the population of an associated state retains the right to make another choice—including, possibly, full independence from the principal state—in the future. Recognition of a right to continuing self-determination was likely a key source of international support for the outcome of free association in the Cook Islands and Niue cases.

Unless this general consensus dissolves and Cassese's view prevails, the matter of continuing self-determination may continue to inject future uncertainty into any agreement arrived at between the parties in the present. However, given the record of international law as a gradually evolving body of principles applied to ever-changing global realities—not to mention a possible, sustained backlash emerging against the instability embodied in the unprecedented political tumult in the Middle East and North Africa commencing in early 2011—it is not inconceivable that support for a strict interpretation of the right to continuing self-determination may begin to slip away, rendering this concern moot, by the time, possibly years down the road, that it must again come under review.

Although far from ideal, a revised autonomy proposal could provide that a right of secession may be examined in the future subject to agreement between the autonomous government of Western Sahara and Morocco, similar to the consultative mechanism in place between autonomous regional and Papuan national authorities with respect to the outcome of Bougainville's deferred referendum on independence. Even should the principle of continuing self-determination not evolve, assuming a successful autonomy arrangement, the passage of time might be expected to dull its edge. In that case, a decision on independence, if taken, will be postponed to a much later date—at which point the parties may have had a chance to reevaluate the wisdom and peril of an abrupt move toward independence.

The achievement of genuine progress over Western Sahara need not be held hostage to disagreements at present over how and when to administer a popular referendum—although crucial to the Autonomy Plan's ultimate success, these are issues that can be negotiated. The preceding cases demonstrate that there is no fixed time frame within which a referendum must be held. Despite Miguel's assertion that the unavailability of a choice "between diverse options" is incompatible with international law on referendums over self-determination,[93] the Cook Islands and Niue cases illustrate that there is no strict requirement that a ballot provide for the full range of choices discussed in General Assembly Resolution 1541, such as independence, free association, or integration.

What the preceding cases have in common with the proposed plan for free association between Western Sahara and Morocco is recognition of the need to substitute, as the basis for ending the conflict, a comprehensive, negotiated political settlement achieved over time, in place of presently unworkable or unattractive alternatives, such as a contentious referendum on independence, open-ended talks, or continued armed conflict. In this way, the Autonomy Plan provides new opportunities for resolving the dispute over Western Sahara—an aim which has become imperative in light of the Arab uprisings and the resultant unsettling of the traditional relationship between the ruler and ruled in the Middle East and North Africa.

However, this by itself may not be enough. Some improvements to the Autonomy Plan may be needed to ensure that a future political arrangement meets the minimum threshold for legislative, executive, and judicial powers obtained in comparable free association and other high autonomy cases. These improvements may include the removal of language expressly ruling out the outcome of independence for Western Sahara, a clarification of what veto powers, if any, Morocco seeks to retain with regard to Western Sahara's internal affairs, and a commitment by Morocco not to unilaterally modify any political arrangement that it ultimately agrees to. The Autonomy Plan might also clarify that the legislature of an autonomous Western Sahara possesses general powers, restricted only by specific grants of authority to Morocco, and accord its judiciary a heightened degree of judicial independence from the host state. All of these concerns will of course be impacted by the direction and process of regionalization, if it includes the Western Sahara rather than treating it as a separate entity with powers beyond the other regions of Morocco.

Overall, while the Autonomy Plan is far from a flawless blueprint for resolving the Western Sahara dispute, its entry into the debate has greatly improved the chances of achieving, through peaceful means, a compromise outcome acceptable under international law.

NOTES

1. The views expressed in this paper are the views of the author, and do not reflect the views of the US House of Representatives, its committees, or members.

2. United Nations, "Secretary-General Hails 2010 as Landmark Year for Special Committee on Decolonization in Message to Organizational Meeting," February 25, 2010, www.un.org/News/Press/docs//2010/gacol3199.doc.htm.

3. Hurst Hannum, *Autonomy, Sovereignty, and Self-Determination* (Philadelphia: University of Pennsylvania Press, 1990), 41. Despite the breadth of possibilities represented by the fourth option, Hannum has pointed out that this flexibility has not yet been utilized to justify emergence from dependent status to any novel constitutional or other arrangement, although he notes that "it does represent a rare and welcome recognition of the potential for new inter- and intra-state relations."

4. J. Peter Pham, "Not Another Failed State: Toward a Realistic Solution in the Western Sahara," *Journal of the Middle East and Africa* 1, no. 1 (2010): 11.

5. Pham, "Not Another Failed State," 21.

6. Pham, "Not Another Failed State," 11.

7. Michla Pomerance, *Self-Determination in Law and Practice: The New Doctrine in the United Nations* (Leiden: Martinus Nijhoff Publishers, 1982), 1.

8. Pomerance, *Self-Determination in Law and Practice*, 10.

9. International Court of Justice, *Western Sahara Advisory Opinion* (October 16, 1975), www.icj-cij.org/docket/files/61/6195.pdf.

10. Karen Knop, *Diversity and Self-Determination in International Law* (Cambridge, UK: Cambridge University Press, 2002), 132–33.

11. Knop, *Diversity and Self-Determination in International Law*, 132–33.

12. Knop, *Diversity and Self-Determination in International Law*, 132–33.

13. Gregory H. Fox, "Self-Determination in the Post-Cold War Era: A New Internal Focus," *Michigan Journal of International Law* 16 (1995): 733.

14. Hannum, *Autonomy, Sovereignty, and Self-Determination*, supra note 2, 473–74.

15. Robin C. A. White, "Self-Determination: Time for Re-Assessment?" *Netherlands International Law Review* 28 (1981): 154.

16. Pomerance, *Self-Determination in Law and Practice*, supra note 6, 74.

17. Laurence S. Hanauer, "The Irrelevance of Self-Determination Law to Ethno-National Conflict: A New Look at the Western Sahara Case," *Emory International Law Review* 9 (1995): 176–77.

18. "Western Sahara: Out of the Impasse," *International Crisis Group*, Middle East/North Africa Report, no. 66 (June 11, 2007).

19. Abdelhamid El Ouali, *Saharan Conflict: Towards Territorial Autonomy as Right to Democratic Self-Determination* (London: Stacey International, 2008).

20. Richard Falk, "Self-Determination under International Law: The Coherence of Doctrine vs. the Incoherence of Experience," in *The Self-Determination of Peoples*, ed. Wolfgang Danspeckgruber (Boulder: Lynne Rienner Publishers, 2002), 41.

21. Falk, "Self-Determination under International Law," 41.

22. Falk, "Self-Determination under International Law," 42.

23. Steven Hillebrink, *The Right to Self-Determination and Post Colonial Governance* (The Hague: T.M.C. Asser Press, 2008), 26.

24. Thomas Musgrave, *Self-Determination and National Minorities* (Oxford: Oxford University Press, 2000), 95.

25. Hannum, *Autonomy, Sovereignty, and Self-Determination*, supra note 2, 384.

26. Hurst Hannum and Richard B. Lillich, "The Concept of Autonomy in International Law," *American Journal of International Law* 74 (1980): 858–89.

27. Hannum, *Autonomy, Sovereignty, and Self-Determination*, supra note 2, 467.

28. Hannum and Lillich, supra note 25, 859, 888.

29. Hillebrink, *The Right to Self-Determination*, supra note 22, 85–86.

30. Antonio Cassese, *Self-Determination of Peoples: A Legal Reappraisal* (Cambridge, UK: Cambridge University Press, 1995), 73.

31. Hillebrink, *The Right to Self-Determination*, supra note 22, 50–51. See also Hannum, supra note 2, 384–85.
32. Hannum, *Autonomy, Sovereignty, and Self-Determination*, supra note 2, 384–85. See also Hillebrink, supra note 22, 51.
33. Hannum, *Autonomy, Sovereignty, and Self-Determination*, supra note 2, 385.
34. Hillebrink, *The Right to Self-Determination*, supra note 22, 52.
35. Hannum, *Autonomy, Sovereignty, and Self-Determination*, supra note 2, 387.
36. Hannum, *Autonomy, Sovereignty, and Self-Determination*, supra note 2, 387.
37. Hannum, *Autonomy, Sovereignty, and Self-Determination*, supra note 2, 387.
38. Hannum, *Autonomy, Sovereignty, and Self-Determination*, supra note 2, 387.
39. Hannum, *Autonomy, Sovereignty, and Self-Determination*, supra note 2, 385–86.
40. Hannum, *Autonomy, Sovereignty, and Self-Determination*, supra note 2, 387–88.
41. Hillebrink, *The Right to Self-Determination*, supra note 22, 53.
42. Hillebrink, *The Right to Self-Determination*, supra note 22, 82.
43. Hillebrink, *The Right to Self-Determination*, supra note 22, 77.
44. Hillebrink, *The Right to Self-Determination*, supra note 22, 71.
45. Hillebrink, *The Right to Self-Determination*, supra note 22, 76.
46. Hillebrink, *The Right to Self-Determination*, supra note 22, 76.
47. Rodd McGibbon, "Secessionist Challenges in Aceh and Papua: Is Special Autonomy the Solution?," *East-West Center Washington*, Policy Studies 10 (2004): 6.
48. "Aceh: A New Chance for Peace," *International Crisis Group*, Asia Briefing no. 40 (August 15, 2005).
49. McGibbon, "Secessionist Challenges in Aceh and Papua," supra note 46, 7.
50. McGibbon, "Secessionist Challenges in Aceh and Papua," supra note 46, 10–11; Michael Morfit, "The Road to Helsinki: The Aceh Agreement and Indonesia's Democratic Development," *International Negotiation* 12, no. 1 (2007): 114.
51. McGibbon, "Secessionist Challenges in Aceh and Papua," supra note 46, 25.
52. McGibbon, "Secessionist Challenges in Aceh and Papua," supra note 46, 25.
53. McGibbon, "Secessionist Challenges in Aceh and Papua," supra note 46, 25.
54. Ted Gurr, *Peoples Versus States: Minorities at Risk in the New Century* (Washington, DC: United States Institute of Peace Press, 2000).
55. McGibbon, "Secessionist Challenges in Aceh and Papua," supra note 46, 69.
56. "Aceh: So far, so good." International Crisis Group, supra note 47. See also Morfit, "The Road to Helsinki," supra note 49, 117.
57. Edward Aspinall, "The Helsinki Agreement: A More Promising Basis for Peace in Aceh?," *East-West Center Washington*, Policy Studies 20 (2005): viii.
58. Aspinall, "The Helsinki Agreement," viii; Morfit, "The Road to Helsinki," supra note 49, 138.
59. "Aceh: So far, so good." International Crisis Group, supra note 47, 6.
60. *Memorandum of Understanding between the Government of the Republic of Indonesia and the Free Aceh Movement* (2005), https://peaceaccords.nd.edu/site_media/media/accords/Aceh-Indonesia_Memorandum_of_Understanding_2005.pdf.
61. "Aceh: Post-Conflict Complications," *International Crisis Group*, Asia Report no. 139 (October 4, 2007).
62. "Indonesia: Pre-Election Anxieties in Aceh," *International Crisis Group*, Asia Briefing no. 81 (September 9, 2008.)
63. "Indonesia: Pre-Election Anxieties in Aceh."
64. Hillebrink, *The Right to Self-Determination*, supra note 22, 122–23.
65. John Connell, "New Caledonia: An Infinite Pause in Decolonization?" *The Round Table* 92, no. 368 (2003): 126.
66. Hillebrink, *The Right to Self-Determination*, supra note 22, 125, 128.
67. Hillebrink, *The Right to Self-Determination*, supra note 22, 131.
68. Connell, "New Caledonia," supra note 64, 130–31. See also Nic Maclellan, "The Noumea Accord and Decolonisation in New Caledonia," *Journal of Pacific History* 34, no. 3 (1999): 245.
69. Maclellan, "The Noumea Accord," supra note 67, 245.

70. Hillebrink, *The Right to Self-Determination*, supra note 22, 132.
71. Anthony J. Regan, "The Bougainville Political Settlement and the Prospects for Sustainable Peace," *Pacific Economic Bulletin* 17, no. 1 (2002): 115.
72. Regan, "The Bougainville Political Settlement," 117–18.
73. Regan, "The Bougainville Political Settlement," 114.
74. Regan, "The Bougainville Political Settlement," 119–20.
75. Regan, "The Bougainville Political Settlement," 120.
76. Regan, "The Bougainville Political Settlement," 120.
77. Regan, "The Bougainville Political Settlement," 120.
78. Regan, "The Bougainville Political Settlement," 114.
79. Regan, "The Bougainville Political Settlement," 126–27.
80. Hannum, *Autonomy, Sovereignty, and Self-Determination*, supra note 2, 389.
81. Hannum, *Autonomy, Sovereignty, and Self-Determination*, supra note 2, 389.
82. Carlos Ruiz Miguel, "The 2007 Moroccan Autonomy for Western Sahara: Too Many Black Holes," *Grupo de Estudios Estrategicos (Madrid)* (Analysis no. 196) (June 15, 2007). See also Stephen Zunes, "Western Sahara: Self-Determination and International Law," *The Middle East Institute*, Viewpoints no. 6 (April 2008); Yahia Zoubir, "Stalemate in Western Sahara: Ending International Legality," *Middle East Policy* 14, no. 4 (2007): 158–77.
83. El Ouali, *Saharan Conflict*, supra note 18, p. 13.
84. Anna Theofilopolou, "Western Sahara—How to Create a Stalemate," *United States Institute of Peace*, Peace Brief, May 2007.
85. Anouar Boukhars, "Simmering Discontent in the Western Sahara," *Carnegie Endowment for International Peace*, March 2012: 16.
86. *Memorandum of Understanding*, supra note 59, p. 6.
87. El Ouali, *Saharan Conflict*, supra note 18, 151.
88. El Ouali, *Saharan Conflict*, supra note 18, 150.
89. Miguel, "The 2007 Moroccan Autonomy," supra note 81, p. 4.
90. El Ouali, *Saharan Conflict*, supra note 18, 152.
91. Miguel, "The 2007 Moroccan Autonomy," supra note 81, p. 4.
92. International Court of Justice, *Western Sahara Advisory Opinion*, supra note 8.
93. Miguel, "The 2007 Moroccan Autonomy," supra note 81, p. 4.

ELEVEN

The Use and Development of Natural Resources in Non-Self-Governing Territories

Glynn Torres-Spelliscy[1]

Western Sahara's 266,000-km² landscape is dominated by the vast and impregnable Sahara Desert. With less than 0.02 percent arable land,[2] and annual rainfall averaging between 26 mm to 76 mm,[3] it is one of the least densely populated, and most environmentally challenged, areas of the world.[4] Yet, Western Sahara is not a desert wasteland. Although the full extent of its natural resources remains largely unexplored, available evidence suggests that these resources could provide significant opportunities for economic development in the territory. On land, Western Sahara harbors one of the world's largest deposits of phosphates, a key component of fertilizers.[5] Offshore, its 1100-km-long Atlantic coastline is replete with fishing stocks. In addition, recent discoveries of oil reserves in geologically similar neighboring countries have fueled oil speculation in the territory. There is also a small, but developing, agricultural industry. But despite its potential, a decades-long political conflict over the juridical and factual control of the territory has prevented its people (known as the Sahrawi) from developing the territory's natural resources and realizing their full economic potential.[6]

The legal status of Western Sahara has been disputed since November 1975. Prior to that time, Spain was universally recognized as the administering power under Chapter XI of the UN Charter.[7] In 1974, pursuant to General Assembly Resolution 1514,[8] the Declaration on the Granting of Independence to Colonial Countries and Peoples, Spain began organizing efforts to conduct a referendum on the territory's future political status.[9] Western Sahara's neighboring states, Morocco and Mauritania, both asserted sovereignty based on claims of historic ties with the territory and its people, and successfully lobbied the General Assembly to adopt Resolution 3292 requesting an advisory opinion from the International Court of Justice (ICJ) on the legal status of the territory.[10] The ICJ ruled in October 1975, rejecting both countries' claims of sovereignty.[11]

A month later, in November 1975, approximately 350,000 Moroccan civilians marched across the border with Western Sahara in support of Moroccan sovereignty.[12] In a desire to avoid a military conflict, Spain negotiated the Madrid Accords, purporting to transfer its administrative responsibilities under the charter to both Morocco and Mauritania.[13] An armed conflict between a Western Saharan independence movement, the Popular Front for the Liberation of the Saguia el Hamra and Rio de Oro, known as the Polisario, and Moroccan and Mauritanian forces followed. As a result, thousands of Sahrawi refugees fled across the border into Algeria.[14] Spain physically withdrew from the territory in February 1976. In the following days, the Polisario announced the formation of a government-in-exile, the Saharan Arab Democratic Republic (SADR).[15] In 1979, Mauritania withdrew from the territory and renounced its claims. In 1988, the Polisario and Morocco entered into a cease-fire, and in 1991, the parties agreed to a Settlement Plan which provided for a referendum to determine the territory's ultimate political fate.[16] However, to date, a referendum has not been held and Morocco continues to control the majority of the territory.

The Spanish withdrawal from the territory and alleged divestment of its administrative responsibilities created a vacuum as to the legal authority responsible for the territory. Legally, Spain did not have the authority to effect a unilateral transfer of its administrative obligations.[17] Consequently, Morocco is not the *de jure* administrator of the territory, and its status in the territory is legally ambiguous. Given that the Western Sahara continues to be designated a non-self-governing territory (NSGT) by the UN, and remains primarily under Moroccan control, there is a strong argument that Morocco should be classified as the *de facto* administrator of the territory; consequently, the laws governing *de jure* administering powers under the charter would be informative by analogy. Other authors have suggested that Morocco is best classified as an occupying power under international law, and that the laws of occupation should therefore govern its use of the natural resources of the territory. Both bodies of law, fortuitously, come to relatively similar conclusions: the economic development of Western Sahara's natural resources does not require, *a priori*, the resolution of the political conflict over the territory's sovereignty, provided that such development is done in the interests of, and in coordination with the peoples of the territory.

The UN Charter provides the basic legal framework governing the administration of NSGTs. It has given rise to the universally accepted principle of customary international law that the people have "permanent sovereignty" over the territory's natural resources.[18] However, this principle only provides general guidelines, rather than specific prescriptions, with respect to behavior. Consequently, there is an open question as to how this principle applies to actual development activities in NSGT. As of 2012, the ICJ has yet to rule on the issue. The cases that have come before it have been resolved or dismissed prior to final judicial resolution.[19] Therefore, we must look to evidence from other sources, such as state practice and General Assembly resolutions, to ascertain whether there exists an *opinio juris*, that is, a legal opinion, with respect to the meaning of "permanent sovereignty over natural resources" in NSGT.

A review of these sources suggests that international law does not impose an absolute bar on the economic development and exploitation of the natural resources of NSGT.[20] Indeed, the law recognizes that such a prohibition may actually be harmful to the interests of the territory and its people.[21] Rather, the prevailing *opinio juris* imposes a conditional bar on such development activities that can be satisfied upon a showing that the proposed activities are in the best interests of, and are done in consultation with, the people of the territory.[22] Provided this two-part test is meaningfully satisfied, economic development of a NSGT's natural resources is "compatible with the Charter obligations of the Administering Power, and in conformity with the General Assembly Resolutions and the principle of 'permanent sovereignty over natural resources' enshrined therein."[23]

This chapter will be divided into four parts. Part I will explore Western Sahara's natural resources, including phosphates, fisheries, and the potential for oil and natural gas. Part II will examine the legal status of the territory and Morocco's presence therein.[24] Part III will analyze the international legal regime governing the use and exploitation of natural resources in NSGT. Finally, Part IV will discuss whether current economic activities in Western Sahara comply with international law.

RESOURCES OF WESTERN SAHARA

Western Sahara's natural resources imbue the territory with significant economic potential. In the 1970s, as Spanish control of the territory was winding down, both the UN and World Bank noted that Western Sahara, with its phosphate reserves and fishing stocks, could be one of the wealthiest countries in the region.[25] The possibility that oil and natural gas could be discovered within the territory has only added to its potential economic viability.[26] However, the full extent and viability of Western Sahara's natural resources remains largely unexplored as a result of the ongoing political conflict. Nonetheless, even if its economic resources were demonstrated to be significantly less valuable than currently predicted, the principles of international law, discussed in part III, would not be affected. International legal principles relating to the development of the natural resources of NSGTs are not dependent on the value or viability of such resources.[27]

Nonrenewable Resources

Phosphate Reserves in Western Sahara

Phosphates are one of the primary components of most fertilizers,[28] and a critical factor in agricultural production levels worldwide.[29] Morocco holds the largest phosphates reserves in the world, controlling over 35 percent of global exports of phosphate rock, and 51 percent of global exports of phosphoric acid.[30] Western Sahara also possesses significant phosphate reserves,[31] and Morocco and Western Sahara combined control approximately half of all the world's reserves.[32]

Phosphates were first discovered in Western Sahara near Bou Craa, southeast of the capital city of Layounne. Since buying out Spanish interests in 2002,[33] the Bou Craa mine has been operated solely by Phosboucraa, a 100-percent-owned subsidiary of the Moroccan state-owned company, Office Chérifien des Phosphates (OCP).[34] The output from the Bou Craa mines has historically been small. In 2010, approximately 2.6 million tons of phosphate rock was mined,[35] which accounted for just 6 percent of OCP's annual phosphate sales.[36] Further, according to the Moroccan government, the phosphate that is mined from Bou Craa is of a "lower grade and therefore requires significant process and investment to be transformed into market-grade phosphate."[37] Nonetheless, the estimated reserves are significant (approximately 132 million tons) and if fully exploited, could offer significant profit potential.[38] The value of Western Sahara's phosphate reserves is further inflated by the possibility of uranium extraction from the rock.[39] A 2009 report from Morocco's Office National des Hydrocarbures et des Mines (OHNYM) noted that Morocco's "south provinces" (i.e., Western Sahara) offer good "perspectives for uranium occurrences in the coastal basin as well as in the Precambrian basement."[40]

Oil and Natural Gas Exploration in Western Sahara

The discovery of oil off the coast of Mauritania,[41] which shares many geologic similarities with Western Sahara, has sparked significant oil speculation in Western Sahara.[42] As oil analyst Helen Campbell notes, Western Sahara's "waters hold the 'end' of a reserves belt,"[43] that if fully exploited could cause Western Sahara to become "one of the leading oil producing countries in West Africa."[44] Exploration has, however, remained limited, and no oil or gas had been discovered (or at the least reported) as of August 2012.[45]

The potential value of any oil and gas reserves has led both Morocco and SADR to issue limited, competing exploration licenses to international oil companies. In some cases, these licenses have overlapped.[46] Within a year of the discovery of oil in neighboring Mauritania, Morocco's ON-HYM had executed various licensing agreements allowing research and evaluation activities in Western Saharan territory. To date, Morocco has designated eight blocks of varying size, for oil exploration in Western Saharan territory,[47] resulting in exploration licenses with at least five corporate partners.[48] Although much of the work remains in the pre-exploratory phase, there are some indications that further exploration, including drilling, could "commence in the 2013 timeframe."[49]

Beginning in May 2005, SADR engaged in its own series of licensing initiatives with respect to onshore and offshore oil exploration in Western Sahara.[50] This initial round of offerings led to nine separate licenses issued to eight different companies.[51] On October 25, 2007, SADR initiated a second round of petroleum and natural gas licensing.[52] Unlike the licenses issued by Morocco, the licenses issued by SADR do not provide a company with rights to immediately begin exploration activity.[53]

Renewable Resources

Fishing Stocks in Western Sahara

Fishing is a major source of revenue for Morocco, accounting for approximately 15 percent of total Moroccan exports, and worth about US$1 billion annually.[54] Two of the most important catches in the Moroccan industry are sardines and cephalopods, both of which, according to the UN Food and Agricultural Organization, have been overfished in Moroccan waters.[55] Comparatively, the supplies of such stocks in the adjacent waters of Western Sahara are still abundant.[56] There is little doubt that Moroccan interests are fishing in Western Saharan waters; however, estimates with respect to the percentage of Morocco's annual catch landed in Western Sahara's waters vary, ranging from 40 percent[57] to 90 percent.[58]

In December 2011, the European Parliament declined to consent to the renewal of the 2007 Moroccan-EU Fisheries Partnership Agreement (FPA)[59] and, as a result, it was terminated.[60] The Parliament's action was based on the recommendations of two separate EU Parliamentary Committees. The EU Budget Committee maintained that the FPA, which consumed 25 percent of the EU's fisheries budget, was not cost efficient.[61] Under the terms of the FPA, the EU agreed to make a €144.4 million financial contribution to Morocco, with annual payments of €36.1 million.[62] Of that total, €13.5 million was to be paid in direct support of the Moroccan fishing industry.[63] Under Article 2(6) of the First Protocol, Morocco had "full discretion" regarding how the funds would be spent, and there was no requirement that the local Sahrawi population be consulted.[64] The EU Development Committee also recommended against the renewal of the FPA, concluding that it did not provide a sufficient developmental impact, nor did it adequately address the issue of Western Sahara.[65] In withholding its consent, the European Parliament called on the European Commission to "negotiate a new, more environmentally and economically beneficial deal that takes into account the interests of Western Sahara."[66] In April 2012, EU Fisheries Commissioner, Maria Damanaki, traveled to Morocco to begin negotiations on a new fisheries deal.[67]

Agriculture Industry

With only a small amount of arable land suitable for agricultural development, Western Sahara's agricultural industry is still in its infancy. Nonetheless, there is some evidence of increasing levels of production, particularly with respect to tomatoes.[68]

On February 16, 2012, the European Parliament voted to approve an agriculture trade agreement with Morocco that calls for trade liberalization and reductions in tariff levels.[69] The Agriculture Agreement does not explicitly exclude products from Western Sahara, and, as a result, during the Parliamentary vote the Rapporteur for the Parliament's Committee on International Trade, José Bové, argued that it potentially breached international law.[70] Bové concluded that,

> Several times over the past few months, the rapporteur has raised the question of the territorial range of the agreement between the European Union and Morocco. . . . As the Commission and Parliament's Legal Service hold diverging views on this issue, the rapporteur feels unable to guarantee that this free trade agreement will comply with the international treaties binding the European Union and all its Member States.[71]

The Parliament, however, ultimately rejected Bové's concerns and approved the agreement. During the debate, the European Commissioner for Enlargement and European Neighborhood Policy distributed a fact sheet to parliament members, which, with respect to Western Sahara, stated that, "[s]o far there is practically no agricultural activity in Western Sahara (only 300 hectares close to Dakhla) and there is no exploitation of resources in agriculture."[72] Following reports that there actually was significant agricultural production in Western Sahara,[73] a group of parliamentarians sought clarification from the Commission on the previous statements. On May 23, 2012, the Commission responded that after receiving further information from Morocco it was clear that there were "about 500 hectares, of which 350 hectares are already exploited," of land being used for agricultural activity in Western Sahara.[74]

THE POLITICO-LEGAL STATUS OF WESTERN SAHARA AND MOROCCO UNDER INTERNATIONAL LAW

Under international legal principles, a state in *de facto* control of a territory has three possible legal classifications: sovereign, administrator, or occupier. The first of these categories, sovereignty, carries a significantly different set of rights as compared to the last two. A state exercising sovereign control over a territory has the right to exploit its natural resources, largely without international interference.[75] However, legally, there is no sovereign state that controls Western Sahara. Neither SADR nor Morocco meets the requisite criteria. Although SADR is currently recognized by some fifty states internationally, as well as various international organizations, it is not recognized by any members of the UNSC, nor is it formally recognized by the UN.[76] Factually, SADR has never exercised full and effective control of the territory. With respect to Morocco, the ICJ rejected its claims of sovereignty in 1975.[77] Its recent autonomy proposal appears to have the support of powerful interests, including the United States,[78] the UNSC,[79] and European powers France and Spain.[80] Yet, to date, no state has officially recognized Moroccan sovereignty over the territory.

Legally, Western Sahara is considered by the UN to be a NSGT.[81] Under the charter, a NSGT is defined as a territory that has "not yet attained a full measure of self-government."[82] Western Sahara's status as a NSGT, however, is somewhat unique. Of the sixteen remaining territories designated as NSGTs, Western Sahara is the only territory where the existence or identity of the state responsible for its administration under chapter XI of the charter is unclear.[83] Prior to 1975, Spain was the undisputed administering power. For thirteen years, Spain transmitted the information required of an administering power under Article 73(e),[84] and it was officially recognized as the administering power by General Assembly Resolution 2072.[85] However, on November 14, 1975, under the terms of the Madrid Accords, Spain agreed to the establishment of a temporary tripartite administration of the territory with Morocco and Mauritania, and made a commitment to fully withdraw from the territory in the first months of the following year.[86] In February 1976, Spain withdrew and sent a letter to the UNSG declaring that, "Spain considers itself henceforth exempt from any responsibility of an international nature in connection with the administration of [Western Sahara]."[87]

Spain's purported unilateral divestment of its administrative responsibilities, along with its physical withdrawal from the territory, put Western Sahara in a unique position. It is considered a NSGT, yet it has no *de jure* administrator. This is because, from a legal perspective, the Madrid Accords were of no force and effect with respect to the transfer of administrative power. As UN Legal Counsel and Under-Secretary-General for

Legal Affairs, Hans Corell, noted in his 2002 opinion, discussed in detail here:

> The Madrid Agreement did not transfer sovereignty over the territory, nor did it confer upon any of the signatories the status of an administering Power—a status which Spain alone could not have unilaterally transferred. The transfer of administrative authority over the territory to Morocco and Mauritania in 1975, did not affect the international status of Western Sahara as Non-Self-Governing Territory.[88]

As a result, there is a legal vacuum with respect to the legitimate governing authority for the territory, which leaves open the question as to what Morocco's role is, and what legal regime governs its behavior. The unique reality of Western Sahara renders an answer to this question difficult under international legal principles. Although Morocco is not the *de jure* administrator of the territory, it does act as a *de facto* administrator; consequently, the laws governing administering powers under the Charter will be informative by analogy.[89] Some scholars have suggested that if Morocco is not the *de jure* administrator of the territory, then it must be an occupier.[90] In 2010, Hans Corell stated that "[t]he argument can be made that Western Sahara in reality is occupied by Morocco."[91] The General Assembly has also made reference to the "continued occupation of Western Sahara by Morocco."[92] However, under a close examination, the laws of occupation are not directly on point, either. Significantly, the UN identifies Western Sahara as a NSGT, as compared to an occupied territory.[93] Therefore, in ascertaining the rules applicable to Morocco's economic activities in Western Sahara, we will be guided primarily by the principles underlying the laws of colonial administration; however, for completeness, we will also consider the laws of occupation. Fortuitously, the principles underlying both legal regimes are based on the same fundamental understanding: the people of territory maintain permanent sovereignty over their natural resources, and consequently, economic exploitation is only permitted to the extent that it is done in consultation with, and for the benefit of, the local population. The origin and development of this principle is discussed in detail in the next section.

ECONOMIC DEVELOPMENT OF NATURAL RESOURCES OF NSGT UNDER INTERNATIONAL LAW

To understand the legality of economic development activities relating to natural resources in NSGTs, we look to both treaty and customary international law.[94] Treaties are legally binding agreements that lay out the rights and obligations of their parties. International customary law is a general state practice accepted as law.[95] This means that if a state practice is motivated by a belief that it is legally required, as compared to merely politically opportune, it has arguably become a principle of customary international law binding on all members of the international legal community.[96] Because of the objective difficulty in determining the "belief" of state parties, courts look to other indicators to establish whether such a legal opinion (known as *opinio juris*) exists, including forms of "soft law," such as General Assembly resolutions.[97] As the ICJ has noted,

> General Assembly Resolutions, even if they are not binding, may sometimes have normative value. They can, in certain circumstances, provide evidence important for establishing the existence of a rule or the emergence of *opinio juris*. To establish whether this is true of a given General Assembly resolution, it is necessary to look at its content and the conditions of its adoption; it is also necessary to see whether an *opinio juris* exists as to its normative character. Or a series of resolutions may show the gradual evolution of the *opinio juris* required for the establishment of a new rule.[98]

The primary treaty governing the administration of NSGT's is the UN Charter. The Charter emphasizes the importance of self-determination in creating "conditions of stability and well-being which are necessary for peaceful and friendly relations,"[99] and in strengthening universal peace.[100] Legal obligations with respect to NSGTs are laid out in chapter XI of the Charter. Article 73 directly establishes the paramountcy of the rights of the indigenous populations in such territories:

> Members of the United Nations which have or assume responsibilities for the administration of territories whose peoples have not yet attained a full measure of self-government recognize the principle that the interests of the inhabitants of these territories are paramount, and accept as a sacred trust the obligation to promote to the utmost, within the system of international peace and security established by the present Charter, the well-being of the inhabitants of these territories.[101]

This "sacred trust" includes an obligation on administering powers to promote "the well being of the inhabitants of [the] territories," including promoting "constructive measures of development . . . with a view to the practical achievement of the social, economic and scientific purposes set forth in this Article."[102] The Charter, however, does not prescribe specific rules of behavior governing how the right of self-determination should be exercised with respect to the exploitation of natural resources in NSGT. We must therefore look to other evidence to determine whether an *opinio juris* has arisen with respect to such development activities.

The right of self-determination for NSGTs was first articulated in 1960, when the General Assembly adopted Resolution 1514, the Declaration on the Granting of Independence to Colonial Countries and Peoples. Resolution 1514 provides that, "all peoples have the right to self-determination; by virtue of that right they freely determine their political status and freely pursue their economic, social and cultural development."[103] The right to self-determination has now been unquestionably established as a principle of customary international law.[104] With respect to the use of natural resources, the right of self-determination includes, as a corollary, the right of the peoples of the territory to maintain "permanent sovereignty over their natural resources." This principle was first articulated in 1962 by General Assembly Resolution 1803, Permanent Sovereignty Over Natural Resources, which provides that, the "right of peoples and nations to permanent sovereignty over their natural wealth and resources must be exercised in the interest of their national development and of the well-being of the people of the State concerned."[105] Further, it provides that the, "[v]iolation of the rights of peoples and nations to sovereignty over their natural wealth and resources is contrary to the spirit and principles of the Charter of the United Nations and hinders the development of international co-operation and the maintenance of peace."[106] The right of permanent sovereignty over natural resources has since been affirmed in numerous treaties and General Assembly Resolutions.[107] For example, Common Article 1(2) of the International Covenant on Civil and Political Rights and the International Covenant on Economic Social and Cultural Rights (Morocco is a state party to both Covenants) provides, "all peoples may, for their own ends, freely dispose of their natural wealth and resources without prejudice to any obligations arising out of international economic co-operation, based upon the principle of mutual benefit, and international law. In no case may a people be deprived of its own means of subsistence."[108]

The principle of permanent sovereignty over natural resources is "indisputably part of customary international law," and therefore binding on all members of the international community.[109] But, what exactly does the principle of permanent sovereignty prescribe with respect to the actual economic development of the natural resources of a NSGT by an administering power, or in the case of Western Sahara, a *de facto* administering power?

This was precisely the question put to Hans Corell, former Under-Secretary-General for Legal Affairs and the Legal Counsel of the United Nations, in 2002 by the president of the UNSC. On February 12, 2002, Corell released his opinion.[110] The Corell opinion closely analyzed decisions of the ICJ, state practice, and applicable General Assembly Resolutions in determining whether an *opinio juris* had developed with respect to the application of the right of permanent sovereignty over natural resources to particular development activities in a NSGT.

First, Corell noted that the ICJ has not yet ruled on the issue. The cases that have been brought before it were either settled or dismissed prior to final judicial resolution.[111] Next, Corell examined recent state practice for evidence of *opinio juris*. Corell acknowledged that the evidence of such practice is relatively sparse due to the few remaining NSGTs; nonetheless, he was able to identify several relevant precedents.[112] First, Corell noted that during the period of Spanish control of Western Sahara, Spain freely conceded that profits derived from the exploitation of the territory's natural resources, which consisted primarily of phosphate production at the time, were to "be used for the benefit of the Territory."[113] Moreover, Spain "recognized the sovereignty of the Saharan population over the Territory's natural resources and that, apart from the return of its investment, Spain laid no claim to benefit from the proceeds."[114]

The most recent example cited by Corell, and perhaps most analogous, related to the administration of East Timor by the United Nations Transitional Administration in East Timor (UNTAET). Prior to achieving full independence, and subsequent to Indonesia's departure, East Timor was administered by UNTAET. UNTAET, however, was not officially recognized as an administrator under Article 73 of the Charter. Consequently, much like Morocco, UNTAET was acting as a *de facto*, rather than *de jure*, administrator of the territory. As *de facto* administrator, UNTAET entered into several agreements relating to the economic development of the territory's natural resources on behalf of the East Timorese people. As Corell pointed out, "[i]n concluding the agreement for the exploration and exploitation of oil and natural gas deposits in the continental shelf of East Timor, UNTAET, on both occasions, consulted fully with representatives of the East Timorese people, who participated actively in the negotiations."[115] Indeed, a review of the record demonstrates that the negotiating team was comprised of both UTAET officials and representatives of the National Council of Timorese Resistance (CNRT), an East Timorese independence group that led the struggle against the Indonesian occupation.[116]

In addition to state practice, numerous General Assembly Resolutions have also addressed the issue of resource exploitation in NSGT. These General Assembly Resolutions consistently recognize that the people of NSGTs possess "inalienable rights ... to their natural resources," as well as a right "to establish and maintain control over the future development of those resources."[117] As Corell pointed out, the guiding principle under the General Assembly Resolutions is the maximization of the interests of the people of the territory:

> In recognizing the inalienable rights of the peoples of Non-Self-Governing Territories to the natural resources in their territories, the General Assembly has consistently condemned the exploitation and plundering of natural resources and any economic activities which are detrimental to the interests of the peoples of these territories and deprive them of their legitimate rights over their natural resources.[118]

The General Assembly has, however, also recognized the potential benefits of economic development in NSGT. For example, in Resolution 50/33, the General Assembly affirmed "the value of foreign economic investment undertaken in collaboration with the peoples of the Non-Self-Governing Territories and in accordance with their wishes in order to make a valid contribution to the socio-economic development of the Territories."[119]

> The body of General Assembly resolutions therefore demonstrates an attempt by the international community to achieve a balance between the rights of the population to permanent sovereignty over their natural resources, and the potential benefits of the economic development of those resources. Consequently, after reviewing the available evidence, Corell concludes, [t]he recent State practice, though limited, is illustrative of an *opinio juris* on the part of both administering Powers and third States: where resource exploitation activities are concluded in Non-Self-Governing Territories for the benefit of the peoples of these territories, on their behalf, or in consultation with their representatives, they are considered compatible with the Charter obligations of the administering Power, and in conformity with the General Assembly resolutions and the principle of "permanent sovereignty over natural resources" enshrined therein.[120]

In December 2008, at a conference in South Africa, Corell once again addressed the issue of Western Sahara, and reiterated his position that economic contracts are illegal if they are "done in disregard of the interest *and* wishes of the people of Western Sahara [and that] Morocco would have to engage in proper consultations with persons authorized to represent the people of Western Sahara before such activities would be allowed."[121] In 2009, the European Parliament Legal Service reversed a prior position and concurred with Corell, stating that, "compliance with international law requires that economic activities related to the natural resources of a Non-Self-Governing Territory are carried out for the benefits of the people of such Territory, *and* in accordance with their wishes."[122]

The laws of occupation start from the same basic premise as the laws relating colonial administration—permanent sovereignty of the resources of a territory rests with the people of the territory. Under Article 43 of the Hague Regulations, the fact of occupation does not vest the occupier with sovereign rights.[123] With respect to the use of natural resources, Article 55 of the Hague Regulations, provides that an occupying power, "shall be regarded only as administrator and usufructuary of public buildings, real estate, forests, and agricultural estates belonging to the hostile State, and situated in the occupied country. It must safeguard the capital of these properties, and administer them in accordance with the rules of usufruct."[124]

The term "usufruct" denotes a "right to use and enjoy the fruits of another's property for a period without damaging or diminishing it, although the property might naturally deteriorate over time."[125] The rules of usufruct, in general, provide that an occupying power cannot take actions that cause permanent changes to the territory, nor can it engage in activities that are detrimental to the peoples of the territory.[126] Consequently, "the extraction and export of natural resources from an occupied territory, which both damages and diminishes the 'capital' of the property," is illegal.[127] As international law does not distinguish between renewable and nonrenewable resources with respect to the laws governing economic activities in NSGTs,[128] the economic development and exploitation of any natural resources would likely present significant legal issues under the laws of occupation.[129]

In conclusion, the prevailing *opinio juris* concerning the application of the principle of permanent sovereignty over natural resources in NSGTs provides that: (1) economic activity, including the development of natural resources, is not strictly prohibited by international law, (2) provided that such activity or exploitation is conducted for the benefit of the peoples of the territory, and (3) in consultation and coordination with their representatives.[130]

APPLICATION OF LEGAL PRINCIPLES TO WESTERN SAHARA

Economic Development of the Natural Resources of Western Sahara and the Interests of the Sahrawi People

Evidence as to whether resource development activities currently ongoing in Western Sahara benefit the Sahrawi population (many of whom continue to reside in refugee camps in Algeria) is disputed. With respect to Western Sahara's phosphate reserves, there is compelling evidence that Moroccan interests are trading phosphates from the Bou Craa mines on the international market.[131] As discussed earlier, the mine at Bou Craa is 100 percent owned and operated by Phosboucraa, a subsidiary of the Moroccan state-owned, Office Chérifien des Phosphates, (OCP). According to OCP's 2010 Annual Report, Phosboucraa's net profit was approximately US$15 million in 2010.[132] OCP has stated that the economic activities of the mine have "directly benefitted and are in the interests of the local population."[133] OCP points to its use of locally sourced goods, a commitment to hiring the local population, including Sahrawis, as well as a commitment that "all net income generated by Phos-Boucraâ has been reinvested in the region."[134] OCP claims that since 2002, it has invested more than US$420 million on operating and capital expenditures related to the mines, and over US$1.3 billion on personnel costs in the territory.[135] Critics on the other hand, argue that the Sahrawi population has been marginalized from the Bou Craa workforce; for example, they cite figures that only approximately 10 percent of the workforce self-identify as Sahrawi.[136]

Morocco also appears to financially benefit from fishing that takes place in Western Saharan waters. In support of the legality of such activities, Morocco asserts that it has invested significant resources into the fishing industry in Western Sahara, and that its investments outweigh the totality of the profits from the trade agreements.[137] For example, the Southern Development Agency has allegedly spent significant sums in rehabilitating and developing coastal fishing villages and ports.[138] Critics, however, maintain that the Sahrawi population has not benefitted from such investments,[139] and that many of the constructed fishing villages remain empty or populated entirely by Moroccans.[140]

With respect to the newly adopted Agricultural Agreement between Morocco and the EU, the EU Parliament has requested that the Commission "ensure that the agreement is fully consistent with international law and benefits all the local population groups affected."[141] The recent statement by the European Commission, discussed above, that 350 hectares of land in Western Sahara is currently being exploited for agricultural development raises substantial legal concerns.[142]

Morocco's issuance of licenses for oil exploration, which, at this stage, appear to be for the non-exploitative exploration of potential oil resources, do not necessarily breach international law on their face. However, as Corell concluded, "if further exploration and exploitation activities were to proceed in disregard of the interests and wishes of the people of Western Sahara, they would be in violation of the international law principles applicable to mineral resource activities in Non-Self-Governing Territories."[143] Consequently, recent announcements by oil companies that exploratory drilling could commence as early as 2013[144] could raise significant legal concerns. Further, to the extent that Morocco has received any financial payments related to the oil exploration licenses it has issued, "in the absence of the participation of and benefit to the people of Western Sahara," Morocco may have violated international law.[145]

In further support of the legality of its activities, Morocco points to significant investments, totaling approximately US$2.5 billion since 1976, that it has allegedly made in developing the economic infrastructure of Western Sahara, including the development of roads, housing, schools, and hospitals.[146] Sahrawi activists, however, argue that the Moroccan government has been using economic incentives to lure settlers from the north to populate Western Sahara, and that the indigenous population has largely been marginalized and has not benefitted from these economic development activities.[147]

Economic Development of the Natural Resources of Western Sahara and Coordination with the Sahrawi People

Whether or not the economic development activities in the region benefit the local population is only one of the conditions required for the legal exploitation of natural resources of NSGTs under international law. As discussed earlier, to be legal, such economic development activities must also be performed in consultation and coordination with the representatives of the people of the territory.

From a political and legal perspective, perhaps the most vexing question with respect to the consultation requirement is how to determine the proper representative of the people of a NSGT. As Hans Corell pointed out in 2008, this is not an easy task.[148] The UNGA has recognized the Polisario as the "representative of the people of Western Sahara,"[149] and SADR, which was established by the Polisario, is currently recognized by approximately fifty states, as well as the African Union (AU), as the legitimate government of Western Sahara.[150] The Moroccan government, however, has consistently refused to recognize the legitimacy of SADR, accusing it of being pawns of the Algerian government,[151] and as providing fertile grounds for terrorist activity.[152] Ultimately, the decision to recognize a foreign government, or governmental entity, and establish diplomatic ties is a political decision by the government of the recognizing state.[153] International law does not mandate recognition. However, if Morocco wishes to develop the natural resources of Western Sahara, they will need to coordinate and consult with representatives of the Sahrawi people.

Advocates for Morocco point to the fact the current inhabitants of Western Sahara regularly participate in elections for the Moroccan legislature.[154] Further, they argue that the views of Western Sahara are considered through groups like the Royal Advisory Council for Saharan Affairs (CORCAS) established in 2006,[155] as well as local government. Participation in the Moroccan government, however, does not necessarily fulfill the self-determination rights of the Sahrawi population under international law, nor does it satisfy their rights of permanent sovereignty over their natural resources.[156] Indeed, the representativeness of such institutions is questionable given the large number of Sahrawis still living in refugee camps in Tindouf, Algeria, who do not participate in the elections. Moreover, Sahrawi advocates argue, the population currently residing, and voting, in Western Sahara consists primarily of northern migrants, who by some estimates "are now thought to outnumber indigenous inhabitants by as many as two to one."[157] On the SADR side, the Sahrawis in the Algerian refugee camps participate in elections for the Sahrawi National Council, which is the parliamentary assembly of SADR, with the most recent election occurring in December 2011.[158]

To date, there is no evidence to suggest that there has been collaboration or consultation with respect to particular development projects involving Western Sahara's natural resources. The topic, however, has reached the agenda in the political negotiations being conducted under the auspices of the UN. The latest negotiations between Morocco and SADR took place over three informal rounds between March 2011 and March 2012. In June 2011, the parties, for the first time, "requested the assistance of the United Nations Secretariat in proposing a framework for reflection for future exchanges on natural resources."[159] In July 2011, the parties agreed to hold an "expert-level meeting in Geneva on natural resources and to begin building a common database of existing natural resources and how they are being exploited."[160] The expert meetings occurred in November 2011, where both sides presented evidence as to the use of natural resources in the territory. The parties agreed to "attempt to build a commonly agreed database as a basis for further discussion."[161] In March 2012, the parties met again and agreed to provide information that would allow experts "from the United Nations Environment Programme (UNEP) to begin building a database as a foundation for future discussions on the state of the environment and natural resources, including an examination of the legal aspects of current exploitation."[162] Although no resolution has yet been reached, these negotiations are a positive step.

CONCLUSION

As the seemingly intractable political conflict in Western Sahara continues toward its fourth decade, and as tens of thousands of Sahrawis still struggle to make ends meet in refugee camps in Algeria,[163] the need for a prompt and effective resolution of issues concerning the use and development of the natural resources of the territory has never been more urgent. As discussed previously, international law does not apply an absolute bar to the development of such resources. The law clearly recognizes that economic development activities could be beneficial to the local population. At the same time, the law recognizes the need to ensure that the rights of the inhabitants of the territory to self-determination are protected. Consequently, it imposes two conditions on the development of natural resources in NSGTs: first, any such activities must be, objectively speaking, in the interest of the local population; and second, they must be done in consultation and coordination with the local population. Provided these two conditions are met, the economic development of natural resources in a NSGT, like Western Sahara, is permitted.

The current efforts of the parties to address the use and exploitation of natural resources in the negotiations occurring under UN oversight represent a positive step in the process. The UN should urge the parties to quickly provide the agreed-upon information to the UNEP, and to establish a consultative process whereby decisions with respect to the use and development of the natural resources of the territory, for the benefit of the people and the territory, could be reached.

NOTES

1. The views and opinions expressed in this article are those of the author alone, and all errors, to the extent there are any, are the responsibility of the author alone.
2. "The World Factbook, Western Sahara—Geography," *Central Intelligence Agency*, last modified June 20, 2012, www.cia.gov/library/publications/the-world-factbook/geos/wi.html.
3. R. H. Hughes and J. S. Hughes, *A Directory of African Wetlands* (Switzerland: Gland, 1992), 87, http://ramsar.wetlands.org/Portals/15/WESTERN_SAHARA.pdf(accessed May 24, 2012). In comparison, for example, in 2009 Morocco averaged 346 mm annually. "Average Precipitation in Depth (mm per year)," *World Bank Food and Agriculture Organization*, http://search.worldbank.org/quickview?name=Average+%3Cem%3Eprecipitation%3C%2Fem%3E+in+depth+%28mm+per+year%29++&id=AG.LND.PRCP.MM&type=Indicators&cube_no=2&qterm=precipitation(accessed May 24, 2012).
4. "2012 Midyear Population and Density Report," *US Census Bureau*, www.census.gov/population/international/data/idb/informationGateway.php (accessed May 24, 2012)
5. Toby Shelley, "Natural Resources and the Western Sahara," in *The Western Sahara Conflict: The Role of Natural Resources in Decolonization*, ed. Claes Olsson (Uppsala: Nordiska Afrikainstitutet, 2006), 19.
6. Stephen Zunes, "The Future of Western Sahara," *Foreign Policy in Focus* (July 21, 2007),www.fpif.org/articles/the_future_of_western_sahara (accessed on June 24, 2012). See also "Why the Maghreb Matters: Threats, Opportunities, and Options for Effective American Engagement in North Africa," *Potomac Institute for Policy Studies and the Conflict Management Program at Johns Hopkins University* (2009), www.whythemaghrebmatters.org/NorthAfricaPolicyPaper032509.pdf(accessed July 4, 2012).
7. United Nations, *Charter of the United Nations* (October 24, 1945), 1 UNTS XVI, Chapter XI, art. 73–74.
8. United Nations General Assembly, "Resolution 1514 (XV) (December 14, 1960) [on independence], A/RES/1514. http://daccess-dds-ny.un.org/doc/RESOLUTION/GEN/NR0/152/88/IMG/NR015288.pdf?OpenElement.
9. United Nations, "Letter from the Permanent Representative of Spain to the United Nations to the Secretary General (August 20, 1974)," A/9714.
10. United Nations General Assembly, "Resolution 3292 (XXIX) (December 13, 1974) [on the Spanish Sahara]," A/RES/3292, http://daccess-dds-ny.un.org/doc/RESOLUTION/GEN/NR0/738/94/IMG/NR073894.pdf?OpenElement.
11. International Court of Justice, *Western Sahara Advisory Opinion* (October 16, 1975), www.icj-cij.org/docket/files/61/6195.pdf.
12. United Nations, "Letter from the Permanent Representative of Morocco to the President of the United Nations Security Council (October 18, 1975)," S/11852.
13. United Nations, "Declaration of Principles on Western Sahara by Spain, Morocco and Mauritania (November 19, 1975)," S/11880, Annex III.
14. "The Legal Issues Involved in the Western Sahara Dispute: The Principle of Self-Determination and the Legal Claims of Morocco," *New York City Bar Association*, June 2012: 14,www2.nycbar.org/pdf/report/uploads/20072264-WesternSaharaDispute--SelfDeterminationMoroccosLegalClaims.pdf(accessed June 25, 2012).
15. "The Legal Issues Involved in the Western Sahara Dispute."
16. "The Legal Issues Involved in the Western Sahara Dispute," 15.
17. United Nations, "Letter from the Under-Secretary-General for Legal Affairs, the Legal Counsel, addressed to the President of the Security Council (January 29, 2002)," S/2002/161, para. 6 (hereinafter "2002 Corell Opinion").
18. United Nations, "Letter from the Under-Secretary-General for Legal Affairs," para. 14.

19. United Nations, "Letter from the Under-Secretary-General for Legal Affairs," para. 15.
20. United Nations, *Charter of the United Nations* (October 24, 1945), 1 UNTS XVI, Chapter XI, art. 73. The UN Charter defines a NSGT as "territories whose peoples have not yet attained a full measure of self-government."
21. United Nations General Assembly, "Resolution 57/132 (February 25, 2003) [on economic activities in Non-Self Governing Territories]," A/RES/57/132).
22. "2002 Corell Opinion," supra note 16, para. 24.
23. "2002 Corell Opinion," supra note 16, para. 24.
24. For a review of the author's position on the issue of self-determination under international law, please see "The Legal Issues Involved in the Western Sahara Dispute: The Principle of Self-Determination and the Legal Claims of Morocco," *New York City Bar Association*, supra note 13.
25. Pedro Pinto Leite, "International Legality Versus Realpolitik: The Cases of Western Sahara and East Timor," in *The Western Sahara Conflict: The Role of Natural Resources in Decolonization*, ed. Claes Olsson (Uppsala: Nordiska Afrikainstitutet, 2006), 16.
26. Congress of the United States, "Letter to The Honorable Barack Obama" (Washington, DC, April 3, 2009), http://moroccanamericanpolicy.com/wsdocs/233letter.pdf(accessed July 5, 2012).
27. See e.g., United Nations General Assembly, "Resolution 2621 (XXV) (October 13, 1970) [on independence]," A/RES/2621, para. 3(9). "The question of territorial size, geographical isolation and limited resources should in no way delay the implementation of the declaration."
28. "Where Might You Encounter Phosphates Today?" *Phosphate Facts*, www.phosphatesfacts.org/uses_apps.asp (accessed July 1, 2012).
29. James Elser and Stuart White, "Peak Phosphorus," *Foreign Policy*, April 20, 2010, www.foreignpolicy.com/articles/2010/04/20/peak_phosphorus (accessed July 5, 2012).
30. Office Chérifien des Phosphates, *2010 Annual Report*, 12, www.ocpgroup.ma/sites/default/files/ra-2010-ang.pdf (accessed July 5, 2012).
31. Hans Morten Haugen, "The Right to Self-Determination and Natural Resources: The Case of Western Sahara," *Law, Environment and Development Journal* 3, no. 1 (2007): 72–81, 75,www.lead-journal.org/content/07070.pdf(accessed on July 1, 2012).
32. Haugen, "The Right to Self-Determination and Natural Resources," 77. This has led some authors to speculate that Morocco's motivation for gaining control over Western Sahara is, in part, a desire to establish and maintain control over the international phosphate trade.
33. "Report on Legal Issues Involved in the Western Sahara Dispute: Use of Natural Resources," *New York City Bar Association*, April 2011, www.nycbar.org/pdf/report/uploads/20072089-ReportonLegalIssuesInvolvedintheWesternSaharaDispute.pdf (accessed June 20, 2012); OCP, *2010 Annual Report*, supra note 29, 48. See also Virginia Thompson and Richard Adloff. *The Western Saharans: Background to Conflict* (Croom Helm, 1980), 175. Prior to 2003, Spain and Morocco co-managed the mine. Spanish involvement dates to the Madrid Accords, through which Spain maintained a 35 percent control of the Bou Craa mines. In 2002, OCP took over full control of the mine.
34. OCP, *2010 Annual Report*, supra note 29, 13.
35. OCP, *2010 Annual Report*, supra note 29, 13.
36. "Morocco's Commitment to the Economic and Social Development of the Sahara," *Moroccan American Center for Policy*, 2012: 4–5, www.corcas.com/Portals/Al/Templates/NewFolder/NewFolder/development-sahara-2012.pdf (accessed on August 14, 2012) (hereinafter "MACP 2012 Report").
37. "Morocco's Commitment," 5.
38. "Report on Legal Issues Involved in the Western Sahara Dispute: Use of Natural Resources," *New York City Bar Association*, supra note 32, 15.
39. "Bou Craa: Western Sahara," *Atlas of Our Changing Environment* (blog), June 12, 2008, http://unepatlas.blogspot.com/2008/06/bou-craa.html (accessed on June 20, 2012); "Uranium from Phosphates," *World Nuclear Association*, www.world-nuclear.

org/info/phosphates_inf124.html (accessed June 20, 2012). Phosphate rock typically contains between 70 to 200 ppm uranium, and sometimes up to 800 ppm. During the processing of phosphate rock to make fertilizers, uranium can be extracted.

40. "Uranium Prospects in Morocco," *National Office of Hydrocarbons and Mines (Morocco)* (ONHYM), (2009): 3, www.wsrw.org/files/dated/2010-02-20/uranium_in_morocco_02-09_english.pdf (accessed June 20, 2012). In 2002 and 2004, Morocco engaged in exploratory surveys for potential uranium by conducting "[t]wo airborne geophysical campaigns by magnetometry and pectrometry." The geological surveys allegedly identified several uranium anomalies indicative of potential reserves.

41. Judy Maksoud, "Production Ramps Up Off West Africa," *Offshore* 62, no. 5 (May 2002): 38. See also "Successful Cormoran-1 exploration well offshore Mauritania," Tullow Oil plc Press Release (London, January 10, 2011), www.tullowoil.com/index.asp?pageid=137&newsid=685 (accessed June 21, 2012).

42. Helen Campbell, "Oil Companies Very Keen on Western Sahara," *Oilbarrel.com*, May 14, 2005, www.wsrw.org/a193x1971 (accessed on June 21, 2012.)

43. Campbell, "Oil Companies Very Keen on Western Sahara."

44. Helen Campbell, "The Top Frontier Oil Companies: Potential, Exploration Ppportunity and Risks," *Business Insights* (April 2010): 84. According to a report prepared by Netherland, Sewell and Associates for San Leon Energy, Ltd., the "Tarfaya prospect has gross unrisked probable prospective oil of 711.3m bls, although the top-end estimate is 3,878.6m, giving the Tarfaya deposit much potential."

45. Campbell, "The Top Frontier Oil Companies," 79.

46. Campbell, "The Top Frontier Oil Companies," 84. For example, "[w]hile the SADR awarded the Bir Lahlou and Hagunia to Europa Oil and Gas, and Bojador to Maghreb and Osceola, Morocco has awarded blocks including some of the same acreage to Island Oil and Gas under the 'Tarfaya' and 'Zag' license areas.

47. "Morocco carves out new oil blocks in the occupied territory," *Western Sahara Resource Watch*, July 17, 2011, www.wsrw.org/a105x2063 (accessed June 21, 2012). As of July 2011, Morocco had "four blocks for the exploration of oil in Western Sahara." By August 2011, Morocco established an additional four new oil blocks.

48. "List of Companies Partnering with ONHYM at February 27, 2012," *National Office of Hydrocarbons and Mines (Morocco)* (ONHYM),www.onhym.com/en/HYDROCARBURES/PartenariatetCoop%C3%A9rationP%C3%A9trole/Listedespartenaires/tabid/325/language/en-US/Default.aspx?Cat=30(accessed June 22, 2012). See also "Activity Report 2010," *National Office of Hydrocarbons and Mines (Morocco)* (ONHYM): 10,www.onhym.com/pdf/Activity%20report%202010.pdf(accessed June 22, 201). The firms include Kosmos Energy, San Leon Energy plc, Longreach Oil & Gas Ventures Ltd., Tangiers Petroleum Ltd. and Teredo.

49. "Operations-Morocco," *Kosmos Energy*, www.kosmosenergy.com/operations-morocco.php (accessed June 22, 2012).

50. "SADR Offshore Oil and Gas License Offering," SADR Petroleum Authority Press Release (May 17, 2005), www.sadroilandgas.com/press_releases/Media%20Pack%20-%20Press%20Release%20English.pdf (accessed June 22, 2012); "SADR Onshore Oil & Gas License Offering," SADR Petroleum Authority Press Release (January 17, 2006), www.sadroilandgas.com/pdfs/SADR%202006%20Onshore%20Oil%20Gas%20License%20Offering.pdf (accessed June 22, 2012). The initial offering was for offshore blocks only. In 2006, SADR expanded the initiative to include onshore blocks.

51. "SADR Offshore Oil & Gas License Awards," SADR Petroleum Authority Press Release (March 23, 2006), www.sadroilandgas.com/pdfs/permits06.pdf (accessed June 22, 2012). The companies are Ophir Energy Company Ltd, Premier Oil (SADR) Limited, Europa Oil & Gas plc, Maghreb Exploration Limited, Osceola Hydrocarbon Limited, Nighthawk Energy Limited, Encore Oil Plc, and Comet Petroleum (SADR) Ltd. Press Release.

52. "2008 Minerals Yearbook: Morocco and Western Sahara," *U.S. Geological Survey* (September 2010): 5. See also "Sahrawi Arab Democratic Republic Announces Second

Petroleum Licensing Round," SADR Petroleum Authority Press Release (October 25, 2007),www.sadroilandgas.com/pdfs/25_10_07_bir%20lahlou_25th%20october_2007.pdf. (accessed June 22, 2012). This second licensing round consisted of six offshore blocks (Tah, Zug, Jreifia, Farsia, Imlili, and Amgala) and three onshore blocks (Umdreiga, Smara, and Tichla).

53. "Frequently Asked Questions," SADR Petroleum Authority, June 8, 2005, www.sadroilandgas.com/pdfs/FAQ.pdf (accessed June 23, 2012). SADR notes that "in the intervening period the licensee can obtain legacy (existing) data and review and rework the data to determine what else is required and can be acquired upon commencement of the first exploration term."

54. Shelley, "Natural Resources and the Western Sahara," supra note 4, 17.

55. Shelley, "Natural Resources and the Western Sahara," supra note 4, 18.

56. Shelley, "Natural Resources and the Western Sahara," supra note 4, 18.

57. Aidan Lewis, "Morocco's fish fight: High stakes over Western Sahara," *BBC News Africa*, December 15, 2011, www.bbc.co.uk/news/world-africa-16101666 (accessed August 16, 2012).

58. Shelley, "Natural Resources and the Western Sahara," supra note 4, 18.

59. European Parliament, *Fisheries Partnership Agreement between the European Community and the Kingdom of Morocco, First Protocol* (May 29, 2006), Council Regulation EC No 764/2006, 2006 O.J. (L141), http://eur-lex.europa.eu/LexUriServ/LexUriServ.do?uri=CELEX:32006R0764:EN:NOT (accessed July 10, 2012).

60. Council of the European Union, "Council Decision," 2012/15/EU, (2012) O.J. (L 6),http://eur-lex.europa.eu/LexUriServ/LexUriServ.do?uri=CELEX:32012D0015:EN:NOT.

61. European Parliament, *Opinion of the Committee on Budgets for the Committee on Fisheries on the Proposal for a Council Decision on the Conclusion of a Protocol between the European Union and the Kingdom of Morocco Setting out the Fishing Opportunities and Financial Compensation Provided for in the Fisheries Partnership Agreement between the European Community and the Kingdom of Morocco* (November 9, 2011), 2011/0139(NLE),www.europarl.europa.eu/sides/getDoc.do?pubRef=-%2f%2fEP%2f%2fNONSGML%2bCOMPARL%2bPE-472.388%2b03%2bDOC%2bPDF%2bV0%2f%2fEN(accessed on July 12, 2012)

62. European Parliament, *Fisheries Partnership Agreement*, supra note 58, First Protocol, art. 2.

63. European Parliament, *Fisheries Partnership Agreement*, supra note 58, First Protocol, art. 6.

64. European Parliament, *Fisheries Partnership Agreement*, supra note 58, First Protocol, art. 2(6).

65. European Parliament, *Opinion on the draft Council Decision on the Conclusion of a Protocol between the European Union and the Kingdom of Morocco Setting out the Fishing Opportunities and Financial Compensation Provided for in the Fisheries Partnership Agreement between the European Community and the Kingdom of Morocco* (November 8, 2011), 2011/0139(NLE),www.europarl.europa.eu/sides/getDoc.do?pubRef=-%2f%2fEP%2f%2fNONSGML%2bCOMPARL%2bPE-472.277%2b02%2bDOC%2bPDF%2bV0%2f%2fEN(accessed July 12, 2012).

66. Steven Hedlund, "EU-Morocco Fisheries Agreement Rejected," *SeafoodSource.com*, December 15, 2011, www.seafoodsource.com/newsarticledetail.aspx?id=13302 (accessed June 25, 2012).

67. "EU/Morocco Agreement Negotiations Begin," *The Fish Site*, April 23, 2012, www.thefishsite.com/fishnews/16980/eu-morocco-agreement-negotiations-begin (accessed June 25, 2012).

68. "The Tomato Barons of the Occupied Western Sahara," *Western Sahara Resource Watch*, June 19, 2012, www.wsrw.org/a105x2312, (accessed August 22, 2012).

69. European Parliament, "Resolution on the Agreement between the EU and Morocco Concerning Reciprocal Liberalisation Measures on Agricultural Products and

Fishery Products," P7 TA-PROV(2012)0055 (2012) (hereinafter "Agricultural Agreement").

70. European Parliament, *Recommendation on the Draft Council Decision on the Conclusion of an Agreement in the Form of an Exchange of Letters between the European Union and the Kingdom of Morocco Concerning Reciprocal Liberalisation Measures on Agricultural Products, Processed Agricultural Products, Fish and Fishery Products, the Replacement of Protocols 1, 2 and 3 and Their Annexes and Amendments to the Euro-Mediterranean Agreement Establishing an Association between the European Communities and Their Member States, of the one part, and the Kingdom of Morocco, of the Other Part* (February 1, 2012), A7-0023/2012, 8,www.europarl.europa.eu/sides/getDoc.do?pubRef=-//EP//NONSGML+REPORT+A7-2012-0023+0+DOC+PDF+V0//EN. See also Göran Färm et al., *Written Explanations of Vote on European Parliament Document PV 16/02/2012—8.7* (February 16, 2012), www.europarl.europa.eu/sides/getDoc.do?type=CRE&reference=20120216&secondRef=ITEM-009&language=EN&ring=P7-RC-2012-0048#4-187-000(accessed on July 12, 2012).

71. European Parliament, *Recommendation on the Draft Council Decision on the Conclusion of an Agreement in the Form of an Exchange of Letters between the European Union and the Kingdom of Morocco*.

72. European Parliament, *Written Question E-002451/2012 Agricultural Activity in Western Sahara* (March 9, 2012), P7_QE(2012)002451.

73. "Conflict Tomatoes," *Western Sahara Resource Watch*, February 2012, www.wsrw.org/files/dated/2012-02-13/conflict_tomatoes_14.02.2012.pdf (accessed August 15, 2012). See also Fiona Govan, "King of Morocco to be Biggest Benefactor of EU Trade Agreement," *The Telegraph*, January 29, 2012, www.telegraph.co.uk/news/worldnews/africaandindianocean/morocco/9047659/King-of-Morocco-to-be-biggest-benefactor-of-EU-trade-agreement.html (accessed July 12, 2012).

74. European Parliament, *Answer to Question No. E-002451/12* (May 23, 2012), P7_RE(2012)002451.

75. United Nations General Assembly, "Resolution 1803 (XVI) (December 14, 1962) [on natural resources], A/RES/1803(XVII); United Nations, *International Covenant on Civil and Political Rights* (December 16, 1966), 999 UNTS 171 and 1057 UNTS 407 / [1980] ATS 23 / 6 ILM 368 (1967), art. 1(2); United Nations, *International Covenant on Economic, Social and Cultural Rights* (December 16, 1966), 993 UNTS 3/ [1976] ATS 5/ 6 ILM 360 (1967), art. 1(2).

76. Zunes, "The Future of Western Sahara," supra note 5.

77. International Court of Justice, *Western Sahara Advisory Opinion*, 12. See "The Legal Issues Involved in the Western Sahara Dispute: The Principle of Self-Determination and the Legal Claims of Morocco," *New York City Bar Association*, supra note 13: 79–87.

78. Congress of the United States, "Letter to The Honorable Barack Obama," supra note 25; See also Zunes, "The Future of Western Sahara," supra note 5, which details American support for the autonomy plan.

79. United Nations Security Council, "Resolution 1813 (April 30, 2008) [on the extension of the MINURSO mandate]," S/RES/1813 (2008). "Taking note of the Moroccan proposal presented on 11 April 2007 to the Secretary-General and welcoming serious and credible Moroccan efforts to move the process forward towards resolution."

80. Ignacio Cembrero, "Spain Favored Morocco's Autonomy Plan for Western Sahara," *El Pais*, December 15, 2010, http://elpais.com/elpais/2010/12/15/inenglish/1292394041_850210.html (accessed July 2, 2012); "Press Briefing," *Ministère des affaires étrangères et européennes (France)*, March 14, 2012, ,www.diplomatie.gouv.fr/en/global-issues/defence-security/conflicts-and-crisis/the-western-sahara-issue/article/sahara-q-a-excerpt-from-the-daily (accessed July 2, 2012). "As the Ministre d'Etat reaffirmed on Monday in New York, we believe that Morocco's Autonomy Plan, which is now the only realistic proposal on the table, constitutes a sound and credible basis for a solution. The continuation of the status quo is not in anyone's interest."

81. "Milestones in the Western Sahara Conflict," *United Nations Mission for the Referendum in Western Sahara (MINURSO)* ,http://minurso.unmissions.org/LinkClick.aspx?fileticket=b67SKR4JLik%3D&tabid=9540&language=en-US(accessed June 25, 2012); "The Legal Issues Involved in the Western Sahara Dispute: The Principle of Self-Determination and the Legal Claims of Morocco,"
New York City Bar Association, supra note 13. The UN Special Committee on Decolonization (the 4th Committee) designated Western Sahara as a non-self-governing Territory in 1963.
82. United Nations, *Charter of the United Nations*, art. 73.
83. United Nations, *Non-Self-Governing Territories*,www.un.org/en/events/nonselfgoverning/nonselfgoverning.shtml.
84. "2002 Corell Opinion," supra note 16, para. 5.
85. United Nations General Assembly, "Resolution 2072 (XX) (December 16, 1965) [on Western Sahara]," A/RES/2072.
86. United Nations, "Declaration of Principles on Western Sahara by Spain, Morocco and Mauritania (November 19, 1975)," supra note 12.
87. United Nations, "Letter from the Representative of Spain to the Secretary General" (February 26, 1976), A/31/56—S/11997.
88. "2002 Corell Opinion," supra note 16, para. 6–7.
89. "2002 Corell Opinion," supra note 16, para. 8.
90. See, for example, Christine Chinkin, "The Laws of Occupation" (paper, Conference on Multilateralism and International Law with Western Sahara as a Case Story, Pretoria, December 2008), www.unisa.ac.za/contents/faculties/law/docs/10chinkin.pdf (accessed July 11, 2012).
91. Hans Corell, "Western Sahara—status and resources," *New Routes*, Vol. 15 (April 2010): 10-13,www.life-peace.org/index.php/download_file/view/53/143/(accessed July 2, 2012).
92. United Nations General Assembly, "Resolution 34/37 (November 21, 1979) [on Western Sahara]," A/Res/34/37.
93. Elizabeth Samson, "Is Gaza Occupied?: Redefining the Status of Gaza Under International Law," *American University International Law Review*, 25, no. 915 (2010): 915, 964. Palestine, for example, is not listed on the NSGT list by the UN, and is considered by the UN to be occupied territory.
94. For a full discussion of the parameters of treaty and customary international law, see Lori Damrocsch, et al., *International Law: Cases and Materials*, 4th Ed. (St. Paul, MN: West Group, 2001), 56–159.
95. International Court of Justice, *Statute of the International Court of Justice*, art. 38(1)(b).
96. See Damrosch, *International Law: Cases and Materials*, supra note 93.
97. International Court of Justice, *Advisory Opinion on the Legality of the Threat or Use of Nuclear Weapons* (July 8, 1996), para. 64–73.
98. International Court of Justice, *Advisory Opinion on the Legality*, para. 70.
99. United Nations, *Charter of the United Nations*, art. 55.
100. United Nations, *Charter of the United Nations*, art. 1(2).
101. United Nations, *Charter of the United Nations*, art. 73.
102. United Nations, *Charter of the United Nations*, art. 73.
103. United Nations General Assembly, "Resolution 1514," supra note 7, para. 2 (December 14, 1960).
104. See International Court of Justice, *Case Concerning East Timor (Portugal v. Australia)* (June 30, 1995), 90. The Court found that the principle of self-determination was "one of the essential principles of customary international law."
105. United Nations General Assembly, "Resolution 1803," supra note 74, para. 1, 7.
106. United Nations General Assembly, "Resolution 1803," supra note 74, para. 1, 7.
107. "2002 Corell Opinion," supra note 16, para. 14.

108. United Nations, *International Covenant on Civil and Political Rights,* supra note 74, art.1; International Covenant on Economic, Social and Cultural Rights, supra note 74, art. 1.
109. "2002 Corell Opinion," supra note 16, para. 14.
110. "2002 Corell Opinion," supra note 16, para. 14.
111. The *Case Concerning East Timor (Portugal v. Australia)* was dismissed for lack of jurisdiction because one of the states involved, Indonesia, was not a participant in the proceedings; *Certain Phosphate Lands in Naura (Naura v. Austrialia)* was settled after the judgment on preliminary objections.
112. "2002 Corell Opinion," supra note 16, para. 18.
113. "2002 Corell Opinion," supra note 16, para. 18.
114. "2002 Corell Opinion," supra note 16, para. 18.
115. "2002 Corell Opinion," supra note 16, para. 20.
116. "Fact Sheet 18," *UNTAET Office of Communication and Public Information,* December 2001, www.un.org/en/peacekeeping/missions/past/etimor/fact/fs18.pdf. See also Press Briefing of Hansjoerg Strohmeyer, January 19, 2000, 2012, www.un.org/en/peacekeeping/missions/past/etimor/DB/sbr1901.htm (accessed August 14, 2012).
117. "2002 Corell Opinion," supra note 16, para. 10. See also United Nations General Assembly, "Resolution 35/118" (December 11, 1980) A/Res/35/118, Annex para. 7; United Nations General Assembly, "Resolution 52/78 (December 10, 1997), A/RES/52/78, para. 7; United Nations General Assembly, "Resolution 54/91(December 6, 1999)," A/RES/54/91, para. 10; United Nations General Assembly, "Resolution 55/147 (December 8, 2000)," A/RES/55/147, para. 10; United Nations General Assembly, "Resolution 56/74 (December 10, 2001)," A/RES/56/74, para. 10.
118. "2002 Corell Opinion," supra note 16, para. 22.
119. United Nations General Assembly, "Resolution 50/33 (February 9, 1996)," A/RES/50/33; United Nations General Assembly, "Resolution 66/83" (December 9, 2011), A/RES/66/83.
This principle was reiterated in December 2011, when the General Assembly voted 170-2 (with 2 abstentions) to adopt Resolution 66/83 on economic and other activities which affect the interests of the peoples of the NSGT.
120. "2002 Corell Opinion," supra note 16, para. 24.
121. Hans Corell, "The Legality of Exploring and Exploiting Natural Resources in the Western Sahara" (paper, Conference on Multilateralism and International Law with Western Sahara as a Case Story, Pretoria, December 2008), www.havc.se/res/SelectedMaterial/20081205pretoriawesternsahara1.pdf, 240 (accessed July 11, 2012) (emphasis in original).
122. An unofficial copy of the July 13, 2009, opinion is available at www.wsrw.org/index.php?parse_news=single&cat=105&art=1346 (accessed on June 24, 2012) (emphasis added).
123. The Hague, *Convention (IV) Respecting the Laws and Customs of War on Land* (October 18, 1907), art. 43.
124. The Hague, *Convention (IV) Respecting the Laws and Customs,* art. 55.
125. Bryan A. Graner, ed., *Black's Law Dictionary,* 8th ed. (St. Paul, MN: West Group, 2004), 1580.
126. Valentina Azarov, "Exploiting a 'Dynamic' Interpretation? The Israeli High Court of Justice Accepts the Legality of Israel's Quarrying Activities in the Occupied Palestinian Territory," *EJIL Talk! (blog),* February 7, 2012, www.ejiltalk.org/exploiting-a-dynamic-interpretation-the-israeli-high-court-of-justice-accepts-the-legality-of-israels-quarrying-activities-in-the-occupied-palestinian-territory/ (accessed on July 2, 2102).
127. Michael A. Lundberg, "The Plunder of Natural Resources During War: A War Crime?," *Georgetown Journal of International Law* 39, no. 3 (2008): 495, 515.
128. Hans Corell, "The Legality of Exploring and Exploiting Natural Resources in the Western Sahara," supra note 120, 242.

129. In 2012, the rules of usufruct were the subject of a controversial decision by the Israeli High Court in HCJ 2164/09 *Yesh Din v. The Commander of the Israeli Forces in the West Bank et al.* An Israeli human rights organization had challenged Israeli mining activity in the Palestinian Occupied Territories as illegal under international law. The High Court found that the "prolonged occupation" of the West Bank by Israel necessitated an "adjustment of the laws of occupation" to the political reality of the situation (para. 10). The court reasoned that ceasing economic activities might be extremely detrimental to the local economy and population (para. 13). Consequently, the Israeli Court found that the mining activity was not illegal. The opinion was met with significant criticism by international legal scholars as ignoring the rights of the local population and infringing on their right to self-determination. An Expert Legal Opinion, *Petitioner's Motion for an En Banc Review, HCJ 2164/09 Yesh Din v. Commander of IDF Forces in West Bank et al.*, was filed January 29, 2012, stating that "the decision is erroneous and stands in direct contradiction with the laws of occupation in light of their wording, spirit and purpose."

130. "2002 Corell Opinion," supra note 16, para. 24.

131. C. Wilson, "Foreign Companies Plundering Western Sahara Resources: Who Is Involved and What Is Being Done to Stop This?" in *International Law and the Question of Western Sahara*, eds. Karin Arts and Pedro Pinto Leite (Leidin: IPJET, 2006), 270.

132. Office Chérifien des Phosphates, *2010 Annual Report*, supra note 29, 48. The report notes a net profit of 134 million MAD. For our purposes, this was converted to US dollars at a rate of 0.1123 USD/MAD, giving a total of approximately US$15.05 million.

133. "Phosphate Rock from Western Sahara," Potash Corp. Press Release (April 2011), www.phosboucraa.com/pages/POT_Western-Sahara-Rock-Position.pdf (July 12, 2012).

134. "Phosphate Rock from Western Sahara."

135. "MACP 2012 Report," supra note 35, 6.

136. Erik Hagen, "The role of natural resources in the Western Sahara conflict, and the interests involve," (paper, Conference on Multilateralism and International Law with Western Sahara as a Case Story, Pretoria, December 2008), https://my.unisa.ac.za/portal/tool/d26779f1-02ca-4b84-81c3-5a3989ddcc02/contents/faculties/law/docs/15hagen.pdf, 293 (accessed July 11, 2012). See also Shelley, "Natural Resources and the Western Sahara," supra note 4, 200.

137. "MACP 2012 Report," supra note 35, 5.

138. Shelley, "Natural Resources and the Western Sahara," supra note 4, 20. See also, "Morocco Dreams of New Monster Port in Western Sahara," *Western Sahara Resource Watch*, December 29, 2010, www.wsrw.org/a105x1770 (accessed on August 16, 2012).

139. Lewis, "Morocco's Fish Fight," supra note 56.

140. Shelley, "Natural Resources and the Western Sahara," supra note 4, 18–20; Haugen, "The Right to Self-Determination and Natural Resources," supra note 30, 78.

141. "Agricultural Agreement," supra note 68, para. 12.

142. European Parliament, "Answer to Question E-002451/2012 (May 23, 2012)," P7_RE(2012)002451.

143. "2002 Corell Opinion," supra note 16, para. 25.

144. "Operations-Morocco," *Kosmos Energy*, supra note 48.

145. "Report on Legal Issues Involved in the Western Sahara Dispute: Use of Natural Resources," *New York City Bar Association*, supra note 32, 32–33.

146. "MACP 2012 Report," supra note 35, 1.

147. Lewis, "Morocco's Fish Fight," supra note 56.

148. Hans Corell, "The Legality of Exploring and Exploiting Natural Resources in the Western Sahara," supra note 120, 239–40.

149. United Nations General Assembly, "Resolution 34/37 (November 21, 1979) [on Western Sahara]," para. 7.

150. Zunes, "The Future of Western Sahara," supra note 5.

151. "The Legal Issues Involved in the Western Sahara Dispute: The Principle of Self-Determination and the Legal Claims of Morocco," *New York City Bar Association*, supra note 13, 14.

152. "Al-Qaeda Threat in N. Africa," *Morocco on the Move*, February 3, 2012, http://moroccoonthemove.wordpress.com/2012/02/02/al-qaeda-threat-in-n-africa-rising-warns-icts-urges-closing-polisario-camps-which-are-recruiting-ground-for-terrorists/ (accessed July 12, 2012).

153. Damrocsch, *International Law: Cases and Materials*, supra note 93, 292. International law distinguishes between acts involving the recognition of a government, as compared to the recognition of a state.

154. Ali Haidar, "Elections Giving Rise to More Enthusiasm in the Southern Provinces than in the Northern Ones," *Sahara News*, November 21, 2011, www.sahara-news.org/index.php?option=com_content&view=article&id=241:elections-giving-rise-to-more-enthusiasm-in-the-southern-provinces-than-in-the-northern-ones&catid=1 (accessed on August 14, 2012).

155. *Royal Advisory Council for Sahara Affairs*, www.corcas.com (accessed August 15, 2012)

156. See "The Legal Issues Involved in the Western Sahara Dispute: The Principle of Self-Determination and the Legal Claims of Morocco," *New York City Bar Association*, supra note 13, for a full discussion of the rights of self-determination of the Sahrawi people.

157. Lewis, "Morocco's Fish Fight," supra note 56.

158. United Nations Security Council, *Report of the Secretary-General on the Situation Concerning Western Sahara* (April 15, 2012), S/2012/197, 2.

159. United Nations Security Council, *Report of the Secretary-General on the Situation Concerning Western Sahara*, 4.

160. United Nations Security Council, *Report of the Secretary-General on the Situation Concerning Western Sahara*, 4.

161. United Nations Security Council, *Report of the Secretary-General on the Situation Concerning Western Sahara*, 6.

162. United Nations Security Council, *Report of the Secretary-General on the Situation Concerning Western Sahara*, 6.

163. "2012 UNHCR Country Operations Profile—Algeria," *Office of the UN High Commissioner for Refugees*, www.unhcr.org/pages/49e485e16.html# (accessed July 13, 2012). According to the UNHCR website, the government of Algeria estimates the Saharawi refugee population as significantly higher, at approximately 165,000.

TWELVE

Refugees, Humanitarian Aid, and the Displacement Impasse in Sahrawi Camps

Aomar Boum

On March 25, 2006, King Mohammed VI gave a speech in Laâyoune, a northern town in the Western Sahara, where he officially declared the establishment of the Royal Advisory Council for Saharan Affairs (CORCASM, *Conseil Royal Consultatif des Affaires Sahariennes*). The CORCAS would play the role of an advisory committee to the king and his government on issues related to the Western Sahara. Mohammed VI urged the members of CORCAS:

> To propose initiatives for the *return and integration* of your *fellow citizens held captive in the Tindouf camps,* so that they may come back to their merciful, forgiving homeland. Indeed, Morocco guarantees them the freedom and dignity they need to contribute to the construction of their country, a nation that derives its strength from its unity and democratic system.[1]

The king reiterated the call of his late father Hassan II on November 6, 1998, when he launched the famous political campaign "the country is clement and merciful," urging Sahrawi families and individuals in camps around the Algerian military base of Tindouf to return back to their "homeland." Since the late 1980s and after the United Nations negotiated a cease-fire between the Moroccan government and the Polisario Front in 1991 (Spanish abbreviation of Frente Popular de Liberación de Saguía el Hamra y Río de Oro), Morocco has focused on the camps' population and tried to encourage Sahrawis to relocate from Tindouf camps to cities in

Western Sahara. The dossier of refugees (or what Morocco calls *detainees/ al-muhtajazun*) represents one of the most important elements of the political battle between Morocco and the Polisario since the conflict began in 1975.

In my contribution to this volume, I look at the relationship between Sahrawi refugees, humanitarianism, and the future of the camps in Algeria. I describe their management and their internal structures through what I call the *feminization of the camp*. By focusing on children and women, the SADR leaders bring attention to the psychological and traumatic experience of the conflict and life in the camps. The doctrine of feminization puts the focus on the vulnerability of women and children as refugees of the protracted conflict. My argument is framed within the context of a larger body of studies on Western Sahara as well as general theories on humanitarian aid and conflict.

Nordstrom looks at the girls and women as the human face of war/ conflict frontlines. Nordstrom notes how "children and girls are . . . constantly used as symbols of war, starvation, forced displacement and other calamities. Every war has the obligatory 'horror photo' of the child. . . . Images of victim girls function as political symbols: as policy justification, as military propaganda to engender nationalists' loyalties, and to call people to arms."[2] In a similar way, and although Fiddian-Qasmiyeh describes Sahrawi women as "dynamic individuals who are engaging with socio-political challenges which they face," she argues that Sahrawi women are represented as "mothers and carers . . . or as passive refugees waiting for aid, as examples of 'generic' images of refugees."[3]

In *Shadows of War*, Nordstrom talks about the shadows of conflict and their institutionalization through a discussion on the relationship between war, aid, and illicit economy. Using stories from different conflict regions, she argues how "'extra-state' exchange systems—[or what she calls] 'shadow' networks—are fundamental to war, and in a profound irony, are central to processes of development, for good or bad."[4] Refugees are part of the expanding institutionalized economies of conflicts. In a rare editorial by a Moroccan journalist, Ali Anouzla highlights how important it is for both political camps to engage with the real issues that face ordinary Sahrawi refugees by moving beyond the psychological obstacle of political propaganda and participating in a constructive negotiation beyond political defamation.[5]

Both the Polisario and Morocco have made the refugees a moral issue in their international diplomatic wars over the contested region of Western Sahara. While the Moroccan government describes the Sahrawis as "captive prisoners" in desolate camps run by the Polisario under the watchful eye of the Algerian military, the Polisario perceives itself as the national liberation movement at the forefront of the Sahrawis' fight for the establishment of the Sahrawi Arab Democratic Republic (SADR).[6] Since the beginning of the conflict, the camps around Tindouf are perceived in the Polisario narrative as a safe haven where Sahrawi nationalism and SADR bureaucratic structures are temporary exercised as refugees dream for their ultimate return to their homeland in what Moroccan authorities call the "southern Moroccan territories." These clashing historical memories dominated both Moroccan and SADR narratives of Sahrawis as refugees and detainees.

In this article I draw on the experiences of Moroccan prisoners of wars who spent a considerable portion of their lives in Polisario prisons before they were released after 2000. Yet few scholars have considered the importance of the narratives and experiences of those Moroccans taken prisoner between 1976 and 1991 in the Western Saharan wars. In 2004, I interviewed several who happened to be residents of villages where I did my fieldwork on the Jews of the Sahara.[7] Our conversations partly focused on their lives in Western Sahara before their capture by the Polisario at the beginning of and during the war. We also discussed their daily lives in the prisons of the SADR's camps. Included in this article is a description of daily life in the camps and an analysis of Sahrawi refugees' decision making and displacement as they struggle to survive the harsh realities of the Sahara including the heat, cold, shortage of water, sand storms, and restricted mobility as well as human impact of the war and cease-fire. This information is framed through personal narratives collected among those Sahrawi returnees who either fled or were released as prisoners of war from Sahrawi camps around Tindouf. Several of my informants were returnees who fled the camps and resettled in Goulmime, Tata, and Assa.

One of them, Brahim, talked about the camp as a space of punishment. In poetic words, he notes:

> When you are surrounded by the *hamada* for thirty years you will do your best to run away from the heat and the cold of the desert. In normal circumstances the desert never beat us as Sahrawi people because it was our home. These camps have destroyed us today because they made us lifelong prisoners. We used to move around with restrictions. Every Sahrawi yearns for the day the camps are taken down.[8]

In January 2002, the Polisario released 115 Moroccan prisoners of war, some of whom were native to the southern provinces of Tata and Goulmime.[9] In 2005, the United States mediated the Polisario's release of what it considered "all remaining prisoners of war" held in its camp prisons for more than twenty years.[10] This operation completed the release of more than two thousand Moroccan prisoners.

This article uses these interviews to describe and discuss the internal social organizations, daily life, and administrative structures inside the Polisario/SADR-run camps around Tindouf. How women and children emerge as the international face of the camp is highlighted, and how the role of aid has become the pivot of household security within the camps as Sahrawi families struggle to maintain their traditional nomadic livelihoods is underlined.

MORALITY POLITICS: CONFLICT AND HUMANITARIAN AID[11]

The SADR's diplomatic strategy to galvanize global support for its independence movement has focused on framing the Sahrawi refugee problem as a moral issue. On the one hand, the Polisario has garnered support and acquired international sympathy by picturing Sahrawi refugees as defenseless people failed by the international community. Since its founding on November 26, 1975, the Sahrawi Red Crescent (SRC) has been at the forefront of the Polisario/SADR public relations highlighting the precarious existence of refugees and their struggle for survival in a harsh desert environment where water is scare and food insufficient. For example, Bouhabaini Yahya, the president of the SRC, and other Sahrawi officers have raised the exploitation of fish along the Western Saharan coasts by the European Union (EU) generating revenues that exceed 1 billion euros to the Moroccan treasury. The SRC laments that while Sahrawi children and women suffer from hunger, the Moroccan government illegally exploits their wealth and violates international legitimacy to their land and its natural resources.[12]

The Moroccan government, on the other hand, has designated the humanitarian plight of these refugees as a "warehousing strategy"[13] by the Polisario and Algeria to pressure Morocco to negotiate a solution to the conflict. Bihi, who spent seventeen years in a camp prison, noted, "Abdelaziz and his junta were always careful to make the conflict about the suffering of women and children. When foreigners visit the camps, they have to see hungry children and struggling women. Nobody cared about us although we are Sahrawis too."[14] As the Polisario connects the realities of Sahrawi people to the harsh conditions of the desert, its leadership also highlights the role of struggling women in Sahrawi nationalism and state building by stressing their role in the management of the daily affairs of the camps. The international community is therefore morally obliged based on humanitarian principles to support and take care of vulnerable refugees especially malnourished children as long as the conflict continues.

In *Condemned to Repeat?: The Paradox of Humanitarian Action*, Terry contends that refugee camps are humanitarian sanctuaries where combatants and corrupt leaders take advantage of camps as "safety zones"[15] where civilians are manipulated not only by fighting parties but also nongovernmental organizations (NGOs), outside political forces, and even intellectuals. Although humanitarianism intends to empower refugee population, it makes them rely on emergency relief operations and make them "passive dependents on the competence of outsiders."[16]

Research on the Western Saharan conflict has largely focused on its regional and global political implications.[17] In the last decade, however, specialists and scholars have begun to show a growing interest in the daily lives of refugees in Sahrawi camps.[18] This scholarship largely assumes that self-governing democratic social and economic structures within Sahrawi camps make them models of political efficiency.[19] In her work on Sahrawi refugees, Fiddian-Qasmiyeh examines the treatment of Sahrawi children and women as "active agents constructing and maintaining their camps,"[20] despite the harsh realities of exile, war, and famine. The position of the Polisario's leadership veils the tragic realities of displacement and turns Sahrawi women, children, prisoners, and disabled and elderly men into symbolic disenfranchised faces of the camps. By shifting the discourse from refugees as passive victims to active participants and organized agents in state formation, SADR effectively uses a public relations political strategy about refugees who struggle against a "colonial power" (Morocco) and are in need of "international friends" such as the World Food Programme, the European Commission's Humanitarian Office, and the United Nations High Commissioner for Refugees (UNHCR) in their fight for independence.

In her introduction to *Do No Harm: How Aid Can Support Peace—Or War*, Anderson argues:

> When international assistance is given in the context of a violent conflict, it becomes a part of that context and thus also of the conflict. Although aid agencies often seek to be neutral or nonpartisan toward the winners and losers of a war, the impact of their aid is not neutral regarding whether conflict worsens or abates. When given in conflict settings, aid can reinforce, exacerbate, and prolong the conflict; it can also help to reduce tensions and strengthen people's capacities to disengage from fighting and find peaceful options for solving problems. Often an aid program does some of both: in some ways it worsens the conflict, and in others it supports disengagement. But in all cases aid given during conflict cannot remain separate from that conflict.[21]

Instead of alleviating the short term suffering of refugees, protracted aid becomes part of the hurdles toward a quick solution to the conflict. It creates a sense of independence among the refugees especially when their livelihood is based on herding and nomadism.

During a short interview in Goulmime, Salek captured this reality when he stated how "food aid as much it is needed throughout the camps is a curse. It creates animosity between individuals and families. It pushes people to steal and it has turned many Sahrawis into vultures who live off the backs of their brothers in the camps."[22] Miloud described how agents with strong allegiance to the Polisario/SADR administration distributed monthly rations of sugar, tea, barley, and wheat among refugee families throughout the camps.[23] This created over time a network of individuals who enriched themselves from aid. Salek argued that geographic camp placement around the military city of Tindouf reinforces dependence on aid and reliance on the Polisario/SADR as the intermediary between the camp population and international state and NGO donors.

"REFUGEE CITIZENS" AND "SELF-GOVERNING CAMPS"

In 1975, the Polisario established Sahrawi refugee camps around the military city of Tindouf in the Algerian interior desert. The UNHCR reported that these desert settlements became home to some 165,200 refugees in 2004 despite the fact that there is no official and reliable census on the camps' population. The refugees represented different Arab, Berber, and black African populations from the tribes of Tekna, Oulad Delim, Laarousiyyin, Oulad Tidrarin, and Rguibat as well as their fractions and subfractions. As the camps began to take shape, the Polisario leadership focused on erasing tribal distinctions as well as racial and ethnic differences, making nontribal affiliation an integral part of the SADR constitution. In 1976, the SRCS provided a detailed description of the contexts in which the camps were established and the conditions of the refugees focusing on the plight of women and children:

> Refugee camps are set up in the heart of the desert where waterholes are rare. The climate is hostile. . . . Most of the refugees are women and children. People are living in impoverished "tents" or completely in the open. The refugees are in poor health. . . . Considerable numbers of children are affected by severe malnutrition. There are many newborn babies in the camps. Their mothers, exhausted, have too little milk to feed them. . . . The food ration of family of six who had eaten nothing for two days was a handful of already used tea leaves and small pieces of dry bread. The parents gave it all to their children.[24]

At the beginning, this focus on women and children within the camp minimized many potential social conflicts and tensions that emerged from the displacement of Sahrawi families. Instead of engaging in their traditional tribal fights, Sahrawis backed by the Algerian government turned their attention to a national independence war with the Moroccan forces and organized themselves as "refugee citizens" in four main temporary camps named after cities in the contested Western Saharan territories.

Although the Sahrawi population was forced to settle in a fixed space and abandon its nomadic life to a large extent, the camps "did not arise from a discursive vacuum, but connected to a series of traditional narratives that facilitated the integration of the dramatic circumstances of the exile in a new coherent historical plot, constructed around the central idea of the Sahrawi nation."[25] These camps include Laâyoune, Awsard,

Smara, and Dakhla. A fifth camp called Rabouni housed the central administration of the SADR including the different ministries, the SRC, and the Parliament. Another camp called the 27th of February was built as a women's vocational school not far from Rabouni. The February 27 camp symbolizes the Polisario/SADR's *feminization* of the conflict, putting women at the center of its national independence movement. Each year, a number of women relocate from the four different camps around Tindouf and settle in the February 27 camp with their children. At the completion of their vocational studies they return to their original camp and are replaced by a new cohort. The camp also houses the office of the National Union of Sahrawi Women, which is annually attended by Sahrawis around Tindouf as well as international visitors and organizations.

With the exception of the February 27 camp, an appointed governor (*wali*) manages the daily affairs of the camp. Camps are divided into a number of districts (*daira*). These governors serve as representatives of Mohammed Abdelaziz, the president of the SADR and the Polisario Secretary General.[26] Districts are organized into neighborhoods with their own schools, administrative buildings, and clinics. At the neighborhood level, the SADR uses a number of employees to administer the daily affairs of the local families including the distribution of food aid.

The organizational structures and effective management tactics within the refugee camps have led to a perception among many international observers and scholars of Sahrawi refugees that the Polisario/SADR camps are models of efficient governance.[27] Mundy hails the Sahrawi refugee camps as the most unique examples of participatory democracy in the world.[28] The focus on the management of aid largely by women veils how the Polisario/SADR exerts its power in the camps. The discourse of female empowerment throughout the camps obscures how the male political leadership through soft power appoints friendly governors and even sympathetic loyal female leadership in the camps.

The geographic closeness of the Rabouni to Tindouf in comparison with other camps provides an insight into the surveillance strategies of the Polisario throughout the different camps. All the major national institutions such as the Parliament and National Council are located in the administrative camp Rabouni. Despite the fact that Algeria has given free reign to the Polisario to self-manage its refugee camps within its southwestern borders, refugees' movement between and outside the camps is largely controlled by the Algerian military. By emphasizing the role of women especially through the February 27 camp and its school and educational training, the SADR successfully diverts any regional and international attention from local forms of corruption, mismanagement, and human rights abuse within the camps.

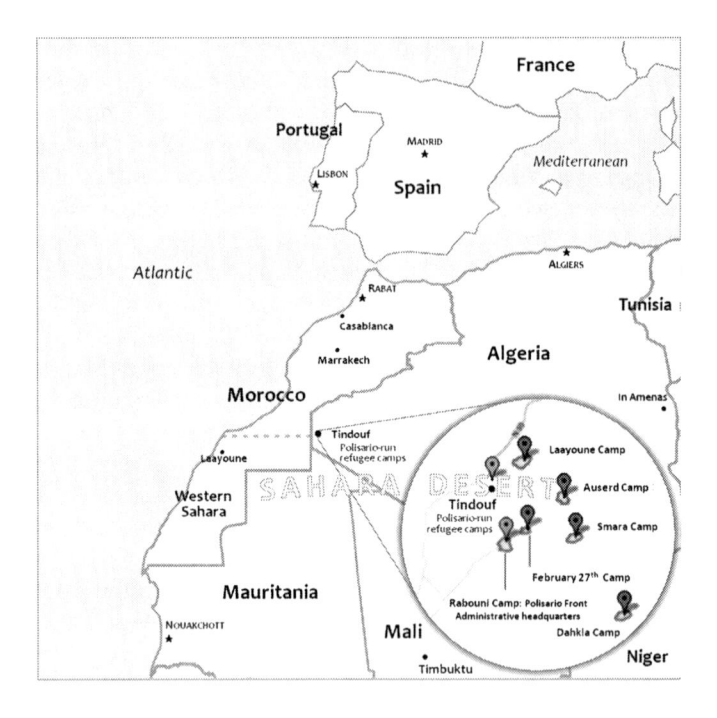

Figure 12.1.

AGENTS OF CHANGE? WOMEN, YOUTH, AND THE FUTURE OF "SAHRAWI NATION"

Women have always played a major role in traditional Sahrawi society. Before the conflict began, women were key to the management of the home/tent (*khayma*) in the absence of their husbands or male relatives who attended their flock of sheep, goats, and camels far from their camps. In her work on women during the early years of the SADR, Amoretti notes that:

> Running the tent in the rigorous environmental conditions of the Sahara implies assumption of the duty of guaranteeing the family's livelihood, in that this is not only a matter of technical skill in erecting and dismantling the tent/house, of utilizing the materials necessary for its upkeep and of fitting it out with the essential furniture, but also of planning how the resources, food and otherwise, should be put to use.[29]

As the Sahrawi society shifted from constant movement in search of grazing lands to becoming settled refugees around Tindouf, women's duty to manage the camps expanded in the absence of men who joined the army. Since 1975, the management of daily camp activities was relegated to women; at the same time, the Polisario began to establish schools throughout the camps. In the absence of fathers and brothers, women managed the camps, their tents, and ran the schools. In an interview with the *New Internationalist*, Moma Sidi Abdehadi, president of the Union of Women and member of Polisario's National Secretariat, described the central role that women played in the building and administration of the camps:

> It was women who had to take primary responsibility for building the camps: in a sense we were at the front, but just a different front from the men and we had to take responsibility for health, education, water, sanitation, everything. . . . This society is run very much by women: the staff of the nurseries is 100-per-cent female, administration is 85-per-cent female and education 70-per-cent female.[30]

The emphasis on women's role in the administration of the camp and the early education of children was meant to create a national consciousness, a sense of shared purpose and social cohesion among camp inhabitants, limiting the appeal of tribal bonds. While the Moroccan government saw children and women as victims of SADR's political propaganda, the Polisario described them as "resilient children who have accepted the responsibility of being the 'Sahrawi's nation's future and its route for self-sufficiency through education and training."[31]

As women become SADR's internal image of resilient survival and sustainable development, children and students have been the face of the camp in Europe, Cuba, Syria, Algeria, Libya, and, to an increasing degree, the United States and Qatar. By the 1990s, the educational policies of the Polisario managed to put a basic infrastructure base within the camps building primary schools in each camp, and two major boarding secondary schools. These early educational projects eliminated illiteracy not only among women but also children. At the university level, the Sahrawi Ministry of Education built many partnerships with friendly states that granted academic scholarships to Sahrawi students and hosted them as they pursued their undergraduate and graduate training.[32] The majority of Sahrawi youth were sent mostly to Spain and Cuba. In his assessment of the educational experience in the camps, García notes that the "Camps became an educative experiment with spectacular results: 100 percent of the population has access to education. . . . Cuba has fostered, educated and given a university degree to more than 5,000 Sahrawis, including 200 doctors. . . . Definitely, the Camps are a focal point that expands a progressive and cosmopolitan logic in the enigmatic life of the deep desert."[33] This optimistic view of the Cuban experience has been challenged by Sahrawi parents who had their children literally taken from them for programs in Cuba despite their parents' opposition.[34] Many of the children grow up lacking sufficient parental ties, especially if family members have been able to flee to Morocco.

Sahrawi youth also benefited from summer vacations sponsored by families in Europe and recently in the United States.[35] After the age of ten, Sahrawi children become eligible for educational and vocational summer trips outside the camps in mostly European cities. In their host countries, they are exposed to a comfortable life. As they return back to the camp at the end of their summer vacation, contacts between the families are maintained to the extent that host families sometimes pay visits to the camps. These social connections with families abroad are seen as a source of revenue for many families. Within the camps, Sahrawi families fight for spots for their children in Spain or the United States to guarantee themselves occasional monetary gifts.

Unlike the majority of Sahrawi males who arrived in the camps in 1975, younger Sahrawi born during the war and after the 1991 cease-fire have had the possibility of attending universities in Cuba, Syria, South Africa, Algeria, and other Western countries.[36] Following the truce agreement between Morocco and the Polisario, weary soldiers began to join the camps to settle for long periods without work. Before the war, nomadic life and fishing provided stable and secure livelihoods for many Sahrawis. After the war, camel herding decreased because of the fighting and droughts. Many Sahrawis could not venture into the desert because of mines, which killed most of the herds. A psychological shift began to take place among the population of the camp. In the past, the livelihood of Sahrawi people was based largely on movement and nomadic life. The shift to sedentarization after fifteen years of war and without stable and secure resources created a new culture of insecurity among an aging male population with limited skills.

Sahrawi men perceived camps at the beginning of the conflict as a temporary stage and planned to return back to their traditional way of life. The temporary camp became a fixture at the end of war as the Polisario and the Algerian authorities controlled refugees' movements within and outside the camp. For instance, migration to neighboring Mauritania and movement to coastal Algerian cities were seen as a threat to the existence of camps. Therefore checkpoints between the different camps as well as Tindouf and the Mauritania border were enforced to limit any refugee population decline. The refugees' limited financial resources and the Moroccan military sand wall (known as the *berm*), have made it easy for the SADR authorities to restrict refugee movements outside the camps.

RESISTANCE INSIDE THE CAMPS

The Polisario/SADR have promoted the idea that the training of women and men as nurses, teachers, and doctors in European, African, and Latin American friendly countries prepares its general population for a future independent nation-state. San Martin argues that the camps are "an example of participatory governance and, since the late 1990s when a limited cash economy was introduced in the camps, also an example of an imaginative social entrepreneurialism."[37] Despite this success and the ability of many Sahrawi graduates to secure stable jobs in the camps upon their return, many fail to find stable jobs adding to the overall dependency on international food aid agencies. As corruption within the camps increases with the diversion of humanitarian assistance to Polisario leaders and Sahrawi families compete for the remaining limited resources, protests against the SADR's leadership has been on the rise.

The *Khat al-Shahid*[38] (Line of the Martyr) splintered from the Polisario on July 4, 2004, accusing the SADR of corruption, nepotism, and marginalization of other factions within the camps. *Khat al-Shahid* has called for reform with the SADR/Polisario to face the challenges of the global and regional changes that have taken place in the international community. Until recently the Polisario has always projected a unified political front. *Khat al-Shahid* succeeded in gaining support in the camps, "where more and more citizens are frustrated about living in dire exile conditions during thirty-five years and with little or no advance in the negotiations since the 1991 ceasefire."[39]

The rise of internal and external Sahrawi opposition to President Mohamed Abdelaziz and his supporters among the Polisario's leadership and within the camps' population signaled a shift in the prospect of self-determination and raised questions about the future of survival on international aid. Activists within *Khat al-Shahid* argue that the Polisario management of the camps is totalitarian and call for a democratic opening that would include all players and social factions within and outside Sahrawi society. For instance, many Sahrawis have been critical of the political appointment by SADR of administrators based on family connections and blood relations. Jadiya Hamdi, the Minister of Culture and the wife of Mohamed Abdelaziz, is one of the most criticized cases. *Futuro Sahara*, an independent Sahrawi newspaper established in 1999, is one of the most outspoken and critical voices of the SADR's internal management of the camps and the Polisario's approach to the conflict. Its motto is as a free press that serves the national cause and does not sanctify individuals. This internal fracturing within the Polisario political bloc is largely the outcome of social malaise, corruption, and unemployment.

Life in the camp is no longer seen as transitory. Mustafa notes how when he was in prison that "even the Polisario's prison guards were tired of long days without anything to do. At least I was a prisoner of war. When the war ended they felt like prisoners in the camps that were supposed to give them the chance for freedom. Time pushes even the most disciplined fighters to be critical of the leadership who could move freely to Algerian cities and outside the camp while the rest feel that they are in prison." The physical impacts of the rampant malnutrition, harsh desert environment, limited health system, and polluted water are the daily concerns of the local population. Camp fatigue and its psychological impact are mainly experienced by the younger generation, which "knows nothing but camp life and does not necessarily share the ideals of the elders."[40] Political experts and academic scholars of the conflict have given less attention to the psychological well-being of individual refugees because Sahrawi society focuses largely on family unity and group solidarity. The absence of advanced medical care does not allow human rights organizations to understand the potential impact of exile on the mentality and psychological well-being of refugees.[41]

CONCLUSION

The Polisario and Morocco are faced with the dilemma of projecting the human face of the conflict, which has been marginalized by political and ideological debates. The 2010 uprisings in the Western Saharan camps at Gdeim Izik[42] highlight larger issues of political governance and economic empowerment of Sahrawis on both sides of the conflict. Since 1975, the Polisario/SADR has managed to link life in the camps to the memory and prospect of a future independent Sahrawi nation. More than thirty-five years after the beginning of the conflict, tens of thousands of refugees still live in camps that bear the names of important cities in Western Sahara.[43] Others resettled in Europe and other parts of the world. Thousands are still living in Mauritania. Yet, despite transnational displacement and migration, the Polisario is keen on sustaining the memory of encampment, loss, and exile in the main camps around the Tindouf region in southwestern Algeria. However, as the years go by, the camp is no longer a desirable place given the environmental challenges, mismanagement, isolation, and economic struggles that refugees face on a daily basis.

A large number of refugees from different backgrounds have chosen to leave the different camps legally or illegally in search of a better life. Some went back to Morocco and benefited from the gifts that the Moroccan state provides to returnees. Yet, the majority are still trapped in desolate lands with limited access to water and food and other resources controlled by the SADR. As Morocco and the Polisario continue to fight this war in new venues and through different means, the humanitarian crisis of the refugees continue unabated while their humanity is left to die slowly. The feminization of the Western Sahara conflict has created a perceptual barrier to recognizing the disguised discrimination that continues in the camps. For the international community, women and girls continue to represent the face of the harsh realities of the camps. At the same time, they are still socially required to take care of their elderly parents even when peer male citizens leave the camp for a better life. Today, many male Sahrawis go back to the camp and marry female Sahrawis. However, they rarely leave the camp with their new wives who generally stay in the camp making sure that Sahrawi national identity survives the global cultural impact of migration. As bearers of the Sahrawi identity, however shaped by the more than thirty-five years of exile, women have little power with which to change the realities in the camps or at the negotiating table.

In the face of the protracted displacement of Sahrawi refugees, Morocco and the Polisario continue to disagree on the political terms for resolving the conflict and the refugees are still at the center of their intermittent and unsuccessful peace negotiations. In the absence of any immediate solution, many refugees are turning to illicit activities including drug and arm trafficking along the Sahara desert to survive. Many observers also claim that ordinary refugees are joining terrorist cells, especially al-Qaeda of the Islamic Maghreb (AQIM) as they face a bleak economic future.[44] The fall of the government of Qaddafi, an early financial and political supporter of the Polisario/SADR, has also pushed some refugees to join organized crime gangs along the porous borders of Mauritania, Algeria, and Mali, especially as Europe and African funding sources dry out.

This contradiction between the visible images of "heroic" female/ young Sahrawi refugees and the grim realities of life in the camps, from a circumscribed and confined physical and emotional space to the erosion of the roles of the male population, is increasingly frustrated by the lack of resolution of the conflict and defines the dilemma of the refugees existence. The shifting regional environment, with greater international attention to the terrorism and criminal activities across ungoverned spaces, threatens to marginalize the humanity of the refugees. With the siphoning off of international aid by Polisario/SADR officials, the disjointed opportunities for the young and ambitious, and the dissipation of the national ethos due to the prolonged stalemate, the future for the refugees is more than uncertain, it is a growing calamity. Political realities, which for so long have blocked the true appraisal of the plight of the Sahrawi refugees, may in fact be the vehicle for its resolution as regional actors face the challenge of avoiding yet another failed state scenario in the region.

NOTES

1. King Mohammed VI, "Royal Advisory Council for Saharan Affairs," (speech, Laâyoune, March 25, 2006), *Royal Advisory Council for Saharan Affairs*, www.corcas.com/eng/SearchResults/FoundingSpeech.aspx. (author's italics)

2. Carolyn Nordstrom, "Girls and War Zones: Troubling Questions," in *Engendering Forced Migration: Theory and Practice*, ed. Doreen Indra (New York: Berghahan Books, 1999), 65. See Diana Cammack, "Gender Relief and Politics during the Afghan War," in *Engendering Forced Migration: Theory and Practice*, ed. Doreen Indra (New York: Berghahan Books, 1999), 94–123; and Patrick Matlou, "Upsetting the Cart: Forced Migration and Gender Issues, The African Experience," in *Engendering Forced*

Migration: Theory and Practice, ed. Doreen Indra (New York: Berghahan Books, 1999), 128–45.

3. Elena Fiddian-Qasmiyeh, "Representations of Sahrawi Refugees' "Educational Displacement" to Cuba: Self-Sufficient Agents or Manipulated Victims of Conflict?," *Journal of Refugee Studies* 22, no. 3 (2009): 328.

4. Carolyn Nordstrom, *Shadows of War: Violence, Power, and International Profiteering in the Twenty-first Century* (Berkeley: University of California Press, 2004), 11.

5. Ali Anouzla, "Al-sahra': sou'u al-fahm al-kabir," *Lakome*, December 1, 2011, www.lakome.com/أرى/106-editorial/11135-2011-12-28.html (accessed March 21, 2013).

6. Teresa Smith, "Al-Mukhtufin (the disappeared): A Report on Disappearances in Western Sahara," in *War and Refugees: The Western Sahara Conflict*, eds. Richard Lawless and Laila Monahan (London: Pinter, 1978), 139–49.

7. Aomar Boum, *Memories of Absence: How Muslims Remember Jews in Morocco* (Stanford, CA: Stanford University Press, forthcoming).

8. All the names are pseudonyms. Personal communication, April 5, 2004.

9. "Polsiario Releases 115 Moroccan Prisoners," *afrol News*, January 3, 2001, www.afrol.com/News2002/wsa001_release_pows.htm (accessed March 21, 2013).

10. "Polisario Releases all Remaining Prisoners of War" *IRIN*, August 18, 2005, www.irinnews.org/Report/55912/WESTERN-SAHARA-Polisario-releases-all-remaining-Moroccan-prisoners-of-war (accessed March 21, 2013).

11. Despite the numbers given by UNHCR, its budget directed to refugees in general and Sahrawis in particular in Algeria is more than 28.2 million dollars for the year 2012–2013. However, we should be aware of the fact that these official numbers do not reflect the reality of how much refugees benefit from these allocated numbers. Also, there are no agencies on the ground that oversea the flow of donations and their sources.

12. "SRC Calls on UN to Allow Saharawi Refugees to Benefit from Western Sahara Wealth," *Saharawi Journalists and Writers Union*, November 2, 2010, www.upes.org/bodyindex_eng.asp?field=sosio_eng&id=2047 (accessed March 21, 2013).

13. This phrase was coined by the Moroccan American Center for Policy, an organization based in Washington, DC, that lobbies for Moroccan interests in the United States.

14. Personal communication, March 12, 2004.

15. Fiona Terry, *Condemned to Repeat?: The Paradox of Humanitarian Action* (Ithaca, NY: Cornell University Press, 2002), 27.

16. Mary Anderson, "Development and the Prevention of Humanitarian Emergencies," in *Humanitarianism across Borders: Sustaining Civilians in Times of War*, eds. Thomas Weiss and Larry Minear (Boulder, CO: Lynne Rienner, 1993), 30.

17. John Damis, *Conflict in Northwest Africa: the Western Sahara Dispute* (Stanford, CT: Hoover Institution Press, 1983); Stephen Zunes and Jacob Mundy, *Western Sahara: War, Nationalism and Conflict Irresolution* (Syracuse, NY: Syracuse University Press, 2010).

18. Pablo San Martin, *Western Sahara: The Refugee Nation* (Cardiff: University of Wales Press, 2010); Sophie Caratini, *La république des sables: anthropologie d'une révolution* (Paris: L'Harmattan, 2003); Anne Lippert, "The Saharawi Refugees: Origins and Organization, 1975–85," in *War and Refugees: The Western Sahara Conflict*, eds. Richard Lawless and Laila Monahan (London: Pinter, 1987), 150–66; James Firebrace, "The Saharawi Refugees: Lessons and Prospects," in *War and Refugees: The Western Sahara Conflict*, eds. Richard Lawless and Laila Monahan (London: Pinter, 1987), 167–85; Tara Deubel, "Between Homeland and Exile: Poetry, Memory and Identity in Sahrawi Communities" (PhD Dissertation, University of Arizona, 2010); Elena Fiddian-Qasmiyeh, "'Paradoxes of Sahrawi Refugees' Education Migration: Promoting Self-Sufficiency or Renewing Dependency?," *Comparative Education* 47, no. 4 (2011): 433–47.

19. Jacob Mundy, "Performing the Nation, Pre-figuring the State: The Western Saharan Refugees, Thirty Years Later," *The Journal of Modern African Studies* 45, no. 2 (2011): 275-297.

Refugees, Humanitarian Aid, and the Displacement Impasse in Sahrawi Camps   275

20. Fiddian-Qasmiyeh, "Representations of Sahrawi Refugees'," 323.
21. Mary Anderson, *Do No Harm: How Aid Can Support Peace—Or War* (Boulder, CO: Lynne Rienner, 1999), 1.
22. Personal communication, May 10, 2004.
23. Personal communication, March 20, 2004.
24. *A People Accuses* (Sahrawi Red Crescent/Polisario Front Information Service, 1976), 56.
25. Pablo San Martin, "Nationalism, Identity and Citizenship in the Western Sahara," *Journal of North African Studies* 10, no. 3 (2005): 565–92.
26. Aomar Boum, "Abd al-'Aziz Muhammad," in *Dictionary of African Biography*, eds. Emmanuel Akyeampong and Henry Louis Gates (Oxford: Oxford University Press, 2011), 13–14.
27. Elena Fiddian-Qasmiyeh, "Protracted Sahrawi Displacement: Challenges and Opportunities and Beyond Encampment," *Refugee Studies Center*, Forced Migration Policy Briefing 7 (May 2011): 1–42.
28. Mundy, "Performing the Nation"; Barbara Harrell Bond, *Imposing Aid: Emergency Assistance to Refugees* (Oxford: Oxford University Press, 1986); Barbara Harrell Bond, "The Experience of Refugees as Recipients of Aid," in *Refugees: Perspectives on the Experience of Forced Migration*, ed. A. Ager (London: Pinter, 1999), 136–68; Eftihia Voutira and Barbara Harrell Bond, "'Successful' Refugee Settlement: Are Past Examples Relevant?," in *Risk and Reconstruction: Experiences of Resettlers and Refugees*, eds. M. M. Cernea and C. McDowell (Washington, DC: World Bank, 2000), 56–76.
29. Biancamaria Scarcia Amoretti, "Women in the Western Sahara," in *War and Refugees: The Western Sahara Conflict*, eds. Richard Lawless and Laila Monahan (London: Pinter: 1987), 118.
30. Natali Dukic and Alain Thierry, "Saharawi Refugees: Life after the Camps," *Forced Migration Review* 2 (1998): 20.
31. Fiddian-Qasmiyeh, "Representing Sahrawi's Refugees'," 336.
32. Antonio Vellos de Santisteban, *La educación en el Sahara Occidental* (Madrid: UNED, 1993).
33. Alejandro García, *Historias del Sahara. El Mejor y el Peor de los Mundos* (Madrid: Los Libros de la Catarata, 2001), 331–32 (quoted in San Martin, "*Nationalism, Identity and Citizenship in the Western Sahara*," 568).
34. "Report of an Independent Committee of Inquiry into Allegations of Violations of Human Rights, Crimes, Abuses and Various Other Irregularities Brought against the Polisario Front." *European Strategic Intelligence and Security Center* (October 2006).
35. Elena Fiddian-Qasmiyeh, "The Pragmatics of Performance: Putting 'Faith' in Aid in the Sahrawi Refugee Camps," *Journal of Refugee Studies* 24, no. 3 (2011): 533–47.
36. Dawn Chatty, Elena Fiddian-Qasmiyeh, and Gina Crivello, "Identity With/out Territory: Sahrawi Refugee Youth in Transnational Space," in *Deterritorialized Youth: Sahrawi and Afghan Refugees at the Margins of the Middle East*, ed. Dawn Chatty (New York: Berghahan Books, 2010), 37–84.
37. San Martin, "Nationalism, Identity and Citizenship in the Western Sahara," 568.
38. The name was chosen as a reference to El Ouali Mustapha EL Sayyed, Polisario's first leader, killed in military action in 1976.
39. "Sahrawis Awake to Government Opposition," *afrol News*, October 11, 2010, www.afrol.com/articles/36743 (accessed March 21, 2013).
40. Dukic and Thierry, "Saharan Refugees," 20.
41. Dukic and Thierry, "Saharan Refugees," 20.
42. Anouar Boukhars and Ali Amar, "Trouble in Western Sahara," *Journal of the Middle East and Africa* 2, no. 2 (2011): 220–34.
43. Toby Shelley, *Endgame in the Western Sahara: What Future for Africa's Last Colony* (London: Zed Books, 2004).
44. Anouar Boukhars, "Simmering Discontent in Western Sahara," *Carnegie Endowment for International Peace*, March 2012, http://carnegieendowment.org/2012/03/12/simmering-discontent-in-western-sahara/a2ah.

THIRTEEN
Western Sahara

A Conflict on the Fringes of New Regional Dynamics

Khadija Mohsen-Finan

FOUNDATIONS OF THE CONFLICT

The dispute over Western Sahara is the longest-standing unresolved conflict in Africa. Unlike other regional conflicts, it receives very little media attention. This lack of media attention, coupled with an absence of debate on the issue, does little to promote understanding of the conflict. When the conflict broke out in 1975, Hassan II opted for a "case closed" policy; he thought he would manage to defeat the Polisario Front quickly without having to expose the issues underlying the Saharan conflict.

In fact, the conflict's origins date back to the colonial legacy and to disagreements over the Saharan borders drawn when Morocco and Algeria gained independence in 1956 and 1962. When the French and Spanish colonial governments divvied up the Sahara, they established zones of influence that later became state borders.

Previously, Mauritanian President Mokhtar Ould Daddah had also claimed this territory populated with nomadic tribes on behalf of the Sahrawis living in his country, and his slogan "We are all Sahrawis" is still well known. In 1957, Sahrawis from the ALM (Moroccan Liberation Army) attacked Spanish troops in the Tarfaya region, prompting Spain and France to lead a joint offensive known as *Operation Écouvillon* in February 1958 to end the insurrection. At the same time, King Mohammed V affirmed his desire to pursue policies to return the Sahara to Morocco.

In 1960, the UN adopted Resolution 1514, which recognizes peoples' right to self-determination, and under the 1963 Charter of the Organization of African Unity (OAU), members are bound to respect the "inviolability of the colonial borders." Morocco rejected this article in the case of the Western Sahara. Thus, the emergence of the Western Sahara issue must be viewed in the context of decolonization in the 1960s. The UN normalized the right to self-determination, the right to independence was recognized as an option, and integration into another state became possible provided popular will was taken into account. Resolution 1514 stipulates in paragraph 6 that "any attempt aimed at the partial or total disruption of the national unity and the territorial integrity of a country is incompatible with the purposes and principles of the Charter of the United Nations." This statement, referring to Algerian decolonization, was intended to prevent a division of Algeria that would have allowed France to keep the Algerian Sahara, since according to the UN, any secession would be a detriment to the colonial state.

Noting the resolution, Morocco denounced the Spanish occupation of the Sahara and Ifni as a violation of its national unity and territorial integrity, and it claimed status as a "state dismembered" by colonization.[1] In direct response to Morocco's claim, Resolution 1514 was supplemented with another resolution: 1541. In addition to the establishment of a sovereign and independent state, this resolution also refers to "free association" and "integration with an independent State"—different scenarios that necessarily had to reflect the choice of the people.

Starting in 1966, both the UN and the OAU began to urge Spain, the colonial power governing Western Sahara, to withdraw from the territory through a UN-supervised process granting self-determination to the local inhabitants. At the time, there was general agreement in international bodies on this process on the basis of anticolonialism and Morocco, Mauritania, and Algeria all agreed to this principle until the end of 1973. However, Spain did not leave the territory. On the contrary, General Franco's government went to even greater lengths to protect Spanish interests in the region through various means, such as granting home-rule status in September 1973 and gradually setting up a form of self-determination that would preserve Spain's influence.

After having set in motion a referendum process intended to end the Spanish presence in the Sahara, and before rallying the people of the region and "recovering" the territory, Morocco realized that referring to the principle of self-determination could risk stirring up genuine Saharan nationalism. In effect, rather than follow either of the two countries (Spain or Morocco), the people in question might decide to speak on their own behalf and represent their own ambitions. The international context of decolonization, which had reached its peak during the 1960s, had not entirely dissipated yet.[2]

These constraints prompted the Moroccan monarchy to abandon all references to the principle of self-determination without actually engaging in an open dispute. Hassan II then decided to place the Sahara issue in a regional framework by forming a united and common front with his neighbors in the Maghreb against the Spanish colonial power. To gain the support of its neighbors Morocco first needed to resolve its conflicts with Algeria and Mauritania. The two Ifrane treaties in January 1969 and the Tlemcen treaty in May 1970 settled the Algerian-Moroccan dispute; and in January 1970, Morocco officially recognized the Mauritanian state.

Despite uniting in a "coalition" to rid the region of the last vestiges of colonization, the main leaders of the Maghreb states appeared to have been driven by ulterior motives. While it was referencing texts on self-determination in referring to the Saharan people, Morocco was also evoking its "historic rights" and the territorial vision of "Greater Morocco," both of which led Rabat to consider granting territorial concessions first to Algeria, by renouncing its claim on Tindouf, and then to Mauritania, by recognizing its independence. Yet it had no intention of extending these same concessions to the Sahara, which it wanted to "recover" at any cost for the sake of its own territorial integrity. In this course of action, Morocco implicitly introduced a sizable ambiguity. In the name of this territorial integrity, and in reference to "Greater Morocco," Rabat chose to renounce some of its claims while maintaining others. This territorial strategy became even more complex when Morocco joined forces with Mauritania (a territory it had been claiming up to that point) in its quest to recover the Sahara in the name of unfinished decolonization.

Despite this, the Saharan issue began to take on a Maghrebian dimension starting in 1970 with the arrival of Algerian and Mauritanian actors on the scene. Morocco, Algeria, and Mauritania formed an agreement to step up the decolonization process in the Sahara and to oppose all Spanish plans to remain in the territory. This agreement gave rise to the demand formulated by the three countries at the Agadir Summit (1974) for a referendum on self-determination "after evicting the Spanish army and government, whose presence would distort the vote."

With the prospect of building the Arab Maghreb Union (AMU), the desire to liberate the Sahara was in keeping with the Maghreb rationale, since this territory could serve as a link between the bordering countries. However, this regional rationale was short-lived because each of the states in the region had its own interests. Morocco had embarked on a course of concessions to the other two countries. Mauritania, fearing a Moroccan expansion near its borders, expressed the desire to acquire a share of Western Sahara's potential riches. Meanwhile, Algeria worried that the 1972 border agreement with Morocco would not be ratified. Concerned about possible Moroccan regional hegemony, Algeria did not appreciate Morocco's territorial expansion and the strengthening of its economic base.

These concerns would expose the strategic calculations of each nation and shatter the consensus on the notion of self-determination that had been so strongly proclaimed at the Agadir Summit. Hegemonic rivalries, along with the fear of political regimes that were fundamentally different, were one of the two main factors that determined the regional actors' involvement in the Saharan war. The other factor was related to how the main states used this conflict to consolidate their power.

INVOLVEMENT OF MAGHREBIAN ACTORS IN THE CONFLICT

The Saharan war broke out in a context marked anew by the Algerian-Moroccan rivalry that had been dormant since the Ifrane Treaty (1969). This is often presented as the main and only factor, but there were others that undeniably conditioned the bordering countries' involvement in this conflict, such as the Algerian-Libyan struggle over control of the Polisario Front or even Ould Daddah's desire to assert his country at the regional level. In addition to the hegemonic factor, the governments of these countries also used the Saharan issue to consolidate their young states. Of course, regardless of the reasons for this conflict and the purposes it served, it would have never come about without the arrival of a new actor on the regional scene that Morocco deliberately denied—the Polisario Front—which initially developed a transnational ideology before establishing a "state" from its exile in Tindouf—the Sahrawi Arab Democratic Republic (SADR), self-proclaimed in 1976.[3]

The start of the conflict coincided with a period of détente between Algeria and Morocco following a long period of tension characterized by the Sand War.[4] Independent Algeria had reneged on the agreement signed by Ferhat Abbas on the restoration of certain territories to Morocco, and proclaimed its support for the principle of respecting the borders imposed on African states by the colonial powers. In January 1969, Houari Boumedienne went to Ifrane and signed a twenty-year treaty in which the two countries agreed to "submit all outstanding issues between them to bilateral committees." A policy of détente was instituted, which explains why Algeria initially refused to come to the aid of the Polisario Front.[5]

The Algerian government's attitude changed considerably after Morocco announced its Green March to "recover" what Rabat considered to be Saharan provinces amputated from Morocco. In its official discourse, Algiers criticized Rabat for renouncing the principle of self-determination. The Moroccan initiative to march on the Sahara clearly signified that Hassan II was turning his back on the tripartite coordination established in 1970 at the Nouadhibou Summit. It also reawakened the old demons of "Greater Morocco" that Algiers had believed to be completely buried after Rabat recognized Mauritania's independence and signed the Ifrane

Agreement giving Algeria possession of Tindouf. Algeria's fear was even more real insofar as the Ifrane Agreement had not been ratified by Morocco. During the fall of 1975, the Algerian political elite took a new line on the need to protect the revolution by denouncing that which could be perceived as a threat against it. Any form of cooperation with Morocco and another state, any diplomatic expression, any aid was seen by Algeria as an assault on its own revolution and a denial of its hegemony. The Algerian military greatly influenced the executive branch. It felt that by capitulating before the Moroccan initiative to march on the South, Algeria ran the risk of exposing itself to other Moroccan claims to other parts of the Algerian Sahara.

These tensions, which took hold at the onset of the conflict, would leave a lasting mark on the evolution of the Saharan issue. The other two regional actors, Libya and Mauritania, have adopted varying positions over the years. Libya, which was the first country to provide military and financial support to the Polisario Front, hesitated to engage in a Maghrebian conflict but was later won over in 1983 by the idea of a union with Morocco. For Mauritania, however, the occupation of Tiris El Gharbia (southern province in the Sahara) had a far more strategic implication. It allowed this fledgling nation to push back the borders of a potentially expansionist Morocco that had still been claiming Mauritania as a Moroccan province only a few years before. Through this occupation, Mauritania was asserting itself on the regional level and especially vis-à-vis Morocco.

Thus, hegemonic, strategic, and geopolitical factors conditioned these countries' involvement in the Saharan conflict, albeit in different ways. These factors supplanted the Maghreb solidarity that Hassan II had sought to combat Western colonialism. From the mid-1970s on, the Saharan conflict has been a distinctly Maghrebi issue, despite Mauritania's withdrawal from the conflict at the end of that decade. After the July 1978 military coup d'état, Mauritania no longer had the means to wage a war, even though it could have taken advantage of the situation to rally support for the government and overcome tribal and ethnic divisions.

Initially, the conflict benefited all of the countries bordering the Sahara, helping to consolidate their young nations.[6] Up until the beginning of the 1980s, this bloody conflict proved to be a formidable tool for Morocco to promote unity around the throne and to bolster a legitimacy badly tarnished by crises in the early 1970s — a decade marked by riots, worker and student strikes, and two military coups d'état against the king. Morocco's involvement in the conflict allowed the monarch to send an unruly army, which had been expressing its own political agenda, to the Sahara. With his monarchy potentially isolated, Hassan II managed to transform the Saharan issue into a national cause. This transformation enabled him to engage the left-wing opposition in political dialogue, which had been broken off when he dissolved the parliament in July 1965. He was thus able to dissuade his adversaries from their agenda of challenging the monarchy in exchange for recognition and limited participation in government institutions.

On the Algerian side, the conflict helped to preserve the extremely delicate balance between the proponents and opponents of economic reforms and political openness within the army and the military intelligence service (*"la Sécurité militaire"*). The collapse of oil prices in 1986 deprived Algeria of some of the resources that had enabled it, both financially and ideologically, to pursue the conflict through the Polisario Front without compromising its international status.

Throughout these years, Morocco refused to engage in any negotiations over this region; it asserted the "Moroccanness" of this area in the name of its "territorial integrity." However, with their in-depth knowledge of the terrain, the Sahrawis inflicted some serious setbacks on the FAR (Royal Armed Forces). To avoid a collapse of the Moroccan monarchy, which would have been perceived as a failure of the West, Morocco obtained financial support from the monarchies of the Gulf and weapons from the United States and France, though these countries refrained from recognizing Morocco's right to the Sahara or the validity of its claim to the region. For its part, Spain provided humanitarian support to the Sahrawis, while avoiding any involvement on the Moroccan side and even less so on the Algerian side.

In 1981, Hassan II attempted to shift the balance of power to his country. He opted for a new diplomatic, military, and political strategy. He accepted the principle of self-determination (Nairobi 1981) and had several defensive walls built to protect the inhabited, phosphate-rich zones from Sahrawi enemy incursions. Operating in this manner, he transformed a guerrilla war that benefited the Polisario Front into a war of attrition and placed the dispute in the context of international law.

The monarch believed this strategy, which enjoyed considerable outside support, would certainly ensure his victory. Two major events occurred in 1988 that further reinforced his conviction. First, after twelve years of broken relations, the Algerian government restored diplomatic relations with Morocco. Second, the Polisario Front's leadership experienced a serious crisis due to the Reguibat tribe's autocratic hold over other Sahrawi tribes. Consequently, many Sahrawis from Tindouf left the Polisario Front to join forces with Morocco and responded to the king's call to "return to the lenient and merciful homeland."

In this extremely difficult context for the Polisario Front, Hassan II called upon "all lost souls motivated by good intentions to return to the homeland."[7] He thereby positioned himself as a father appealing to the "scattered" and "forgotten" sons of a past union between what he called the *Greater South* and the Moroccan monarchy. In reality, however, these repeated appeals broadcast over the radio from Mahbes, the closest Moroccan town to Tindouf, revealed the king's strategy. It consisted in stepping up efforts to win over more people, which, according to his plan, would cause a mass exodus from the ranks of the enemy and thereby render futile any efforts to hold a referendum on self-determination.

The king's "clemency" reflected a sultanic tradition according to which a kingdom of tribes expands as more people pledge allegiance to the king. However, in referring to this tradition, Hassan II removed the Saharan conflict from its international rationale—a rationale he recognized, moreover, when he accepted the principle of self-determination in 1981—and inserted it into a regionalization policy through integration of the Saharan people into Morocco.

This dual reference to tradition and international law set the tone for how Morocco would manage the conflict, inevitably introducing a sort of schizophrenia. In Hassan II's mind, he alone could combine these two references by making them coexist. The effects of this recourse to dual meaning were felt later. Rabat, in fact, was only open to discussing a referendum that would serve to underscore "its rights," whereas Algiers could not accept such a solution without giving the impression of capitulating on this issue.

Under these circumstances, given the Moroccan strategy put in place during the 1980s, the Sahrawi belligerents, who were now involved in a disadvantageous war of attrition, incessantly reiterated their desire to have a referendum on self-determination held under the aegis of the UN. For nearly two decades, Morocco was betting on a decrease in Algerian support for the Polisario and trying to convince itself that this support was solely the will of President Boumedienne.

After Boumedienne's death, Rabat quickly perceived in his successor, Chadli Bendjedid, as a man open to rapprochement between the Maghreb's two great capitals. During the Algerian civil war (1992–1998), Hassan II was also betting on his neighbor being weakened. The arrival of President Bouteflika in 1999 stirred up genuine hope, which was echoed in the Moroccan press. However, the changes at the head of the Algerian executive did not alter the situation. The convergence of views among the Algerian army, the security services, and the president of the republic concerning the Saharan issue—and more generally the issue of Moroccan-Algerian relations—seriously contradicted all those who had thought that Algeria's support for the Polisario was merely an obsession of Boumedienne. None of his successors turned out to be Rabat's longed-for "man of compromise."

In spite of this, Algeria's policy on the Sahara has changed considerably since 1988. Decision makers shifted their focus from negotiations between Morocco and the Polisario Front to the UN-proposed peace plan, a shift that allowed them to avoid taking a radical position. The referendum that Algeria would continue to support represented an honorable exit plan in which Algiers could still show a minimum of support for the Polisario Front without actually agreeing to a peace on Morocco's terms. However, according to this game, which was so perfectly orchestrated by the army, the president of the republic was not to challenge this minimal support in any way. This was the implicit order that was probably not understood by President Mohamed Boudiaf.[8] He increasingly disagreed with the army, first over how to manage the Islamist issue and then over the Saharan issue. The Algerian defense staff never forgave him for having brought a bilateral perspective to the issue, just as Morocco wanted.[9]

THE REFERENDUM OPTION

The September 1991 cease-fire agreement called for a referendum to be organized starting in January 1992. However, the referendum was never held because the parties failed to agree on the composition of the electorate. Several factors contributed to the difficulty in compiling a register of eligible voters. Whether in 1992, or today, if a referendum were to be held, none of the parties would be assured a clear victory. This concern over the vote drove the various actors to try to swell the ranks of the electorate likely to vote their way on the fate of the disputed territory.

Granted, the stakes of this referendum were extremely high for all the parties. Morocco's political life was so heavily mortgaged by the sacred cause of recovering the Saharan provinces that the monarchy could not venture into an electoral affair without the assurance of a clear victory. The vote was crucial to the Polisario Front because it would cease to exist both as a regional and international actor in the event the referendum failed. Thus, for the protagonists, when it came to preparing the voter lists, the only factor that appeared to be malleable was the composition of the electorate. Given the importance of this vote, each of the parties had its own interpretation of how the voter lists should be updated. The Polisario Front wanted to use the registry created by 1974 Spanish census as the basis of voter identification;[10] while Morocco wanted to include all the Sahrawis who, for economic or political reasons, had been forced to emigrate to Morocco or Mauritania since the 1950s.

Between these two options, more than one hundred thousand voices were at stake—voices that could make all the difference in the case of a vote. These attempts to outdo each other in increasing the ranks of the electorate ultimately derailed the plan to hold a referendum. Beyond that aspect, though, three distinct factors more thoroughly explain the failure of the referendum process. First, in belatedly accepting (in 1981) the idea of a referendum to decide the future of the territory, the Moroccans thought they would be able to closely control the composition of the electorate, in particular by bringing people from southern Morocco to polling stations.[11]

The second factor touches on an issue that remains central and relates to the definition of a Sahrawi. Given the various movements of peoples and the criteria established on various occasions for defining a Sahrawi, who would actually be considered a Sahrawi nowadays? Finally, the third factor concerns the failure of the various UN plans for resolving the conflict to take into account all aspects of the issue, such as refugees.[12]

In an effort to revive the struggling peace process, James Baker was named UN Special Envoy for Western Sahara in 1997. Baker proposed peace plans on three occasions (in 2001, 2002, and 2003); they were all rejected. These plans were based on a gradual process, for example, in the 2001 plan, during the first phase (four to five years), Saharan self-rule would be established under Moroccan sovereignty. Following this period, a referendum on self-determination would determine the territory's sovereignty. The plans in 2002 and 2003 did not mimic this initial phase and instead provided a governing role for the Polisario Front.

These proposals did have some advantages. First, they would have prevented either of the actors from being able to claim a complete and definitive victory over the adversary, at least in the initial phase. They had the additional advantage of involving all concerned or interested parties, including Algeria, and also specifying the role that Washington and Paris could play. Finally, they took into account the specificities of the Sahara and recognized, at least implicitly, a distinctiveness that could be equated to an identity of its own.

In spite of the advantages, however, there were clearly difficulties in applying these measures. For example, the 2001 framework agreement called for "broad autonomy" and the election of an assembly by Sahrawi voters alone. This assembly's powers would be limited to four basic functions (local taxes, law enforcement, education, and culture), while diplomacy, defense, and national security, that is, the attributes of sovereignty, would fall under the exclusive purview of the Moroccan state. These measures raised a number of questions. How would this assembly be elected? What would its true prerogatives be, particularly in the area of education? Which Sahrawis would be considered to be legitimate and representative? How would Saharan specificities be taken into account in school textbooks?

Moreover, the establishment of an ethnically based autonomy could prove difficult for the central government to manage. First, other regions, particularly those like the Rif that had rebelled in the past, might be tempted to demand the same autonomy. In addition, recognition of a regional entity based on ethnicity could, in the long run, strengthen ethnic identity and undermine the concept of citizenship in the state. Finally, this new more decentralized institutional architecture would have an impact on the monarchy, which had "developed a role for itself as guardian of national unity and of Moroccan Islam, while centralizing its power."[13] Furthermore, despite the risks it entailed, self-rule was not designed to be the end goal, but rather a transitional phase prior to holding a referendum. Consequently, this begged the question: How could a referendum be possible four or five years after autonomy would take effect, when efforts to organize a referendum in the 1990s had failed?

In reality, these various UN peace plans essentially did nothing to change the situation because each of the parties continued to hold firm to its position—self-determination for the Polisario Front and self-rule for Morocco. They merely shifted the conflict to the diplomatic arena. The situation became so inextricable that the UNSC routinely refused to make any decisions on the thorny issue of Western Sahara. The resolutions adopted regularly straddled the issue in such a way that all the parties found enough reason for satisfaction. The secretary-general's reports always highlighted the impasse without attributing it to either actor, or even both, and regularly noted that "the UN would not impose a solution."[14] To a large extent, the inertia was fueled by the UN's inability to move beyond the conflicting interpretations. Meanwhile, the conflict continued on the diplomatic level in a clash of views over the principles of autonomy and self-determination that was difficult to resolve.

AUTONOMY VERSUS SELF-DETERMINATION: THE DIFFICULTY IN REACHING A COMPROMISE

Defending the principle of self-determination seemed almost natural to Algeria, given that it owed its own independence to a self-determination referendum held in 1962. Placing the Polisario Front's struggle within the framework of decolonization and officially supporting this movement in its effort for independence in the name of a people's right to self-determination, Algeria continually reiterated its demand for this method of resolution. Backed by Algeria in its fight for a territory it considered to be its own, the Polisario Front harnessed all the great myths of Third World resistance and insisted that the Sahara was still a territory under the colonial yoke. It could not, therefore, back down on its demand for self-determination. The Saharan belligerents' unwavering posture concerning the form of resolution can be explained by the ideological reasons that served as the basis for their involvement in the conflict.

By contrast, Morocco appears to have wavered between autonomy and self-determination since 1966. In June 1966, during a meeting of the Committee of Twenty-four in Addis Ababa, the Moroccan representative to the UN reasserted Morocco's demands and evoked Spain's blunt refusal before concluding: "Given that until now the Spanish government does not appear to have accepted liberation (of Ifni and the Sahara) by means of negotiation and following the formula of pure and simple restitution to Morocco, the Moroccan government proposes that independence be granted as soon as possible."[15] On other occasions, such as the

1981 OAU summit in Nairobi, Morocco reaffirmed its call for self-determination for the Sahara. At that time, it was seeking a referendum in order to counter a process that favored the SADR. Similarly, Moroccan Prime Minister Filali and Interior Minister Driss Basri, in Houston in 1997, also defended the principle of self-determination.

Should this be viewed as a paradox on the part of a monarchy that sometimes called for autonomy and sometimes self-determination? In reality, Hassan II felt both options could be complementary. In advancing his now-famous expression "save for the stamp and the flag, everything is negotiable," the king was presenting the attributes of sovereignty that should come under Rabat's purview. But he added, "Sooner or later, our propriety in the Sahara will have to be filed with the United Nations land registry." In other words, although he found the idea of self-rule attractive, even going so far as to tout the merits of the German *Länders*, he was not ruling out a referendum, which would bring international recognition of this autonomy.

A true shift in the monarchy's position on the conflict came about during the latter half of the 1990s. The change was barely perceptible because the two main stakeholders managing this issue, the king and his minister of interior, Driss Basri, had vastly different points of view. According to Basri, controlling the polls was the key to ensuring a Moroccan victory that would be definitive and indisputable since it would be validated by a vote. The objective of moving Moroccans around from the southern parts of the country over several years was to increase the number of voters favorable to Morocco in the event a referendum were held.

While Basri was betting on the vote, boasting of "having always managed to organize elections the way he intended,"[16] Hassan II's advisors managed to convince him to abandon this option. Based on a survey conducted in the main towns of Western Sahara, they realized that the majority of the population canvassed would most likely vote against incorporating this region into Morocco. Shortly before his death, Hassan II opted for autonomy. Succeeding his father in July 1999, Mohammed VI embraced autonomy as the solution to this conflict, implicitly ruling out the self-determination option based on independence. Demonstrations calling for independence, which routinely occurred in Western Sahara's main cities, likely reinforced his conviction concerning the need to rule out the referendum option:

> In 2007, Morocco proposed a plan for autonomy. Rabat presented this plan stating, In response to a call from the international community, the kingdom of Morocco is moving forward in a positive and constructive way by pledging to support an initiative to negotiate an autonomous status for the Saharan region in the context of the kingdom's sovereignty and national unity.

The plan specified that the kingdom would guarantee all Sahrawis their role in regional institutions and bodies. It also noted that the Saharan people would:

> democratically manage their own affairs through legislative, executive, and judicial bodies with exclusive jurisdiction. They will have the necessary financial resources to develop the region in all fields and will actively contribute to the kingdom's economic, social, cultural life.[17]

In reality, although the Moroccan plan was presented as a basis for negotiations, it lacked precision and clarity. First, it was vague concerning the type of autonomy and what powers would be transferred. Insofar as the king's powers would still be maintained by the state, this would mean (although not explicitly stated) an autonomy at the regional level only and thus an asymmetrical system of territorial organization. This type of configuration is, in fact, often considered in the context of resolving conflicts related to demands for autonomy. However, there were no specific details about the management of Western Sahara's resources, such as fishing or phosphates. Moreover, justice was not mentioned in the list of state prerogatives. Thus, in Morocco, where justice is rendered in the name of the king, could it be conceivable that the procedure would be different in a regional setting?

In the different points set forth, the degree to which powers would be asymmetrical was not specified. Yet, this attribution of reciprocal powers could serve as the basis for negotiations. Beyond these aspects, if the protagonists were to agree to this peace plan, which the Polisario Front continues to reject, it would transform Morocco's land base and its internal government structure, which could have an impact on its political identity.

If the region were to be given autonomy, Morocco would have to strike a balance between formal state sovereignty and true autonomy for a population that needs to assert its right to independence. It is not simply a matter of granting some degree of liberty to a region in Morocco, but to the Sahrawi people, whose identity has not been diminished after thirty-five years of conflict and who will be capable of fiercely negotiating their self-rule when the time comes. By granting autonomy to the Sahara, Rabat would, in fact, be implicitly recognizing the Sahrawi identity—the very same identity that the Polisario Front has been asserting and Morocco has not formally recognized until the 2011 Constitution. Could the proposal to grant regional autonomy to the Sahara be construed as a partial victory in the Polisario Front's struggle to be recognized as an entity with a separate identity from the Moroccans? Moreover, this option could gain widespread acceptance and result in other demands by regions in Morocco whose populations might be tempted to assert their identity or quite simply their own specificities. If this were to occur, would it result in a successful federalism, which some observers already see as the natural configuration of the kingdom, or a fragmentation of a central government eclipsed by local identities and liberties? Again, the 2011 Constitution may provide the instrument for balancing these competing currents between the central government and the regions of Morocco by implementing the mandate for regionalization, devolving administrative powers to the local authorities, which has been strongly supported by the king.

DEMONSTRATIONS IN SAHARAN TOWNS

In 1976, when Morocco integrated Western Sahara into the kingdom as a "recovered territory" by setting up a Moroccan government and extending national elections to this region, Rabat was in all likelihood attempting to establish an irreversible trend. It was a matter of providing the Sahrawis who had chosen to remain in this region with the same standard of living as other Moroccan regions. The plan also aimed to attract those who had taken refuge in Tindouf and to acclimate the international community to the idea that the Sahara, which Rabat had chosen to develop at great expense, could not be anything but Moroccan.

While a government was being set up—proof of the Sahara's integration into the kingdom as confirmed by the extension of Moroccan elections and extending the Interior Ministry's authority to Laguira (the most southern point of the Western Sahara)—the monarchy undertook a series of projects to promote economic development in these regions and to erase the long-standing lag vis-à-vis other regions in Morocco brought about during Spanish colonization. Under this development policy, the capital of Western Sahara, Laâyoune, was supposed to be a showcase city, symbolizing both the possibility of successful integration of the Sahrawis and the achievements of Morocco's development efforts in this region. It was a powerful symbol. This small, desert-climate village built by the Spanish in the 1930s was promoted to the rank of imperial city on the same level as some of Morocco's thousand-year-old cities.

Over the span of a few years, huge investments were made in Laâyoune, much more so than in other Saharan towns. These were designed to help the inhabitants forget the harsh climate and to show what needed to be done given the inadequacy of infrastructures inherited from the Spanish period. As a symbolic city, it was also supposed to attract Moroccans from "the North" in order to create a melting pot of peoples. The monarchy encouraged this internal migration by offering compensation in the form of higher salaries to offset the harsh living conditions in this stark city in the middle of the desert. Starting in the mid-1980s, the aim of creating such a melting pot was to make the native Sahrawis a minority, thereby progressively eliminating their hegemony and gradually erasing their specificity and, by extension, their identity. Two groups of people came to settle here, some for just a few years, others—more courageous—for good. Moroccans from towns just north of the Sahara and even from northern Morocco came in search of higher wages and subsidized goods. There were also people commonly called Sahrawis who came from the southern regions of Tan Tan, Tarfaya, and Goulimine.

Among the natives of Western Sahara, Laâyoune had a large population of Teknas, a tribal group who had settled there in the past or more recently.[18] Some of their descendants settled in Laâyoune, carrying on the merchant tradition of their elders and maintaining "traditional ties" with the government in Rabat.

They formed an elite group that Hassan II relied on to govern the territory. He granted them import licenses, for example, so that they could conduct large volumes of trade between Morocco and the Canary Islands via Laâyoune. In exchange for their allegiance and loyalty, Hassan II involved them in the region's most dynamic economic activities: trade, fishing, and construction. Gradually, these privileges were extended to other Sahrawis who helped the monarchy govern the territory peacefully; Hassan II awarded them civil service positions, known as *king's counselors*. The king thus managed to establish a group of co-opted elites who served as both a source of support and a showcase. These hand-picked Sahrawis symbolized the success that was possible and the integration of this "minority" into the Moroccan political system.

With time and with Mohammed VI's succession to the throne, however, the patronage ties that had been so instrumental in the monarchy's management of the Saharan territory and people began to weaken. The relationship between the king and the new generation of Sahrawis changed considerably. The young monarch did not subscribe to the logic of co-opting Sahrawi elites by reason of their tribal or ethnic group. The younger generation of Sahrawis no longer benefited from special treatment, and the practices formerly employed by Hassan II and his interior minister Driss Basri were gradually abandoned.

In parallel with the monarchy's change in attitude, young Sahrawis became immersed in the changes underway in the country over two decades.[19] The emergence of a civil society in Morocco and the demands formulated by Moroccans in the area of human rights in the 1990s did not go unnoticed by the Saharan populations. The birth of an independent press at the end of the decade changed the way the Saharan issue was understood in Morocco. The other event that marked a significant change in governance was the government's experiment in attempting to reconcile citizens with their own history. In January 2004, King Mohammed VI established an Equity and Reconciliation Commission (IER) tasked with shedding light on acts of violence committed by the government against its opponents from 1956 to 1999.[20] Thus, the government took over the task of accounting for the "Years of Lead" and decided, of its own accord without being prompted by any crisis, to build a national consensus based on financial and moral reparations for the injustices that occurred. Naturally, victims of all the various episodes of violence should have been represented. But this was not the case. Sahrawis were significantly underrepresented in public hearings, comprising only 2 percent of the victims interviewed even though 23.58 percent of all claims came from the three regions in Western Sahara. While this underrepresentation was indicative of the government's strategy of leaving current acts of violence out of the reconciliation process, the face of the Islamist victim or even the Sahrawi victim was absent from the hearings and debates. Nevertheless, "Morocco integrated the Sahrawis as a component of collective memory as if it had been done through state coercion."[21]

Now that they were integrated into the Moroccan landscape, young generations of Sahrawis certainly felt affected by the new dynamics at work on the national level. This led some of them to redefine their identity while trying to reposition themselves politically.[22] When these activists demonstrate, burn the Moroccan flag, and chant self-determination slogans, they redefined themselves with respect to their past, with respect to the older generations of co-opted elites, and with respect to Moroccans, with whom they would have to merge in the context of Saharan autonomy.

Although they do not really identify with the Moroccan government, they have not joined forces with the Polisario Front either, and their demands are more similar to those of other citizens, even though they raise the specter of self-determination. Their demands draw on a new framework of reference, one of human rights, individual and political liberties, and international law. To a certain extent, their ambitions are comparable to those of unemployed graduates in Morocco, with the exception that Sahrawis have an otherwise formidable weapon for negotiating with the government. In talking about self-determination and allowing some doubt to linger about the possibility of independence, they are raising the bar high enough to be taken into consideration. In so doing, however, they are implicitly putting themselves in a governor-to-governed relationship, acting in the context of a national entity. At the same time, with the regularity of their demonstrations and the means they use, especially when they invoke universal rights, they are directly or implicitly calling the attention of the international community to Rabat's management of this territory.

THE SAHARA CONFLICT AND THE NEW REGIONAL DYNAMIC

Can the Western Sahara issue resist the influence of the new dynamic at work in the region? Insecurity in southern Morocco, and more specifically in the Sahel, and the popular uprisings that have occurred in the region since January 2011 are new factors that call for a reassessment of the

Saharan conflict. In addition to the usual problems of a disadvantaged region, the Sahel along with southern Morocco is currently part of a vast zone under severe threat now that Al-Qaeda in the Islamic Maghreb (AQIM) has managed to set up operations there for the long haul.[23] Extremely determined, this terrorist organization is taking advantage of the proliferation of weapons circulating in the region since the Libyan revolution. In fact, the fall of Colonel Gaddafi sparked a massive return of some 3,000 to 4,000 Tuaregs of Malian or Nigerian origin to their respective countries.[24] With their extensive experience, these "former combatants" returned to their countries well equipped with arms. These seasoned troops were not without political plans.[25] The National Movement for the Liberation of Azawad demanded the "Azawad people's right to freely choose its government, to have self-determination and, if so desired, to be independent."

The emergence of this new movement, along with another Islamist-inspired group—*Ansar Eddine*, which had controlled northern Mali since April 2012—has sparked a resumption of the Tuareg rebellion under new forms and with new means. Naturally, their new found capabilities are linked to the fall of the Gaddafi regime and to the connections that these guerrillas now have with AQIM, to the point of even having established economic alliances. Unfortunately, at this time, the self-rule aspirations of the Tuaregs have been submersed by the radical Islamist bent of their former allies who have taken over the northern Mali territory, drawing other extremists to their cause.

These "Libyans"[26] are reconfiguring the region and, at the same time, have the means to destabilize it.[27] Like elements of AQIM, they maintain ties throughout the region. These different groups need the ground knowledge that nomadic tribes have, and they could be tempted to cooperate with elements of the Polisario Front. Although these links have yet to be proven,[28] the fight against AQIM requires mobilization of all nations in the region, effective cooperation with the United States[29] and France, and peace in the region, which would entail a resolution of the Saharan conflict. The coexistence of AQIM elements, Tuareg "veterans" from Libya, and elements of the Polisario Front in a vast region that has traditionally been vulnerable to trafficking of all sorts (drugs, cigarette smuggling, weapons, etc.) poses an even greater threat given that the countries of the region are especially weak (Niger and Mali). This reassessment of the Maghreb and Sahel zone from the security angle could prompt the Americans and Europeans to get involved in seeking a peaceful solution to the Saharan conflict. The fight against AQIM must first start with bringing peace to the region through dealing with issues of self-determination and recognition of ethnic and cultural diversity.

Although the security parameters, primarily the effects of the fall of Colonel Gaddafi's regime, highlight the dangers of not resolving this conflict, the "Arab Spring," as it is commonly called, lends an anachronistic aspect to this conflict. Indeed, the popular Arab uprisings that began in January 2011 show that the old principles of political governance no longer have a place. Even in places where they are not being directly challenged, they appear out of touch and irrelevant to history.

Certainly, the Arab revolutions underway since 2011 have originated from the streets, shaking up regimes through a tidal wave unleashed by society. Angry protesters have expressed their disillusionment with their regimes' incapacity to reinvent themselves and redefine their social contracts to reflect realities of the contemporary world. Although the effects of these uprisings have not yet been fully assessed, what is certain is that the citizens are now experiencing political action in an entirely new form, in a context where expression has been freed. A new concept of politics has been born and, with it, new actors—citizens placing new demands on governments. Sparked in Tunisia, this movement has affected the entire region, even though some of the countries are experiencing this political transformation differently based on their political history, economic structure, political regime, and external constraints. But the reconfiguration underway no doubt weighs heavily on them all. This time of profound political transformation is also turning regional geopolitics upside down. The AMU is being rethought, and the Union for the Mediterranean will also be reconsidered in the context of renewed relations between the EU and its neighbors to the south. These changes have become necessary due to the fact that civil societies have managed to break the unspoken consensus between their governments and international actors. The standards governing international affairs are changing insofar as global politics are no longer dictated by the imperatives of power alone but also by social pressures voiced by public opinion.

Despite this, the actors in the Saharan conflict are still locked in well-defined political attitudes that have already shown their limits. Morocco continues to push the territorial integrity envelope within the context of autonomy, and Sahrawis and Algerians are still making self-determination for independence their cardinal principle.

Yet, the traditional parties in this conflict may no longer be the only ones. The April 2012 report by the UNSG[30] reexamines the difficulties in breaking the deadlock and finding a solution to the conflict. According to the report, the problem lies in the fact that the belligerents continue to hold fast to their positions regardless of the recent upheavals in the region. It notes that the effects of the regional and international environment, along with domestic developments, will force the parties to take "the people of Western Sahara" into account. By introducing the concept of "people," the report is attempting to move past the ossified, rigid nature of the situation and place it in the context of the Arab Spring.

In the modern sense of the term, the people, as a free and autonomous entity, can no longer be marginalized or excluded from the ongoing negotiations over the sovereignty of this territory. It is the people who will ultimately decide whether they choose to live independently or with a system of self-rule under Moroccan sovereignty. Of course, the first difficulty lies in defining this "Saharan people," but already, the old paradigms appear to be completely ineffective and outdated.

NOTES

1. After its independence, all of Morocco's territorial claims were formulated in the name of Rabat's concept of "Greater Morocco." At the time of independence, the leader of the *Istiqlal Allal Al Fassi* party had contested the La Celle-Saint Cloud agreements, accusing them of solidifying the colonial borders in the region. The outlines of this map, published in *Istiqlal*'s journal *Al Alam* (July 7, 1956), stretched over a large portion of the Sahara and the Tidikelt oasis, over all of Spanish Sahara, Mauritania, and the northwest tip of Mali, and included other territories as well, such as the Ifni enclave and Ceuta and Melilla. This concept of Moroccan territory was based on the kingdom's past ties or rights with these countries. Al Fassi also criticized France for maintaining its grip on the majority of the "Tunisian Sahara," the "Algerian Sahara," and what it called "Eastern Morocco" in order to turn them into "southern" territories under the authority of Algeria's general government. France's goal in conquering the Sahara was to attain complete unity and security for the French colonial empire, in particular through the establishment of the Common Organization of the Saharan Regions (OCRS). Following the discovery and development of mineral resources in the Saharan region, it stepped up its efforts to incorporate the Sahara into France.

2. Claude Bontems, *La Guerre du Sahara Occidental* (France: Presse Universitaires de France, 1984).

3. Tony Hodges, *Western Sahara: The Roots of a Desert War* (Westport, CT: Lawrence Hill and Company, 1983).

4. The "Sand War" was a military conflict between Morocco and Algeria in October 1963. Hostilities ended on November 5, but the OAU did not manage to broker a formal cease-fire until February 20, 1964. Several factors contributed to the outbreak of this conflict: the absence of a precisely delineated border between Morocco and Algeria, Moroccan irredentism on the notion of "Greater Morocco," the discovery of major mineral resources in the disputed area, and Algeria's refusal to reconsider the borders inherited from the colonial period, pursuant to the promise made by the then GPRA president Ferhat Abbas to Hassan II on July 6, 1961.

5. Algeria even voted for the resolution asking the ICJ to issue an advisory opinion on the Saharan issue.

6. Khadija Mohsen-Finan, *Sahara Occidental: Les Enjeux d'un Conflit Régional* (Paris: CNRS Editions, 1997).

7. Official document of the Moroccan Ministry of the Interior.

8. A founding member of the FLN, he opposed Algeria's top political leaders. He spent twenty-eight years in exile in Morocco before being recalled to Algeria during the crisis of January 1992 to head up the *Haut Comité d'Etat* [High Council of State], an interim body for managing the state. He was assassinated in Annaba on June 29, 1992.

9. *Jeune Afrique (Paris)*, No. 1624, February 20–26, 1992. When interviewed by the Middle East Broadcasting Corporation and the Algerian Press Agency on February 3, 1992, Mohamed Boudiaf stated, "If there is a genuine desire to manage the Saharan problem—and if it is sincere on our part and on the part of the Moroccans, whom we know and with whom I have discussed the issue—we will find a solution to this issue as quickly as possible so that we can continue building the Arab Maghreb."

10. Prior to withdrawing from their colony, the Spanish conducted a population census in 1974 that counted 74,000 Sahrawis. This figure, consolidated by the UN, indicated a total of 70,204 eligible voters spread throughout Tindouf, Mauritania, and

Western Sahara. With the agreement of all the parties, the UN decided that this census should serve as the basis for determining the electorate.

11. This plan, developed by Moroccan Interior Minister Driss Basri, was based on a broader strategy. When Spain pulled out of Western Sahara, Morocco, which was defending the theory of historic rights, interpreted this departure as Spain handing over the territory, just as it had done with Tarfaya in 1958 and Ifni in 1969. However, Ifni and Tarfaya did not have the same status as the Spanish Sahara. All the same, Morocco cultivated this ambiguity in particular by integrating Tarfaya into Western Sahara, a region that official documents refer to as "the Saharan provinces."

12. The repatriation of some 40,000 to 50,000 Sahrawi refugees to Tindouf created numerous problems for the UNHCR because the cost of moving and resettling them was not included in the conflict resolution plan.

13. Malika Zeghal, *Les Islamistes Marocains, le Défi à la Monarchie* (Paris: La Découverte, 2005).

14. "Le Conseil de sécurité refuse de trancher le dossier du Sahara occidental," *Le Monde*, May 3, 2007.

15. Francisco Villar, *El Proceso de Autodétermination del Sahar* (Valencia: Fernando Torres, 1982).

16. Discussion with Driss Basri, Paris, September 2006.

17. Abdelhamid El Ouali, *Autonomie au Sahara, Prélude au Maghreb des Régions* (London: Stacey International, 2008).

18. Members of this tribe had always been present in the Saguia el-Hamra region as well as in the Tarfaya region in southern Morocco. Generally, they were sedentary in the North and nomadic in the South, where they traded in caravans and had good relations with the Moroccan central government. Some branches of the tribe (Izarguin, Ait Lahcen, and Yaggout) swore allegiance to the king.

19. Throughout the 1990s, the Moroccan monarchy began to change how the country's political system operated by opting for a system of alternating political power. In addition to creating a new group of elites through an alliance with the former government opposition party Socialist Union of Popular Forces (USFP), the monarchy decided to open up the political arena by creating more public space. Independent newspapers, debates on previously taboo subjects, and a new way of managing human rights were intended to bring closure to the Years of Lead that had tarnished the country's image abroad.

20. Frédéric Vairel, "L'Instance Equité et Réconciliation au Maroc: Lexique International de la Réconciliation et Situation Autoritaire," in *Après le conflit la réconciliation*, ed. Sandrine Lefranc (Paris: Michel Houdinard, 2006); Khadija Mohsen Finan, "Mémoire et réconciliation nationale au Maroc," *Politique étrangère*, no. 2 (2007).

21. Omar Brousky, "La redéfinition de l'identité Sahraouie," *Annuaire de l'IE-Med* (2007).

22. Omar Brousky, "La redéfinition de l'identité Sahraouie."

23. On January 24, 2007, the Algerian GSPC (Salafist Group for Preaching and Combat) morphed into AQIM and adopted a new combat strategy that brought the former GSPC to the forefront of the world jihadist scene. Two thousand seven was an especially bloody year in Algeria. However, this terrorist organization soon showed its limits, proving to be incapable of moving beyond the Algerian front and hitting targets in Europe, as it had initially planned. In addition, AQIM was unable to federate jihadist groups in the Maghreb. Consequently, in order to compensate for these setbacks at the local jihad and regional Maghreb levels, and its failure to reach European targets, AQIM thought that the southern Algerian flank was the only alternative for achieving its international objectives.

24. Refugees from the 1990s or recent emigrants, who took part in the fighting between Colonel Gaddafi's "mercenaries" and the rebels during the Libyan Revolution.

25. On October 16, 2011, two Tuareg movements, the *Mouvement national de l'Azawad* (National Movement of Azawad, or MNA), and the *Mouvement Tuareg du*

Nord Mali (Northern Mali Tuareg Movement, or MTNM), merged and formed the *Mouvement national de libération de l'Azawad*.

26. Naturally, this also includes combatants returning from Libya, just as Algerian Islamic combatants who had been trained in Afghanistan were in the past referred to as "Afghans."

27. "La Situation dans les pays de la zone Sahélienne," *L'Assemble Nationale (France)*, Foreign Affairs Committee Report, March 6, 2012, www.assemblee-nationale.fr/13/rap-info/i4431.asp.

28. Moroccans are the only ones to give credence to the hypothesis of AQIM collaborating with the Polisario Front. This theory, which has never been proven, came to the forefront after three humanitarian workers (two Spanish and one Italian) were kidnapped on October 23, 2011. At the time, Rabat accused the Polisario of having ties to AQIM. In the end, AQIM was not behind the kidnapping. The *Mouvement pour l'unicité et le jihad en Afrique de l'Ouest* (MUJAO) claimed responsibility and demanded a thirty-million-euro ransom.

29. France and the United States have a presence in the region but have chosen to refrain from direct intervention against AQIM. In 2002, the Americans launched the "Pan Sahel Initiative" to assist countries in the region. This was replaced by the TSCTP Initiative in 2005, which includes five additional states (Morocco, Algeria, Tunisia, Senegal, and Nigeria). The objectives of this $10 million/year program are to fight terrorism, to cooperate with France and nations in the region, especially in the area of intelligence, and to conduct joint military exercises under the NATO umbrella.

30. United Nations Security Council, *Report of the Secretary-General on the situation concerning Western Sahara* (April 15, 2012), S/2012/197, www.un.org/ga/search/view_doc.asp?symbol=S/2012/197.

Conclusion

A Realistic Solution to the Western Sahara Conflict

J. Peter Pham

A sparsely populated, wind-scorched desert land covering an area slightly larger than Great Britain—albeit with virtually no water and barely fifty square kilometers of arable land—whose primary export commodity, rock phosphates,[1] is recoverable in better quality and larger quantities elsewhere, the Western Sahara would seem an unlikely candidate to be the object of one of Africa's longest-running and most bitter territorial disputes, one with profound implications for both regional security and economic development as well as international stability and order. And yet, now well into its fourth decade, the "question of Western Sahara," as it is termed in the nomenclature of the UN, is one of those challenges which, defying multiple efforts by the international community to facilitate its "solution," despite increasingly dire warnings, recently reiterated by UN Secretary-General (UNSG) Ban Ki-moon and others, that "the rise of instability and insecurity in and around the Sahel" and the risk of "spillover" from the fighting in Mali, requires "an urgent settlement" of this "ticking time bomb."[2]

Until now, with the ambiguous exception of a small group of journalists and scholar-activists among some of whom passionate advocacy has often gotten the better of learned inquiry,[3] this issue has been largely passed over by researchers and generally ignored by policymakers, many of whom thought the status quo could be maintained indefinitely. However, upheavals in the Sahel and the Sahara in the aftermath of the North African revolutions of 2011—not least of which was the collapse, in March 2012, of the constitutional government in Mali and the takeover of the northern two-thirds of the country by al-Qaeda's regional affiliate and allied extremists, a development precipitating a French-led military intervention in early 2013 and the subsequent deployment of a UN stabilization force—have contributed not only to the increasing recognition of the need to resolve this "frozen conflict" once and for all, but also the growing conviction that any workable arrangement must be based on a sober calculus of state viability and regional stability. In fact, an expanding body of literature acknowledges that the integration of and sustainable development in the countries of the Maghreb and the Sahel as well as the security interests of the broader international community requires a defusing of tensions, but in a manner consonant with the principles of political pragmatism to avoid the specter of a state failure in a geopolitically sensitive region.

HISTORICAL CONTEXT

As Osama Abi-Mershed and Adam Farrar note, while "history cannot answer the 'core question' of the conflict," historical knowledge can contribute to a better understanding of the conflict's roots and the narratives employed by those involved in it. To this end, one of the great ironies of the conflict over the Western Sahara is that, for all its attendant bitterness, it evinces none of the characteristics usually found in ethnic conflicts in which minority groups have struggled for self-determination. In fact, in this case the parties to the conflict are defined by none of the "ascriptive differences, whether the indicium of group identity is color, appearance, language, religion, some other indicator of common origin, or some combination thereof."[4] By religion, language, and appearance, the inhabitants of the Western Sahara are virtually indistinguishable from those of the southern part of Morocco.[5] Not surprisingly, with the exception of the colonial period beginning in the nineteenth century when Spain managed to take control "by invoking 'historic' rights based on the unstable occupation for a few years by trading companies constantly attacked by a population hostile to the implantation of foreign powers on its territory," the "cultural and effective ties of this region predominate over every other allegiance."[6]

From at least the Muslim conquest of North Africa in the seventh century CE, the various nomadic tribes inhabiting what is today designated "Western Sahara" on most maps owed allegiance to the rulers of Morocco—that is, with the exception of periods when "Saharan families, taking the conquerors route in the opposite direction, were, in turn, to impose their domination on Morocco,"[7] as was the case under the Almoravids, the Almohads, and the Sa'dis in the eleventh, twelfth, and sixteenth centuries, respectively. The current Alaouite dynasty, whose first sultan, Moulay al-Rashid, captured Fez in 1666 and took Marrakesh in 1669, establishing the Sherifian Empire that is the precursor to modern Morocco, continued the age-old practice of issuing royal rescripts known as *dahirs* accepting the fealty (*bay'a*) and tribute of the Saharan chieftains and appointing them as *qaids*, or civil governors, over their respective peoples, from whom they also collected taxes in the name of the sovereign.

Joshua Castellino and Elvira Domíguez-Redondo point out that it is the failure of the European conceptual model of the state to account for precolonial structures of political allegiance and governance which led to the 1975 International Court of Justice (ICJ) advisory opinion holding both that the Western Sahara was not *terra nullius* before the European colonization and that while "a legal tie of allegiance had existed at the relevant period" between the Sultan of Morocco and the nomadic peoples of the territory, the latter was nonetheless deemed, more than a little incongruously,[8] materially insufficient to give Morocco clear title to sovereignty.[9]

The historiography behind the ICJ decision runs counter to what I. William Zartman argues is the "central pillar" of Morocco's independence process, the "retrocession," or return, piece by piece, of all territories historically subject to Moroccan sovereignty. Thus the end of the French protectorate and independence on March 2, 1956, was followed a month later by the end of the Spanish protectorate over and the recovery of Tetouan in the northern part of the country. In August 1956, Morocco succeeded in having the international control council for the international zone around Tangier repeal its status and reintegrated the city into the kingdom. It took two more years, until April 1958, for Spain to return the zone of Tarfaya, which was governed under the same colonial regime as the Spanish Sahara immediately to its south.[10] And it was only in 1969, during the reign of King Hassan II, Mohammed V's son and successor, that, after failing to legitimize its continuing occupation by arguing that the enclave was a "historic" part of Spain fully integrated into the Spanish state, Madrid finally ceded back Ifni, on the Atlantic coast of Morocco opposite the Canary Islands, headquarters since 1934 of the governor-general of Spanish Morocco.[11]

What the flawed judgment did feed into, however, was a more modern struggle of the newly independent states of the region to consolidate and, Laurence Aïda Ammour documents, the pursuit, in the context of "the nationalistic and militaristic political culture forged by Algerian leaders during the country's war of independence," of regional geopolitical hegemony defined against Morocco and, consequently, in "military, logistic, political, and financial support" for the *Frente Popular de Liberación de Saguía el Hamray Río de Oro* ("Popular Front for the Liberation of Saqiet al-Hamra and Río del Oro," Polisario Front).

Egged on by Algeria, the Polisario Front demanded full independence for the Spanish Sahara territory following Madrid's relinquishing of the administration of the territory to Morocco and Mauritania on February 26, 1976, launching a guerrilla campaign against the Moroccan and Mauritanian forces that moved in to assume control after the Spanish withdrew. In some instances, units from the Algerian army joined the Polisario forces. As a result of battlefield setbacks, in 1979, Nouakchott eventually gave up its claims, which were taken up by Rabat. While the Polisario forces, with considerable support from the Algerians, acquitted themselves well in the early stages of the fighting, by 1981, however, Morocco was in control of more than 85 percent of the territory and was constructing the "sand berm," a defensive shield consisting of a series of barriers of sand and stone completed in 1987. Since then the Polisario Front has been largely confined to a small zone around Tindouf in southwestern Algeria where, as Aomar Boum notes, it has sequestered tens of thousands of Saharawi refugees in the squalid camps which have recently been the object of UNSG Ban's concerns about conflict spillover. For its part, the Organization of African Unity (OAU) muddied the waters in 1984 by recognizing and admitting to membership the virtual "Sahrawi Arab Democratic Republic" (SADR) that the Polisario Front had proclaimed in 1976. As a result, Morocco left the OAU and has yet to join its successor organization, the African Union (AU), where growing support for the Moroccan position remains blocked by the continuing support for the Polisario Front by a committed minority led by Algeria and South Africa.[12]

In 1991, the United Nations managed to achieve a cease-fire between Morocco and the Polisario Front, monitored by the UN Mission for the Referendum in Western Sahara (MINURSO), a peacekeeping force which, as its name implies, is theoretically supposed to work toward a vote on whether the territory reintegrates into Morocco, affiliates in some other mode with Morocco, or becomes independent. As of early 2013, the UN mission deploys a total of 230 uniformed personnel—including 27 troops, 6 police officers, and 197 military observers from 33 different countries—and 96 international civilian staff in a $61.3 million per year operation.[13] Since the beginning of the MINURSO mission, a series of high-level special representatives of the UNSG and special envoys have come and gone (including former US Secretary of State James Baker III, who served in that capacity from 1997 until 2004), while the disagreement over who should vote, when they should vote, and what they should be voting on has remained essentially unchanged. As Jacques Rousselier observes, depending on one's perspective, the failure to break the deadlock can be seen either as regression or an opportunity to move to a political accord of some sort.

MOVING FORWARD: POLITICAL REALITY AND STRATEGIC IMPERATIVES

In a November 2005 speech commemorating the thirtieth anniversary of the "Green March" by hundreds of thousands of Moroccans into the then Spanish Sahara, Morocco's King Mohammed VI announced that he would begin an internal national dialogue within Morocco on the subject of possibly granting autonomy to the country's southern provinces (i.e., the Western Sahara) and would present proposals to the UN once a consensus had been reached. As part of the process of consultation, in 2006,

Mohammed VI revived the Royal Advisory Council for Saharan Affairs (CORCAS) as a consultative body for proposals relating to the kingdom's southern provinces.[14] The 141 members of CORCAS included leaders representing the various Moroccan political parties, tribal sheikhs, elected delegates from women's groups and youth organizations, and representatives of civil society.[15]

In April 2007, Rabat sent a proposal to UNSG Ban Ki-moon that included not only an elected local administration—including executive, legislative, and judicial branches—for the "Saharan Autonomous Region" that would be created, but also ideas about education and justice and the promise that financial resources would be forthcoming to support them in addition to whatever revenues can be raised locally.[16] Under the "Moroccan Initiative for Negotiating an Autonomy Statute for the Sahara Region,"[17] the only matters that would remain in control of Rabat would be defense and foreign affairs as well as the currency, while the "Sahara Autonomous Region" would have broad powers over local administration, the economic sector, infrastructure, social and cultural affairs, and the environment[18]

Samuel J. Spector places the proposal in the juridical context of international legal principles which provide for resolving self-determination disputes somewhere "in the *between* the status quo and full independence." It should also be viewed against the backdrop of the revolutionary changes which swept across North Africa and the Middle East beginning in late 2010 and the Moroccan response with the adoption of a new constitution in the July 1, 2011, referendum and the November 25 election under the new charter of a government of the moderate Islamist Justice and Development Party (PJD), led by Abdelilah Benkirane. Significant hallmarks of the constitutional reform with direct bearing on the Western Sahara dispute include the explicit acknowledgment of Morocco's pluralist national culture—which is described as "enriched and nourished by African, Andalusian, Hebrew, and Mediterranean influences"—and its provision for the passage of organic legislation to further devolve power to the country's regions.[19]

It is important to note, as Edward M. Gabriel and Robert M. Holley do, that the autonomy proposal has, moreover, been well-received by the international community, which has tended to view it as an important advance. Then US Secretary of State of State Hillary Rodham Clinton, for example, has reaffirmed that "there has been no change in policy"[20] on the part of Washington and reiterated that support for the autonomy initiative is firmly rooted in American policy as something "that originated in the Clinton administration . . . was reaffirmed in the Bush administration and it remains the policy of the United States in the Obama administration."[21]

An indispensable part of any solution will also be, as Glynn Torres-Spelliscy writes in chapter 11, the sustainable development of the territory's natural resources for the benefit of the local population and in consultation with them. Not only is this legally permissible, it is imperative given the political and social fragility of the region in general and temptations—and dangers—presented by the growing nexus of radicalism and organized criminality in particular. Adding further stress is the marginalized Western Sahara's susceptibility to ethnic and other social divisions, as Anouar Boukhars reports.

Given the alternative to movement forward—allowing the current situation, especially in the Sahrawi camps of southern Algeria to continue to fester, to say nothing of the threat of renewed conflict and additional state failure in Africa and in the already volatile Sahelian zone at that—it is certainly in the interests, not only of the peoples directly affected, but also of states in the region and other members of the international community that, as Khadija Mohsen-Finan makes clear, the Western Sahara conflict needs to be reassessed. The security challenges which have multiplied across the region, especially since the fall of the Muammar Gaddafi regime in Libya, highlight the dangers of not resolving the conflict as has the growing geographical and operational reach of al-Qaeda in the Islamic Maghreb (AQIM).[22] In fact, it should not be forgotten that Polisario-linked figures have played more than cameo roles in recent troubles throughout the region, ranging from recruiting mercenaries to defend Gaddafi to providing AQIM's allies in northern Mali with both fighters and, in one notorious case, Western hostages to trade for ransom.[23]

And yet, as Stephen J. King observes in his chapter, the Polisario Front remains "caught up in a revolutionary vision that may no longer be viable given international concerns with stability and security in the region and beyond," even while its pretensions serve to obstruct the very rapprochement between Morocco and Algeria which is the condition *sine qua non* for effective regional security cooperation in the immediate term and, over the long haul, the regional integration which would deliver the sustained economic growth and prosperity necessary to meet the expectations of the populations of the Maghreb and the Sahel, especially the burgeoning youth segment.

For the sake of regional stability and development as well as the security and interests of the larger international community, the dispute over the Western Sahara cannot continue to be relegated to the status of a "forgotten conflict" peripheral to world affairs. Of course, whatever solution adopted, if it is to have any chance of being viable and sustainable over time, must not only respect the principles of international law, but also necessarily be founded on geopolitical reality. Interesting, the man who oversaw the establishment of a cease-fire between Morocco and the Polisario Front and set in motion the deployment of MINURSO more than two decades ago also outlined the contours a pragmatic framework for resolving the conflict. In his memoirs, former UNSG Javier Pérez de Cuéllar wrote:

I was never convinced that independence promised the best future for the inhabitants of the Western Sahara. There number, however counted, is less than 150,000, and aside from its phosphate deposits the land is poor, offering meager prospects of viability as a separate country. Such political leadership as exists is not impressive and in some cases is not Sahrawi in origin. A reasonable solution under which the Western Sahara would be integrated as an autonomous region in the Moroccan state would have spared many lives and a great deal of money. The Maghreb countries were in the best position to pressure Polisario to accept such a solution since Polisario was largely dependent upon them, especially Algeria, for support. They chose not to do so, even though in conversations with me President Chadli [Bendjedid] seemed prepared to support such an outcome. . . .

As the years passed, Morocco was able to strengthen its position in competing with Polisario, first militarily but subsequently in its political position within the Western Sahara, which it cultivated with substantial economic assistance. I believe that . . . that if the referendum is ever held, there will be majority support for integration with Morocco.[24]

It is imperative that such a realistic perspective informs the path forward to resolve a conflict that has gone on for far too long. To this end, policymakers and analysts would do well to bear in mind that while Morocco without the Western Sahara is diminished, the Western Sahara without Morocco is largely wasteland—albeit one with considerable potential for mischief in a part of the world that has already amply demonstrated its vulnerability to ethnic fissures, extremist militancy, and criminal networks.

NOTES

1. Despite frequent references in some of the literature describing the region as being "resource-rich"—thereby imputing a materialistic motivation for Moroccan interests there—it should be noted that, in fact, the phosphates of the Western Sahara are of a lower quality and represent just 2.4 percent of Morocco's total reserves.

2. United Nations Secretary-General Ban Ki-moon, quoted in Tim Witcher, "Ban says Western Sahara Risks Being Drawn into Mali War," *Agence France-Presse*, April 9, 2013, www.google.com/hostednews/afp/article/ALeqM5iOnupKvBuc8I_WTR3J5BnNCFnmEw?docId=CNG.566cbe22180951c72bc8d9c6ad6fd9d1.d1 (accessed July 1, 2013).

3. See, *inter alia*, Tony Hodges, *Western Sahara: The Roots of a Desert War* (Westport, CT: Lawrence Hill, 1983); Yahia H. Zoubir and Daniel Volman, eds., *The International Dimension of the Western Sahara Conflict* (Westport, CT: Praeger, 1993); Toby Shelley, *Endgame in the Western Sahara: What Future for Africa's Last Colony?* (London: Zed, 2004); Stephen Zunes and Jacob Mundy, *Western Sahara: War, Nationalism, and Conflict Irresolution* (Syracuse, NY: Syracuse University Press, 2010); and Erik Jensen, *Western Sahara: Anatomy of a Stalemate*, 2nd ed. (Boulder, CO: Lynne Rienner, 2011).

4. Donald L. Horowitz, *Ethnic Groups in Conflict*, 2nd rev. ed. (Berkeley: University of California Press), 17–18.

5. See Lloyd Cabot Briggs, *Tribes of the Sahara* (Cambridge, MA: Harvard University Press, 1960).

6. Robert Rézette, *The Western Sahara and the Frontiers of Morocco* (Paris: Nouvelles Éditions Latines, 1975), 36.

7. Rézette, *The Western Sahara and the Frontiers of Morocco*, 38.

8. See Jean Chappez, "L'Avis Consultatif de la Cour Internationale de Justice du 16 Octobre 1975 dans l'Affaire du Sahara Occidental," *Revue Generale de Droit International Public* 80, no. 3–4 (1976): 1132–87.

9. International Court of Justice, *Western Sahara Advisory Opinion* (October 16, 1975), 12ff, www.icj-cij.org/docket/files/61/6195.pdf (accessed July 1, 2013); see also B. O. Okere, "The Western Sahara Case," *International and Comparative Law Quarterly* 28, no. 2 (April 1979): 296–312.

10. See C. R. Pennell, *Morocco Since 1830: A History* (New York: New York University Press, 2000), 292–96.

11. See Guadalupe Pérez García, "La Falacia Histórica Sobre la Colonia de Ifni," *Historia y Comunicación Social* 8 (2003): 207–22.

12. See Terence McNamee, Greg Mills, and J. Peter Pham, *Morocco and the African Union: Prospects for Re-engagement and Progress on the Western Sahara*, Brenthurst Discussion Paper 1/2013 (Johannesburg: Brenthurst Foundation, 2013).

13. United Nations Mission for the Referendum in the Western Sahara, "Facts and Figures," April 30, 2013, www.un.org/en/peacekeeping/missions/minurso/facts.shtml (accessed July 1, 2013).

14. See King Mohammed VI, "Royal Advisory Council for Saharan Affairs" (speech, Laâyoune, March 25, 2006), *Royal Advisory Council for Saharan Affairs*, www.corcas.com/eng/SearchResults/FoundingSpeech.aspx (accessed July 1, 2013).

15. Perhaps the most interesting member of CORCAS is one Khalil Rkibi, a retired noncommissioned officer of the Royal Moroccan Army living in Kasbah Tadla and, rather tellingly, the father of Mohamed Abdelaziz, chief of the Polisario Front and self-proclaimed president of the "Sahrawi Arab Democratic Republic" (Khalil Rkibi's two other sons, a surgeon and a lawyer, respectively, are also Moroccan citizens, both residing in the kingdom).

16. United Nations, "Letter dated 11 April 2007 from the Permanent Representative of Morocco to the United Nations addressed to the President of the Security Council (April 11, 2007)," S/2007/206, http://daccess-dds-ny.un.org/doc/UNDOC/GEN/N07/307/48/PDF/N0730748.pdf?OpenElement (accessed July 1, 2013).

17. Kingdom of Morocco, "Moroccan Initiative for Negotiating an Autonomy Statute for the Saharan Region," April 10, 2007.

18. For a detailed commentary on the provisions of the autonomy proposal, see Abdelhamid El Ouali, *Saharan Conflict: Towards Territorial Autonomy as a Right to Democratic Self-Determination* (London: Stacey International, 2008), 144–53.

19. See J. Peter Pham, "Morocco's Momentum," *Journal of International Security Affairs* 22 (Spring 2012): 13–20.

20. Secretary of State Hillary Rodham Clinton, "Remarks with Moroccan Foreign Minister Taieb Fassi-Fihri," (remarks, Marrakesh, Morocco, November 2, 2009), www.state.gov/secretary/rm/2009a/11/131229.htm (accessed July 1, 2013).

21. Hillary Rodham Clinton, interview with Fouad Arif, *Al-Aoula Television*, November 3, 2009, www.state.gov/secretary/rm/2009a/11/131354.htm (accessed July 1, 2013).

22. See J. Peter Pham, "The Dangerous 'Pragmatism' of Al-Qaeda in the Islamic Maghreb," *Journal of the Middle East and Africa* 2, no. 1 (January–June 2011): 15–29.

23. Three aid workers, one Italian and two Spaniards, were kidnapped from a Polisario-controlled camp in southern Algeria in October 2011 and eventually transferred to the control of the Movement for Unity and Jihad in West Africa (MUJAO), which extorted a ransom of €15 million for their release in July 2012. See "Rebels: $18.4 Million Paid for Hostage Release," *Associated Press*, July 20, 2012, http://bigstory.ap.org/article/rebels-184-million-paid-hostage-release (accessed July 1, 2013).

24. Javier Pérez de Cuéllar, *Pilgrimage for Peace: A Secretary-General's Memoirs* (New York: Palgrave Macmillan, 2006).

Index

Abd al-Hafid, Sultan, 12
Abd ar-Rahman, Moulay, 10–11
Abdelaziz, Mohamed, 79, 86, 188
Aceh, Indonesia: assessment of outcome in, 224; autonomy and, 218, 219–220; breakthrough in, 219; GAM and, 218, 218–219; Helsinki and after, 218–219; history of relevance, 218; MoU and, 218–219, 219, 220; powers to be exercised by, 226; self-determination and, 218–220; self-government principles and, 220; Special Autonomy Plan, 218
African crusade: aims of, 5; Almohads and, 5; Almoravids and, 5, 24n3; Ferdinand III and, 5; gold and, 5–6; history of, 5–7; Marinids and, 5; Treaty of Alcáçovas-Toledo and, 6–7
African Union (AU): deadlock in, 146–149; diplomacy and, 146–149; principles of, xxiii
Agadir Summit, 279
Agdim Izik camp, 202
agents of change, 268–270
aggressive claiming: Algeria and, 57–58; Arab League and, 58; border treaty and, 58–59; contested Saharan geography and, 56–57; Hassan II and, 58–59; as Morocco's first policy, 56–61; OAU and, 58
agriculture industry, 240–241
Ait Lahssen tribe, 192
Ait Oussa tribe, 192
Algeria: aggressive Moroccan claiming and, 57–58; Amgala oasis and, 18; AU influence of, xxiii; autonomy and, xiii; *The Battlefield, Algeria 1988–2002, Studies in a Broken Polity* (Roberts), 115n16; border treaty and, 58–59; conflict and, 282, 283–284; GPRA and, 57; hydrocarbons and, 147; independence and, xiii; Maghrebian actors and, 282, 283–284; military and, xxi; Mohammed V and, 57; Polisario backed by, 76; self-determination and, xi, xiii
Algerian foreign policy: ANP and, 99–101; battle for Sahara, 93; border issue, 93–94; conclusions about, 112–113; defense, 102; diplomacy and, 99–107, 101–102, 110–112, 112; diplomacy decline and, 101–102, 112; diplomacy toward Libya, 111–112; diplomacy toward Northern Mali, 110–111; GWOT and, 102–104; inequalities in territorial makeup and, 98–99; land as sovereignty issue, 92–95; Mauritania tactical rapprochement and, 109; Morocco tactical rapprochement and, 109–110; overview, 91–92; pipeline, 94–95; projecting power and, 106–107; regional behind-the-scenes diplomacy and, 110–112; regional initiatives in awkward position, 108–109; regional security and, 104–106; road-paving, 94–95, 114n5; road project and, 109, 117n42; secret meetings and, 111, 117n48; space-time antinomy and, 95–98; state within a state and, 99–101; tactical rapprochement and, 109–110; terrorism and, 106–107, 116n28–116n29; unilateral initiatives in awkward position, 108–109; war legacy and, 99–107; way forward

regarding, 108–112
allegiance (*bay'a*), 7
Almohads, 5
Almoravids, 5, 24n3; trans-Saharan exchanges and, 9
ALN. *See* National Liberation Army
Amgala oasis, 18
Ammour, Laurence Aïda, xxi
Anderson, Mary, 265
Anglo-Moroccan Treaty, 12, 25n44
Annan, Kofi, 65, 132; Baker and, xii
ANP. *See* National Popular Army
Anzoula, Ali, 262
AQIM. *See* Al-Qaeda in the Islamic Maghreb
Arab League, 58
Arab Maghreb Union (UMA): June 2012 meeting of, 110, 117n46; Morocco's defensive confirming and, 63
al-A'raj, Ahmad, 7
Arslan, Shakib, 13
Assembly of the Forty, 39
as you possess (*uti possidetis*), 15, 26n57
AU. *See* African Union
Aubry, Martine, 155
autonomy: Aceh and, 218, 219–220; Bougainville and, 221–223; compromise and, 286–289; executive and judicial, 217; free association and, 214–215, 225–229; Hannum and, 214–215; Morocco and, xiii, xviii, xxv–xxvi, 227; Morocco Saharan policy and, 66–68; New Caledonia and, 221–223; as only option, xiii; overview of issues surrounding, xxi–xxv; Pérez de Cuellar and, 64, 70n17; plan assessment and, 225–229; Polisario and, xiii; powers associated with, 214–215; self-determination and, 214–215, 225–229, 286–289; Special Autonomy Plan, 218. *See also* Initiative for Negotiating an Autonomy Statute for the Sahara Region
Autonomy Plan. *See* Initiative for Negotiating an Autonomy Statute for the Sahara Region

Babana, Ould, 37
Bafour, 38
Baker, James, III: Annan and, xii; Baker initiatives and, 20–21; Bush administration and, 174–175; FA and, xxiii, 171; four options proposed by, 171; Houston agreement and, 65; inflexibility of, 174–175; Peace Plan for the Self-Determination of the People of Western Sahara and, 134–135, 174–175; Polisario and, 20–21, 83–84; political compromise formula of, 170; SADR and, 83–84; Sahrawis and, 46, 51n106; stronger mandate and, 171; three-year delay and, 66; voter identification and, 132
Ban Ki-Moon, 209, 297
barak (divine charisma), 7
Barikallah, Haj Ahmed, 116n36
Basiri, Mohammed Sidi Ibrahim: *Harakat Tahrir* and, 73–74; *Al-Shihab* and, 74
Basri, Driss, 64, 70n18, 171, 295n11; Hassan II and, 287; police brutality and, 198
Bassiri, Muhammad Embarak, 15, 26n55

The Battlefield, Algeria 1988–2002, Studies in a Broken Polity (Roberts), 115n16

bay'a (allegiance), 7
Belghzal, Abdelmajid, 203
Bella, Ben, 58
belonging to no one (*terra nullius*), 211
Bendjedid, Chadli, 62, 283
Benkirane, Abdelilah, 301
Bens, Francisco, 49n75
Berbers, 31, 38, 49n87
Berm (defensive walls), xv
bias, xv
Bihi (prisoner of war), 264
Bilad Shinguitti, xvii; international standards and, 35–36; spelling of, 47n9; territoriality and, 33–36; two political systems within, 34–35

Bled el-Makhzen (domain of sovereignty), 32–33
Bled es-Siba (domain of suzerainty), 32–33, 40
bloggers, bias and, xv
border: issue, 93–94; treaty, 58–59
Bou Craa mines, 238
Boudiaf, Mohamed, 284, 294n8–294n9
Bougainville: assessment of outcome in, 224; constitutional modifications and, 227; history of relevance, 222; interim autonomy and deferred referendum and, 221–223; peace agreement elements, 222; self-determination and, 221–223
Bouhali, Mohamed Lamine Ould, 105, 116n35
Boumedienne, Houari, 58–59
Bourguiba, Habib, 58
Bouteflika, Abdulaziz, 59, 101–102, 103, 105, 107, 115n27, 147
Boutros Ghali, Boutros, 65
Bové, José, 240
Brahim (prisoner of war), 263
Brahimi, Lakhdar, 147
British Somaliland. *See* Somaliland
Brzezinski, Zbigniew, 179
Buba, Shar, 9–10
bunker state, 100, 115n21
Bush administration: Baker and, 174–175; moves forward, 175–176; US and Moroccan policy evolution and, 173–175, 175–176

Calixtus III, Pope, 6
Campbell, Helen, 238
Castile, Treaty of Alcáçovas-Toledo and, 6–7
Catalan Atlas (Cresques), 6
cease-fire: defensive confirming and, 64; migration wave, 194–195; US and Moroccan policy evolution and, 165–166
La Celle-Saint Cloud agreements, 294n1
Cembrero, Ignacio, 188
CEMOC. *See* General Staff Joint Operations Committee

CEN-SAD. *See* Community of Sahel-Saharan States
central state apparatus (*makhzan*), 7–8
Chandora, Ali, 10
Charter for Peace and National Reconciliation plan, 115n27
children: agents of change and, 268–270; education and, 269; summer vacation and, 270; Tindouf refugee camps and, 266
Chirac, Jacques, 154
Clinton, Hillary, 176, 301; State Department alignment with, 179–180; US policy and, 163, 179–180
Clinton administration, 166–171
colonial rule: borders and, 278, 294n1; group identity and, 72; history of, 10–12; Ma' al-Aynayn and, 12; Mackenzie and, 11; Protectorate of Río de Oro and, 11; Sahrawis and, 72; Sherifian Empire and, 36–38; Treaty and Convention on Commerce and Navigation and, 10–11
Committee of the 24, 50n90
Common Organization of the Sahara Regions (OCRC), 95, 114n7
Community of Sahel-Saharan States (CEN-SAD), 108–109, 117n41, 146
compromise, 170, 171–173, 286–289
conflict: Agadir Summit and, 279; Algeria and, 282, 283–284; AQIM and, 291–292, 295n23, 296n28–296n29; autonomy *versus* self-determination and, 286–289; colonialism and, 278, 294n1; foundations, 277–280; Franco and, 278; Green March and, 280–281; Hassan II and, 281–282, 282–283; historical context, 298–300; Ifrane and Tlemcen treaties and, 279; Libya and, 281; Maghrebian actors in, 280–284; Mauritania and, 281; media attention, 277; Morocco and, 281–282, 282–283; new regional dynamic and, 291–293; *Operation Écouvillon* and, 277; origins, 277–280; Polisario and, 280; political

reality and, 300–303; referendum option and, 284–286; Saharan towns demonstrations and, 289–291; Sand War and, 280, 294n4; shadows of, 262; solution to, 297–303; strategic imperatives, 300–303; UN Resolution 1514 and, 278; *Western Sahara: War, Nationalism and Conflict Irresolution*, 23. *See also* history, of conflict; intergroup conflicts dynamics; Maghrebian actors, in conflict
conflict dynamics. *See* intergroup conflicts dynamics
conflict resolution phase: FA and, 133–135; self-determination referendum and, 129; Settlement Plan and, 129–131; UN and, 128–138; UNSC Resolutions and, 135; voter identification and, 131, 132
Congress of the Wilaya, 79
constitution: July 2011 Moroccan, 204; Polisario, 74–75; SADR, 78–79
constitutional modifications, Autonomy Plan and, 227–228
Cook Islands: assessment of outcome in, 223; constitutional modifications and, 227; executive and judicial autonomy and, 217; free association and, 216–217, 217; history of relevance, 216; legislative core power and, 216; popular consent and, 217–218; powers to be exercised by, 226; self-determination and, 216–218; settling on free association, 216–217
CORCAS. *See* Royal Advisory Council of Saharan Affairs
Corell, Hans, 242
Corell opinion, 244–245, 246
coups, 20
Cresques, Abraham, 6
crisis management phase: Green March and, 124, 125–127; UN and, 124–128; UNGA and, 127–128; UNSC and, 125–127; US and, 125; West Irian precedent and, 124, 138n16

customary law, 243–244

Daddah, Mokhtar Ould, 277
Dakhilis, 191
Dakhla: demographic changes in, 192; description of, 191; ethnic tension and, 189–192; fishing and, 191, 206n18; military stationed at, 192; socioeconomic development in, 192, 206n22; violence in, 189–190
Dawhat an-Nashir (ibn 'Ali ibn 'Askar), 7
decolonization, 213; Morocco Saharan policy and, 60; nationalism, resistance and, 12–17; range of outcomes for, 213–214; self-government and independence and, 213–214; UN Decolonization Committee, 42, 50n90; UNGA and, 43, 50n91, 120
decolonization paradigm: self-determination, independence and, 121–122; UN and, 120–122; UNGA resolutions and, 120
defensive confirming: cease-fire and, 64; diplomatic strategy, 62; Moroccan military campaign and, 61–62; Morocco's policy of, 61–66; referendum of confirmation and, 63; sedentarization and, 62; UMA and, 63
democratic spirit, akin to (*jema'as*), 33, 47n33
demonstrations, Saharan towns, 289–291
Department of Intelligence and Security (DRS), 100, 115n23
diplomacy: African continent policy divisions and, 142–146; Algerian foreign policy and, 99–107, 101–102, 110–112, 112; AU deadlock and, 146–149; conclusions about, 83–159; EU debates and, 155–157; Europe and, 149–157; France favoring Morocco and, 154–155; Hassan II and, 145; hydrocarbons and, 147; Libya and, 111–112; Mohammed VI and, 145–146; Morocco's isolation and, 144–146; Morocco's lack of

consistency in, 160n13; Morocco's policies reform and, 145; Northern Mali and, 110–111; overview about, 141–142; SADR in OAU and, 142–144; Spanish balancing game and, 149–153
divine charisma (*barak*), 7
Dlamini-Zuma, Nkosazana, 148
domain of sovereignty (*Bled el-Makhzen*), 32–33
domain of suzerainty (*Bled es-Siba*), 32–33, 40
Do No Harm: How Aid Can Support Peace — Or War (Anderson), 265
DRS. See Department of Intelligence and Security

East Timor, 130, 245
Economic Community of West African States (ECOWAS), 111, 117n47
education, 269
ethnic tension: background about, 187–188; Dakhilis and, 191; Dakhla and, 189–192; human rights improvement and, 189, 205n6; Morocco accountability and, 188, 205n2; patterns of, 187–192; al-Wahda neighborhood, 190
EU. See European Union
Europe: France favoring Morocco, 154–155; Sahrawi question and, 149–157; Spanish balancing game and, 149–153
European Union (EU), 155–157

FA. See Framework Agreement
Fascism, 13

al-Fasi, Allal, 14

Ferdinand III, of Castile, 5
Ferrer, Jaime, 6
Fiddian-Qasmiyeh, Elena, 265
fishing: Dakhla and, 191, 206n18; stocks, 239–240
FLN. See National Liberation Front
FLU. See Fusion and Liaison Unit
Framework Agreement (FA), xxiii; achievements of, 136–137; Baker and, xxiii, 171; conflict resolution phase and, 133–135; political compromise formula and, 170; welcomed by US, 173
France: favoring Morocco, 154–155; Moroccan Army of Liberation and, 73
Franco, Francisco, 278
Free Aceh Movement (GAM), 218, 218–219
free association: autonomy and, 214–215; Autonomy Plan as pathway to, 225–229; Cook Islands and, 216–217, 217; criteria, 229; Hillebrink and, 215; Niue and, 216–217, 217; popular consent and, 229–230; self-determination and, 214–215, 225–229
fronteiras (military outposts), 6–7
Front for the Liberation of the Sahara from Spanish Domination, 15
Fusion and Liaison Unit (FLU), 108, 117n40
Futuro Sahara (newspaper), 271

Gaddafi, Muammar, 142–143, 291, 295n24, 302
GAM. See Free Aceh Movement
Garcia Lopez, Bernabe, 188
General Staff Joint Operations Committee (CEMOC), 114n1
geography: contested Saharan, 56–57; Western Sahara, 39–40
Giscard d'Estaing, Valéry, 154
global war on terrorism (GWOT), 102–104
gold: African crusade and, 5–6; trans-Saharan exchanges and, 8
Gonzalez, Felipe, 152
GPRA. See Provisional Government of the Algerian Republic
Green March, 17; crisis management phase and, 124, 125–127; Hassan II and, xi; Maghrebian actors and, 280–281; UN and, 124, 125; UNSC and, 125–127

Hadrami, Omar, 79
Haidar, Aminatou, 188

Hakim, Ibrahim, 79
Hamdi, Jadiya, 271
Hannum, Hurst, 214–215
Harakat Tahrir. *See* Movement for the Liberation of Seguia el-Hamra and Río de Oro
Hassan II, King: aggressive claiming and, 58–59; Basri and, 287; conflict and, 281–282, 282–283; critical period for, 60; death of, 142; diplomacy and, 62, 145; diplomatic strategy of, 62; electorate and, 65; Green March and, xi; ICJ opinion and, 16–17; Maghrebian actors and, 281–282, 282–283; military coups and, 20; Morocco's isolation and, 144–145; nation building and, xx; plot against, 69n8; referendum of confirmation and, 63; Tekna tribe and, 193; UN and, 7; UN Settlement Plan and, xii
Helsinki, 218–219

al-Hiba, Ahmad, 12

Hillebrink, Steven, 215
history, of conflict, 298–300; African crusade, 5–7; Baker initiatives and, 20–21; colonial rule, 10–12; conclusion, 22–24; Fascism and Socialism and, 13; Green March and, 17; ICJ Advisory Opinion and, 16–17; independence movements and, 15; internationalization of conflict, 17–22; long arc of, 5–10; MINURSO and, 19–22; Moroccan Army of Liberation and, 14–15; nationalism, resistance, decolonization, 12–17; overview of, xvi–xvii, xvii–xx, 3–4; Polisario and, 17–19; religious reformist movements and, 13; Sharifian authority consolidation, 7–8; trans-Saharan exchanges, 8–10; UNGA resolutions and, 15–16
Hollande, François, 155
Horowitz, Donald, 204
housing, 201–202
Houston agreement, 65, 83

humanitarian aid: morality politics and, 264–265; UNHCR budget and, 274n11
human rights: accountability for, 188, 205n2; Morocco's improvement in, 189, 205n6, 290, 295n19
hydrocarbons, 147

ibn Abdallah, Mohammed, 10
ibn 'Ali ibn 'Askar, Muhammad, 7
ICJ. *See* International Court of Justice
Ifrane treaties, 279
Implementation Committee, 143, 159n5
impossible dual paradigm: FA and, 133–135; self-determination referendum and, 129; Settlement Plan and, 129–131; UN and, 128–138; UNSC Resolutions and, 135; voter identification and, 131, 132
independence: Algeria and, xiii; Bougainville and, 221–223; decolonization paradigm and, 121–122; *Harakat Tahrir* and, 73–74; Al-Istiqlal and, 14; movements, 15, 73–74; New Caledonia and, 221–223; Pérez de Cuellar and, 303; Polisario and, xiii, 75–87; right to, 122–123, 138n8; self-government and, 213–214
Indonesia. *See* Aceh, Indonesia
Indyk, Martin, 173
Initiative for Negotiating an Autonomy Statute for the Sahara Region (Autonomy Plan): assessing, 225–229; assessment parameters regarding, 210; constitutional modifications and, 227–228; flaws, potential, of, 210; as free association pathway, 225–229; international community and, 210; judicial powers specified in, 228; overview about, 210; powers outlined in, 226; powers retained by Morocco in, 227; preamble of, 225–226; Sayed, El-Ouali Mustapha, on, 226; veto powers and, 226; as viable, 211
intergroup conflicts dynamics: Agdim Izik camp and, 202; CORCAS and,

203–204; direct aid programs and, 200–201, 208n53; ethnic tension patterns, 187–192; housing and, 201–202; job creation and, 207n40; July 2011 Moroccan constitution and, 204; Laâyoune violence and, 197–198; migration and, 192–197; new, 197–203; overview, 187; police brutality and, 198; roots of conflict, 192–193; school system and, 201, 208n54; shared ethnic identification and, 198; Smara and, 207n43; social and economic aid policy and, 197, 207n39–207n40; way forward regarding, 203–205
International Court of Justice (ICJ): Hassan II and, 16–17; Morocco Saharan policy and, 59–60; 1975 Advisory Opinion of, xvii, 16–17; normative phase and, 122–123; Polisario and, 78; right to independence and, 122–123, 138n8; self-determination and, 211–212; UN and, 122–123
international law, 241–247
Islamist Justice and Development Party (PJD), 301
Ismail, Moulay, 10
Israeli usufruct example, 258n129
Istiqlal party, 14, 56–57, 294n1

Jackson, Robert P., 200
Jawdar, Pasha, 9

al-Jazuli, Muhammad, 7

jema'as (akin to democratic spirit), 33, 47n33
Jensen, Erik, 20, 23, 195
Jimenez, Trinidad, 152

Al-Kainan. *See* Mahmoud, Haddi Hamed

Keita, Modiba, 58
Khat al-Shahid (Line of the Martyr): creation of, 271; democratic bent of, 271; Polisario and, 85–86

al-Khattabi, Abdelkrim, 14

Khelil, Chakib, 147
Kissinger, Henry, 125
Kodjo, Edem, 143

Laâyoune, 206n30, 289–290; Agdim Izik camp and, 202; intergroup conflicts dynamics and, 197–198
Lahbib, Ayob, 80
Lalumière, Catherine, 156
Latin America, Sahrawis and, 44, 50n98–50n99
laws of occupation, 246, 258n129
League of Nations, 13
Libya, 292, 296n26; Algerian diplomacy toward, 111–112; Maghrebian actors and, 281
Line of the Martyr. *See* Khat al-Shahid

Ma' al-Aynayn, Tindouf, 12
Mackenzie, Donald, 11
Madrid Agreement, 77
Maghrebian actors, in conflict, 280, 282, 283; Algeria, 282, 283–284; Bendjedid, 283; Green March and, 280–281; Hassan II and, 281–282, 282–283; Libya, 281; Mauritania and, 281; Morocco, 281–282, 282–283; Polisario, 280; Sand War and, 280, 294n4
Mahjoub, Mohamed, 116n32
Mahmoud, Haddi Hamed: background about, 199; transfer of, 199
Mahmoud inspired violence: events leading to, 199; factors accounting for, 199–200; international context and, 200; liberalization process and, 199–200; resource distribution mismanagement and, 199
makhzan (central state apparatus), 7–8
Mali: Algerian diplomacy toward Northern, 110–111; Morocco and, 57

al-Mansur ad-Dhahbi, Moulay Ahmad, 8, 9, 57

Maqil, 38

maquis power, 99, 115n16
Maria Aznar, José, 152
Marinids, 5

al-Matghari, Shaykh, 7

Matutes, Abel, 152
Mauritania: Bilad Shinguitti and, 33–36; formation of, 30–38; Maghrebian actors and, 281; modern political parties and, 37; modern state and, 37–38; Polisario defeat of, 75–76; self definition during colonization, 34; tactical rapprochement with, 109; territorial bifurcation and, 41; Treaty of Fés and, 37; two political systems and, 34–35
Mbeki, Thabo, 148
Medelci, Mourad, 110
media attention, 277
Médiène, Mohamed, 112
Memorandum of Understanding (MoU), 218–219, 219, 220
Messahel, Abdelkader, 91
migration: cease-fire wave of, 194–195; first phase of, 192–193; intergroup conflicts dynamics and, 192–197; 1980s wave of, 194; successive phases of, 194–197; Tindouf camp wave of, 195–197
military: Algeria and, xxi; Dakhla and, 192; *fronteiras* and, 6–7; Hassan II and, 20; Moroccan military campaign, 61–62; Polisario and, 75–87
Military Committee for National Salvation, 18
military outposts (*fronteiras*), 6–7
Mission of United Nations for the Organization of a Referendum in Western Sahara (MINURSO): history and, 19–22; Morocco and, 43, 50n92; Pérez de Cuellar and, 64; Polisario and, 43, 50n92, 82; SADR and, 82; US and Moroccan policy evolution and, 166–167
Mitterrand, François, 154

Mohammed V, King, 56; Algeria and, 57
Mohammed VI, King, 66; continuity and change under, 145–146; CORCAS and, 21, 84–85, 261; diplomacy and, 145–146; patriot or traitor comment by, 22; regionalization and, 67–68, 68; third way and, 142; Tindouf refugee camps and, 261
Mohsen-Finan, Khadija, xxi–xxii
Moors: etymology of term, 48n54; origins of, 37; Sahrawis and, 72
Moran, Fernando, 151
Moroccan Army of Liberation: history, of conflict, and, 14–15; Sahrawis and, 73
Moroccan Autonomy Plan, xix
Moroccan Wall, building of, 18–19
Morocco: accountability for human rights and, 188, 205n2; advanced status granted to, 157, 162n55; autonomy and, xiii, xviii, xxv–xxvi, 227; autonomy plan future, xxv–xxvi; Autonomy Plan powers retained by, 227; colonial influence and, 36–38; conflict and, 281–282, 282–283; contested Saharan geography by, 56–57; diplomacy and, 144–146, 154–155, 160n13; as economic partner with Spain, 153, 161n37; formation of, 30–38; France favoring, 154–155; Green March and, 17; human rights improvement and, 189, 205n6, 290, 295n19; identity of, xx; isolation of, 144–146; July 2011 constitution of, 204; Maghrebian actors and, 281–282, 282–283; Mali and, 57; MINURSO and, 43, 50n92; Mohsen-Finan on, xxi–xxii; policy reform and, 145; Polisario and, xv, 61, 77–78; possession arguments of, 77–78; protests in, 86; retrocession process of, 55, 56; sovereignty and, xi, xii, xiii; tactical rapprochement with, 109–110; territorial bifurcation and, 41; three-pronged strategy of, xxiii; Treaty of Fés and, 36–37; unipolar

world order and, 20; UNSC Resolution 1813 and, 21–22. *See also* United States and Moroccan policy evolution

Morocco Saharan policy: aggressive claiming, 56–61; Arab League and, 58; autonomy and, 66–68; border treaty and, 58–59; compromise shift in, 171–173; conclusions about, 68–69; decolonization and, 60; defensive confirming, 61–66; ICJ and, 59–60; monarchy and, 56; offensive bargaining, 66–68; overview of, 55–56; Polisario and, 61; retrocession and, 55, 56; of sedentarization, 62; UMA and, 63; UNGA and, 59. *See also* United States and Moroccan policy evolution

MoU. *See* Memorandum of Understanding

Moulay Hassan, Sultan, 11, 12

Mouloud, Mustapha Salma Ould Sidi, 196

Movement for the Liberation of Seguia el-Hamra and Río de Oro (*Harakat Tahrir*), 15, 26n55, 73–74

Mubarak, Hosni, 143

Muhammad IV, Sultan, 11

MUJAO. *See* Movement for Unity and Jihad in West Africa

Mundy, Jacob, 23

Mustafa (prisoner of war), 271

Nairobi meetings, 143

Nambia. *See* South West Africa/ Nambia

nationalism, 12–17, 23, 72–75

National Liberation Army (ALN), 57

National Liberation Front (FLN), 57

National Popular Army (ANP), 99–101

nation-building, xx–xxi

natural gas, 238–239, 253n44, 253n46, 254n53. *See also* hydrocarbons

natural resources, xix–xx; agriculture industry, 240–241; conclusions about, 250–251; Corell opinion and, 244–245, 246; customary law and, 243–244; fishing stocks, 239–240; historical background and, 235–236; international law and, 241–247; international law and NSGTs and, 242–247; laws of occupation and, 246, 258n129; legal framework regarding, 236–237; legal principles application to, 247–249; nonrenewable, 238–239, 252n32, 252n39–253n40, 253n44, 253n46, 254n53; oil and natural gas, 238–239, 253n44, 253n46, 254n53; overview of, 235; phosphate reserves, 238, 252n32, 252n39–253n40; politico-legal status regarding, 241–242; renewable, 239–241; Sahrawi people's coordination and, 248–249; Sahrawi people's interests and, 247–248; Torres-Gillepscy and, xix–xx; treaty law and, 242–243; UNGA and, 245–246, 257n119; uranium, 238, 252n39–253n40; usufruct and, 246, 258n129; of Western Sahara, 237–241

New Caledonia: assessment of outcome in, 224; constitutional modifications and, 227; history of relevance, 221; interim autonomy and deferred referendum and, 221–223; self-determination and, 221–223

New Zealand, 216–218, 226, 227

Nezzar, Khaled, 79–80, 99, 115n18

NGO. *See* non-governmental organization

Niue: assessment of outcome in, 223; constitutional modifications and, 227; executive and judicial autonomy and, 217; free association and, 216–217, 217; history of relevance, 216; legislative core power and, 216; popular consent and, 217–218; powers to be exercised by, 226; self-determination and, 216–218

nomadic tribes: identity and, 40–41; Sahrawi and, 38–39; territorial bifurcation and, 41

non-governmental organization (NGO), 180

nonrenewable natural resources, 238; oil and natural gas, 238–239, 253n44, 253n46, 254n53; phosphate reserves, 238, 252n32, 252n39–253n40; uranium, 238, 252n39–253n40

non-self-governing territory (NSGT), 242–247. *See also specific territory*

Nordstrom, Carolyn: shadows of conflict and, 262; women as symbols of war and, 262

normative phase: ICJ and, 122–123; right to independence and, 122–123, 138n8; UN and, 122–123; Visiting Mission and, 123, 138n10

Northern Mali, 110–111

Nouméa Accord, 221

NSGT. *See* non-self-governing territory

OAU. *See* Organization of African Unity

Obama administration: current circumstances and, 177–178; security and, 176; steps for moving forward for, 178–181; US and Moroccan policy evolution and, 176–177

OCRC. *See* Common Organization of the Sahara Regions

offensive bargaining, 66–68

oil, 238–239, 253n44, 253n46, 254n53. *See also* hydrocarbons

Operation Écouvillon, 277

Organization of African Unity (OAU), xii; aggressive Moroccan claiming and, 58; Implementation Committee and, 143, 159n5; Nairobi meetings and, 143; Polisario and, 81–82; SADR in, 81–82, 142–144; 20th Summit of, 144; UN Charter Articles 33 and 52 and, 143, 159n2

Pacific Islands, 137

Parsley Island crisis, 152

Partido De La Union Nacional Saharaui (PUNS), 74

Partido Socialista Obrero Espanol (PSOE), 151

Peace Plan for the Self-Determination of the People of Western Sahara: achievements of, 136–137; Baker and, 134–135, 174–175; Bush administration and, 174–175; inflexibility of, 174–175

Pérez de Cuellar, Javier, 129; autonomy and, 64, 70n17; independence and, 303; MINURSO and, 64; Polisario and, 82; UN Settlement Plan and, xii

Philippe III, 36

phosphate reserves: Bou Craa mines and, 238; extent of, 238; low quality of, 297; as nonrenewable natural resource, 238, 252n32, 252n39–253n40; political motivations surrounding, 252n32; uranium and, 238, 252n39–253n40

pipeline, 94–95

PJD. *See* Islamist Justice and Development Party

police brutality, 198

policy analysts, bias and, xv

Polisario. *See* Popular Front for the Liberation of Saguia al-Hamra and Rio de Oro

political reality, 300–303

popular consent, 217–218, 229–230

Popular Front for the Liberation of Saguia al-Hamra and Rio de Oro (Polisario): Algerian backing of, 76; AQIM and, 292, 296n28; autonomy and, xiii; Baker and, 20–21, 83–84; battle plan of, 18; campaigns of, 17–19; conclusions about, 86–87; conflict and, 280; CORCAS and, 84–85; diplomatic successes of, 80–81; establishment of, 74–75; formal constitution of, 74–75; founders of, 15; ICJ opinion and, 78; ideological orientation of, 79; independence and, xiii, 75–87; internal fracturing of, 271; internal practices of, 79–80; Khat al-Shahid and, 85–86; Madrid Agreement and, 77; Maghrebian actors and, 280; Mauritania defeat and, 75–76; military and diplomatic independence wars, 75–87; military defeats of, 76–77; military victories of, 75–76; MINURSO and, 43, 50n92,

82; Moroccan military campaign against, 61–62; Moroccan Wall and, 18–19; Morocco Saharan policy and, 61; Morocco's possession arguments and, 77–78; Morocco standoff with, xv; new generation and, 189; OAU and, 81–82; origins of, xx; overview about, 71; Pérez de Cuellar and, 82; prisoners of war release by, 263; recent events and, 83–87; referendum and, 82–83; roots of, 71–72; Sahrawi nationalism origins, 72–75; Sayed, El-Ouali Mustapha, and, 74; self-determination and, xi, xiii; Spanish census and, 284, 294n10; SPLA and, 74; Tindouf refugee camps and, 80; UNSC Resolution 1754 and, 85. *See also* Sahrawi Arab Democratic Republic

Portuguese: explorations, 6; Treaty of Alcáçovas-Toledo and, 6–7

Primary Popular Congresses, 79

prisoners of war: Bihi, 264; Brahim, 263; interviews overview, 263; Mustafa, 271; Polisario's release of, 263

Protectorate of Río de Oro, 11

Provisional Government of the Algerian Republic (GPRA), 57

PSOE. *See Partido Socialista Obrero Espanol*

PUNS. *See* Partido De La Union Nacional Saharaui

Al-Qaeda in the Islamic Maghreb (AQIM), 291–292, 295n23, 296n28–296n29, 302

al-Qa'im, Muhammad al-Mahdi, 7

Qotbi, Mehdi, 154

Rabouni, 267
Rachid, Khalihenna Ould, 203
rapprochement, 109–110
realist paradigm: Green March and, 124, 125–127; UN and, 124–128; UNGA and, 127–128; UNSC and, 125–127; US and, 125; West Irian precedent and, 124, 138n16

referendum: Bougainville and, 221–223; of confirmation, 63; conflict resolution phase and, 129; Houston agreement and, 83; New Caledonia and, 221–223; option, 284–286; Polisario and, 82–83; US and Moroccan policy evolution and, 165–166; voting issues, 82–83. *See also* Mission of United Nations for the Organization of a Referendum in Western Sahara

refugees: Anderson and, 265; conclusions about, 272–273; cost of repatriation of, 295n12; Fiddian-Qasmiyeh and, 265; as moral issue, 262–263, 264–265; Salek, 265; SRC and, 264; Terry and, 264; as tools, xxiv–xxv; UNHCR and, 181, 274n11; UNHCR budget and, 274n11. *See also* Tindouf refugee camps

Reguibat tribe, 192
religious reformist movements, 13
renewable natural resources, 239; agriculture industry, 240–241; fishing stocks, 239–240
repatriation, cost of, 295n12
resistance, 12–17, 270–272
resolutions: self-determination, xi; UN, xii, 278; UNGA, xi, 15–16, 120, 209; UNSC, 21–22, 85, 132, 135
retrocession, 55, 56
Revolutionary Movement of the Blue Men, 15
Río de Oro, 14, 15
road-paving, 94–95, 114n5
road project, 109, 117n42
Roberts, Hugh, 115n16
Romeva, Raül, 157
roots of conflict, 192–193
Ross, Christopher, 67, 169, 176; UNSC Resolution 1754 and, 85
Royal Advisory Council of Saharan Affairs (CORCAS): members, 301; Mohammed VI and, 21, 84–85, 261; Polisario and, 84–85; poor performance of, 203–204; Rachid and, 203
Rquibate (tribal confederation), 191, 206n16

Saadians: rise of, 7; success of, 7–8
SADR. *See* Sahrawi Arab Democratic Republic
Saharan Liberation Army, 15
Sahel, trans-Saharan exchanges and, 8, 25n26
Sahnoun, Mohamed, 147
Sahrawi Arab Democratic Republic (SADR), xxiii; African states that recognize, 150–151; African states that support, 148; Baker and, 83–84; constitution, 78–79; CORCAS and, 84–85; diplomatic successes of, 80–81; establishment of, 17–18, 78; ideological orientation, 79; internal fracturing within, 271; internal practices of, 79–80; Khat al-Shahid and, 85–86; MINURSO and, 82; OAU and, 81–82, 142–144; Pérez de Cuellar and, 82; recent events and, 83–87; referendum and, 82–83; Tindouf refugee camps and, 80; unipolar world order and, 20; UNSC Resolution 1754 and, 85
Sahrawi Peoples Liberation Army (SPLA): crushing of, 75; establishment of, 74
Sahrawi question: EU debates, 155–157; Europe and, 149–157; France favoring Morocco in, 154–155; Spanish balancing game and, 149–153
Sahrawi Red Crescent (SRC), 264
Sahrawis: agents of change and, 268–270; Baker and, 46, 51n106; Basiri and, 73–74; colonialism and, 72; conclusions about, 45–46; defined, 38, 48n62; geopolitical backdrop and, 30–38; *Harakat Tahrir* and, 73–74; as independent, 72; Latin America and, 44, 50n98–50n99; Moors and, 72; Moroccan Army of Liberation and, 73; nationalism origins, 72–75; natural resources and coordination with, 248–249; natural resources and interests of, 247–248; nomadic character of, 38–39; overview about, xv, 29–30; Polisario and, 74–75; protests by, 86; PUNS and, 74; radicalization of, xv; refugees as tools, xxiv–xxv; Sayed, El-Ouali Mustapha, and, 74; Sherifian society and, 31–33; SPLA and, 74; territorial bifurcation and, 41; territory *versus* identity and, 42–45; women and, 268–270. *See also* Popular Front for the Liberation of Saguia al-Hamra and Rio de Oro
Salek (refugee), 265
Salek, Mahjjoub, 85–86
Sand War, 280, 294n4
Sayed, Baba, 80
Sayed, El-Ouali Mustapha, 17, 74, 226
scholarship bias in, xv
school system, 201, 208n54
sedentarization: defensive confirming and, 62; Tindouf refugee camps and, 270
Selassie, Haile, 58
self-determination: Aceh and, 218–220; Algeria and, xi, xiii; alternatives to, 209, 232n3; autonomy and, 214–215, 225–229, 286–289; Bougainville and, 221–223; case studies, 216–223; case studies assessment, 223–224; compromise and, 286–289; conflict resolution phase and, 129; Cook Islands and, 216–218; decolonization-era framework of, 213; decolonization paradigm and, 121–122; decolonization range of outcomes and, 213–214; definitions of, 212–213; evolution of, 211; examples of, xviii–xix; free association and, 214–215, 225–229; ICJ and, 211–212; New Caledonia and, 221–223; Niue and, 216–218; options ahead, 229–231; overview of issues surrounding, xxi–xxv, 209–211; Polisario Front and, xi, xiii; post–Cold War era and, 212–213; resolutions of UNGA, xi, 15–16; statutory phase and, 121–122; understanding law of, 211–213; voter registration and, 129. *See also* Peace Plan for the Self-Determination of the People of

Western Sahara self-government: Aceh and, 220; independence and, 213–214
Settlement Plan: conflict resolution phase and, 129–131; East Timor and, 130; Hassan II and, xii; as sketchy agreement, 129–130; South West Africa/Nambia and, 130; stalemate, 131; voter identification and, 131, 132
Shadows of War (Nordstrom), 262
Sharifian authority: consolidation, 7–8; al-Mansur ad-Dhahbi and, 8; rise of, 7; Saadians success and, 7–8

ash-Shaykh, Muhammad, 7

Sherifian Empire, xvii; *Bled el-Makhzen* and *Bled es-Siba* and, 32–33; colonial influence and, 36–38; society and, 31–33; Treaty of Fés and, 36–37; tribal communities and, 31–32

Al-Shihab (periodical), 74

Sidati, Mohamed, 156
Sliman, Moulay, 10
Smara, 207n43
Socialism, 13
Somaliland, 136, 140n60

de Soto, Alvaro, 148

Soudan, François, 202
Souilem, Ould, 196
South Sudan, 221
South West Africa/Nambia, 130
sovereignty, xi, xii, xiii, 32–33, 92–95
space-time antinomy, 95–98
Spain: balancing game of, 149–153; census and, 284, 294n10; diplomacy, 149–153; as economic partner with Morocco, 153, 161n37; end of occupation by, 165–166; Franco and, 278; Front for the Liberation of the Sahara from Spanish Domination and, 15; Green March and, 17; Moroccan Army of Liberation and, 73; as noncommittal, xxii; occupation end and, 165–166; self-determination resolutions and, xi
Special Autonomy Plan, 218
Spector, Samuel, xviii, 301
SPLA. *See* Sahrawi Peoples Liberation Army
SRC. *See* Sahrawi Red Crescent
statutory phase: self-determination, independence and, 121–122; UN and, 120–122; UNGA resolutions and, 120
strategic imperatives, 300–303
Sudan. *See* South Sudan
summer vacation, 270

tactical rapprochement, 109–110
Tamek, Ali Salem, 188, 205n5
Tartag, Othman, 112, 117n51
Tekna tribe, 192–193, 290, 295n18
terra nullius (belonging to no one), 211
terrorism: Algerian foreign policy and, 106–107, 116n28–116n29; GWOT and, 102–104
Terry, Fiona, 264
Tindouf refugee camps, 80; conclusions about, 272–273; conditions, 266; cost of repatriation to, 295n12; described, 266; entrepreneurialism and, 270; management of, 267; map of, 268; migration wave out of, 195–197; Mohammed VI and, 261; overview, 266; participatory governance and, 270; Rabouni and, 267; resistance inside, 270–272; sedentarization and, 270; spring of 2010 and, 208n59; 27th of February camp and, 266–267; women and children in, 266
Tlemcen treaty, 279
Tokelau, 224
The Torch. *See Al-Shihab*
Torres-Gillepscy, Glynn, xix–xx
Touré, Sékou, 144
Trans-Sahara Highway, 94, 114n5
trans-Saharan exchanges: Almoravids and, 9; Buba and, 9–10; commodities included in, 8; history regarding, 8–10; Jawdar and, 9;

Sahel and, 8, 25n26; sociocultural and intellectual, 8–9
treaties: Anglo-Moroccan Treaty, 12, 25n44; border, 58–59; Ifrane, 279; law, 242–243; Tlemcen, 279; Treaty and Convention on Commerce and Navigation, 10–11; Treaty of Alcáçovas-Toledo, 6–7; Treaty of Fés, 36–37; Treaty of Solidarity and Cooperation, 58–59
Tuareg, 291, 295n25
Tuquoi, Pierre, 152
27th of February camp, 266–267

UEMOA. *See* West African Economic and Monetary Union
UMA. *See* Arab Maghreb Union
UN. *See* United Nations
UNGA. *See* United Nations General Assembly
UNHCR. *See* United Nations High Commissioner for Refugees
unipolar world order, 20
United Nations (UN): Charter Articles 33 and 52, 143, 159n2; conflict resolution phase, 128–138; crisis management phase, 124–128; Decolonization Committee, 42, 50n90; decolonization paradigm, 120–122; framing issues, actors, processes, 122–123; Green March and, 124, 125; Hassan II and, xii, 7; ICJ and, 122–123; impossible dual paradigm, 128–138; MINURSO and, 19–22; normative phase, 122–123; overview of role of, 119–120; phases of involvement of, 119–120; realist paradigm, 124–128; Resolution 1514, 278; resolutions, xii, 278; Settlement Plan and, xii; statutory phase, 120–122; Visiting Mission and, 123, 138n10; West Irian precedent and, 124, 138n16
United Nations General Assembly (UNGA): crisis management phase and, 127–128; decolonization and, 43, 50n91, 120; decolonization resolutions, 120; Morocco Saharan policy and, 59; natural resources and, 245–246, 257n119; Resolution 1541, 209; Resolution 2229, 16; resolutions, xi, 15–16, 120, 209; right to independence and, 122–123, 138n8; self-determination resolutions of, xi, 15–16
United Nations High Commissioner for Refugees (UNHCR), 181, 274n11
United Nations Security Council (UNSC): crisis management phase and, 125–127; Green March and, 125–127; Resolution 1342, 132; Resolution 1541, 135; Resolution 1598, 135; Resolution 1754, 85, 135; Resolution 1813, 21–22
United States (US): Framework Agreement welcomed in, 173; realist paradigm and, 125; steps for moving policy forward for, 178–181; UN crisis management phase and, 125; Western Sahara as low priority in, xxiii; Western Sahara policies overview, xxiii–xxiv
United States and Moroccan policy evolution: Baker's peace plan and, 174–175; Bush administration moves forward, 175–176; Bush administration's election and, 173–175; cease-fire and, 165–166; Clinton, Hillary and, 163, 179–180; Clinton administration policy change and, 166–171; conclusions about, 181–182; current circumstances, 177–178; development assistance and, 179; failed referendum attempt and, 165–166; interagency policy review and, 168; MINURSO's mission and, 166–167; Moroccan compromise shift and, 171–173; NGO, civil society, local government programs and, 180; Obama administration verbal support and, 176–177; overview about, 163–164; political compromise formula and, 170; private US investment and, 180; referendum and, 165–166; regional stability concerns and, 166–171; renewed tensions and, 174–175;

Spanish occupation end and, 165–166; steps for moving US policy forward, 178–181; unambiguous policy statement and, 179; UNHCR and, 181; US foreign assistance and, 180; US/Moroccan relationship tensions and, 167–168; visiting Western Sahara and, 179
UNSC. *See* United Nations Security Council
uranium, phosphate reserves and, 238, 252n39–253n40
US. *See* United States; United States and Moroccan policy evolution
usufruct (right to use of an other's property): Israeli example, 258n129; natural resources and, 246, 258n129
uti possidetis (as you possess), 15, 26n57

van Walsum, Peter, 21, 66, 67, 176, 176–177
Villemont, Régine, 155
Visiting Mission, UN, 123, 138n10
voter: identification, 131, 132; registration, 129

Wad-Ras, Terms of, 11

al-Wahda: neighborhood, 190; subsidies to, 195

Waldheim, Kurt, 124
War of Ifni, 14
War of the Sands, 15

Wattasids, 7
West African Economic and Monetary Union (UEMOA), 146
Western Sahara: geographic parameters of, 39–40; geopolitical backdrop of territory and people, 30–38; internal situation future, xxv–xxvi; natural resources of, 237–241; nomadic character of, 38–39; overview of situation in, xi–xiii, xv; territory and identity in, 38–41; US policies overview, xxiii–xxiv; US priorities and, xxiii. *See also specific topic*
Western Sahara Collective, xvi
Western Sahara: War, Nationalism and Conflict Irresolution (Zunes & Mundy), 23
West Irian precedent, 124, 138n16
Wilaya. *See* Congress of the Wilaya
women: agents of change and, 268–270; camp management and, 268–269; education and, 269; home management and, 268; national consciousness and, 269; Tindouf refugee camps and, 266; 27th of February camp and, 266–267

Yahya, Bouhabaini, 264

Zartman, I. William, xx
Zion, Muhammad Ould, 78
Zunes, Stephen, 23

About the Contributors

EDITORS

Anouar Boukhars is a nonresident scholar in Carnegie's Middle East Program and an associate fellow at the Madrid-based think tank FRIDE. He is also an assistant professor of international relations at McDaniel College in Westminster, Maryland, and the author of *Politics in Morocco: Executive Monarchy and Enlightened Authoritarianism* (2010). His 2012 Carnegie publications include: *The Paranoid Neighbor: Algeria and the Conflict in Mali, Simmering Discontent in the Western Sahara,* and *The Drivers of Insecurity in Mauritania*. In 2013, he coedited with Fred Wehrey the book *Perilous Desert: Sources of Saharan Insecurity*. Boukhars is a former fellow at the Brookings Doha Center, where he published *Political Violence in North Africa: The Perils of Incomplete Liberalization* and *Fighting the Growth of Terrorist Networks on the Maghreb*. His other publications have appeared in a large number of journals and leading newspapers, including *Journal of Conflict Studies, International Political Science Review, European Security, Terrorism Monitor,* and *Columbia International Affairs Online*. Boukhars has lectured in several universities and provided advice to governments, businesses, and different community groups. He currently provides consultancy serivces to private and government institutions in the United States and abroad.

Jacques Roussellier is an instructor at American Military University and an international political consultant. His current research concentration is on security in North Africa, including the Western Sahara dispute, terrorism, and sovereignty. Previously, he worked for the World Bank Group, the United Nations, and the Organization for Security and Cooperation in Europe. Roussellier served as a spokesperson for MINURSO from 1999–2001 and is the author of *Quicksand in the Western Sahara? From Referendum Stalemate to Negotiated Solution* (International Negotiation, 2005).

CONTRIBUTORS

Osama Abi-Mershed is associate professor of history at Georgetown University and director of the Center for Contemporary Arab Studies in the Edmund A. Walsh School of Foreign Service. He teaches courses on

North Africa, the Middle East, and the Western Mediterranean (medieval and modern); on Arab and Ottoman societies in the nineteenth and twentieth centuries; and on colonial and postcolonial Franco-Maghribi relations. His academic research focuses on the ideologies and practices of modernization in nineteenth-century Algeria, and on the processes of state- and nation-making in colonial France and North Africa. He is the author of *Apostles of Modernity: Saint-Simonians and the French Civilizing Mission in Algeria* (Stanford University Press, 2010) and editor of *Trajectories of Education in the Arab World: Legacies and Challenges* (Routledge, 2009). He holds a PhD in history from Georgetown University (2003), a MA in international affairs from George Washington University (1997), a MBA in International Finance from George Washington University (1988), and a BA in economics (1985) from the American University of Beirut.

Laurence Aïda Ammour is research fellow at *"Les Afriques dans le monde"* at the Bordeaux Institute for Political Science and consultant in international security and defense at *GéopoliSudconsultance* (www.geopolisudconsult.com.)

Aomar Boum researches how Moroccan Muslims remember, picture, and construct Jewishness and Moroccan Judaism. He has published numerous peer-reviewed articles on the history, historiography, and politics of Jewish-Muslim relations in Morocco. Although his work focuses on Saharan Jewries, he has also written on other Middle Eastern ethnic and religious minorities including Shia, Bahai, Christians, Ibadi, Berbers, and Haratine. He has also published on larger political, social, historical, educational, economic, and environmental issues in North and sub-Saharan Africa and Morocco in particular. He co-authored the *Historical Dictionary of Morocco* (Scarecrow Press, 2006 and 2013) and is the author of *Memories of Absence: How Muslims Remember Jews in Morocco* (Stanford University Press, 2013).

Joshua Castellino was appointed professor of law and head of Law Department, Middlesex University, UK, in September 2007. From 2000 to 2006, he was a member of the teaching faculty at the Irish Centre for Human Rights National University of Galway, Ireland. He played a major role in the development of the Irish Centre for Human Rights and is currently an adjunct member of faculty and the driving force behind the Irish Centre's acclaimed annual Minority Rights Summer School. Professor Castellino is a specialist in minority rights and has written two books on the subject: *Minority Rights in Asia: A Comparative Legal Analysis*, coauthored by Dr. Elvira Dominguez Redondo (Oxford University Press, 2006) and *International Law and Indigenous Peoples* (Ashgate, 2003).

Elvira Domínguez Redondo is senior lecturer in law at Middlesex University, UK, and adjunct lecturer of the Irish Centre for Human Rights, NUI Galway, Ireland. She is the coauthor with Joshua Castellino of *Minority Rights in Asia: A Comparative Legal Analysis* (Oxford University

Press, 2006) and *Los Procedimientos Publicos Especiales de la Comisioan de Derechos Humanos de Naciones Unidas* (Tirant lo Blanch, 2005).

Adam Farrar holds a BA in Middle Eastern studies and a BA in psychology from the College of William and Mary (2010), and a MA in Arab studies from the Georgetown University Center for Contemporary Arab Studies (2012). His research interests include Islamic intellectual history, expression, and articulation of identity, and political, intellectual, and religious movements in the Middle East and North Africa. In pursuit of these interests, he has coauthored an annotated bibliography on an early Muslim sect known as the Kharijites, written on the formation of Moroccan national identity, and presented a paper that examines the two principal Islamist movements in Morocco, the Justice and Development Party and the Society of Justice and Charity.

Edward M. Gabriel served as US Ambassador to Morocco from 1997 to 2001 and is currently chair of the Moroccan-American Center. He is a Visiting Fellow at the Center for Strategic and International Studies, a member of the Global Advisory Board of George Washington University, a member of the boards of Amideast, the Keystone Center, the Tangier American Legation Museum, the Casablanca American School, and the American School of Tangier. Ambassador Gabriel has an extensive background in international affairs, having convened multilateral policy forums involving national security, environmental, and trade and energy issues. He has been active in advising the US government on Mideast policy matters.

Robert M. Holley served in the US Foreign Service from 1980 to 2002, and was the principal US government interlocutor between the Moroccan government and the Polisario from 1998 to 2001. He is the recipient of an impressive variety of military and civilian awards for his service to his country with the US Army and the Department of State, including the Secretary of State's Career Achievement Award and the Silver Star. Currently, Holley advises the government of Morocco and is the Senior Policy Advisor at the Moroccan American Center for Policy.

Stephen J. King is associate professor of government at Georgetown University. He specializes in comparative politics in the Middle East and North Africa. He is the author of *Liberalization against Democracy: The Local Politics of Economic Reform in Tunisia* (Indiana University Press, 2003) and *The New Authoritarianism in the Middle East and North Africa* (Indiana University Press, 2009). He teaches the following courses: Introduction to Comparative Politics, the Politics of North Africa, Authoritarianism in Comparative Perspective, The Middle East in Comparative Perspective, and Politics of the Third World.

Khadija Mohsen-Finan is a research associate at Institut Des Relations Internationales et Stratégiques (IRIS) and professor at Paris I (Panthéon Sorbonne). She has published many books and articles on the Maghreb, the Western Sahara, Algeria, and Moroccan-Algerian relations.

In particular, she published *Le Maghreb dans les relations internationales* (CNRS éditions, 2011), *Les Médias en Méditerranée* (Actes Sud, 2009), *L'Image de la femme au Maghreb* (Actes Sud, 2008), avec Rémy Leveau *Musulmans de France et d'Europe* (CNRS éditions, 2005), with Malika Zeghal *Les islamistes dans la compétition politique : le cas du Parti de la Justice et du Développement au Maroc* (RFSP, 2006). Dr. Finan holds a PhD in Political Science (IEP Paris) and a degree in history (University of Aix-en-Provence).

J. Peter Pham is director of the Africa Center at the Atlantic Council in Washington, DC. He was previously a tenured associate professor of justice studies, political science, and African studies at James Madison University in Harrisonburg, Virginia, where he directed the Nelson Institute for International and Public Affairs. The author of over three hundred essays and reviews, he is the author, editor, or translator of over a dozen books, most recently *Somalia: Fixing Africa's Most Failed State*, coauthored with Greg Mills and David Kilcullen. He is the also the vice president of the Association for the Study of the Middle East and Africa (ASMEA) and editor-in-chief of its peer-reviewed *Journal of the Middle East and Africa*.

Samuel J. Spector currently works in the US House of Representatives. A graduate of Georgetown University Law Center, he was formerly an independent legal consultant specializing in the Middle East and North Africa. He served as a Fulbright Fellow at Tel Aviv University, as well as project associate for the Long-Term Strategy Project of the Center for Strategic Budgetary Assessments, which examined political change in the Middle East for the Office of the Secretary of Defense. In February 2010 he participated in a fact-finding mission to Western Sahara, and he recently published an article in *Middle East Quarterly* titled "Western Sahara and the Self-Determination Debate."

Glynn Torres-Spelliscy is an instructor at the New School for Public Engagement in New York City and at St. Petersburg College in Florida. He teaches classes on public international law, international politics, international business law, human rights, and international criminal law. He is a member of the Association of the Bar of the City of New York's (ABCNY) United Nations Committee, and a past member of the ABCNY's International Human Rights Committee. While a member of the UN Committee, he coauthored a report concerning the use of natural resources in Western Sahara by Morocco. In October 2010, Torres-Spelliscy addressed the UN on behalf of the ABCNY with respect to humanitarian conditions in Western Sahara and the Tindouf refugee camps. His research focuses on issues of national security and liberty, international human rights, prisoners' rights, and US constitutional issues. From 2002 to 2011, he was an associate in the New York office of the law firm, Arnold and Porter LLP. He holds a JD and MA in international relations from the University of Toronto and a BA with honors from McGill University.

Antonin Tisseron is a research fellow specializing in security issues and counterterrorism in the Maghreb and the Sahel at the Institut Thomas More. He has authored various publications on Morocco and the Western Sahara, including "Geopolitical tangles and the fight against terrorism in the Sahara," and "Western Sahara's Polisario: Crime and Terrorism." Before his fellowship at the Institut Thomas More, Tisseron worked at the French Department of Defense where he focused on problems relating to the modernization of the armed forces and counterterrorism.

I. William Zartman served as the Jacob Blaustein Professor of International Organizations and Conflict Resolution at SAIS for nearly twenty years, where he also directed the Conflict Management and African Studies programs. He has been a Distinguished Fellow of the United States Institute of Peace, Olin Professor at the US Naval Academy, Elie Halévy Professor at Sciences Pô in Paris, and holder of the Bernheim Chair at the Free University of Bruxelles, and received a lifetime achievement award from the International Association for Conflict Management. He is author of a number of books, including *Negotiation and Conflict Management: Essays in Theory and Practice*; *The Practical Negotiator*; *Ripe for Resolution*; *Cowardly Lions: Missed Opportunities to Prevent Deadly Conflict and State Collapse*; *Morocco: Problems of New Power*; and the co-editor of *Terrorist Negotiations: Who Holds Whom Hostage?* and *State Engagement with Terrorists: Negotiating Ends and Means*. He is past president of the Tangier American Legation Institute for Moroccan Studies and past president of the Middle East Studies Association and the American Institute for Maghreb Studies.

CPSIA information can be obtained at www.ICGtesting.com
Printed in the USA
BVOW07*0253230114

342734BV00003B/4/P